Anonymous Anonymous

**Jesuits' Estates Act**

A Complete and Revised Edition

Anonymous Anonymous

**Jesuits' Estates Act**
*A Complete and Revised Edition*

ISBN/EAN: 9783744659277

Printed in Europe, USA, Canada, Australia, Japan

Cover: Foto ©Lupo / pixelio.de

More available books at **www.hansebooks.com**

A COMPLETE AND REVISED EDITION

OF THE DEBATE ON THE

# JESUITS' ESTATES ACT

IN THE

## HOUSE OF COMMONS

OTTAWA, MARCH, 1889

MONTREAL
PRINTED BY EUSEBE SENECAL & FILS
20 ST. VINCENT STREET

# INDEX.

|  | PAGES |
|---|---|
| Mr. O'BRIEN (Muskoka) | 3 |
| Mr. RYKERT (Lincoln & Niagara) | 11 |
| Mr. BARRON (Victoria, O.) | 36 |
| Mr. WALLACE (York, Ont.) | 48 |
| Mr. COLBY (Stanstead) | 53 |
| Mr. MITCHELL (Northumberland) | 59 |
| Mr. McCARTHY (Simcoe N. Riding) | 62 |
| Sir JOHN THOMPSON (Antigonish) | 86 |
| Mr. McNEILL (Bruce N. Riding) | 111 |
| Mr. MILLS (Bothwell) | 113 |
| Mr. CHARLTON (Norfolk, N. Riding) | 134 |
| Mr. MULOCK (York, N. Riding) | 152 |
| Mr. SCRIVER (Huntingdon) | 155 |
| Mr. SUTHERLAND (Oxford, N. Riding) | 158 |
| Mr. McMULLEN (Wellington, N. Riding) | 159 |
| Mr. LAURIER (Quebec, East.) | 161 |
| Sir JOHN A. MACDONALD, (Kingston) | 174 |
| Sir RICHARD CARTWRIGHT, (Oxford, S. Riding) | 183 |

# THE JESUITS' ESTATES ACT.

Mr. FOSTER moved that the House again resolve itself into Committee of Supply.

MR. O'BRIEN (MUSKOKA).

I beg, Sir, to move in amendment :

That all after the word " That " be left out, and the following inserted in lieu thereof: " Mr. Speaker do not now leave the Chair, but that it be resolved, that an humble Address be presented to His Excellency the Governor General, setting forth : 1. That this House regards the power of disallowing the Acts of the Legislative Assemblies of the Provinces, vested in His Excellency in Council, as a prerogative essential to the national existence of the Dominion ; 2. That this great power, while it should never be wantonly exercised, should be fearlessly used for the protection of the rights of a minority, for the preservation of the fundamental principles of the Constitution, and for safe-guarding the general interests of the people ; 3. That in the opinion of this House, the passage by the Legislature of the Province of Quebec of the Act entitled ' An Act respecting the settlement of the Jesuits' Estates ' is beyond the power of that Legislature. Firstly, because it endows from public funds a religious organization, thereby violating the undoubted constitutional principle of the complete separation of Church and State and of the absolute equality of all denominations before the law. Secondly, because it recognizes the usurpation of a right by a foreign authority, namely, His Holiness the Pope of Rome, to claim that his consent was necessary to empower the Provincial Legislature to dispose of a portion of the public domain, and also because the Act is made to depend upon the will, and the appropriation of the grant thereby made as subject to the control of the same authority. And, thirdly, because the endowment of the Society of Jesus, an alien, secret and politico-religious body, the expulsion of which from every Christian community wherein it has had a footing has been rendered necessary by its intolerant and mischievous intermeddling with the functions of civil government, is fraught with danger to the civil and religious liberties of the people of Canada. And this House, therefore, prays that His Excellency will be graciously pleased to disallow the said Act."

I should like to say, in the first place, that, in addressing the House upon this question, which I shall do as briefly as possible, I desire to avoid as far as may be what may be called its religious side, and to confine myself to its constitutional and political aspect. I would further say that I would not have undertaken the serious responsibility of bringing before the House a subject of so delicate a nature, attended with so many difficulties, and so likely to give rise to angry feelings, and possibly to acrimonious discussion, were it not for the very strong sense which I have of what is due to my own convictions on the subject, as well as to the convictions of those whom I represent in this House, and, I will venture to say, to the convictions of the majority of the people of Canada. Now, Sir, one word with regard to my own position in the matter. Had the resolution or any resolutions by my hon. friend the member for North Victoria (Mr. Barron) come before this House in such a shape as to meet the wishes of those who think as I do on this subject, or had they come at such a period in the Session as to have given reason for the probability of a discussion, I should not have interfered. I wish to say further, Sir, that though I was elected as a supporter of the present Administration, and a supporter of their policy so far as that policy could be known, yet, at the same time, during my election contest, and on several subsequent occasions, I said, with the full approbation of my supporters, and I think with the approbation of a great many who did not support me as well, speaking in anticipation of such an Act as that now under review, and speaking in anticipation—because, as we knew, coming events cast their shadow before, and we had had on many occasions indications from various sources and in various quarters, of an attempt to do what I think is inconsistent with the right and privileges of the people of this country — I said that in my place in Parliament I should, regardless of consequences, and regardless of whom it might make or whom it might mar, I should oppose any attempt on the part of any nationality, or any party, or any race, or any religion, to exercise powers, or claim privileges, no guaranteed by treaty, or not secured by subsequent legislation. I am, therefore acting perfectly consistently in moving this resolution, and in taking this step, and not only so, but I would be recreant to my own principles, and recreant to the pledge I gave to those who sent me here, were I to fail in doing so. This resolution which I am about to place in your hands, Mr. Speaker, is, I think, sufficiently explicit, and sufficiently comprehensive, to leave no doubts in the minds of everyone as to what it means. It declares in, I think, reasonable terms, the limit to which the power of disallowance on the part of the Dominion Government should go, and I think, in view of the history of the last twenty years, it ought to meet the approba tion of the House by the declaration that without a full and fearless exercise of the prerogative vested in His Excellency the Governor General by the British North America Act it is impossible that this country can maintain anything like a national existence; I contend, Sir, that while it may be possibly true that an Act may ever be within the four corners of the British North America Act, and although it may be within the literal interpretation of that Act, yet, that if it violates a fundamenta principle of the Constitution—a supposition which is quite possible— or if it in any way interferes with the general interests of the Dominion, if it brings a principle t bear upon the public welfare which the majority of the people consider to be detri mental, even though the Act may originate within that Province, then, Sir, I sa this Government has a right and ought to interfere. I say that this House has th right, as the grand inquest of the nation, to discuss any question of great, nations importance, and especially a question like this which has created a degree of atten tion on the part of the people of this country, which certainly calls for legislativ notice. In the resolution, Sir, I have endeavored, in brief terms, to point out hov we consider that Act violates the Constitution, how it interferes with the rights an privileges of the people, and why it justifies interference as being an Act prejudicia to the general interests of the people. Were I not to say a single word in support o the resolution, I think it would stand before the House as a sufficient manifesto o the sentiment which I and others in this House entertain in regard to the Bill whic we are now about to discuss. Now, Sir, we shall, of course, be met with the conter tion that the Act passed by the Legislature of Quebec is one entirely within th purview of that Assembly—one with which neither this Parliament nor the Goverr ment of the Dominion has anything to do. Before entering into a consideration c that question, it would be well briefly to review the history of the subject. We find then, at the time of the Conquest the Society of Jesuits established and carrying o active operations in all that part of the American continent which was under th jurisdiction of His Most Christian Majesty the King of France ; and far be it from me to say one word derogatory to the manner in which that society performe those great functions. We found them here in possession of estates derived from three sources—chiefly from grants direct from the Crown, from private individual and from purchases by funds out of their own resources ; but all were held by them and necessarily held by them, according to the constitution of the society, for th promotion of the objects they had in hand—these two, I think, mainly : the conver sion of the heathen Indians, and the education of the people of New France. Far b it from me, Sir, to say anything derogatory to the manner in which the first, at an rate, of those works were carried on by the Jesuit missionaries; and I pity the ma who can read without emotion of the hardships, the trials and the sufferings endured by the Jesuit missionaries in their efforts to Christianize the heathen. It is hard for us in these days of luxury and comfort to realize what hardships and sufferings those men went through — sufferings which too often met their only reward in a crown of martyrdom, and which would only be endured from the highest and noblest sense of duty. After the Conquest, the large estates which were possessed by the Jesuit Societies, as well as those possessed by other religious societies, were referred to in the Act of Capitulation ; and so far as the terms of that Act go, that property was secured to them. But, Sir, when the Treaty of Paris came to be made, we find that the reservation made by the Act of Capitulation was not carried out. We find, on the contrary, that while all the rights of property of private individuals were reserved and maintained, those of the various religious communities were expressly exempted, and it was held that those properties had by operation of the law passed into the possession of the Crown. We need not pursue further the history of the estates of the other religious bodies, because we know, as a matter of fact, upon enquiry into the character and operations of these various societies—the Sulpicians and others — that their estates were handed back to them, and have remained in their undisturbed possession ever since. But with regard to the Jesuits a different view was taken ; and is it surprising that a different view should be taken when we consider who and what the Jesuits of that day were ? Although we can only speak in terms of admiration of the operations of those who were carrying on their work in New France ; yet the society at large occupied a very different position, and, Mr. Speaker, had the heads of the society, elsewhere than in Canada, been single-minded and single-hearted, devoted men like Brébeuf and Lallemand, the history of the last century would have been differently written ; the name of Jesuit would not have become a bye-word of reproach throughout all the nations of Europe, and the great Gallican Church, once the bulwark of the French nation, renowned for its independence as well as its piety and learning, would not be dependent on the huge pretensions of ultramontane Rome    That sentiment, I dare say, will not meet with approval on the part of many members of this House. But those who have studied with care the history of Europe during the past three centuries, know that what I have stated is the truth, know that no one has ever more violently opposed the pretensions of the Jesuits than writers of the Roman Catholic Church itself ; and in reference to that, I would say that one of the original grounds on which the society was subsequently suppressed was the fact of its interference with various other religious communities belonging to the Catholic Church. Well, Sir, we find that the Jesuits' Estates were not restored ; and it is not surprising when we consider the position of the society. From the time of Queen Elizabeth downwards the Jesuits had been proscribed in the British realm, and why ? Because it was found that they were enemies of the public peace, that they were determined by every possible means—means which I will not characterize here, because it is not essential to the argument to do so— to overthrow the Protestant succession as established in England ; that they would lose no opportunity and hesitate at no means to accomplish that object. Fortunately for the liberties of Europe and the peace of the world their efforts were unsuccessful. At the same moment, if they had not been actually expelled, they were on the point of being expelled from every country in Europe, just at the time when the question of the legality of their estates came before the law officers of the Crown ;— from Spain, the country where they had their origin, by the Government of His Most Catholic Majesty the King of Spain ; from Naples, under the very shadow of the Pontifical chair. In France, they were brought before the High Court of Paris, the highest tribunal in France, one might almost say in Europe, and there their transactions were a matter of judicial investigation, and the result of that investigation was, that they were suppressed and expelled from France ; and, only a few years later, as everyone knows, in 1773, Pope Clement XIV, pronounced their suppression and abolition in terms which can leave no possible doubt as to his intention to do away with and abolish the society entirely. I say, considering all these things, considering the odor in which the society stood with regard to the Church of Rome itself, considering its actions with regard to the realm of England in times past, it is not surprising that the British Government felt mistrust towards the body they found established in their own country, and hesitated in giving them the means to carry on operations which they would be censurable if they had not regarded as dangerous to the State. Because, why should they suppose that a Jesuit in Canada would act from different principles or motives from what the same men did when they had access to the shores of England? But they did not confiscate the estates, and the term used in the Act is an improper one. They took the opinion of the law officers of the Crown, as to the title of these estates, and that opinion clearly established that the estates had lapsed to the Crown, and that the Crown of England had a right to do with them as it pleased. In 1865, the question of the title to these estates was referred to Sir James Marriot, Judge Advocate General, and in giving his opinion, he said:

"That the order never had in France any legal establishment as part of the civil and ecclesiastical constitution of the realm, having refused the conditions on which it was admitted, because those terms were radically subversive of the whole order. Their title, therefore, to estates in Canada had no better qualification than those titles had by the laws and constitution of the realm of France previous to the Conquest. This society differed from other societies in that it had nowhere any corporate existence. All its property was vested in its General living at Rome, who was neither a French nor a British subject, and could not be either, and, therefore, could not avail himself of the 4th article of the Treaty, being neither an inhabitant of Canada nor a subject of the King of France."

Matters appear to have remained in *statu quo* until 1775, the year after the suppression of the society by the Pope, when, in the instructions to the Governor General, Sir Guy Carleton, it was ordered:

"That the society be suppressed and dissolved, and no longer continued as a body corporate or politic, and all their rights, possessions, and property shall be vested in us for such purposes as we may hereafter think fit to direct or appropriate."

Well, at the same time, all the other religious societies were permitted to retain possession of their property, and anyone will easily understand from what I have said the distinction the Government made between these various bodies. They judged the one by its historical record, and they judged, I think the people will say rightly, in assuming that it was not a society to which they could give encouragement or which they could permit to carry on operations such as the society had been carrying on previously. A similar statement was given later on by the Attorney General and the Assistant Attorney General of Lower Canada, in which they said:

"The nature of their institution prevented them, individually, from taking anything under the capitulation of all Canada, and to their society under one head domiciled at Rome, nothing was granted or could be legally or reasonably be supposed to be conveyed, but even that head, and with it the whole society, wheresoever dispersed, was finally dissolved and suppressed in 1773, so that the existence of the very few members of the order in this Province can in no shape be construed as forming a body, corporate or politic, capable of any of the powers inherent and enjoyed by communities. * * * As a derelict or vacant estate, His Majesty became vested in it by the clearest of titles, if the right of conquest alone was not sufficient, but even upon the footing of the proceedings in France and the judicial acts of the Sovereign Tribunals of that country, the estate in this Province would naturally fall to His Majesty and be subjected to his unlimited disposal, for, by those decisions, it was established, upon good, legal and constitutional grounds, that from the nature of the first establishment, or admission, of the society into France, being conditional, temporary and probational, they would, at all times, be liable to expulsion, and having never complied with, but rejected the terms of their admission, they were not even entitled to the name of a society; wherefore, and by reason of the abuses and destructive principles of their institution they were stripped of their property and possessions."

However, although the legal title was in His Majesty, as representing the Crown of Great Britain, according to this opinion, the Jesuits certainly had no reason to complain of harsh treatment, for they were allowed to remain in possession of their estates untill 1800, when the last survivor of the Order in Canada died. It was not until after that, the Crown took possession of the property, and when they did take possession of the property, the Crown did not confiscate it for any purpose of their own, but, as for as they could, having the legal title, executed the equitable trusts attached to the title; and after much negociation and a good deal of dispute, conveyed the title to the Province of Quebec, in trust for educational purposes. In that position the property remained until the passsage of the Act we are now discussing. Now, I have rather gone out of the way in referring to the legal title of these estates, because in his correspondence Mr. Mercier expressly admits that the Jesuits have no legal title, that their claim was only a moral one; but I have referred to the legal question and to the action of the Government to show upon what very flimsy foundation even this moral claim rests. I contend there was no claim moral, legal, or equitable, on the the part of the Jesuits; I contend that the property had absolutely passed into the possession of the Crown and that the Crown had the power to deal with it as they choose, and the disposition made of the property was one eminently consistent with the objects for which the property had been given to the society. Instead of making the property a present to Lord Amherst, as they had been pressed to do, they handed it over to the Province of Quebec for educational purposes, and thus, as far as possible, carried out the trusts which were attached to the title in this property. Having done so, the Crown parted with the interest they had in it, and the property became that of the Province, but only upon trust for educational purposes. That trust the Province accepted in 1831 by its own legislation, and I contend that having taken that trust, the Province have now no right or power to dispose of the property in the way suggested. Now, among the first of the grounds upon which we claim this Act should be disallowed is the ground that it violates a fundamental principle of the Constitution by endowing a religious society. It matters not by what means that endowment is made or how the money is to be divided, the fact remain that, even after the disposition which has been suggested as likely to take place, a portion of this money, at any rate, goes direct to the Jesuits, and forms a practical, distinct, and direct endowment of a religious society. That, I contend, violates a fundamental principle of our constitution, established in this country for years, namely, that all denominations shall be equal before the law, and that there shall be no vestige of a state church in any part of the Dominion. That principle was laid down in unmistakable terms when the Clergy Reserves of Upper Canada were secularized. Not merely did the secularization of the reserves establish that principle, but the Act by which that secularization was accomplished laid down the principle as well. The Act recites the necessity of:

" Removing all semblance of connection between Church and State."

The Rectory Act of 1850 says :

" Whereas the recognition of legal authority among all religious denominations is an admitted principle of colonial legislation, and whereas, in the state and condition of this Province, to which such a principle is peculiarly applicable, it is desirable that the same should receive the sanction of direct legislative authority, recognizing and declaring this same as a fundamental principle of our civil policy."

It may be contended that was not an Act binding upon the Dominion, but it was an Act to which Upper and Lower Canada united gave their assent, and those who sat in Parliament then, the predecessors of hon. gentlemen now sitting here, representing the same constituencies, gave their assent to the principle, by their votes upon the

Clergy Reserve Bill, that all religious denominations should hereafter cease to be state-supported. Is it a proposition to be tolerated, that while the right to the Clergy Reserves was thus set aside for the sake of an abstract principle, this society should be allowed to stand in a totally different position, and that they should receive compensation for estates to which they have no title, while similar rights are to be denied the other bodies to which I have alluded? Is it to be tolerated that the grants made by George III to the people of the Protestant faith in the Province are to be set aside as contrary to a principle, and yet the grants made to the Jesuits by the King of France are to be held sacred so as to allow compensation to be made to them? I do not think the people of this country will agree to that contention; but that is practically the conclusion to which we are asked to come in regard to this Bill. Another strong point in relation to this Bill is a matter peculiarly affecting the Province of Quebec. I have said that these lands were given to Canada in trust for educational purposes. That trust was accepted and recognized in 1831. The grant was accepted and confirmed by the Legislature at that time, and it was reaffirmed by the United Parliament of Canada in 1856, and again at a later period. The fund was specially set apart for superior education, and the reference which is made to that in the British North America Act clearly establishes that the Province of Ontario has an interest in that fund, and therefore that Province has something to say in regard to the disposition of it, because it is the same estate which is dealt with, and that estate has never been parted with, but has been kept as a separate trust for special purposes; and, by the British North America Act, that trust is accepted and is made a part of the Dominion. The Province of Ontario has a direct interest in that fund, and, therefore, that trust is not one wich the Province of Quebec as a right to deal with in any way whatever. It is a direct breach of trust, and a breach of a contract which was entered into by themselves, and was broken without any reason being adduced, any proposition being made, or any ground being shown. On that ground it is claimed that the power of disallowance should be exercised on behalf of the minority, because this grant of $400,000 is taken directly from the funds of the Province to which all contribute alike; and to say that $60,000 is voted as a sort of compromise, or as a bribe to the Educational Board of the Protestants of the Province, does not affect it. They are bribed with their own money to agree to a grant to a religious institution, and, if it is a compromise, it is a compromise of truth and a compromise of principle. One other ground of objection, and a very strong ground of objection, arises from the terms of the Act, in which the leave of His Holiness the Pope of Rome is asked to dispose of the estate which the Province had no right to dispose of. Can they think they could better their right to dispose of that estate by asking the consent of the Pope? Can they imagine, when they have no right to dispose of it, that they can supply the defect in their title by asking the Pope of Rome to make it good? Mr. Mercier says, in his correspondence:

"Under these circumstances, I deem it my duty to ask Your Eminence if you see any serious objection to the Government's selling the property, pending a final settlement of the question of the Jesuits' Estates."

I must say that is a very remarkable sentence to be found coming from the representative of a Government in a British Legislature—

"The Government would look on the proceeds of the sale as a special deposit to be disposed of here after, in accordance with the agreements to be entered into between the parties interested, with the sanction of the Holy See."

And this is a sentence which shows that Mr. Mercier was so affected by the atmosphere of Rome, where he was at that time, as absolutely to have lost his head—

"As it will perhaps be necessary upon this matter to consult the Legislature of our Province, which is to be convened very shortly, I respectfully solicit an immediate reply."

It was perhaps necessary to consult the Provincial Legislature, but it was absolutely necessary to consult the Pope of Rome ; and this is the answer which is made :

"The Pope allows the Government to retain the proceeds of the sale of the Jesuit Estates as a special deposit to be disposed of hereafter with the sanction of the Holy See."

It is contended, and very likely it will be contended in this House, that the grant of free religious liberty to the Roman Catholics of Quebec at the time of the Conquest carried with it the right of appeal to the Pope, that this is incidental to the right which was granted to them. I say that is untenable, and the British Government took very good care that no such ideas should enter into the minds of the people ; because they took such good care to avoid that, that when the Quebec Act was passed in 1791, they made a distinct provision in regard to it. That Act is the charter of the religious as well as the civil liberties of the Roman Catholics of Quebec, and there we find the following words :—

"It is declared that His Majesty's subjects professing the religion of the Church of Rome, of and in the said Province of Quebec, may have, hold and enjoy the free exercise of the religion of the Church of Rome, subject to the King's supremacy declared and established by an Act made in the first year of the reign of Queen Elizabeth, over all the dominion and countries which then did or thereafter should belong to the Imperial Crown of this Realm."

It is mere child's play to pretend, in the face of this Act under which the religious liberties of these people are granted, which would not otherwise have existed, this Act which set aside in their favor a great part of the Statute law of England, that they have any right to appeal to the Pope or to pretend that the Queen's supremacy does not exist, or that they have any privilege or any right in this country which is not controlled by the Act of Supremacy. In order still further to render it impossible that these people should entertain any idea that they were not subject to the control of England in regard to these matters, and to prevent any idea that they could appeal to the Pope of Rome in the past, or that they might take any such position at any time, I will quote the instructions given to Governor Murray in 1762, when he received the following admonition :—

"You are not to admit of any ecclesiastical jurisdiction of the See of Rome, or of any other foreign ecclesiastical jurisdiction in the Province under your jurisdiction."

And again, in 1775, Governor Carleton is reminded :—

"That all appeals to or correspondence with any foreign ecclesiastical jurisdiction of what nature or kind soever, be absolutely forbidden under very severe penalties."

There can, therefore; be no doubt that the Act of Supremacy was in force, and that the rights and privileges guaranteed were controlled by the Act, and that for some years they were so controlled ; because, if I am not mistaken, no appointments were made by the Pope for many years subsequent to the Conquest. Of course, as time went on, the restrictions were relaxed and many things were allowed to be done which were contrary to the Act of Supremacy, but it is quite evident that that was toleration and not a grant. It is quite evident, I think, from these facts, that it cannot be consonant with the religious liberty guaranteed by the Quebec Act, to allow an appeal to the Pope, or to recognize his jurisdiction as being of any authority in the affairs of the Provinces. I think, Mr. Speaker, it is a contention which hardly needs to be made in this House, it is a contention which need hardly more than be stated, that to pass an Act of Parliament by the Lieutenant Governor, the Assembly and the Legislative Council of a Province, and so expressed that the validity of that Act shall be dependent upon any foreign jurisdiction whatever — I say it is almost childish to contend that such an Act can be constitutional. I have heard it said that this correspondence forms no part of the Act. Well, if it is not intended to form part of the Act, what is it put there for ? A clause of the Act expressly makes it a part of the Act; it would be a mere legal quibble to contend that it is no part of the Act, because without it the Act would be meaningless and would have no force at all. The agreement set forth in the correspondence is the very essence of the Act. It may be contended as a legal proposition that it is not part of the Act, but that is a proposition which will never commend itself to the common sense of the people at large. I say it is hardly worth while to argue that no Province, no Assembly, no Parliament under the British Crown, much less a Provincial Parliament, which has only a delegated power, can make an Act which is valid by the assent of any other power ; because the affirmative implies also the negative, and if assent is necessary to make an Act valid, clearly inaction on the part of the referree would condemn the Act. The Act is made absolutely dependent upon the will of a foreign power. It matters not whether it is Pope or President, Kaiser or King, it does not matter who the authority is, it cannot be constitutional for the Parliament of this country to pass an Act which depends for its validity upon any foreign jurisdiction whatever. I have heard it contended that it would be a precisely analogous case were the Province of Ontario to make a grant to the Synod of the Diocese of Toronto, and that the distribution of the grant was made subject to the control of the Archbishop of Canterbury. Well, I think that such an Act would be absolutely invalid for the same reason, because the Provincial Legislature has no right to delegate its power to a foreign power, or to do anything that would diminish its own power, or the power of the Crown. But, moreover, there is no analogy between the two cases, because the Archbishop of Canterbury would still be a subject of the British Crown, whereas, in other cases, the foreign power is not so. But I do not think that the analogy is needed, because it cannot be contended that an Act is constitutional which depends for its validity upon the exercise of any foreign jurisdiction. But I will leave the constitutional question to be argued by the lawyers, if they think it worth while to spend their time in doing so ; but I am very sure of this, that whatever the lawyers may say, the people of this country will be satisfied with the proposition that it is unconstitutional, and that it ought to be unconstitutional, for any Parliament in this country to pass an Act whose validity is made to depend upon the affirmation or the negation of any foreign jurisdiction, no matter what that jurisdiction may be. Now, Sir, in the resolution which I have read, we take another ground as one upon which this Act should be disallowed. We say it should be disallowed, because we contend that the endowment of the Society of Jesus, an alien, secret and politico-religious body, is fraught with danger to the civil and religious liberties of the people of Canada. Why do we say that ? Because we find from the history of that society during the last 300 years, that wherever its operations have been known they have in various ways interfered with the functions of civil government, they have interfered with the independence of other religious bodies, and they have taught a system of morality which cannot be inculcated generally without destroying, not only the independence, but also the morality of the people. It may be said, perhaps it will be said, that all these are idle tales. It may be said that the principles and practices of this society are so altered, in conformity with modern usages and modern views, that the ideas which formerly prevailed, no longer have existence. But, unfortunately, there are too many modern writings, too many modern records, which contradict that view of the case, and make it impossible for us to believe that this society has so altered its principles, so departed from its previous practices, that it can now be recognized as a society which can be established and encouraged in this Dominion, or in any other country inhabited by Her Majesty's subjects. The weapons used by this society may possibly have changed.

There may be the same difference between what the society was at the time of the Conquest, at the time when it was in its very worst position, at the time when the English Government were called upon to deal with it, and when the European Governments of Catholic countries, and also the Roman Catholic Church itself, were obliged to suppress it—I say, there is the same difference between the society in those days and the society as it manifests itself to-day, that there is between the muskets used by Wolfe on the Plains of Abraham and the rifles that were used by General Wolsely in Egypt; the weapons may be different, but the power behind them remains the same. If we may contrast the documents that we find in our library, if we may read the statements published within the last fifteen or twenty years, we find the same doctrines inculcated, we find there is no change such as would justify us in giving our assent to the establishment of this order in our country. Sir, a Jesuit is a being abnormal in his conditions; he has no family ties, no home nor country. He is subject absolutely to the will of his superior. I say that such a system, that such an order, being subject to an irresponsible power, must be dangerous, as it always has been dangerous to every community in which it has existed. I admit there have been in this society men of high attainments, men of high moral worth, but that does not render the society less dangerous. It has not rendered it less dangerous in the past, that wherever that there was work to be done, whether the work was good or bad, there were always the right men to do it. It is because we know from their own writings, from their practice, from their history in times past, that such is the case, that we say that in this free country it is not desirable to allow the existence of a society which inculcates principles more or less repugnant, not only to our civilization, but to every principle that unites communities in every condition of life. For these reasons, Mr. Speaker, and for many others which might be adduced in respect to the constitutionality of the Act, we say it should be repealed; we say the Government should exercise with discretion this power of disallowance, but that it should disallow this Act; we say that the majority of the people of the Dominion desire that this should be done. I know that the vote on my resolution this evening, or to-night, or to-morrow, or whenever it may be taken, will imply a very strong contradiction to this statement; but nevertheless, I am quite willing that the decision of this question should go from the jury of this House to the jury of the people, and I venture to say that the time has come judging not only by the passage of this Act, which is but one among a number of incidents, but by other events, when we have a right to say to hon, gentlemen in this House and to the people of this country, just as we said to our American cousins with respect to commercial affairs : " Canada is not for sale." So we say to them here, and we will say it elsewhere : ." This Dominion must remain British and nothing else, and no power or authority, no jurisdiction, foreign, civil, religious or otherwise, shall be allowed to exercise power which will interfere with its affairs." Mr. Speaker, the resolution is in itself, I think, so comprehensive that it is not necessary I should further occupy the time of the House in enlarging upon it. As I said at the beginning, it is so clear and comprehensive that the country will understand what it means, and members of this House will understand what they are voting for ; and such being the case, not desiring to prolong the discussion, not desiring to say one word more than is absolutely necessary to sustain the position I take in reference to this question, I beg to place this motion, Mr. Speaker, in your hands.

Mr. RYKERT (LINCOLN & NIAGARA).

I think, Mr. Speaker, that if the predictions of the hon. gentleman are correct as regards the feelings of the country upon this question, then it is absolutely useless for me to say one word to this House. I entirely dissent from the proposition or from the assertion of the hon. gentleman, that the great majority of the people of this country are in favor of the disallowance of this Act in question, and I unhesitatingly assert that the majority of the people of this Dominion are not in favor of its disallowance. The hon. gentleman h is taken that ground; I cannot tell from what source he gets his information, except from the public press, but I venture to say that if the Province of Ontario were canvassed to-day, without prejudice, without religious bigotry, the people fully understanding the question, the vast majority of the people would dissent from the proposition of the hon. gentleman. We are told outside of this House, and inside of this House, that certain religious bodies and certain bodies in this country are in favor of disallowance. We are threatened, Sir, by the public papers and the public organs throughout this country with decapitation, and with being driven from Parliament if we dare, upon the floor of Parliament, to assert our right to declare that his Act is constitutional. I am told, Sir, and the public press repeats it day after day, that no Orangemen dare stand upon the floor of Parliament and speak in favor of allowing this Bill to go into operation. I, Sir, am an Orangeman, and I will dare so to speak. I speak as an Orangeman, and I say : that I fulfil all the tenets of my order, and that I am just and right in supporting the Government in the course it has taken. I speak upon this question because we are told and threatened by papers that if we favor allowance we will be exterminated from the order. Sir, it is one of the first principles of the Orange Order that there should be civil and religious liberty for t all. Allow me to quote one portion of the constitution of that order, and when I do so, I do not think that any person will say that I am not justified in taking the stand I am taking here to-day. It says :

" Disclaiming an intolerant spirit, the Association demands as an indispensable qualification, without which the greatest and the wealthiest may seek admission in vain, that the candidate shall be deemed incapable of persecuting or injuring anyone on account of his religious speeches; the duty of every Orangeman being to aid and defend all loyal subjects of every religious persuasion in the enjoyment of their constitutional rights."

I say, Sir, that I fulfil the precepts of the order, in standing up to defend the action of the Government in refusing to disallow this Bill. I would be sorry to incur the hostility of a large portion of the people of the Province, as my hon. friend (Mr. O'Brien) says, but, Sir, I have upon another occasion had an opportunity of facing public opinion on a similar question, and I am prepared to go back to my constituents on this issue, and when I put the question fairly before them, and when they fully understand it, I have no doubt they will say I was right in supporting the Government, and that the Government was right in pursuing the course it did. I am not prepared to join this crusade, or this unholy alliance against my Roman Catholic fellow-countrymen ; I am not prepared, Sir, as one professing strong Protestant views and professing the principles of the Protestant religion, to join in this crusade, and, as I said before, this unholy alliance against my Roman Catholic fellow-countrymen. Day after day we see the press endeavoring to inflame the public mind on this question ; we see them day after day trying to stir up religious animosity and strife in every portion of this community, but that unfortunate spirit, I am glad to say, has not yet reached the Orange Order. It has reached the public through a certain class of ministers in this country, who seem determined, at whatever cost, to drive Pope and Popery from this country, That seems to be the ground-work of the whole opposition of this class to which I refer, and I think I will be able to show, before I sit down, that that is their whole aim. I am familiar with the history of the past in this country, I am familiar with what took place prior to Confederation, when. Sir, in the old Parliament of Canada the great fight was against Lower Canadian domination. What was the cry then ? It was : " We are trampled upon by our Roman Catholic fellow-countrymen." Fortunately for this country, our people united at the time of Confederation, they threw aside their religious differences and joined together for the common good of their common country. Is it to be said that after twenty-one years of our existence, one section of the people of this country is to be found fighting against a large body of their

Roman Catholic fellow-citizens and urging us to throw a stumbling block in the way of the progress of the Confederation. We must remember that in this country we have made great national progress by joining together and throwing aside those religious cries. We have done all that we could do to perpetuate a good feeling upon this continent, and I am happy to say, Sir, that the united action of Catholics and Protestants of Canada has led us to-day to a prosperous and progressing condition. I would like to know if we ought to accept the advice of my hon. friend from Muskoka (Mr. O'Brien) and send the firebrands throughout this country to array one religion against another. What must be the inevitable result of that? The result will be that it will drive every Protestant member of Parliament from the Province of Quebec, and I would not blame the Roman Catholics for that; I think they would be justified in doing so, if the Protestants of Ontario would adopt the same course in that Province and drive out every Roman Catholic member. But I believe that any person who takes a fair view of the question will not say that it is a right course to pursue. I say, Sir, that this agitation is an attempt upon the part of a certain portion of the Protestants of Ontario, not to stand by the minority in Lower Canada, but over the heads of the Jesuits to attack the Roman Catholic faith I am not here to-day to defend the Jesuits, nor am I here to speak of their past history, but I may be permitted, before I sit down, to quote one or two observations in connection with their past history from competent authorities, in opposition to what my hon. friend says. I did hope that upon the discussion of this question nothing of the history of the past would be imported, but that we might be allowed to consider it on its merits, as to whether the Government were right or wrong in refusing to disallow the Bill. The people of the Province of Ontario have been inflamed and fired, as I said before, by enthusiasts and fanatics upon the question. I will take the ground in opposition to them, and I think I will be able to show to the House and to the people of this country the position which those I have referred to occupy on this question. The first paper which seems to have taken up the crusade is the *Mail*. It was said a few days ago that the *Globe* had made a wonderful somersault, but I venture to assert that the *Mail* took a greater somersault on this question than the *Globe*. The *Mail* has occupied several different positions in the matter, and we find that in the wind-up it calls on the people of this country to " prevent the encroachment of the French into the Province of Ontario." Some time ago the *Mail* said, referring to the Provincial Legislature on the Jesuit question :

" They have exceeded their powers."

And it goes on to say :

" We are ready, however, to argue the question on the narrower ground and to maintain that in endowing religious propagandism out of the public taxes, the Legislature of Quebec has exceeded its powers."

Mark you, Sir, the *Mail* says that " the Legislature has exceeded its powers ; " and what are we to do then, are we to disallow this Bill ? No; you must not disallow it, but you must go to the courts to seek for a remedy. The *Mail* further says :

" Acts done in excess of legal powers do not call for the use of a veto ; they are void, and will be declared void by the courts of law. A veto is a political, not a judicial power, and is given as a political safeguard. It is given to the national Government of Canada, to guard the nation against action, on the part of any of the members, injurious to its interest as a whole, to its honor, or to its unity."

In this extract this paper takes the ground that the Act is *ultra vires*, that it is beyond the power of the Local Legislature, and as such it should be fought in the courts. Then the *Mail* takes another stand, and on the 22nd of March it says :

" A French Canadian contemporary says : ' The *Mail* rests is whole case against the Jesuits upon the alleged unconstitutionality of the Estates Act.' This is a mistake. The strongest objection to both Acts is that they are contrary to the public interest. The prerogative of disallowance is frequently exercised on this high ground against measures that are perfectly constitutional and *intra vires* of the Provincial Legislatures."

Sir, if that be the case I will be prepared to show that it is not in accord with the views taken by those celebrated law ournals of the Province of Ontario, which took altogether another ground, and which ground has convinced the *Globe* newspaper that it was wrong in pronouncing in favor of the allowance of the Act. You will see from this that the *Mail* commences by declaring the Act *ultra vires* and unconstitutional, and, in the end, that it demands the disallowance of the Bill upon the ground that it is against public policy. It is hard to tell upon what ground that paper chooses to take its stand upon this question. Day after day we have been favored with the history of the Jesuits and their rascalities and misdeeds in days gone by, of which my hon. friend speaks so feelingly ; and the *Mail* newspaper usually winds up by calling on the Protestants of Ontario to put an end to the encroachment of Popery in this country. On the 14th of March, we find this language, which I commend to my friends from Lower Canada :

" If the British and Protestant element in Quebec will not save itself, we must try to save it for our own sakes. That the abandonment of Quebec to the Ultramontane and the Jesuit will be the death of Canadian nationality is clear enough. But Ontario will not be safe. Our eastern gate has already been opened by the perfidious hand of the vote-hunting politician, and French and Roman Catholic invasion is streaming through. The French priest, it is true, cannot formally import into Ontario his Church establishment and his system of tithes. But this matters little if he can thrust out the British population and plant in its room a population which will be under his away, and from which he can wring practically any payments which he thinks fit. The assessor, moreover, will be his creature, and he will be able to distribute the burden of local taxation between the faithful and the heretic pretty much at his pleasure. He will, to all intents and purposes, detach eastern Ontario from the British and Protestant civilization, of which it now forms a part, and annex it to the territory of the French race, which is also the dominion of the priest. No distortion of facts by sophistical rhetoric, no hypocritical protests against race feeling, will hide from us either the gravity or the imminence of this result."

After its long labor of the last three or four months in portraying the history and misdeeds of the Jesuits, this paper holds this question up as a sort of bugbear to frighten the people of Ontario into opposition to the Government, and finally winds up by coming out in its true colors and saying that they must prevent the encroachment of the Roman Catholic Church and the French Canadians in Ontario. Now, we find that for a long time the late organ of some hon. gentlemen opposite was very strong on this question. It discussed it from all points of view, both on its merits and on its constitutional aspects, and on several occasions it has taken a very strong stand in favor of the Bill being allowed, and in support of the contention of the present Government. But while this strain runs through all the editorials, you will find in them a strong feeling against the Dominion Government, and a desire to excite against that Government not only the Protestants of Ontario, but the Orangemen as a body. With that object in view it calls attention to the fact that on the 12th of July, which is a famous day in the history of Orangemen, the Tory Lieut. Governor of Quebec allowed the Jesuit Bill. That was done to inflame Orange feeling against this Government. It went on to say :

" These citations clearly show that the Liberals, if they were in office at Ottawa now, could not disallow the Jesuits' Estates Act without enormous inconsistency. With equal clearness these citations show that the Conservatives are not only free to disallow the Act, but are bound in consistency to disallow it if they believe it to be wrong in principle and unjust to the Protestant minority."

Then, on the 4th of March, it pointed out the danger that this country was running into, and that the result must be the breaking up of Confederation. It says :

" Again we ask, should the Bill be allowed or disallowed? A Protestant of a practical turn of mind may well answer : ' I can't tell—it's six of one and half-a-dozen of the other.' The truth is that the people of Ontario are at the cross-roads where they must decide either to continue with or separate from a Quebec that is ever becoming more thoroughly Roman Catholic. If Ontarians wish to perpetuate the Confederation they will quietly accept Sir John's allowance of the Jesuits' Bill. If they can't stomach that allowance they may as well face the truth like honest men and acknowledge that they really do not think the Confederation worth preserving. The course of the *Globe* has been, and will be, perfectly straightforward. We do not mean to blame Sir John Macnonald——."

Do you believe that? I do not, for one :—

" We do not mean to blame Sir John Macdonald if he stands by his disallowance theories and vetoes the Bill. We will not in any way aid any persons who may endeavor to excite race and creed passions over the affair. If the people of Ontario hold great meetings to press for disallowance, and if they otherwise signify that they are sincerely desirous to enter upon a serious struggle with Quebec, we will advise them that the end can be nothing else than the destruction of the Confederation, and that it would be incomparably better for all concerned that the Federal compact should be quietly dissolved now than dissolved after and in consequence of a long, bitter conflict that would be, at best, a savage verbal struggle, and at worst one marked by riot, bloodshed and civil war."

These were the predictions of the late organ of the party of hon. gentlemen opposite, and, if the consequences were to be such as the *Globe* newspaper predicted, one would suppose that the Government of the country were justified in allowing that Bill. But, Sir, on the 16th of March, a day, I suppose, ever memorable in Room No 6 in this House, we find that the *Globe* newspaper made the somersault, and I venture to assert that no public paper in this country ever made such a somersault. We have also the opinions of other papers. I will only read a few, and I do this, not with the view alone of being heard in this House, but I have to answer to my constituents, and I want to place my case before them should I ever ask them for their suffrages again. The London *Advertiser* of March 14, says :

" From the quotation given by Dr. Grant from Mr. Mercier's speech in moving the Legislature into Committee on the resolutions, it is clear that the purpose was not to acknowledge any authority in the Pope in the legislative affairs of the Province, but to secure finality in a dispute long pending."

The Hamilton *Times* of October 19, after waking up to the sudden conversion of the *Globe*, deals with the question from the constitutional point of view, and I commend its language to my hon. friend from Muskoka :

" By some it is claimed that the mention of the Pope's name as a party to the Bill renders it unconstitutional. We cannot decide so intricate a question as that, though it appears to us that the Pope stands in the same relation that contractor Onderdonk or any other foreigner would occupy with respect to the payment of public funds. So far as our light goes we should oppose the disallowance of the Bill, though we reserve the right to hear and consider evidence on the point that the Bill is unconstitutional. The idea that Ontario and the rest of the Dominion will have to supply the money to pay the Jesuits should not have weight in the discussion."

I may quote from another organ of hon. gentlemen opposite, the Belleville *Ontario*, of the 19th of March, which gives the *Globe* a certificate of character :

" The vacillating policy of the Toronto *Globe* of late years on almost every public question is without precedent in Canadian journalism. Its latest somersault on the Jesuit Bill is enough to restore the founder of this ever-powerful paper to life again. The *Globe's* flop over has caused a feeling among the Liberals at Ottawa little short of disgust for the men who at present are responsible for its policy, if such it can be called."

Now, Sir, I propose briefly to show—and this is a point my hon. friend has avoided —the feeling in the Province of Quebec on this important question ; because, while

I appreciate the effort of my hon. friend to defend the rights of the people of Ontario, I think also he might have had something to say with regard to the opinion of the minority in the Province of Quebec. We heard nothing from the hon. gentleman concerning the Bill of 1887. He steadily avoided that question, and confined his argument wholly to the Bill now under consideration. We are here to-day for the purpose of considering whether or not this Bill should be allowed or disallowed ; but behind that question is another one. Should the Bill of 1887, incorporating this society, have been allowed or disallowed? The hon. gentleman said nothing about that. No one has spoken about it in Parliament or out of Parliament. It was allowed to pass, and thus we recognized, in not disallowing that measure, the right of the Province of Quebec to incorporate the Jesuits. Having done so, the question arises, is it just and right to go further, and supplement that measure by giving money to this order ? What is the opinion of the people of the Province of Quebec on that subject ? I can appeal to the leader of the Third party for his views. I find throughout the whole of this controversy on this question, that the newspaper controlled by my hon. friend (Mr. Mitchell), supported the Mercier Government. Although he pointed out that such an Act was inexpedient, he always took the ground that the Bill was a fair one in the interests of the country.

    Mr. MITCHELL. That is good authority.

    Mr. RYKERT. Very good, but I want to give a better one.

    Mr. MITCHELL. Question.

    M. RYKERT. I will give the authority of the Montreal *Gazette*, which I look upon as a good authority, expressing the opinion of the English-speaking people of the Province of Quebec very fairly. The *Gazette* has had several editorials on the question, from one of which I propose to quote a few observations, in order to satisfy at any rate, the people of the Province of Ontario, that while they are so exercised about the rights of the minority in Quebec, the minority in that Province, which is well able to take care of itself, has taken no exception to the legislation passed :

> " Excepting the Huntingdon *Gleaner*, we are not aware that any newspaper in this or any other Province of the Dominion interested itself in the matter. The Protestant Committee of the Council of Public Instruction silently acquiesced on securing its sixty thousand dollars. There was a slight ruffle as to how to apply the money, but that was all. The Protestant members of the Legislature did not take the trouble to divide the House upon it; the leading spirits of Mr. Mercier's Protestant following thought it a very reasonable measure, and not one word of dissent was heard from anybody, clerical or otherwise. The Bill in its various stages appeared in the telegraphic summaries of the newspapers of the Dominion, with no more emphasis than any bill to incorporate a trading company."

So that you see while this matter was being discussed in the Quebec Legislature, and while the people were made aware of what was going on from day to day, and the minority of Quebec had every opportunity of expressing their dissent and making known their opposition, if there was anything wrong in the Bill, no exception was taken by them either on constitutional grounds or on grounds of public policy. The *Gazette* goes on further to say that :

> " They felt that the true claimant for this property was the Roman Catholic Church in general, and that church was represented by its ecclesiastical head, and not by a recently incorporated body of ecclesiastics governed by a foreign general, no matter how estimable they might be."

I commend this to the attention of the hon. member for Muskoka (Mr. O'Brien) :

" Now, in the face of these threats of extra provincial intervention, Roman Catholics, no matter what they think, must, in self-respect, close their ranks."

That is the opinion of a Protestant paper in the Province of Quebec.—

" If there be one principle clear in a Parliamentary Government, it is the right of the representatives of the people to dispose of the money of the people. It is one of these self-evident principles which, if men's minds were not heated by religious and political passion, no one would dream of disputing."

But there is another authority which I will cite, because I find that persons belonging to the same church are trying to foment discord and religious disturbance in Ontario on this question. I will cite the opinion of the Rev. Dr. Campbell, of the city of Montreal, Presbyterian clergyman, who discussed the question in all its merits. In a letter published some time ago he says :

" That is reason sufficient why we in Canada, Protestants and Roman Catholics alike, should be very slow to afford them any encouragement in our country. But we failed—we who should have vigorously protested against their establishment and endowment,—to make our voices heard at the moment when our views might have influenced the situation. The Protestant representatives in the House of Assembly did not oppose the two measures as stoutly as they ought to have done, and the people failed to petition the Legislature against the Bills. Not having availed themselves of their constitutional rights while the measures were under discussion, they virtually put themselves out of court. It is not fair either to the local authorities or to those at Ottawa for us now to make an outcry. Mr. Mercier was justified in concluding, while the Bills were before the Assembly, that there was no very strong sentiment against them in the Province, or else the Legislature would have been flooded with petitions against them, as it always is when there are proposals before it directly affecting the people's pockets. Nor have we any right to feel greatly disappointed that the Federal authorities did not put themselves in an embarrassing position to shield us from the consequences of our own neglect of our interests, when they could urge a constitutional plea to rid themselves of responsibility in the matter."

That is the opinion of a gentleman whose opinion is worth having, and who addressed a letter some time ago to the Montreal *Witness* in which he expresses those views. But let us look at what was done in the Legislature. We find that in the Legislature, when the matter was under discussion, different members spoke upon the question. We find that Hon. M. Lynch, a Protestant member, spoke, and I have taken this extract from the paper to show that he who represented the interests of Protestants was fully alive to the importance of the question under discussion and expressed his opinion at the time :

" Notwithstanding what may be thought in some quarters, there is nothing in the Bill alarming in its character. We are living in an age where wisdom prevails, living in an age in which freedom is supposed to exist the world over, and nowhere in the dominions of Her Majesty does liberty prevail more than in the Province of Quebec. *** Is it possible that the intelligent public opinion of the Province of Quebec should deny those Jesuit Fathers the civil rights we have granted to every one else ? "

Then we have the opinion of several gentlemen in the Upper House. Among them, Mr. Starnes, who said :

" I approve of the Bill as it is, for that question should have been settled long ago. Protestants and Catholics ought to be satisfied with the manner in which the question is now settled."

The Hon. David Ross also said :

" Some newspapers have shown me up as the friend of the Jesuits and as a bad Protestant, because I lent my assistance to the settlement of this question. I will answer it by saying that I am neither a friend nor an enemy of the Jesuits. We had to deal with a question of justice, and I gave it my support. The Protestants themselves entertain the belief that the Jesuits deserve some compensation for the estates taken away from them. Moreover, the Protestants whom I represent in the Cabinet, are well satisfied with the settlement of this question, as you have heard the hon. councillor for Wellington express it, and with the indemnity which falls to their lot."

So that you will see Protestant public opinion to-day in Quebec is strongly in favor of the Bill and the settlement made, and against disallowance. I am glad to see also that while the Orange body has seen fit to pass resolutions as a body in favor of disallowance, there are some Lodges in the Province which have had the courage of their convictions, which have stated the question broadly and have not seen fit to endorse the action of the Grand Lodge. I find at a meeting of L. O. L., 152, Dorchester township, a strong resolution was passed condemning the Quebec Government for passing the Jesuits' Estates Bill, and expressing the opinion that a number of the Orange lodges had acted unwisely in condemning the Dominion Government for not disallowing the measure, as they firmly believed that if an injustice had been done, redress would be better secured by the various Protestant denominations taking united action in pressing the claims of the Protestant body. The resolution goes on further to express the hope that that course will be followed, so that the legal opinion may be tested. As I said a few minutes ago, an effort has been made to fire the public mind in the Province of Ontario by calling on the people to form organizations with a view of putting down the Roman Catholic religion in that Province and also throughout this country. We find that Mr. Hughes has taken a very active part in this matter. I mention him because, day after day, his name is cited as an authority on the subject, and only last night I find it reported that he addressed a meeting in the Pavilion in Toronto upon this important question. But, after reciting, as my hon. friend from Muskoka (Mr. O'Brien) has done, all the misdeeds of the Jesuits, he winds up by asking the people of this country to establish an organization similar to one existing in Scotland, and proposes the following as the objects :—

" The objects of the Alliance are :—(a) The defence of our common Christianity ; (b) the exposure of the errors of Popery and Infidelity ; (c) the instruction of Roman Catholics in Bible truth ; and (d) the maintenance and promotion of the great Scriptural principles of the Scottish Reformation.
" The membership of the Alliance is composed of persons of all the Protestant denominations, and various political opinions, who are thoroughly agreed that the Papacy is an enemy to national and social prosperity, and to personal freedom, and who are resolved to resist the aggressions in the Empire by every possible means."

So you will see that the sum and substance of the arguments of those people in the Province of Ontario is, first, to inflame the public mind by reciting historical reminiscences, and then to arouse a certain feeling in favor of the Protestant religion. I find, also, that the Rev. Mr. Ross says :

" The Church of Rome in the Province of Quebec is established and endowed in violation of the said principle. We hereby request the Dominion Government to take steps to secure the revision of the British North America Act, so as to lead to the disestablishment and disendowment of said church in said Province."

It is thus evident that nearly all these gentlemen run in the same direction. I am glad, however, to find that, conspicuous among many people in the Province of Ontario, are men of larger minds, men such as the Rev. Principal Grant, who has expressed himself on several occasions in regard to this matter, and has published a letter in the public press which I will do him the justice of quoting. He is as much interested in the welfare of Protestantism as anyone in the Province of Ontario, and he has seen fit to discuss this question on its merits and to publish his views in the press. He says :

" If the matter was to be settled at all, and before giving an opinion on that point, let us remember that the great majority of the people of Quebec are Roman Catholics. I do not see what else Mr. Mercier could have done than require the sanction of the Pope to the bargain. It may seem astonishing to Protestants that Roman Catholics should acknowledge a man living in Rome as the head of their church. But they do. Protestants must accept that fact in the same spirit in which all facts should be accepted."

So it is clear that he has not the same dread of the Pope exercising his clerical powers, as far as this Act is concerned, as some gentlemen have. He goes on :

" The grant of money to the Jesuits. But the money was not awarded, and has not been given to the Jesuits. It has been given to the Roman Catholic Church. Doubtless the Jesuits will get some of it. Mr. Mercier, in his speech, quotes a letter, dated 11th October, 1884, from the Secretary of the Propaganda to the General of the Jesuits, promising on the part of the Pope that when the matter was settled they would get a share, the proportion to be subsequently determined."

The House will thus see that there are persons who regard this question from a different standpoint; as also, in this city of Ottawa, the Rev. Mr. Herridge, speaking on the question, stated that it was purely a question of money, and that he could see no reason why there should be any interference on the part of the Government with a Bill which was not, in his opinion, detrimental to the interests of the country or to the policy of the country. The fact is that the people are not thoroughly informed on this question, and in the papers from day to day the historical references are not correct. In fact, they are just as incorrect as some of those which my hon. friend (Mr. O'Brien) made to-day, as I shall point out later. The Ministerial Association in Toronto is composed of a number of men of all denominations, and they could not find out whether the Jesuit Order has ever been suppressed in this country or not, and, after searching for a week, they could not come to a conclusion. And yet these are the men who pretend to guide public opinion. I deny their right to do so, or I say, at all events, that, before they do so, they should first inform themselves as to the facts. Then I find that a resolution was moved by Dr. McVicar and seconded by Dr. Campbell, and what is asked by that resolution is to have a certified copy of the Bill sent to the Queen, and then they say she will disallow it. Why, they do not seem to understand the constitution of this country, when they think that an Act of the Province of Quebec can be sent to the Queen for disallowance, whereas it is only the Acts of this Parliament which are subject to disallowance by the Queen. They are in absolute ignorance of the provisions of the British North America Act. Now, I do not intend to defend the Jesuits, but I am going to quote a few authorities to show that, in this country, at all events, they are not as bad as my hon. friend (Mr. O'Brien) makes them out to be. In his speech, he said he did not propose to discuss the course of the Jesuits in this country, but only to refer to their misdeeds in the past. I will quote from one or two articles on that subject, because it is just as well to understand what Protestants think in regard to the Jesuits. As I said, I do not pretend to make any elaborate argument on the subject, or to defend the Jesuits or their acts, but I find that public men in this country, persons who have written on this question here and in England, are of one accord that the Jesuits of to-day are not the Jesuits of 100 years ago. That is where my hon. friend goes astray. He refers to their intriguing in Europe, and to their determination to upset every State in Europe, and to various acts of theirs which will not commend themselves to anyone ; but he should have also referred to those authorities who took an entirely different view of the subject. In Parkman's work I find this testimony given to the Jesuits :

" The lives of these early Canadian Jesuits attest the earnestness of their faith and the intensity of their zeal ; but it was a zeal bridled, curbed, and ruled by a guiding hand. Their marvellous training in equal measure kindled enthusiasm and controlled it, roused, into action a mighty power, and made it as subservient as those great material forces which modern science has learned to awaken and to govern. They were drilled to a factitious humility, prone to find utterance in expressions of self-depreciation and self-scorn, which one may often judge unwisely when he condemns them as insincere. They were devoted believers, not only in the fundamental dogmas of Rome, but in those lesser matters of faith which heresy despises as idle and puerile superstitions. One great aim engrossed their lives. For the greater glory of God they would act or wait, dare, suffer or die, yet all in unquestioning subjection to the authority of the Superiors, in whom they recognized the agents of divine authority itself."

Then I find that Macaulay—and I do not suppose many in this House will question his authority—in his "History of England," spoke of these men as follows:—

"No religious community could produce a list of men so variously distinguished; none had extended its operations over so vast a space; yet in none had there been such perfect unity of feeling and action. There was no region of the globe, no walk of speculative or active life in which Jesuits were not to be found. They guided the councils of Kings. They deciphered Latin inscriptions. They observed the motions of Jupiter's satellites. They published whole libraries, controversy, casuistry, history, treatises on optics, alcaic odes, editions of the fathers, madrigals, catechisms and lampoons. The liberal education of youth passed almost entirely into their hands, and was conducted by them with conspicuous ability. They appear to have discovered the precise point to which intellectual culture can be carried without the risk of intellectual emancipation. Enmity itself was compelled to own that, in the art of managing and forming the tender mind, they had no equals."

That seems to be entirely in opposition to the views which have been expressed by my hon. friend, and the various assertions as to their practices in the mother country. But we have an authority in this country which I think will also be received in this House. I refer not to the organ of the Third party, but to the Montreal *Gazette*, which, on the 25th June last, speaking of the Jesuits, and knowing well what they are in the Province of Quebec, says :

"There is probably no country in the world in which the Society of Jesus has enjoyed so fair a reputation and so large a share of goodwill from the people generally, without distinction of creed, as have fallen to their lot in Canada. Their piety, humanity and courage are associated with the most heroic and romantic periods in our annals. ' The story of their trials and triumphs on this continent, and especially within the limits of our own land, is one of the most interesting and instructive in the records of missionary labor.' If we except certain works and ambitions which marked some passages in their career, the members of the order in Canada have never forfeited that respect which is due to the faithful prosecution of noble aims."

So you see that we have testimony from the Province of Quebec that at least they have some friends in this country, and that they are not looked upon in the same light as they were in the mother country and on the continent. Now, Sir, one of the arguments of my hon. friend was that the Jesuits are hostile to the Roman Catholic Church. Well, I have read different sermons, that of Father Hand in Toronto and Father Whelan in Ottawa, and I find that they take the view that the Jesuits are in accord with the Church of Rome, as is evidenced by the telegram sent some time ago to Mr. Mercier. He read this telegram, at Laprairie, on July 22, from Rome :

"You cannot be called a rebel against the Bishops of the Province of Quebec for having incorporated the Society of Jesus, when the Holy Father allowed its members to seek incorporation."

So you see that is evidence that they are entirely in accord with the Church of Rome, and are not in the same position as they were in 1773 when they were suppressed by the Pope. But there is another evidence which my hon. friend did not refer to. When they were restored in 1814 we find in the Pope's Bull that he does not refer to them in the same terms as my hon. friend. There we read :

"The Catholic world unanimously demands the restoration of the Society of Jesus. We daily receive the most earnest petitions to this effect from our venerable brethren the Archbishops and Bishops, and from other earnest persons."

This shows conclusively that they are in accord with the Roman Catholic Church, they are subservient to it, they are delegates of that Church in missionary works. Now, my hon. friend, in speaking of the Jesuits in England, has not told all that he might have told. It is true that by the Act of Supremacy, (1 Elizabeth) pains and penalties were placed upon them, but it might be a question whether that Act then applied to this country when it was not a portion of the British Empire. But that is set at rest by the Quebec Act of 1774. The next we hear of the Jesuits in England is the Act 10, George IV, to which my hon. friend did not refer. That Act was passed for the purpose of suppressing them gradually. I will presently show how they have been suppressed in England, and whether they are considered in England to be as obnoxious as my hon. friend represents. That Act is entitled an Act for the relief of His Majesty's Roman Catholic subjects, and was passed on the 13th of April, 1829. The statute says :

" Whereas by various Acts of Parliament certain restraints and disabilities are imposed on the Roman Catholic subjects of His Majesty, to which other subjects of His Majesty are not liable ; and whereas it is expedient that such restraints and disabilities shall be from henceforth discontinued ;
" And whereas Jesuits and members of other religious orders, communities, or societies of the Church of Rome, bound by monastic or religious vows, are resident within the United Kingdom, and it is expedient to make provision for the gradual suppression and final prohibition of the same therein ; be it therefore enacted."

Now, mark you, Mr. Speaker, at that very time, long after the passage of the Quebec Act, we find an English Parliament declaring that it was wise to pass an Act for their gradual suppression. It goes on to say :

" That every Jesuit and every member of any other religious order, community, or society of the Church of Rome, bound by monastic or religious vows, who, at the time of the commencement of this Act, shall be within the United Kingdom, shall within six calendar months after the commencement of this Act, deliver to the Clerk of the Peace of the county or place where such person shall reside, or to his deputy, a notice or statement in the form, and containing the particulars required to be set forth in the schedule to this Act annexed ;
" And be it further enacted : That if any Jesuit or member of any such religious order, community, or society as aforesaid, shall, after the commencement of this Act, come into this realm, he shall be deemed and taken to be guilty of misdemeanor, and being there lawfully convicted, shall be sentenced and ordered to be banished from the United Kingdom for the term of his natural life.
" Provided always, and be it further enacted : That in case any natural-born subject of this realm, being at the time of the commencement of this Act, a Jesuit, or other member of such religious order, community, or society as aforesaid, shall, after the commencement of this Act, be out of the realm, it shall be lawful for such person to return or come into the realm; and upon such his return or coming into the realm he is hereby required, within the space of six calendar months after his first returning or coming into the United Kingdom, to deliver such notice or statement to the Clerk of the Peace of the county or place where he shall reside ;
" Provided also, and be it further enacted : That, notwithstanding anything hereinbefore contained, it shall be lawful for any one of His Majesty's principal Secretaries of State, being a Protestant, by a license in writing, signed by him, to grant permission to any Jesuit, or member of any such religious order community, or society, as aforesaid, to come into the United Kingdom and to remain therein for such period as the said Secretary of State shall think proper, not exceeding in any case the space of six calendar months. "

Now, Sir, that Act was passed to show that there was a desire on the part of the English Government to suppress the Jesuits. At this very time there were hundreds of Jesuits in England, and surely the English Parliament is as desirous of protecting the great Protestant religion, surely the Archbishop of Canterbury and the other Bishops of the Church of England are as desirous as my hon. friend, to protect the Protestant religion ; and if the Jesuits are a obnoxious as they were a hundred years ago, if their precepts and doctrines are as antagonistic to the best interest of the country as my hon. friend pretends, surely the English Government would say : We will put an end to them, and drive them out of the country. Now, Sir, what do we find ? We find that a notorious gentleman who has figured in English parliamentary life, Mr Whalley, in 1875, in the English House of Commons, brought up the question of suppression of the Jesuits. After they had been barely fifty years in the mother country, after a penal clause had been passed making it a crime for them to remain in the country more than six months, this gentleman declared, on the floor of Parliament, that the Jesuits had increased in number from 447 to 1,967. He called upon the English Parliament to drive them out of the country. And what did members say ? They counted out the House, they laughed at him, and they left him there making a speech upon this question. Then, in order not to be outwitted he placed a notice in the paper asking Mr Disraeli, at that time at the head of the Government, what he intended to do ? Mr. Disraeli said :

" There is no doubt that there are in this country members of the Society of Jesus, commonly called Jesuits, and there is also no doubt that their presence in this country is under 10 Geo. IV., known as the Roman Catholic Emancipation Act, a misdemeanor. During, however, the period which has elapsed since the passing of that Act, now nearly half a century, the Government of this country has, I believe, in no instance—none, at least, known to myself—proceeded against any Jesuit for committing a misdemeanor under its preavisions, and, so far as Her Majesty's present advisers are influenced by the circumstances with which they are acquainted, the same policy will continue to prevail. At the same time, I beg it to be understood that the provisions of the Act are not looked upon by Her Majesty's Government as being obsolete, but, on the contrary, are reserved provisions of law which they are prepared to avail themselves of if necessary. "

Now, that does not look like the English people being opposed to the Jesuits ; it does not look as if they were undermining the State and the Protestant religion in England ; on the contrary, they are performing a good work, and they are not the mischievous people that my hon. friend says they are now. But Mr. Whalley was not going to be outgeneralled again. He moved again on July 13, 1875, a motion for a committee, as follows :—

" To enquire into and report to this House as to the residence in this country, in contravention of the Act 10 Geo. IV, of any persons being members of the Order of Jesus, commonly called Jesuits, and as to the names, present residence, and ostensible occupation of such persons ; also, as to the amount and nature of any property vested in, or at the disposal of such persons for the purpose of promoting the objects of such society or order, and, so far as may be practicable, to enquire into and report as to the doctrine, discipline, canons, laws or usages under which such order is constituted, and by which it is directed and controlled. "

What was the result of that motion ? It was that he could not get a seconder for it. After making a speech and showing that the number of priests had increased from 447 in 1829 to 1,967 in 1875—these are exactly the figures he used at that time—notwithstanding the violent speech he made on that occasion, the people of England said : We have no fear of the Jesuits. To day I venture to assert that if anyone will consult history, will look at the Order in England, will visit their colleges at Stoneyhurst and other places, they will find evidence of the fact that the greatest men to-day have been educated there, including Protestants, and men who are as strong in their Protestant faith as is the hon. member for Muskoka (Mr. O'Brien). That is all I intend to say with respect to the Jesuits of England. I do not justify the acts of the Jesuits, but I do say that the men to-day are not the men of 100 years ago, that they do not possess the same feelings and intentions in regard to destruction of British power as they did in those days. To-day you will find those men are desirous of pursuing their holy work without the interference of politicians. The hon. gentleman has referred to the history of Canada. He has not, however, placed altogether a proper construction on the Act of 1774, 14 George III, c. 83. The hon. gentleman read section 5, but he might also have read section 8. Section 5, as stated by the hon. gentleman, goes on to say :

"Sec. 5. And for the more perfect security and ease of the minds of the inhabitants of the said Province, it is hereby declared that His Majesty's subjects, preferring the religion of the Church of Rome, of and in the said Province of Quebec, may have, hold and enjoy the full exercise of the religion of the Church of Rome, subject to the King's supremacy declared and established by an Act made in the 1st year of the reign of Queen Elizabeth, over all the dominions and countries which then did, or thereafter should belong to the Imperial Crown of the realm; and that the clergy of the said church may hold, receive and enjoy the accustomed dues and rights, with respect to such persons only as shall profess the said religion."

Even taking that language as it stands, it appears that the Roman Catholics have a right to carry on their church affairs in the same manner as they had hitherto done, so long as they did nothing contrary to the laws of England. But section 8 goes on to say :

"Sec. 8. That His Majesty's Canadian subjects, within the Province of Quebec, the religious orders and communities only excepted, may also hold and enjoy their property and possessions, together with all customs and usages relative thereto, and all other civil rights, in as large, ample and beneficial manner as if the said proclamation had not been made and as may consist with their allegiance to His Majesty."

So while the Imperial Government would not recognize the supremacy of the Pope in England, yet at the same time they gave the Roman Catholics power to carry on the affairs of the church so long as they did not conflict with the laws of England. The hon. gentleman has referred to the petition of Lord Amherst. I am glad he has referred to that petition, because I think if the hon. gentleman had read the opinions of the law officers of the Crown, he would have come to the conclusion that the Government were right in passing the law giving an annuity instead of land, because the officers of the Crown were not quite certain in regard to the title. It is true that Lord Amherst in 1770, after having performed signal services for England, petitioned the King to have the Jesuits' Estates transferred to him. The petition was referred to the Committee of the Lords of the Privy Council ; they reported in favor of it, and it was referred to Lords Gray and Williams, who reported on May 18, 1790. If anyone will take the trouble to follow their report, he will see that, in their opinion, the subject was surrounded with grave doubts. It discussed the whole question as to where the land came from, and under what power the Jesuits held it; and we have the fact that at the close of their labors the commissioners appointed to investigate the title stood 6 to 2 on the question. But they recommended the Government to take possession of the land. The Government did so. In 1800 they took possession of the land in this country, they placed the sheriff in possession of it, but they would not give it to Lord Amherst's heirs, and they passed an Act in 1803 giving an annuity of £3,000 sterling a year instead of the lands asked for, which the law officers of the Crown recommended should be granted. If hon. members will look at the recital of the Act, they will observe that the words are very significant, and those words are such as to justify me in stating that the law officers of the Crown were not distinctly in favor of the validity of the Crown's title, but had grave doubts in regard to it. The recital goes on to say that :

"In consequence of difficulties arising from local circumstances His Majesty's intentions were not carried into effect."

So hon. gentlemen will see that while these lands were requested to be granted to Lord Amherst, yet when the subject was discussed by the law officers of the Crown such grave doubts surrounded the question that the Government would not grant the lands but granted a money allowance. The next we hear of the Jesuits was on the 17th September, 1791, when they were suppressed in Canada under Royal instructions. Those instructions we find in the Chisholm Papers, page 252. In 1791 we find these instructions :

"It is our will and pleasure—that the Society of Jesuits be suppressed and dissolved, and no longer continued as a body corporate or politic, and all their possessions and property shall be vested in us for such purposes as we may hereafter think fit to direct and appoint ; but we think fit to declare our Royal intention to be that the present members of the said society as established at Quebec shall be allowed sufficient stipends and provisions during their natural lives."

But we have the very significant fact that after that proclamation was issued in 1791, they remained in possession of the estates ten or eleven years, during which they had control over them. We find in the report of the Attorney General and Solicitor-General of England they referred to the fact that Lord Haldimand allowed the Jesuits to remain in possession of the lands for that period. I am not surprised that Mr. Mercier said they had a moral claim, because they appear to have a moral, if not a legal, claim to the estates. Lord Goderich, in a despatch in 1831, sent to the Legislature in that year this question for their disposition. He says :

"The only practical question which remains for consideration is, 'whether the appropriation of these funds for the purpose of education should be directed by His Majesty or by the Provincial Legislature ?
"The King cheerfully, and without reserve, confides that duty to the Legislature, in the full persuasion that they will make such a selection amongst the different plans for this purpose which may be presented to their notice, as may most effectually advance the interests of religion and sound learning amongst his subjects ; and I cannot doubt that the Assembly will see the justice of continuing to maintain under the new distribution of these funds those scholastic establishments to which they are now applied."

We find following that, the Act 2nd William IV, cap 41, goes on to say :

"An Act to make provision for the appropriation of certains moneys arising out of the Estates of the late Order of Jesuits, and for other purposes. "
"Reciting that His Majesty had been graciously pleased to confide without reserve to the Provincial Legislature the apportioning of the funds arising from the Estates of the late Order of Jesuits to the purposes of education exclusively. Enacted that all moneys arising out of the Estates of the late Order of Jesuits shall be placed in a separate chest in the vault wherein the public moneys of the Province are kept, and shall be applied to the purpose of education exclusively, in the manner provided by this Act, or by any Act or Acts which may hereafter be passed by the Provincial Legislature in that behalf, and not otherwise."

If my hon. friend will only consult this Act he will find that it was given exclusively to the Province of Quebec for educational purposes. Subsequent to this we find, and that my hon. friend has also admitted, that the incorporation of St. Mary's College was passed in 1852 by the old Parliament of Canada and that the Jesuit College which this Act incorporated still remains in existence, and is still doing its good work throughout the country, and no fault has been found with it. In 1856 we find that the Act 14-15 Victoria, chapter 54, says :

1. "The estates and property of the late Order of Jesuits whether in possession or reversive, including all sums funded or invested, is to be funded and invested as forming part thereof, and the principal of all moneys which have arisen or shall arise from the sale or commutation of any part of said estate or property, are hereby appropriated to the purpose of this Act, and shall form a fund to be called' The Lower Canada Superior Education Investment Fund' and shall be under the control and management of the Government in Council for the purposes of this Act."
"Apportionment of fund among universities, colleges, seminaries, academies, high and superior schools, and as the Governor in Council shall approve."

So that my hon. friend will see that it would be utterly impossible to claim a portion for the Province of Ontario, because this Parliament has declared that the fund, should be known as the " Lower Canada Superior Education Investment Fund. " Section 5 of that Act says that the apportionnement of the fund shall be amongst, " universities, colleges, seminaries, academies, high and superior schools, and as the Governor in Council shall approve. " But my hon. friend says they have no power to vote the money for ecclesiastical institutions. In this he would appear to be at variance with the *Law Times* and *Law Journal*. Now, Mr. Speaker, I have dealt thus far with the history of the question of the Jesuits, and pointed out to his House the different Acts bearing on the question in England and also in Canada. I wish now to turn my attention to another branch of the subject, and to see in what position we stand when we ask the Government to disallow this Bill. I hold that we have established a constitutional practice in this country, and that the records of Parliament are full of this practice. We have Mr. Todd and other eminent authorities writing on this subject, and I shall briefly allude to them in order that the people of the country may know, as we know in this House, that we have rules and constitutional government by which this Act must be construed, and by which this House must decide whether or not the Government was right or wrong in the course it pursued. At page 358, Todd says :

" The redress of grievances arising out of the operation of Provincial Legislature by which such laws have been enacted : except in cases wherein the Acts complained of have been unlawfully passed, or are open to objection upon grounds that would justify the interference of the Governor General in Council, or the Dominion Parliament, with the law. "

And at page 359 he continues :

" But in all such cases (appeals by petition to the Queen &c) the principle is affirmed that no interposition to the detriment, in any degree, of the established principle of self-government, in matters of local concern, would be permitted or approved, whether on the part of the Imperial or Dominion Government, in their several and appropriate spheres of action, or matters within the acknowledged competency of either tribunal. "

You will see that Todd lays down the very sound principle that all matters of provincial concers come within the jurisdiction of the Legislature and shall not be controlled by this Parliament. Again at page 343 Todd says :

" The British North America Act recognizes and guarantees to every Province in the Confederation the right of local self-government, in all cases within the competency of the provincial authorities, and it does not contemplate or justify any interference with the exclusive powers which it entrusts to the Legislatures of the several Provinces ; except in regard to Acts which transcend the lawful bounds of provincial jurisdiction or which assert a principle, or prefer a claim that might injuriously affect the interests of any other portions of the Dominion, as in the case of Acts which diminish rights of minorities in the particular Province in relation to education, that has been conferred by law in any Province prior to Confederation."

Now, I think the member for Muskoka (Mr. O'Brien) has failed to point out that this Act asserts a principle in violation of the interest of the Dominion, or which affects the rights of the minority within the particular Provinces, because if we understand aright the minority of the Province of Quebec, who thoroughly understand their position and who thoroughly understand what the law was, are themselves prepared to accept at the hands of the Local Government the sum of $60,000 as full and just compensation to them for the amounts they were entitled to for their superior education fund and that while we are so anxious to protect the minority in the Province of Quebec that minority, knowing more than we do, are perfectly satisfied. Todd again says :

" It was manifest that it was the intention of the Imperial Parliament to guard from invasion all rights and powers exclusively conferred upon the provincial authorities, and to provide that the reserved right of interference therewith by the Dominion Executive or Parliament should not be exercised in the interest of any political party or so as to impair the principle of local self-government."

And at page 363 in his work, he continues :

" It has been sometimes worked in repeal of Acts which contained provisions that were deemed to be contrary to sound principle of legislation, and, therefore, likely to prove injurious to the interests or welfare of the Dominion."

You will, therefore, find we have high constitutional authorities on this subject, and authorities which satisfy me that the Government were perfectly right in acting as it has done. We have also the opinions of eminent judges in this country, and my hon. friend has pointed out to judicial authorities in England, in support of his argument. I think that we should quote some of our own eminent authorities, in order to guide the House to a just conclusion on this matter. In the case of Severn against the Queen, Supreme Court Reports, volume 2, page 96, Chief Justice Richards says :

"Under our system of Government, the disallowing of statutes passed by Local Legislature after due deliberation, asserting a right to exercise powers which they claim to possess under the British North America Act will always be considered a harsh exercise of power unless in cases of great and manifest necessity, or where the Act is so clearly beyond the power of the Legislature that the propriety of interfering could be at once recognized."

And Justice Taschereau said :

"There is no doubt of the prerogative right of the Crown to veto any Provincial Act, and that could even be applied to a law over which the Provincial Legislature had complete jurisdiction. But it is precisely on account of its extraordinary and exceptional character that the exercise of this prerogative will always be a delicate matter. It will be always very difficult for the Federal Government to substitute its opinion instead of the Legislative Assembly, in regard to matters within those Provinces, without exposing themselves to be reproached with checking the independence of Parliament in the Provinces. What would be the result if the Province chose to re-enact a law which had been disallowed? The cure might be worse than the disease and fully as grave complications might follow.

"It cannot, therefore, be argued that, because this right exists, we must adopt an interpretation which could lead to the necessity by having recourse by it."

Now, Mr. Speaker, that points out the fact that while this Government has the power to disallow Acts which are strictly within the power of the Local Legislature, yet that very judge declares that it his inexpedient and impolitic in the Government to set its opinion against that of the Local Legislature, because if it did so the Legislature would turn around and re-enact the Bill, and the result would be a conflict between the Provincial Government and the General Government, which all must deplore. We have also certain principles laid down by theright hon. leader of the Government, whom I look upon as a very high constitutional authority, and I think both this House and the country recognize him as such. At any rate, we know that the rules laid down by him in the year 1868 for the guidance of the Government on such questions, have been approved of by Mr. Mowat, the Premier of Ontario, a high legal authority, by the learned gentleman who sits opposite, the hon. member for West Durham (Mr. Blake), by the hon. member for East York (Mr. Mackenzie), and by other hon. gentleman in this House. Those rules were as follows :—

"In deciding whether any Act of a Provincial Legislature should be disallowed, or sanctioned, the Government must not only consider whether it affects the interest of the whole Dominion or not, but also whether it be unconstitutional ; whether it exceeds the jurisdiction conferred on the Local Legislature, and, in cases where the jurisdiction is concurrent whether is clashes with the legislation of the General Parliament.

"As it is of importance that the course of local legislation should be interfered with as little as possible, and the power of disallowance exercised with as great caution, and only in cases where the law of general interests of the Dominion imperatively demand it, the undersigned recommends that the following course be pursued :—

"That on the receipt by Your Excellency of the Acts passed in any Province, they be referred to the Minister of Justice for report, and that he with all convenient speed, do report as to those Acts which he considers free from objection of any kind, and if such report be approved by Your Excellency in Council, that such approval be forthwith communicated to the Provincial Government.

"That he make a separate report, or separate reports, on those Acts which he may consider—
"1. As being altogether illegal or unconstitutional.
"2. As illegal or unconstitutional in part.

" 3. In cases of concurrent jurisdiction as clashing with the legislation of the General Parliament.
" 4. As affecting the interests of the Dominion generally. And that in such report or reports he gives his reasons for his opinions."

These rules have been endorsed by all legal gentlemen in this House, and I think no person can deny that they embody the true and correct principle. We also find, by the Sessional Papers of 1877, page 102, that the hon. member for West Durham recommended that the question as to *ultra vires*, with reference to the Escheats Bill, should be referred to the Supreme Court. Again, in 1876, the hon. gentleman, in regard to an Act respecting the Legislative Assembly, said :

" It appears to the undersigned that several of the provisions are open to very serious questions as being *ultra vires* of a Local Legislature, but almost all of them are contained in an Act of the Legislature of Quebec, upon the same subject which was left in its operation. There are indeed some new provisions, but it could not be advisable upon the principle upon which the Quebec Act was allowed to advise the disallowance of the Act by reason of the insertion of these provisions, and the undersigned feels bound to recommend, that following the precedent referred to, the Act should be left in its operation ; it being quite possible for those who may object to its constitutionality to raise their objections in the courts."

There we have two of the highest legal authorities in this country, as high almost as can be found in any country, the hon. First Minister and the hon. member for West Durham, laying down the principle that upon the question of the constitutionality of an Act the decision of the courts ought to be invoked. We find the *Mail* of 5th February endorsing that view in the following words :—

" There is nothing in the British North America Act to limit the exercise of the veto power. That it shall not be exercised merely on grounds of ordinary policy, unless the Provincial Legislature has exceeded its jurisdiction, is a good general rule, which once more we commend the Government for observing. The authority given to the Provincial Legislature in certain classes of subjects, carries with it, like all authority, a liberty of error which must be respected, so long as the legal power is not exceeded and the error is not manifestly subversive legally or morally of the principle of the constitution or of the great objects of the State."

I have pointed out that the *Mail* in a former article contended that this Act was *ultra vires*, and therefore, the courts should be invoked to decide upon its constitutionality ; and we have affirmed that principle in this House over and over again. It was affirmed in regard to the Streams Bill, the consensus of opinion being that in regard to legislation which was claimed to be unconstitutional, the proper course for the Government to adopt was to let the measure go into operation, and leave those affected by it to contest its constitutionality before the courts. I commend to this House the opinion expressed by the hon. member for West Durham upon that question, and I think hon. gentleman opposite will hardly dissent from it. It is a proposition which, I think, was well conceived, and which, though perhaps not accepted by the House at the time, was in entire accord with the views laid down in 1868 by the right hon. leader of the Government. The hon. member for West Durham said:

" Can any member of this House, who is a real, live lover of the Federal system, find any possible objection to this proposition? Where the law and the general interests of the Dominion imperatively demand it, then and then only shall the power of disallowance be exercised ; but it would impair the Federal principle and injuriously affect the autonomy of the institutions of our several Provinces were this power to be exercised on subjects which are within the exclusive control of the Local Legislatures on the ground that in the opinion of His Excellency's advisers, or of the Canadian Parliament, any such legislation is wrong. * * I admit that, under the constitution of Canada and the Provinces, the Local Legislatures have the power to deprive the subject of his property under these conditions, but I say that if we import into the Constitution of the Confederation a restriction upon that power and declare it, as a majority in this House propose this night to declare, we will declare it to be the right and duty of the Government, whenever the power is to be exercised, to nullify its exercise by disallowing such Acts."

On that occasion the Government declared that the Act should be disallowed, on the ground that it interfered with private rights ; but the general principle laid down was that in all matters of unconstitutionality, the court should be invoked and nobody else. We have also a case almost in point in this country, the case of the New-Brunswick School Law. When that case arose, members of Parliament who were versed in constitutional law expressed opinions which would be entirely in accord with the action taken by the Government of the day. That school law was one to compel the Roman Catholics of New Brunswick to contribute to a system of education which they could not conscientiously avail themselves of. It was a law which affected a large class of the community, and which that class contended interfered with its rights. That Bill was allowed to go into operation, and was not interfered with by the Dominion Government for reasons given by the First Minister, who says :

"The Provincial Legislature has exclusive powers to make laws in relation to education. It may be that the Act in question may act unfavorably on the Catholics or other religious denominations, and if so it is for such religious bodies to appeal to the Provincial Legislature which has the sole power to grant redress.

"The assumption by the Provincial Legislature and Government of Canada of the right to seek the imposition of further limitations of the powers of the Provincial Parliaments is subversive of the Federal character of the Union, tending to the destruction of the powers and independence of the provincial law to the centralization of all power in the Parliament of Canada.

"The people of New Brunswick cannot, and will not, surrender their rights of self-government within the limits of the constitution."

He went on further to say:

" In the case of measures not coming within either of these categories the Government would be unwarranted in interfering with local legislation.

" In the present case there was not a doubt that the New Brunswick Legislature had acted within its jurisdiction, and that the Act was constitutionally legal and could not be impugned on that ground.

" On the second ground which he had mentioned in which he considered the Dominion Government could interfere, it could not be held that the Act in any way prejudicially affected the whole Dominion, because it was a law settling the Common School system of the Province of New Brunswick alone.

" The Government of the Dominion could not act and they would have been guilty of a violent breach of the constitution if, because they hold a different opinion, they should set up their judgments against the solemn decision of a Province in a manner entirely within the control of that Province."

There is the decision of the First Minister, entirely in accord with that of Mr. Justice Taschereau. Judge Taschereau adopts almost the very language of the First Minister in the case I have referred to, the Queen vs. Severn. It seems to me that, that case is on all fours with the case before the House. The hon. the Minister of Inland Revenue (Mr. Costigan) moved the following resolution in this House in 1872 :—

"That the Local Legislature of New Brunswick in its last Session, in 1871, adopted a law respecting Common Schools forbidding of any religious education to pupils, and that that prohibition is opposed to the sentiments of the entire population of the Dominion in general and to the religious convictions of the Roman Catholic population in particular:—That the Roman Catholics of New Brunswick cannot, without acting unconscientiously, send their children to schools established under the law in question and are yet compelled like the remainder of the population, to pay taxes to be devoted to the maintenance of those schools;—That the said law is unjust, and causes much uneasiness among the Roman Catholic population in general disseminated throughout the whole Dominion of Canada, and that such a state of affairs may prove the cause of disastrous results to all the Confederate Provinces;—and praying His Excellency in consequence at the earliest possible period to disallow the said New Brunswick School Law;

In that debate the whole question was thoroughly discussed. The *Globe* thus commented on it :

" The question so far was exclusively a local one, and it would have been well if it could have been fought out and settled in New Brunswick, as it was in past years in Ontario and Quebec. But the Catholic minority determined to make an appeal to the Dominion Parliament, on the ground that by the Confederation Act they were secured in the rights which they allege have now been taken away."

The hon. member for West Durham (Mr. Blake) moved in amendment to that resolution of Mr. Costigan, declaring that it was expedient that the opinion of the law officers of the Crown should be taken :

" That this House regrets that the School Act recently passed in New Brunswick is unsatisfactory to a portion of the inhabitants of that Province, and hopes that it may be so modified during the next Session of the Legislature of New Brunswick, as to remove any just grounds of discontent that now exist ; and this House deems it expedient that the opinion of the law officers of the Crown in England, and, if possible, the opinion of the Judicial Committee of the Privy Council, should be obtained as to the right of the New Brunswick Legislature to make such changes in the School Law, as deprived the Roman Catholics of the privileges they enjoyed at the time of the Union in respect of religious education in the Common Schools with the view of ascertaining whether the case comes within the terms of the 4th sub-section of the 93rd clause of the British North America Act, 1867, which authorizes the Parliament of Canada to enact remedial laws for the due execution of the provisions respecting education in the said Act."

You see, therefore, the opinion of the hon. member for West Durham (Mr. Blake) was that it was not expedient for the House to pass censure upon the Government and disallow that Bill, but on the contrary left the decision with the officers of the Crown. On 29th November, 1872, the law officers of the Crown reported as follows :

" That we agree substantially with the opinion of the Minister of Justice of the Dominion, so far as appears from the papers before us."

Sir J. D. Coleridge and Sir G. Jessell said of it :

" Of course, it is quite possible that the new Statute of the Province may work in practice unfavorably to this or that denomination therein, and therefore to the Roman Catholics ; but we did not think that such a state of things is enough to bring into operation the restricting powers of appeal to the Governor in Council."

It seems to me that this New Brunswick case is much stronger than the one now before us. We had a minority in the Province of New Brunswick of Roman Catholics, who contended that the law passed was a great injustice to them. The first Minister said he recognized the injustice. The law officers of the Crown said the same thing when their opinion was taken in 1875, but they all agreed that the matter was of purely local concern. I would like to ask the hon. member for Muskoka (Mr. O'Brien) if the views of the Catholic minority in the Province of New Brunswick should not be respected as well as those of the Protestant minority in Quebec which is entirely satisfied with the action of the Government. In New Brunswick the Catholics felt that their rights were unjustly dealt with, the Government law officers of the Crown were of the same opinion, and the Government here were of the same opinion but in spite of all that, they all agreed that it was a matter of purely local concern, with which we had nothing to do.

AFTER RECESS.

When the House rose at six o'clock, I was endeavoring to show that in the question of the New Brunswick School Law, the Catholic minority in that Province, had made complaint, in reference to the legislation of that Province, that their rights had been seriously infringed upon. I endeavored to show that the Minister of Justice of that day, the right hon. the Premier of this country had expressed his opinion upon that law, and had stated distinctly that while he sympathized with the Roman Catholics in that Province, yet that the action of the New Brunswick Legislature was entirely within its jurisdiction. I quoted also the authority of several gentlemen, among them the hon. member for West Durham (Mr. Blake). I showed that he moved in amendment to have the matter referred to the law officers of the Crown and also expressed his opinion of the Act. I find that opinion reported in the *Globe* of May 19th, 1872:

"Mr. BLAKE said he*had from time to time considered the constitution with reference to the state of the law in New Brunswick on the subject of schools, and he was free to confess that his opinion had fluctuated, and any expression he might now give was given with great doubt and hesitation. He was free to admit that there was much to support the view that had been put forward in the report of the Minister of Justice on the subject, and that the conclusion of that gentleman might have been fairly reached and might very possibly be correct; but he desired to point out to the House those circumstances with reference to the Act which led his mind very strongly—he would not say conclusively—to a different conclusion.

He moved in amendement that the question be referred to the law officers of the Crown, and they expressed their opinion that the legislation of New Brunswick was entirely within the jurisdiction of that Legislature. Then we have Mr. McDougall, who poses sometimes as a constitutional lawyer, who upon that occasion, gave expression to his opinion as follows:—

"I agree that any interference with the powers that are given to the Local Legislature in the framing of laws unnecessarily through political or national, religious or other motive, except on the broadest public grounds, would be injudicious and improper."

In 1875, the question of the New Brunswick school law was again brought to the notice of this House. A resolution was moved by Mr. Cauchon, seconded by the hon. member for West Durham (Mr. Blake), in which they recited the resolution of the previous year, and asked the intervention of the opinion of the law officers of the Crown. The resolution was as follows:—

"The House regrets that the School Act passed in New Brunswick is unsatisfactory to a portion of the inhabitants of that Province, and hopes that it may be so modified during the next session of the Legislature of New Brunswick as to remove any just grounds of dissatisfaction that now exist. That the House regrets that the hope expressed in the said resolution has not been realized and that an humble address be presented to Her Majesty embodying the resolution and praying that Her Majesty will be graciously pleased to use her influence with the Legislature of New Brunswick to procure such a modification of the said Act as shall remove such grounds of discontent."

That matter was referred to the law officers of the Crown, and upon the 18th October, 1875, there was a despacth from Lord Carnarvon, in which he stated:

"That he laid it at the foot of the Throne, but that he could not advise Her Majesty to take any action in respect of it; that he could not advise the Queen to advise the Legislature of New Brunswick to legislate in any particular direction as that would be undue interference."

Further on he says:

"Holding, as I have already explained, that the constitution of Canada does not contemplate any interference with the provincial legislation, on a subject within the competence of the Local Legislature by the Dominion Parliament, or as a consequence by the Dominion Ministers."

So even the law officers of the Crown were of the opinion that, though sympathizing with the minority in New Brunswick, they could not advise interference with that law or advise the Crown to disallow the Bill. On that occasion, the hon. member for East York (Mr. Mackenzie), who sympathized very strongly with the minority in the Province of New Brunswick and felt that they had been unfairly dealt with, said:

" But there is a higher principle still which we have to adhere to, and that is to preserve in their integrity the principles of the constitution under which we live. If any personal act of mine, if anything I could do would assist to relieve those who believe they are living under a grievance in the Province of New Brunswick, that act would be gladly undertaken and zealously performed; but I have no right, and the House has no right to interfere with the legislation of a Province when that legislation is secured by an Imperial compact to which all the parties submitted in the Act of Confederation. * * *  I have merely to say this, whatever may be our religious proclivities or feelings, whatever may be the feelings that actuate us in relation to local grievances, it is not well that we should endanger the safety of any one of the Provinces in relation to matters provided for in the British North America Act, which is our written Constitution. * *  It is not desirable that we should make the way open or that anything should be done which would excite religious discussions and permeate religious animosities."

That was good advice, and that advice was followed by the House. Now, I come to consider a question which seems to have exercised the mind of the *Globe* newspaper, and that is the articles in the *Law Journal* and the *Law Times*. I have shown. I think, by constitutional authority, that the Act, if it be unconstitutional or *ultra vires*, should be allowed by the Government to take its course, and those who are injured by its operation or aggrieved by it should at once apply to the law courts for redress. The *Law Journal* has declared beyond all question that the Act is *ultra vires*; and, if that be so, according to the practice we have always adopted, the parties should apply to the courts for redress. The *Law Journal* says :

" It will, we think, be conceded, apart from any provisions in Imperial statutes, that it is *ultra vires* the constitutional power of a Colonial Legislature to confer on or delegate to any foreign sovereign, potentate, or tribunal, lawful jurisdiction or authority to determine, or ratify, the distribution of the moneys or properties of the Crown, or now money grants to the subjects of the Crown, within its colonial jurisdiction, are to be distributed. The Imperial Crown may in any proper case agree with another crown or nation to refer to a sovereign, or to arbitrators mutually agreed upon questions affecting its belligerent or territorial rights or claims; but this *regality* of the Imperial Crown is not possessed, nor can it be exercised, by a Colonial Government or Legislature. If it would be *ultra vires* of the Legislature of Ontario to delegate authority to a foreign power—say to the President of the United States—to distribute, or to ratify the distribution of public moneys legally voted (the Clergy Reserve moneys, for instance), it follows that this delegation of authority to the Pope by the Legislature of Quebec must also be *ultra vires*. What would be unconstitutional in Ontario must be equally unconstitutional in Quebec."

The *Law Journal* lays down the proposition that the Act is *ultra vires*. If that be so the authorities show clearly that they must go for redress to the courts ; but what evidence have we in this instance that the Pope is, as they say, a foreign potentate ? The *Law Journal* does not pretend to say how it is, except that, under the Statute of Elizabeth, there were certain documents, or mandates, or judgments issued or sent forth by the Pope, and that those should not be recognized by the authorities in England. But the Statute of Elizabeth was passed under different circumstances from those which exist now, and the position of the Pope to-day, bereft of his temporal power, is entirely different from what it was years ago. Instead of being a foreign power, he is in this case simply an arbiter between two parties in the Province of Quebec. At the time to which my hon. friend from Muskoka alludes, no doubt the Pope did exercise a controlling influence in Europe and over many nations, but now he is bereft of that power and is in a totally different position. The *Law Journal* says this matter is not yet settled, and should be relegated to the courts. That is the position which this Government and all preceding Governments have taken in regard to such a question. Then, as to the *Law Times*. In my judgment, the *Law Times* shows conclusively that it is quite constitutional for the Province to vote money in the way it has. The hon. member for Muskoka (Mr. O'Brien) is entirely at issue with the *Law Times* on that point. If he had read the article in the *Law Times*, he would have found that it holds that the voting of money to ecclesiastical institutions or powers is regarded by that newspaper in an entirely different way from that in which he regards it. I cannot understand, therefore, on what ground the *Globe* made its sudden summersault· The *Law Times* says it is constitutional to vote money for this purpose. Of course, the *Law Times* is in conflict with Mr. Wm. McDougall on that point, but I will refer to him later. The *Law Times* says:

" The constitutional question that arises is not the voting away of public money, be the pretext never so shallow, but the subordination of the sovereign to a foreign authority, and the placing of Her Majesty's public funds at the disposal of the same foreign authority. It is of course an unquestionable and fundamental proposition of law that the Legislature cannot deny the sovereignty of Her Majesty or acknowledge the sovereignty of any other person, especially as under the Constitution it derives its sole authority from an Act passed by the Imperial Parliament. But there is authority for saying that such a proceeding would be unconstitutional."

Then it goes on to refer to the case of the International Bridge Company and the Canada Southern Railway Company, reported in 28 Grant, page 14, showing that the action of Parliament would be unconstitutional in declaring that an Act of that kind could go into operation without the consent of a foreign power. It quotes the decision of Vice-Chancellor Proudfoot as follows:

" If Canada has chosen to pass an Act in terms similar to the New York Act, it derives its validity from the Canadian Legislature, not from the Legislature that originally created it. No express clause was required to exclude the laws of one from operating in the territory of the other; the exclusion arose from the countries forming part of different nationalities with different sovereign powers. Each country has assented to the corporation created by it uniting with the corporation created by the other, and bringing into the union the rights and liabilities conferred or imposed upon it, and certainly Canada has not introduced the provisions of any Act of Congress passed subsequent to the union applying to the united company. Were the Canadian Parliament to endeavor to do so—to say that Canadian subjects and Canadian corporations are to be subject to legislation that might be passed by Congress—it would, I apprehend, be unconstitutional."

And upon that ground the *Law Times* argues that it is unconstitutional in having, as it says, delegated the power to the Pope to say whether the law shall go into operation or not. We have seen that the Act does not depend upon the action of the Pope at all, but the money voted by this Act for a particular purpose is left for the Pope to say how much shall go to one church or another, or to one university or another. Now, we have in our Canadian Parliament enactments which are somewhat at variance with the law as laid down by Mr. Justice Proudfoot. In the Niagara Frontier Bridge Company Act we have a clause to this effect:

" The said company shall not commence the actual erection of the said bridge until an Act of the Congress of the United States of America has been passed consenting to or approving the bridging of the said river, or until the executive of the United States of America has consented to and approved thereof."

We have enacted the same thing in the Niagara Frontier Bridge Company Act. I think I can safely say that the constitutional authorities of this country, who have expressed their opinion upon it, are as reliable and as deserving of our confidence as the expressions of the opinion in the *Law Times* or other papers of the same kind. It seems to me that the *Law Times* could not have carefully considered the question, otherwise it would not have arrived at the conclusion I intend to point out. The hon. member for Muskoka states in his resolution that the Act is not legal, firstly:

" Because it endows from the public funds a religious organization, thereby violating the unwritten but understood constitutional principle of a complete separation of church and state, and the absolute equality of all denominations before the law."

We have an answer to that in the *Law Times*, which says:

" The policy of disallowing a Provincial Act must be determined by responsible Ministers of the Dominion. They are constitutionally answerable to Parliament and the people, and as has frequently been shown, the right to disallow Acts was not granted in order that unconstitutional or invalid legislation might be got rid of, but in order that the more important policy of the Dominion should not be interfered with by the Provinces. The whole course of English history shows a struggle with the ecclesiastical houses to prevent property from falling into their hands. The policy both in England and her colonies has been the same—to prevent the property of the nation from falling into mortmain. But it is a question, not of legality, but of policy, and with the policy of the Governments of the day we have nothing to do."

Whereas, on the other hand, the *Mail* says it is entirely a question of policy with which we have to do, yet the *Law Times* is of a contrary opinion:

"If a particular Province choose to depart from this policy and permit the absorption of property by ecclesiastical orders, it is undoubtedly acting within its constitutional rights. The Governor in Council would also be acting within his constitutional rights in opposing such a policy by disallowing all Acts tending thereto; but it is a question of policy as we have said, and not of law. The Act then must be looked at with regard only to its contents."

So that while the hon. member for Muskoka takes strong ground that no Legislature has a right to vote money for ecclesiastical purposes to seminaries or churches, or anything of the kind in the Province of Quebec, yet the *Law Times* says that they have got absolute power. Now, which authority are we to take? Are we to take that of the *Law Times*, or that of the hon. member for Muskoka, or are we to say that the Government acted strictly within its constitutional rights and privileges by saying : We will not interfere, because they had a perfect right to vote their money; at any rate it is a matter of purely local concern. Now, it is stated that the Pope is an alien, and as such has no right whatever to express an opinion upon this question. If we look at the Treaty of Paris we find that, to a large extent, his authority is recognized so far as is necessary for church purposes. The clause says :

"For her part, Her British Majesty agrees to grant to the inhabitants of Canada the liberty of the Catholic religion. Consequently she will give most precise and effective orders, so that her new Roman Catholic subjects may profess and practise their religion, according to the rites of the Roman Church, in so far as the laws of Great Britain permit."

Now, the law of Great Britain permits the Catholics to carry on the affairs of their church just as they please, so long as they do nothing in conflict with the laws of England. It seems to me, looking at the *Law Times* and *Law Journal*, that they agree with the proposition I laid down, that if an Act be *ultra vires* or unconstitutional, it should not be a subject of discussion, but one which the Government should leave entirely to the jurisdiction of the courts. Now, we have another authority in this House—Mr. Wicksteed, who has been for years the law officer for this House. He has expressed his opinion upon it, and I find in a communicated article this language:

"And as respects the article questioning the constitutionality of the said Act,—it does not seem to me that the English Acts cited in it can apply to Canada, which, when they were passed, was no part of the realm of England, and the inhabitants of which are by subsequent Acts of the Imperial Parliament, guaranteed the free exercise of the Roman Catholic religion, of which the Pope is the head, and his supremacy as such is part of its very essence. The later law derogates from and virtually repeals any former provision contrary to it. The English laws disqualifying Roman Catholics from holding certain offices were never in force in Canada. The money appropriated belonged to the Province, and is granted by its Legislature for the purposes for which the property from which it arises was given by the French King, and the Act of Appropriation is sanctioned by the assent of the Queen, who may, without impropriety, avail herself, in dealing with it, of the advice and assistance of the head of the church and of an ecclesiastical and educational corporation, which, if not legally the same, is morally the representative and successor of that to which the original grant was made, and which, with the Pope, will be bound to use the money in accordance with and solely by virtue of the powers given them by the Act."

So we find that nearly every authority learned in the law who has expressed an opinion, points clearly to the fact that the Government acted entirely within the constitution. But, Sir, these gentlemen who are so terribly annoyed because the Pope has been called in, and has chosen to say how that money belonging to the church shall be distributed, were not so particular a short time ago when the Pope's opinion was asked upon a more important question. In Ireland, not very long ago, when, as we know, dissensions were rampant, when the people of England were looking to Ireland with dismay, were not the people of England glad to have the Pope act as arbitrator? We have here a very important question, and I see nothing in the English courts, in the English Parliament, or in the English Government, protesting against this. On the contrary, they were glad to see the Pope give his opinion on that question. Also, when the question arose upon boycotting and paying rents, the matter was referred to the Pope, and the Pope issued—I do not know what you would call it—a pronunciamento, or whatever it may be, and sent that to Ireland. No fault was found with that. I wonder the hon. member for Muskoka did not find fault with that. He is opposed to Home Rule, as I am myself, but at the same time, he found no fault with the Pope being called in as arbiter to settle this most important of all questions. Now, let us see what the Pope says:

" On several occasions the Apostolic See has given to the people of Ireland (whom it has always regarded with special benevolence) suitable admonitions and advice, when circumstances required, as to how they might defend their rights without injury to justice or the public peace. Our Holy Father Leo XIII, fearing lest in that species of warfare that has been introduced amongst the Irish people into the contest between landlords and tenants, which is commonly called the Plan of Campaign, and in that kind of social interdict, called boycotting arising from the same contest, true sense of justice and charity might be perverted, ordered the Supreme Congregation of the Inquisition to subject the matter to serious and careful examination.
" Hence the following questions were proposed to Their Eminences the Cardinals of the Congregation : Is it permissible, in the disputes between landowners and tenants in Ireland to use the means known as the Plan of Campaign and boycotting ? "
" After long and mature deliberation Their Eminences unanimously answered in the negative, and the decision was confirmed by the Holy Father of Wednesday, the 18th of the present month.
" The justice of this decision will be readily seen by any one who applies his mind to consider that a rent agreed on by mutual consent cannot, without a violation of a contract, be diminished at the mere will of tenant, especially when there are tribunals appointed for settling such controversies and reduced unjust rent within the bounds of equity, after taking into account the causes which diminish the value of the land."

No objection was taken to that. The Pope took steps in these matters as between landlord and tenant, he denounced the plan of compaign, and declared that in his judgment the course taken by supporters and others in the Catholic Church was improper, and he advised them to take a different course. It seems to me that, looking at this question in all its lights, this House is justified in declaring that the Government have acted fairly with the Province of Quebec. Let me briefly refer to the amendment moved by the hon. member for Muskoka (Mr. O'Brien). It states:

" Firstly, because it endows from public funds a religious organization, thereby violating the unwritten but undoubted constitutional principle of the complete separation of church and state and of the absolute equality of all denominations before the law."

I think I have met that objection, and I have read the opinion of the *Law Times*, an authority which the hon. gentleman will not endeavor to controvert. The amendment further states :

" Secondly, because it recognizes the usurpation of a right by a foreign authority, namely: His Holiness the Pope of Rome, to claim that his consent was necessary to empower the Provincial Legislature to dispose of a portion of the public domain, and also because the Act is made to depend upon the will, and the appropriation of the grand thereby made is subject to the control of the same authority."

Let any one look at the Act and he will see that it says nothing with respect to the benefit of the Jesuits. The preamble of the Act shows there was a controversy going on between the church and the Province of Quebec in regard to claims respecting the Jesuits' estates, and with a view to settling that question negotiations were opened with the Pope in order to ascertain how it could be settled amicably. There is not a word in the whole of the correspondence or in the whole of the Act to show that it was a settlement with the Jesuits themselves, but only with regard to the Jesuits' estates. The hon. gentleman has forgotten that point. The hon. member for Muskoka (Mr. O'Brien) entirely fails to point out that there is one word in the Act respecting a settlement with the Jesuits, but that it is for a settlement in regard to the Jesuits' estates, which the Act says were confiscated by Imperial authority; and I have endeavored to show from history that there is considerable doubt with respect to the confiscation and as to whether the estates really were within the possession of the Crown. The Act itself says:

"Whereas it is expedient to put an end to the uneasiness which exists in this Province, in connection with the question of the Jesuits' estates, by settling it in a definitive manner: Therefore Her Majesty, by and with the advice and consent of the Legislature of Quebec, enacts as follows."

It is true that the head of the Jesuits was authorized by the Pope to enter into negotiations, but these negotiations were not with the Jesuits at all, and there is not one word in the Act to show it; it was for the purpose of settling a long standing question as to whether these estates belonged to the church or not. The hon. gentleman says that the Quebec Government are taking out of the Jesuits' estates money and handing it over to the church authorities, that $400,000 is to be placed at the disposal of the Pope and $60,000 at the disposal of the Protestant clergy. Such is not the fact, for there is not a word said about the Jesuits' estates. The Quebec Government has to take the money out of the consolidated revenue, and power is given them by the Legislature, in section 6 of the Act, to sell the estates and apply the money in any way it may think proper. Section 6 says:

"The Lieutenant Governor in Council is hereby authorized to dispose, in the manner he deems most advantageous to the Province, of the whole property, movable and immovable, interests and rights, generally whatsoever of the Province upon the said property known as the Jesuits' estate."

It, therefore, appears that the Lieutenant Governor in Council is authorized to pay out of any public moneys at his disposal, $400,000 under the conditions named, and may make any deed necessary for the full and entire execution of such agreement. The money, therefore, is taken out of the consoliditated fund, and authority is taken to sell the Jesuits' estates and apply the proceeds as the Lieutenant Governor in Council may see fit. It appears to me that upon every ground advanced by the hon. member for Muskoka (Mr. O'Brien), this House is bound to answer his interrogations in the negative and to vote that the propositions made by the hon. gentleman are not in accord either with facts, or with history, or with constitutional law. He says further:

"Thirdly, because the endowment of the Society of Jesus, an alien, secret and politico-religious body, the expulsion of which from every Christian community wherein it had a footing, has been rendered necessary by its intolerant and unchristian intermeddling with the functions of civil government, is fraught with danger to the civil and religious liberties of the people of Canada."

The hon. gentleman forgot to say that there was St. Mary's College, which was a recognized corporation in the Province of Quebec. Yet he deliberately declares they are an alien corporation. What does the Act of 1887 say? It states distinctly that they were incorporated as a body and were recognized as a corporation by the Province of Quebec. Those are the facts, and I leave the House to judge as to their application. I have endeavored to show as briefly as possible, although I have necessarily occupied considerable time in doing so, that the rights of the minority are not interfered with, and I think I have shown that successfully; that the people have acquiesced in and approved both Acts, which is a fact beyond all question; that the feeling raised in Ontario is entirely uncalled for, the minority in Quebec asking for no such support for them. I have pointed out to the satisfaction of this House, I think, that a large amount of ignorance has been displayed by public men in Ontario in discussing this question, and that the hon. member for Muskoka (Mr. O'Brien) was somewhat at fault in his history of the matter. I have also shown that the attacks on the Jesuits, that the historical references made to the past are not with a view so much to condemn the Jesuits as to stab the Roman Catholic Church. That is, at all events, my judgment. I gather that from the resolution passed at the different meetings and the course adopted, a course which in my judgment is not justifiable. I have pointed out that the Jesuits of to-day are not the Jesuits of 100 years ago, that the Province of Quebec are in sympathy with the Jesuits, and I have shown that they are not an alien corporation, and that they are not such people as they are sometimes considered to be in Canada. It is true they were suppressed in 1773, but they were restored in 1814, because the Roman Catholic Church felt that the Jesuits were not at that time the same class of men as they were before; that they did not act as others had acted according to history, but were influenced in their action simply by a desire to promote the best interests of the church. I have shown conclusively that they are entirely in accord with the Roman Catholic Church. I have also shown conclusively that according to our constitution the course taken by the Government was the only proper one, and in support of my statement I have the authority of the *Law Times* and the *Law Journal*. I have also shown conclusively that the Government was justified in voting money for ecclesiastical purposes, and had a perfect right to vote money for Laval University or any other seminary or similar institution, and that if they acted harshly towards any portion of the community it became a question of policy. I have also shown that the Province of Quebec were not bound to give $60,000 to the Protestants which was more than their proportion of the money. It does seem to me, Sir, that it is unwise and inexpedient that this House should discuss a question such as this from the standpoint of my hon. friend from Muskoka (Mr. O'Brien). I think that I have shown that from every point of view the Government was justified in taking the course they have done: that is to leave the matter to the courts to settle, whether or net it is *ultra vires* or unconstitutional. I, Sir, am going to be the last one to join in an unholy crusade against any portion of my fellow-countrymen. To-day, we are joining together for the purpose of building up this great Confederation into a magnificent nation. Is all that we have accomplished for the last twenty-one years to be set at naught? I, Sir, shall not be a party to such a course. While I feel as strong in my Protestant views as any man in this House, I recognize the foundation of Protestant principles: civil and religious liberty. As long as I occupy a seat in this House, even though I be threatened with extermination from my constituency, I shall endeavor to deal out equal justice to all my fellow-contrymen.

## Mr. BARRON (Victoria, O.).

Mr. Speaker, I wish I could content myself with simply giving an affirmative vote to the amendment of my hon. friend from Muskoka (Mr. O'Brien); but, Sir, that has become impossible. Fortunately or unfortunately I do not know which, my name has been more or less intimately associated with the subject-matter of the hon. gentleman's amendment ever since the beginning of this Session, and I feel compelled to supplement the vote that I shall give with some explanation. I do that, Sir, even though my duty is a most unpleasant one and a most painful one indeed, especially so when I remember and am conscious of the fact that in voting and in speaking as I do I am weaning myself for the time being—and only for the time being I hope—from few or many, I don't say which, of the hon. gentlemen around me with whom I have been in such happy accord ever since I have had the honor of a seat in this House. Still more especially it is painful to me, Mr. Speaker, to speak as I do and to vote as I do, when I am conscious of the fact that I am separating myself from the hon. gentleman on this side of the House who leads me and who leads us, and for whom I, in common with hon. gentlemen on this side of the House, as well as with many hon. gentlemen on that side of the House have feelings not only of respect but of the deepest possible affection. But, Sir, even under those circumstances I enjoy the comfort which is that I know that hon. gentlemen on both sides of this House will, at least, give me credit for acting from sincere and honest conviction. Believing that I am in the right, I hope hon. gentlemen will give me their sympathetic attention while I speak to the amendment of the hon. member for Muskoka. I may be permitted in passing to make a few references to the remarks of the hon. member for Muskoka, after which I will come to the speech of the hon. member for Lincoln (Mr. Rykert). I do not refer so much to the remarks that the hon. gentleman for Muskoka made this afternoon as I do to his remarks of a day or two ago, upon the occasion when he gave notice to this House of his intention to introduce the amendment which he has placed, Mr. Speaker, in your hands to-day. I do not wish to be understood even inside or outside of the House as complaining at all of the course of the hon. member for Muskoka. It has been suggested to me that that hon. gentleman's course was in fact forestalling me and taking from me that course which I intended to pursue; but, Sir, I can tell this House that I was gratified beyond measure when the hon. gentleman rose in his seat a day or two ago and announced his intention of doing what he has done to-day. I recognize, and no one in this House can recognize more than I do, how grave and serious this question is, not only in the present but grave and serious in its consequences in future, and I would be foolish indeed if I presume to think that I could give the question the weight and the importance of other hon. gentlemen in this House, I, who am comparatively young and especially so in comparison with the hon. member for Muskoka. I recognize, Sir, that someone older in years, older in experience, and older in position that I am should have taken this matter up, and I, therefore, say again, and I hope hon. gentlemen will believe me, that I was pleased and gratified when the hon. gentleman from Muskoka notified the House a day or two ago of his intention to move his amendment. I do not complain even of his words when he spoke, but I may be permitted to make some reference so as to explain away the inference that his words bore. He gave as his reasons for taking the course which he did, that, inasmuch as my resolution appeared so far down on the Order Paper that likely it would not be reached this Session, he thought it was his duty, under these circumstances, to move in the matter. The very best answer to the statement of the hon. gentleman is that my motion was reached, my motion was made and the papers have since been brought down so that it will be understood. I think that the course I took was right, not as has been suggested by people outside of this House, to evade the matter altogether. In speaking on this question I must be understood as having no feelings whatever against the Jesuit body or even against the Roman Catholics, amongst whom I am happy to say I number many, many friends. I have no sympathy with the clamor which is being made outside of this House, clamor, I may say, without reason. The Jesuits have been in some quarters assailed without argument, and I have no sympathy whatever with the course pursued in those quarters against the Jesuits and against the Roman Catholic body. All that has been said may be true or false; I care not. As far as my investigation and my reading has gone, I confess to believing that much that has been said is false. Even, Sir, taken the maxim, *Finis determinat probitatem actûs*, I believe that it bears no construction such as has been put upon it in certain quarters that " the end justifies the means." But, on the contrary, my reading and education has been such as to inspire me with admiration for the early Jesuit fathers. We need only recall Parkman's account (and he is by no means a very favorable historian toward Roman Catholicism) of the early Jesuit fathers, and we must be inspired and imbued with enthusiasm in our recollection of the work they accomplished in the country. We can recall, all of us, from history, the arrival, in this country, on the unfortunate Father Jogues, his capture by the Iroquois, his cruel and unheard of tortures, his determination to regenerate by baptism, notwithstanding his intense sufferings, his subsequent escape to France, his performing the sacred rites of the mass in his mutilated condition, his return to this country, his recapture and his fearful death at the hands of the father whose child he was trying to save by baptism. The only effect of that will be, the only result can be to inspire us with enthusiasm that such mi-sionaries have lived in years gone by. I approach this grave and serious question entirely relieved from any bias whatever against the Jesuit fathers or against the Roman Catholic Church. Our admiration for them is one thing, our judgment regarding the constitutionality of this Act under discussion is another thing. Now my first serious objection to the Act is that which has been mentioned by the hon. member for Muskoka. I claim, Sir, that the introduction into the Act of the mention of the Pope is such a serious encroachment upon the prerogative of the Crown, as to call for its disallowance at the hands of the Government. The sovereign is the *caput principium et finis* of all legislation; but in this particular case the Legislature of Quebec makes the Pope the end of its legislation. The Pope is given the right, notwithstanding what hon. gentlemen say, to negative this legislation entirely. Suppose the Pope did nothing, the Act would be a dead letter. It cannot be denied that the effect is to give a foreign potentate—and I shall show that the Pope is a foreign potentate—the right to disallow or negative this legislation; and if that is true, the converse must be true : if he has power to negative legislation, power to make an Act of Parliament a dead letter. it must follow logically that he has also the right to affirm legislation. And here we have introduced into a British Act of Parliament the power given to a foreign potentate to negative or affirm legislation. Now, we are taught again and again that the right of assenting to or dissenting from an Act of Parliament is a right so peculiar to the prerogative of the Crown that the sovereign herself cannot delegate it. It is quite true that the Governor General is given the right to assent or to dissent from Acts of Parliament; so are the Lieutenant Governors of the different Provinces ; but they have not the right to delegate that power to anybody else. *Delegata est non potest delegare* is a maxim specially applicable to the Lieutenant Governors of the Provinces in cases of this kind. Now, to show that my contention is well founded, I want to refer to the Statutes. First, I will refer to the Statute of 1 Elizabeth, chapter 1, which has already been referred to, and clause 16 of which reads as follows :—

" That no foreign prince, person, prelate, state or potentate, spiritual or temporal, shall at any time after the last day of this Session of Parliament, use, enjoy or exercise any manner of power, jurisdiction, superiority, authority, pre-eminence, or privilege spiritual or ecclesiastical within this realm or within any other of Your Majesty's dominions or countries that now be, or hereafter shall be, but from thenceforth the same shall be clearly abolished out of this realm, and all other Your Highness' dominions forever. Any statute, ordinance, custom, constitution or any other matter or cause whatsoever to the contrary in any wise notwithstanding."

The hon. member for Lincoln (Mr. Rykert), although he referred to that statute, did not for one moment contend that it was not in force in this country ; but it has been said that because it is an old statute, therefore it is not applicable. Well, I want to read from the Treaty of Paris, and I will read only those portions which bear on my argument. His Britannic Majesty engaged :

" To grant the liberty of the Catholic religion to the inhabitants of Canada ; and to give precise and effectual orders that his new Roman Catholic subjects might profess the worship of their religion according to the rites of the Romish Church, as far as the laws of Great Britain permitted."

I want to emphasise these last words, " as far as the laws of Great Britain permitted," because at the time of the making of that Treaty of Paris this Statute of Elizabeth was in force, so that the treaty did not negative the existence of that statute in this country, but, on the contrary, perpetuated it. Now, the hon. member for Lincoln said that there was a distinction between His Holiness the Pope as a foreign potentate, and as the head of the church. I grant you that; but does anyone mean to say that the Statute of Elizabeth is not directed, as all the statutes of Elizabeth we re to His Holiness the Pope ? No one can argue to the contrary, if he is possessed of, the least atom of historical knowledge. Every one of the penal Statutes of Elizabeth was pointedly directed to His Holiness the Pope, and, therefore, the Treaty of Paris did not discontinue the Statute of Elizabeth or prevent its application to this country. If we want any further legislative authority, let us look at the Quebec Act of 1774, the 5th section of which reads as follows :—

" And for the more perfect security and ease of the minds of the inhabitants of the said Province, it is hereby declared that His Majestys' subjects professing the religion of the Church of Rome at and in the said Province of Quebec may have, hold and enjoy the free exercise of the religion of the Church of Rome, subject to the King's supremacy, declared and established by an Act, made in the first year of the reign of Queen Elizabeth over all the dominions and countries which then did or hereafter should belong to the Imperial Crown of the realm, and that the clergy of the said church may hold, receive and enjoy their accustomed dues and rights with respect to such persons only as shall profess the said religion."

There we have, first of all, the Statute of 1 Elizabeth positively, in a legislative way, disapproving of the Pope in any way, exercising a jurisdiction ; then we have the Treaty of Paris coming after that, not preventing the operation of that statute ; and then we have the Quebec Act of 1774, specially perpetuating that statute in the Province of Quebec. Now, Sir, let me refer to the opinion of a great judge to show that what I say is correct. Mr. Justice Smith, in the case of Corse vs. Corse, reported in the Lower Canada Reports, page 314, said :

" As soon as Canada ceased to belong to France, the public law of France ceased to exist, and the public law of England came in."

Now, it may be said that my construction of that statute is a forced one, is not a fair one, is not consistent with the time in which we are living, in 1888, when it was passed in 1554 ; but I will read from an authority whose name is a household word, well known to every gentleman in this House. I refer to Mr. Todd, who was cited by the hon. member for Lincoln in his attempts to demonstrate the truth of some of his statements. He says :

" The Statute of 1 Elizabeth, chapter 1, known as the the Act of Supremacy, declares that no foreign prince, person, prelate, or potentate, spiritual or temporal shall henceforth use, enjoy or exercise any power, jurisdiction———"

Now, Sir, I want to ask hon. members of this House, how it is possible, if that construction be a correct construction of the Statute of Elizabeth, and I challenge assertion to the contrary to contend that that construction is not infringed upon by the Act passed in the Province of Quebec last Session ? At the very least by it the Pope is exercising the jurisdiction of distributing moneys, if nothing else, which I say is a violation of the statute according to the universal construction thereof. Mr. Todd goes on to say :

"—or authority within the realm, or within any part of the Queen's Dominions: and that all such power or authority heretofore exercised shall be forever united and annexed to the Imperial Crown of this realm. This declaration remains in force to the present day, and it is the statutory warrant for the supremacy of the Crown, in all matters and causes civil or ecclesiastical, throughout the British Empire, as well as for the renunciation of the papal claims therein."

Now, it has been said in the House, and has been written to the press by the hon. member for Bellechasse (Mr. Amyot) that there is a distinction between the Pope in his spiritual capacity, as the head of the church, and the way he has been brought into this statute ; but here we have the opinion of Mr. Todd that his right to exercise papal claims in this country ought not to and does not exist. But, Sir, I shall cite earlier authorities. I understand that some of the gentlemen who are opposed to this resolution rely upon the authority of Lord Thurlow. Now, I ask the attention of this House for a few minutes until I read his opinion regarding the statute :

" By the 1st of Elizabeth, I take it that there is no reason whatever, why the Roman Catholic religion should not have been exercised in this country as well as in that; confining it entirely to that Act, I know no reason to the contrary * * * * for the language of the Act is only this, that no foreigner whatever should have any jurisdiction, power or authority within the realm."

Then I will refer to the language of the celebrated Wedderburn :

" I can see, by the article of this bill, no more than a toleration. The toleration, such as it is, is subject to the King's supremacy, as declared and established by the Act of the 1st of Queen Elizabeth. Whatever necessity there be for the establishment of ecclesiastical persons, it is certain they can derive no authority from the See of Rome, without directly offending against this Act."

Then it may be argued that this statute is not in force now, by reason of some Provincial or Federal legislation which prevents its application in this country. No one who makes that contention could have read the British North America Act, because Imperial legislation, which was in force at the time of Confederation, could not since be repealed or destroyed by any Dominion or Provincial legislation. The 129th section of the British Nort America Act reads as follows :—

" Except as otherwise provided by this Act, all laws in force in Canada, Nova Scotia or New Brunswick at the Union, and all courts of civil and criminal jurisdiction, and all legal commissions, powers and authorities, and all officers, judicial, administrative and ministerial, existing therein at the Union, shall continue in Ontario, Quebec, Nova Scotia and New Brunswick respectively, as if the Union had not been made; subject nevertheless (except with respect to such as are enacted by or exist under Acts of the Parliament of Great Britain or of the Parliament of the United Kingdom of Great Britain and Ireland) to be repealed, abolished, or altered by the Parliament of Canada, or by the Legislature of the respective Provinces, according to the authority of the Parliament or of that Legislature under this Act."

Even if there had been legislation in any way detracting from the Statute 1st Elizabeth, which was undoubtedly in force at the time of Confederation, no legislation, either in this House or in the Province of Quebec, could in any way legally detract from or diminish the extent of the application of that statute. I think I have shown conclusively what is now the statute law of the land, namely, that resulting from the enactments of 1 Elizabeth. But I maintain that the common law. altogether apart from the statute, is such as to prevent the introduction of His Holiness the Pope into this legislation. Some of us can recollect the fact—I only from my reading— that, prior to 1850, the Pope attempted to divide England into different dioceses or divisions, but a statute was passed in 1850 to prevent him from doing so. This statute was the Ecclesiasticals Act of that year. Now, I want to refer to Mr. Todd again, who says, on page 313, that that statute passed in 1850 declaring that the Pope had no power to act as a foreign potentate, either in his individual capacity as head of the church or as a foreign potentate, to divide England into dioceses, had always been the common law of England. Mr. Todd says :

" The Ecclesiastical Titles Act was is substance a declaration of the common law, which was affirmed before the Reformation, and ratified by Parliament some five hundred years ago."

If it was always the common law of the land, Sir, that the Pope could not divide England into dioceses, surely it must have been the common law of the land that he had not the right to distribute money, and that money the money of the State. I would like to know which is the most important—dividing a country into different parcels or dioceses with the view of placing church authorities over each, or distributing certain moneys? If it was the common law of the land that His Holiness the Pope could not divide England into dioceses, it must have been also the common law that he could not distribute moneys in the way provided by the statute aimed at by the amendment now before the Chair. The common law of England became the common law of Canada. On this point Sir Richard West gives his opinion, on the 20th of June, 1720 (see Chalmer's Colonial Opinions, page 510):

"The common law of England is the common law of the plantations, and all statutes in affirmance of the common law passed in England, antecedent to the settlement of any colony, are in force in that colony, unless there is some private act to the contrary, though no statutes, made since these settlements, are there in force, unless the colonies are particularly mentioned."

Mr. MILLS (Bothwell). That is a settlement not a conquest.

Mr. BARRON. No, but it matters not. I maintain on that authority that the common law of England was such at that time that no distribution of moneys could be made by the Pope in England, and that common law became part and parcel of the common law of this country. Some reference has been made to correspondence from officers of the Crown in England, or others is high authority regarding the right of His Holiness the Pope to exercise any jurisdiction in this country. I, refer, in support of my view, to the Royal Instructions to the Duke of Richmond, on his appointment in 1818 as Governor in chief of Upper and Lower Canada, with reference to the inhabitants of Lower Canada:

"That it is a toleration of the free exercise of the religion of the Church of Rome only to which they are entitled, but not to the powers and privileges of it as an established church. * * * * It is our will and pleasure that all appeals to a correspondence with any foreign ecclesiastical jurisdiction, of what nature or kind soever be absolutely forbidden under very severe penalties."

Then as to the royal supremacy, which cannot exist if this Statute is to become law, I will refer also to Mr. Todd who says at page 313:

"The source of the authority of the Crown in ecclesiastical matters and of its jurisdiction in the last resort all over ecclesiastical causes is to be found in the doctrine of the Royal Supremacy. This doctrine is a fundamental principle of the British Constitution. It was authoritatively asserted by Parliament at the era of the Reformation, and it is interwoven with the very essence of the monarchy itself."

Further on he says:

"While by previous enactment, ecclesiastical supremacy had been conferred upon the Crown, as a perpetual protest against the assumptions, by any foreign priest or potentate, of a right to exercise coercive power or pre-eminent jurisdiction of British subjects."

Now, I think I have fairly shown that, at all events, the statute law is against the introduction of the Pope into any matters in this country in the way this statute provides. I will refer now to what I believe to be the objectionable clauses, and I will ask how it is possible for anyone not to admit, in the face of the statute, that these clauses to which I refer certainly make this law an infringement of the law as it is defined by the Statute of Elizabeth. In reply to a letter of Mr. Mercier, Cardinal Simeoni says:

"I hasten to notify you that, having laid your request before de Holy Father at the audience yesterday, His Holiness was pleased to grant permission to sell the property which belonged to the

Jesuit Fathers before they were suppressed, upon the express condition, however, that the sum to be received be deposited and left at the free disposal of the Holy See."

Then, in another place, Cardinal Simeoni replies to Mr. Mercier:

"The Pope allows the Government to retain the proceeds of the sale of the Jesuits estate as a special deposit to be disposed of hereafter with the sanction of the Holy See."

Is it to be said in the British country that we are to be told by a foreign potentate that he allows the Government of this country—a British Government— to "retain the proceeds of the sale of the Jesuit estates as a special deposit to be disposed of hereafter with the sanction of the Holy See?" Yet, allowing this Act is tantamount to saying that we allow the Pope to assume this important position. In another place, Cardinal Simeoni, replying to the question:

"Should authority be given to any one to claim from the Government of the Province of Quebec the property which belonged to the Jesuit Fathers before the suppression of the society, and to whom and how should it be given?"

Says as follows:

"Affirmatively in favor of the Fathers of the Society of Jesus and in accordance with the method prescribed in other places, that is to say, that the Fathers of the Society of Jesus treat in their own name with the civil government, in such a manner, however, as to leave full liberty to the Holy See to dispose of the property as it deems advisable, and, consequently, that they should be very careful that no condition or clause should be inserted in the official deed of the concession of such property which could in any manner affect the liberty of the Holy See."

Then in another place Mr. Mercier appears to acknowledge all that the Pope, through his secretary, demands. He says:

"That the amount of the compensation fixed shall remain in the possession of the Government of the Province as a special deposit until the Pope has ratified the said settlement, and made known his wishes respecting the distribution of such amount in this country."

Now, the letters containing these sentences are a preamble to this statue. They are referred to by a section of this statute and are made part and parcel of the law of Quebec—a British Province—and that the law is that nothing is to be done until the Pope has ratified the settlement and made known his wishes as to the distribution of the Property. There is an admission on the part of a Premier of a British Province that a foreign potentate—for such I claim he is—has the power to ratify British legislation. If he has the power to ratify it, he has the power to nullify it, and that is a power which no one, whether he be the head of a church or not, should possess. Then the statute goes on, in order to give it a sort of meritorious effect, to talk about restitution. In the very front of the statute, it speaks of restitution being necessary to be made to the Jesuit Society. What is restitution? You cannot restore anything to a person who was not at one time or other entitled to it, or to some one who is entitled to claim it on his behalf. I contend that the Jesuit Society, which was incorporated in 1887, has nothing whatever to do with the original Jesuit Society. Suppose a society is incorporated by charter in this Parliament, and for some reason or other it becomes extinct, and fifty years afterwards another society is formed under the same name, can anyone say, will anyone argue, that the society so formed can have any claim to the estates of the former society which has become extinct? Certainly not; and the same state of things exists here, and there can be no principle whatever of restitution involved. Sir, to contend the affirmative is to contend, not for the principle, but for the irony of restitution. I find that the Jesuit Society was incorporated in the year 1678 in France. I shall not trouble the House by reading at length the diploma or letters patent incorporating that society, but, with your consent and the consent of the House, I shall ask permission to hand it in.

Sir JOHN A. MACDONALD. No.

Some hon. MEMBERS. Read.

Mr. BARRON. On the 2nd August, 1761, that Society was dissolved in France, and, if the House is determined to have lengthy words read, I shall read the decrees of dissolution, contenting myself with the bold statement that the Society was incorporated as I have said. The Society was dissolved by the self-same Parliament which originally incorporated it, and the declaration of the King of France at Versailles was:

" Moreover, we ordain, that during one year from the date of the enrolment hereof, nothing shall be ordered, either definitely or provisionally, upon what may relate to the said institutes, constitutions and establishments of the houses of the said society, unless we shall otherwise so ordain."

Then on the 6th August 1761, by another sentence, the Parliament of France, with reference to the report to them made of the doctrine of the Jesuits, made the following provisions:—

" In like manner it is provisionally inhibited and forbidden unto the said priests, and others of the said society, to continue any lessons, either public or private, of theology, philosophy or of the humanities in the schools, colleges and seminaries within the jurisdiction of the court, under penalty of seizure of their temporalities, and under such other penalty as to right and justice shall appertain; and this, from and after the first day of October next, as well with respect to the houses of the said society which are situated at Paris as to those which are situated in the other towns, within the jurisdiction of the court, having within their limits schools or colleges other than those of the said society; and from the first day of April next, only with respect to those which are situated in towns within the jurisdiction of the court, where there are no other schools or colleges than those of the said society, or in which those of the said society shall be found to occupy any of the faculties of the arts or of theology in the university there established, and, nevertheless, in case the said priests, scholars, or others of the said society, shall claim to have obtained any letters patent duly verified in the court, to the effect of performing the said scholastic functions, the court permits the said priests, scholars, and others of the said society, to produce them before the court, all the chambers assembled, within the delays above prescribed, such order, upon view of the same, and upon the conclusion of the King's Attorney General, to be made by the court as to right shall appertain.

" The court most expressly inhibits and forbids all subjects of the King from frequenting, after the expiration of the said delays, the schools, boarding schools, seminaries, noviciates and missions of the said persons styling themselves Jesuits, and enjoins all students, boarders, seminarists and novices to quit the colleges, boarding houses, seminaries and noviciates of the said society, within the delays above fixed; and all fathers, mothers, tutors, curators or others having charge of the education of the said scholars, to withdraw them or to cause them to be withdrawn therefrom, and to concur, each in respect to himself, in carrying into effect this present decree, as good and faithful subjects of the King, zealous for his preservation. The court in like manner prohibits them from sending the said children to any colleges or schools of the said society, held within the limits of the jurisdiction of the court, or out of the kingdom. And as for the said scholars, the court declares all those who shall continue after the expiration of the said delays to frequent the said schools, boarding houses, colleges, seminaries, noviciates and instructions of the said persons styling themselves Jesuits, in whatever place they may be, incapable of taking or receiving any degrees in the universities, or any civil or municipal offices, or of discharging any such public functions. The said court reserving to itself to deliberate on Friday, the 8th day of January next, upon the precautions which it shall judge necessary to take upon the subject of the offenders, if any there be."

Then the society, having been dissolved by the same Parliament that brought it into existence, appears to have got a respite for a short time. But the letters patent were enregistered, and provided :

" Subject, nevertheless to this : That the respite contained in the said letters patent shall take place only to the first of April next, upon which day the provisional decree of the court of the sixth August last shall be executed *ipso jure*, and also without the necessary proceedings to enable the court to render judgment on the *appel comme d'abus*, instituted by His Majesty's Attorney General, prove the bulls, briefs, constitutions, forms of vows, and other regulations relating to the said society, can be suspended, and in like manner without prejudice to the provisional execution of the said *appel comme d'abus*.

"And also subject to this: That the public or private lectures on theology, philosophy or the humanities, held and given by the priests or scholars in all the towns or places within the jurisdiction of the court, without distinction, cannot be provisionally continued after the expiration of the said respite, the whole under the pains contained in the provisional decree of the sixth August last."

Thus I maintain that the same Parliament which brought the Jesuit Society, as a corporate society, into existence, by its decree, dissolved the society. Then, we find that His Holiness the Pope, on the 20th July, 1773, dissolved the society by his celebrated brief *Dominus ac Redemptor*. I shall not ask the House to the reading of that brief which is not necessary for my purpose, and in any event it is familiar to the ear of most hon. gentlemen in this House. A year later, this society was suppressed by royal instructions to the Governor General as follows :—

"That the Society of Jesuits should be suppressed and dissolved, and no longer continue a body corporate and politic, and that all their rights, privileges and property, should be vested in the Crown, for such purposes as the Crown might hereafter think fit to direct and appoint, and the Royal intention was further declared to be that the present members of the said society as established at Quebec, should be allowed sufficient stipends and provisions during their natural lives."

In 1791 there are Royal Instructions to the same effect. The last Jesuit died in 1800; the present society came into corporate existence in 1887, so I maintain that the present society is not in any way connected with the former society; and the principle of restitution does not and cannot apply. This Government, at least, should have returned the Bill, suggesting that it should be altered in some respects, and amongst others, the one to which I referred a few moments age. Even the Bishops of Quebec, or some of them, admitted that the Jesuits were no longer in existence, and they, at the request of the Jesuits, made a claim to the property. I find the following in a petition over the signatures of Joseph, Bishop of Quebec, P. F. Turgeon, Coadjutor of Quebec, and J. S. Lartigue, Bishop of Montreal :

"Your petitioners humbly represent that the Order of Jesuits being exitnct in this country, their natural successors are the Roman Catholic bishops of the diocese."

Then the very Act itself incorporating the Society of Jesuits in 1887, makes no claim whatsoever to their rights as owners of this particular property, so I think it cannot be maintained, on the merits, that they are entitled on any principle of restitution to this property. But it has been said that this property was taken from the Jesuits at the time of the Conquest. I deny that, because at the time of the Conquest it did not belong to the Jesuits. It had become Crown property, like any other Crown lands ; therefore, when the statute now objected to says that the property was confiscated, it states that which is not the case, and the Federal Government should not have sanctioned that mistatement, but they should, at least, have returned the Act to the Government of Quebec to have it amended in the particular. Now, in some pamphlets issued by gentlemen who support the Jesuit Society, I find Twiss referred to as an authority on the law of nations. A gentleman who writes a very able argument in support of the Jesuit case, has quoted from this authority as follows :—

"A victorious nation in acquiring the sovereignty *de facto* over a country, from which it has expelled its adversary, does not acquire any other rights than those which belonged to the expelled sovereign; and to those such as they are with all their limitations and modifications, he succeeds by right of war."

They also refer to De Vattell on the Law of Nations:

" The conqueror, who takes a town or province from his enemy cannot justly acquire over it any other rights than such as belonged to the sovereign against whom he has taken up arms. War authorizes him to possess himself of what belongs to his enemy; if he deprives him of the sovereignty of that town or province, he acquires it such as it is, with all its limitations and modifications.
" One sovereign makes war upon another sovereign, and not against unnamed citizens. The conqueror seizes on the possessions of the state, the public property, while private individuals are allowed to retain theirs. They suffer but indirectly by the war; and the conquest only subjects them to a new master."

Now, I agree with every word of that. Suppose the United States and Great Britain were to go to war—and I think hon. gentlemen in this House on both sides would have but very little doubt as to the result—it would not be said for one moment that Great Britain obtained any rights whatsoever over private property. Now, at the time of the Conquest this property did not vest in the Jesuits at all; it had become extinct, it had become vacant property; therefore, when it is said outside the House, as it has been said inside, that for meritorious reasons, because the property was taken by a method of confiscation, therefore it should be returned to them—I say it was not taken by confiscation, because at the time that Canada was conquered by England this property was not the property of the Jesuits, but was the property of France, having become extinct. We find the opinions of Her Majesty's Attorney General and Solicitor General for the Crown, dated 18th May 1779, stating in regard to this property:

" As a derelict or vacant estate, His Majesty became vested in it by the clearest of titles, if the right of Conquest alone was not sufficient, but even upon the footing of the proceedings in France and the judicial acts of the sovereign tribunals in that country. The estates in this Province would naturally fall to His Majesty, and be subjected to his unlimited disposal, for by those decisions it was established upon good, legal and constitutional grounds, that from the nature of the first establishment or admission of the society into France, being conditional, temporary and probational, they were at all times liable to expulsion, and having never complied with, but rejected the terms of their admission, they were not even entitled to the name of a society; therefore, they were stript of their property and possessions, which they were ordered to quit upon ten days' notice, after having been compelled to give in a full statement of all they had, with the several title deeds, and documents or proofs in support of it. Sequestrators or guardians were appointed to the management of their estates, and in course of time and with a regularity proportioned to their importance, provision was made for the application of them in the various ways that law, reason, justice and policy dictated; and all this was done at the suit of the Crown."

Now, to show further that at the time of the conquest this was vacant property, I refer to Marriott's opinion, 12 May, 1765. He says:

" From all these premises, it seems conclusive that the titles of the society passed together with the dominions ceded to Great Britain (in which dominions those possessions were situated) attended with no better qualifications than those titles, had by the laws and constitution of the realm of France, previous to the conquest and cession of those countries."

I mention that this Quebec Act is objectionable in many important particulars, and is also objectionable in declaring that those estates were confiscated by the British Crown. I say such was not the fact, and is not borne out by the history of the estates. This property has always been treated as having escheated to the Crown, not as having been confiscated by reason of the Conquest. I find Lord Goderich on 7th July, 1831, spoke to this effect:

" His Majesty's Government do not deny that the Jesuits' estates were, on the dissolution of that order, appropriated to the education of the people, and readily admit that the revenue which may result from that property, should be regarded as inviolably and exclusively applicable to that object."

And the Statute of William IV, chapter 41, states to same effect as follows :—

"And it is hereby enacted by the authority of the same, that from and after the passing of this Act, all moneys arising out of the estates of the late order of Jesuits which now are in or may hereafter come into the hands of the Receiver General of this Province shall be placed in a separate chest in the vaults wherein the public moneys of the Province are kept, and shall be applied to the purposes of educat on exclusively, in a manner provided by this Act, or by any Act or Acts which may hereafter be passed by the Provincial Legislature in that behalf and not otherwise."

Then we have the petition of the bishops, to which I have already referred. Does anyone mean to say that if the Province became owners of this property by reason of confiscation, the bishops would say the Jesuits were no longer entitled to it, as they did say in their petition ? It is quite clear, therefore, that the statute is incorrect in that particular, when it states that the property was acquired by confiscation. Then there is another point to which I desire to refer, and it is one to which has not yet been touched upon, and it is this : It is the case that two or more of the properties were acquired by the Jesuits, not from the King of France and not by grants of the Parliament of France, but from private individuals. I do not think anyone will deny that within strict law, and I may say I am speaking from a legal standpoint altogether—and I do not desire to go into the merits or demerits of the Jesuit claim, but to speak of the question from a legal standpoint only,—no one, I think, will deny that it is good and proper law that when property is given to a corporation or society or body of men or to one or more men upon a certain and specific trust, the very moment that the trust is no longer capable of performance the property reverts to heirs of the party from which the property originally came. That this trust was destroyed no one will question. It was destroyed by the Parliament of France. Then if such be the case, the heirs of the donors are not entitled to the property, whoever they may be. But it may be said that I am building up a fictitious case, and therefore, I will quote the language of the Rev. Father Flannery of St. Michael's Cathedral of Toronto, on 17 February, 1889. He said :

"These lands were never given to them by the French Government or by any Government but were the donations of private members of the church who left the lands in possession of the order for religious and educational purposes."

That trust having been destroyed, it will not be denied by any legal gentleman that the property reverts to the original donors. Why, we see only lately that the Seigniory of Sillery was given to a certain body of Indians, and that the property has been taken away from them by this objectionable statute. We remember in 1882 in this House the first Minister, waxing eloquent over the contention that the Rivers and Streams Bill took away one person's property and gave it to another, he contended that the public interests were greatly affected, and that it was his duty for that reason to disallow that Bill. The premises he built did not exist; but if he was right in that action, he should have enquired more closely into the facts regarding this question to ascertain whether the rules he laid down for his own Government, and for succeeding Governments, dit not apply to this particular case. If he was right in disallowing the Ontario Rivers and Streams Bill because, as he said, it took away the property of one man and gave it to another, *a fortiori*, he should have disapproved of this legislation because the trusts created by private donors have been taken away by the Parliament of Quebec, and handed over to other parties that have nothing more to do with them than the man in the moon. In order to show that I am not wrong in my view of this question, I quote a letter dated 20th June, 1879, over the signature of Mr. James McGill:

" It seems to us that it would have been proper by an advertisement to call upon the public for any dormant claims there may be on the Jesuits' estates."

I maintain, moreover, that under the British North America Act this Act is entirely unconstitutional. If I remember rightly (I will not read the particular section) it states that each Province of the Dominion shall have the right to deal with educational matters, reserving the rights of the minority in Quebec, and the minority in the Province of Ontario. No one has ever maintained that that Act gave to the different Provinces of the Dominion the right to make denominational grants, as has been done. There can be not doubt that the Jesuits are a religious institution; and are we to understand that the different Provinces have the right to make religious grants to the different religious bodies ? I think not. I assert that if the leader of the Government had the very least respect for his own past record and his own past utterances, he would have disallowed this legislation just as quickly as he allowed it. Why, we have only to recall the case of the Rivers and Streams Bill of Ontario. In that case he built up the premises which did not exist. He claimed that it gave the right to take away the property of one man and give it to another; and that the general effect upon the whole country would be such that he had a right to disallow the Bill. I say that, applying that principle, he should have disallowed this Bill, and for the reasons given. If it is true that a portion of the property was given originally to the Indians of the Seigniory of Sillery, then I say there are good reasons for disallowing this Bill, as, on the Premier's contention, there was for disallowing the Rivers and Streams Bill of Ontario ; there was good reason to disallow this legislation, if for no other reason than that it took away from the Indians land given to them, as it is said, by France originally. I desire to refer to the remarks of the right hon. leader of the Government on the Rivers and Streams Bill disallowance ; and I may mention that his remarks were coincided in by several hon. gentlemen, and especially by the present Postmaster General and the hon. member for North or South Simcoe. On that occasion the First Minister spoke as follows :—

" I declare that, in my opinion, all Bills should be disallowed if they affect general interests. Sir, we are not half a dozen Provinces. We are one great Dominion. If we commit an offence against the laws of property or any other atrocity in legislation, it will be widely known."

Can any subject be thought of that affects the people more generally than that of religion ? Can any subject be thought of that will affect the people more generally than one respecting the Jesuits' Society. Without reflecting for one moment upon the society, let me point out that this society of Jesus has been legislated against by the countries of Saragossa, La Palantine, Venice, Avignon, Portugal and Segovia, England, Japan, Hungary, and Transylvania, Bordeaux, France, Holland, Tournon and Berne, Denmark, Bohemia, Russia, Naples, and in all Christendom by the Bull of Pope Clement XIV. I maintain that it cannot be said that a society legislated against in all these countries is not of general interest, but it might be said that " this was many years ago and that we are not now in the dark ages." I am quite willing to admit that, but I find that even since, that society was restored by Pope Pius VII, in 1814, it has been legislated against by, and expelled from Belgium, Russia, France, Portugal, Spain, Switzerland, Bavaria and the Italian towns. I refer to that not because I have the least unkind feeling against the Jesuit Society, but I maintain that it cannot be said that that society is not of general interest when we find it has been legislated against in all these different countries. Can it be said that the question is of the deepest possible interest right up to the imaginary line which divides the Province of Quebec from the Province of Ontario, and that the moment you step across to the Province of Ontario it has no interest at all? I certainly say no. Can it be said that anything which will be injurious to the Methodist body in Ontario, that the same body is not more or less affected by it in the

Province of Prince Edward Island ? No. The Baptist community, the Congregational community, and all other denominations, have a touch of sympathy throughout the whole Dominion. Therefor, I say that the words of the right hon. gentleman spoken in 1882 in this House in reference, to the River and Streams Bill, apply to this case. By the authority of the words that he used then, I hold it is a strong argument for this Bill being disallowed to-day. I do not like to charge the hon. Premier with making fish of one and fowl of the other in this matter, but his treatment of the Orange Incorporation Bill in this House cannot be forgotten. He takes only three days to intimate to the Lieutenant Governor of Quebec that he assents to and approves of this Bill, but he is dumb to the enquiry of the Lieutenant Governor of Ontario, to know if he would assent to and approve of the Orange Incorporation Bill, when one word from him, similar to that he gave Quebec, would have incorporated the Orange Society. If he assents and approves of this legislation it follows as a most positive *sequitur* that when he disallowed legislation in the Province of Ontario, and when he disallowed legislation in the Province of Manitoba, because he disapproved thereof, it must follow that by allowing this Statute to become law he does so because he approves of the same. I would like to give the hon. the Premier an opportunity, but I see he his not in the House just now, of denying what he is credited with having said at a certain meeting on the 20th June, 1886. On that occasion he is credited by is organ, *la Minerve*, with saying as follows :—

"To the calumnious hypocrites who represent him as the personification of religious fanaticism."

Sir John replied by saying :

"That he had never in his life set foot in an Orange lodge. * * * I am accused, said Sir John, of being a Protestant, and even of being a bad Protestant. In like manner I have been accused of being an Orangeman, although I have never set foot in a lodge.

I do not know whether to believe that or to believe the statement of one of his *protégés* regarding our Roman Catholic fellow-citizens, that he, or a member of his Government " had no confidence whatever in the breed." I have satisfied myself, at all events, that my conclusions are correct, that this Bill should have been disallowed, and, if possible, that it should be still disallowed, for the reason that it is stricly unconstitutional. Now that I see the Minister of Customs in his seat, I hope that he, occupying the prominent position he does in a certain order which has been mentioned by the hon. member for Lincoln (Mr. Rykert), will not allow this opportunity to pass without giving to some hon. members on this side of the House who think as I do, the benefit of his views. I hope, Sir, they will be in accord with many of those who belong to the society of which I believe he is such——

Mr. BOWELL. An ornament.

Mr. BARRON. Yes; such a great ornament.

Mr. WALLACE (York, Ont.).

I am sure, Sir, that every member in this House must sympathize with the hon. member for North Victoria (Mr. Barron) when he declared how exceedingly painful it was for him to separate himself even for a few moments only from his beloved colleagues, and still more beloved leader. We can all sympathize with the hon. gentlemen, and we can all sympathize with the party that is so painfully distracted at the present moment. I want to refer at the outset to a remark made by the hon. member for Lincoln (Mr Rykert) in the opening of his speech. He stated that a newspaper published in the interests of the Orange Order threatened any member of that order who will dare vote for the allowance of this Bill. I would say to the member for Lincoln, what perhaps he knows himself, that the Orange Order has only one organ in the Dominion, and, Sir, I defy him, and I defy any hon. member of this House to point to any such article in that organ of the Orange Association in Canada. I say, Sir, that the organ has, during this discussion which has agitated the public, the press and public meetings, and which agitation has assumed a pretty violent form in many places—I say that that organ of the Orange Association has set an example of moderation that might well be emulated by other organs, and also by some of the members of the sacred profession in their pulpits. I fancy, Sir, that the hon. gentleman instead of reading an article from the *Sentinel* was reading the *Globe* when it was thundering out its anathemas against the hon. gentlemen opposite if they dared to vote against disallowance. For myself. I propose to be able to dicuss the very important amendment moved by the member for Muskoka (Mr. O'Brien) without any race or religious prejudices or feelings, and purely from a Canadian standpoint. As a Canadian who has the strongest faith in the future of our country and who has watched with pride its rapid march in material progress the united work of all races and of all religions—I hope that this question may be investigated on its merits and entirely apart from any religious feeling. We came to Canada from different countries, or we are the descendants of those who have come here to enjoy and exercise fully our religious convictions. We have flourished under our free institutions in Canada, and in order to do so we must be prepared to respect not only the rights of others, but also their feelings and, to a certain extent, their prejudices as well. Now, Mr. Speaker, two very important Acts have recently been passed by the Quebec Legislature. The first was the incorporation of the Society of Jesus in the year 1887, and in the following year the " Act respecting the Settlement of the Jesuits' Estates." These two Acts bring up the whole question of the Jesuit Order in Canada, as well, perhaps, as the Jesuit Order in other countries. Previous to the Conquest, in 1759. the Jesuits held property which they have received from various sources in trust, for two purposes : for the training and education of the French youth of the country, and also of the aboriginal inhabitants. Now, Sir, their position under the English régime depended upon the terms, first, of the capitulation to Lord Amherst in 1760, and, secondly, upon the terms of the cession to the English Crown by the Treaty of Paris in 1763. Article 32 of the Capitulation reads as follows :—

" The communities of nuns shall be preserved in their constitutions and privileges. They shall continue to observe their rules. They shall be exempted from lodging any military, and it shall be forbidden to trouble them in their religious exercises."

The reply of General Amherst to this request was " Granted." Then, article 33, of the Terms of Capitulation, was as follows—

" The preceding article shall likewise be executed with regard to the communities of Jesuits and Recollets and of the House of St. Sulpice at Montreal. This last and the Jesuits shall preserve their right to nominate to certain curacies and missions as heretofore."

The answer of General Amherst was :

" Refused till the King's pleasure be known."

Now, it will be observed from these facts that the Recollets and the Jesuits received no particular or special rights under the Terms of Capitulation of 1760. The next place where these matters were negotiated and regulated was in the Treaty of Paris in 1763. The only stipulation in that treaty bearing on this question was as follows :—

" His Britannic Majesty agrees to grant the liberty of the Catholic religion to the inhabitants of Canada ; he will consequently give the most effectual orders that his new Roman Cath lc subjects may profess the worship of their religion according to the rites of the Roman Church, as far as the laws of Great Britain permit. His Britannic Majesty also agrees that the French inhabitants, or others who had been the subjects of the most Christian King in Canada, may retire with all safety and freedom whenever they think proper, and may sell their estates, provided it be to subjects of His Britannic Majesty, and bring away their effects as well as their persons, without being restrained in their emigration under any pretence whatever, except that of debts or of criminal prosecutions; the term limited for this emigration shall be fixed for the space of eighteen months, to be computed from the day of the exchange of the ratifications of the present treaty."

Therefore, it is plain that the right secured by the treaty of Paris to the French Canadians was the liberty to worship according to the rites of the Roman Catholic Church, and the limit of the English law as it then stood. They received no further rights under that treaty. Then, Mr. Speaker, there is a great and important distinction between the Jesuits and the Recollets, Sulpicians and others established in Canada. The Recollets and Sulpicians were organized by French subjects in France. The Jesuit Order originated in Spain; it is of no nationality, and it has no law but the will of its General. The next change that took place with reference to the Order of Jesuits was under the Quebec Act of 1774, the result of which was given in the royal instructions to the Governor of Quebec in the year 1775. This made a new departure in the rules governing the Jesuits, and made a very wide distinction between the Recollets and the Sulpicians on the one hand and the Jesuits on the other. For instance, the orders to the Governor in 1775 stated:

" That the society of Romish priests, called the Seminaries of Quebec and Montreal, shall continue to possess and occupy their houses of residence and all other houses and lands to which they were lawfully entitled on the 31st September, 1759, and it shall be lawful for those societies to fill up vacancies and admit new members according to the rules of their foundation."

That was the regulation with regard to the other orders of the Roman Catholic Church. But, Sir, what do we find in reference to the Jesuit Order? An entirely different regulation was meted out to them, and it was as follows:—

" That the Society of the Jesuits be suppressed and dissolved and no longer continue as a body corporate and politic, and all their rights, possessions and property shall be vested in us, for such purposes as we may hereafter think fit to direct or appoint; but we think fit to declare our royal intention to be that the present members of the society, as established at Quebec, shall be allowed sufficient stipends and provisions during their natural lives."

Now, Sir, by order of the British Parliament, in the Royal Instructions given to the Governor of Canada in 1775, while the other orders of the Roman Catholic Church were permitted to remain in Canada, enjoy their property, and continue their work, the Jesuits were suppressed. This took place not only in Canada, but in various countries in Europe. We find that in 1759 the order was suppressed in Portugal; in 1764 it was suppressed in France; and in 1767 it was suppressed in that country where it first had its birth, in Spain; and not only was it suppressed in those countries of Europe, but in all the colonies and possessions of those countries throughout the entire world. Following those events, Pope Clement XIV, the head of the Roman Catholic Church, found that order to be so intolerant, so mischievous in its workings, so inimical to the peace not only of several Governments, but of the church itself, that he determined to suppress and abolish the order. We, therefore find in 1773 a brief from the Pope of Rome, and I will trouble the House while I read a few extracts from that brief. It is adressed to the Catholic Church throughout the world. His Holiness cites many instances of the suppression of religious orders by the Holy See; he recites the many favors and privileges conceded to the Jesuits, and then he says :

" There arose in the bosom of the society divers seeds of discord and dissension, not only among the companions but with other regular orders, the secular clergy, the academies, the public schools and lastly even with the Princes of the states in which the society was received."

The Pope then recites at some length these quarrels ; the accusations, he says :

" multiplied without number, especially with regard to that insatiable avidity of temporal possessions with which it was reproached."

Then he gives an account of some unavailing efforts to reform the society, and adds :

" In vain did these Pontiffs endeavor by salutary constitutions to restore peace to the church, as well as with respect to secular affairs with which the company ought not to have interfered."

After reciting some further efforts he proceeds :

" After so many storms, tempests, and divisions, every good man looked forward with impatience to the happy day which was to restore peace and tranquility ; but, under the reign of this same Clement XIII, complaints and quarrels were multiplied on every side, in some places dangerous seditions rose, tumults, discords, dissensions, scandals, which, weakening or entirely breaking the bonds of Christian charity, excited the faithful to all the rage of party hatreds and enmities."

Then he says :

" After a mature deliberation, we do, of our certain knowledge and the fullness of our apostolical power, suppress and abolish the said company.

" Our will and meaning is that the suppression and destruction of the said society and of all its parts shall have an immediate an l instantaneous effect."

Previous to 1773, the society had been abolished by almost every Roman Catholic country in Europe, and finally, that year it was suppressed in every part of the world by the head of the Roman Catholic Church itself. I think no stronger evidence could be given of the character of that order than the character given to it by Pope Clement XIV. Pope Clement would not have uttered it. He knew the machination of the order, and in this brief he states what he was compelled, though reluctantly, to do in the interests of the church and of civil government. We are told, however, that the society was restored. True, it was restored ; and I will refer briefly to one or two facts in connection with the society after its suppression. In Canada they were allowed, what they were not allowed in any country in Europe, to enjoy in peace and quietness the property they had received in trust. In the countries of Europe, they were not only banished, but were deprived of all their properties of every kind whatsoever. Now, the British Government, after the death of the last member of the order in Canada, in 1800, took possession of the whole Jesuits' states. The Crown held these properties until 1831, when, after some negotiations, they were handed over to the Government of the Provinces of Upper and Lower Canada with the stipulation that the revenues therefrom should be devoted exclusively to the higher education of the young. That stipulation has been carried out up to the present day. But now we find a different state of affairs. We find an Act of Parliament passed in 1887 incorporating this society, and in 1888 an Act giving them $400,000, also giving the Government of the Province of Quebec power to sell this property, which has been estimated and valued at $2,000,000, and to devote the proceeds to any purpose they may think proper :—not to the purposes of education, but to any purpose whatever. Another important feature in this matter is this ? $60,000 are voted for the superior education of the Protestants in the Province of Quebec and $400,000 are voted to the Jesuits. A good deal has been said about the Pope's extraordinary powers in connection with the latter vote. The first point that I would call your attention to is this : That $400,000 is voted, not for the purposes of education not purposes for which the British Government held the property, not for the purpose for which the property was handed, in the first place, in trust, but for any purpose the Quebec Legislature may choose. Not only $400,000, but the entire proceeds of the estates. While from year to year until now the revenues derived from them were devoted to superior education, now power is taken to sell the property and devote the proceeds for other secular purposes, and the $400,000 are to be divided as the Pope may determine. That money is not required in the Act to be devoted at all to the education of the young, but it may be devoted to any purpose. It may be devoted to the propagation of the Roman Catholic religion, or to any other purpose they may think fit. I have carefully looked over the British North America Act, under which the Dominion Parliament and the various Legislatures of this country carry on their operations, and I am unable to see one line of that Act in which power is given to a Local Legislature to vote money for the purposes of any church. Many years ago when severe and bitter contests were going on in this country for the complete separation of the Church from the State, we thought in Canada that we had obtained that complete separation, and that all the churches stood on the same plane in the eye of the law; but if this Act is allowed to go in force, an end is put to that equality and I think it would be a lamentable thing if a law should be passed in any Province giving greater power to one religious denomination than is given another. There are one or two features of this Act of incorporation and the moneys voted which, I think, are deserving of a little attention. We know there is no love between the Jesuit Order and certain other orders in the Roman Catholic Church, and we know through the legislation by which the Jesuits are incorporated, they are given only the right to exercise certain rights, not in the whole Province of Quebec, but only in certain portions. The second clause says:

"The corporation shall not have the right under this Act to possess educational establishments elsewhere than in the Archdioceses of Montreal and Ottawa, and in the Diocese of Three Rivers."

Still further on it says:

"The corporate seat of the corporation shall be in the city of Montreal and another place in this Province, within the present limits of the Archdioceses of Montreal and Ottawa, and of the Diocese of Three Rivers, which may be selected later on by a by-law of the corporation."

That means that in the archdiocese of Quebec, that diocese over which the Cardinal has control, the Jesuits are not allowed any privileges. They are not allowed to establish their headquarters or schools there. As a matter of fact, they are incorporated only in a part of the Province of Quebec. What is a still stranger feature is the fact, that they are incorporated in the Archdiocese of Ottawa. I do not know much about the divisions and boundaries of the dioceses of the Roman Catholic Church, but I am informed that the Archdiocese of Ottawa includes three counties in the Province of Ontario. That it includes the city of Ottawa, and therefore, the society which was incorporated by the Province of Quebec would be incorporated only in portions of the province of Quebec and also in portions of the Province of Ontario. That would be one reason for disallowing the Act that it incorporates a society not only in the Province of Quebec but also in portions of the Province of Ontario. It appears to me, from the reason I have already adduced, from the reasons recorded in the resolution in your hand, and from other reasons, that it would have been better for the peace and happiness of the various portions of this community if this society had not been incorporated and had not received this endowment. In the first place, it diverts money from its lawful object. That money has been, I believe, faithfully administered for the purpose of superior education since the Quebec Government got it in 1831. This Act also recognizes the supremacy of the Pope over the Queen and over the Quebec Government; and it is also bringing into life—

illegally, as I believe—a society which was legally suppressed by the British Government in 1775. As there was no Legislature in Canada until 1791, I believe that Act, not having been repealed, is still law in Canada to-day. I am against this Act for another reason, as I have already said, that I do not believe the Confederation Act gives any such power to vote any such money for any such purpose, and, therefore, though agreeing with the Government in its great and prosperous Dominion, I shall be compelled to vote for the amendment of the hon. member for Muskoka (Mr. O'Brien).

Mr. COLBY (STANSTEAD).

In addressing the House I shall endeavor to confine my remarks very closely to the question now before the Chair. I do not find it necessary, in the discussion of that question, from my standpoint at least, to go into the record, as other speakers have done, of that remarkable order of men, the Society of the Jesuit Fathers, of their beliefs or of their conduct a century or more ago. I do not think that necessary to a proper determination of the question now before the House. Nor shall I go into any close legal consideration of the case, as did the hon. member for North Victoria (Mr. Barron), because I think it must be decided upon other, and broader, and more liberal ideas than can be drawn, from nice legal, fine-drawn, hairspun distinctions; and I think such remarks would have been more applicable in the Quebec Legislature at the time when the Bill referred to was under discussion, than they are in this Parliament at this time. The proposition now before the House, as I understand it, carries an implied censure of the Government for not having disallowed the Act of the Quebec Legislature for the settlement of the Jesuits' estates, and a positive instruction to the Government to disallow it. I think we will all agree that the power of disallowance, which by the Constitution is vested in the Governor General and his advisers, is a power which should be exercised with the greatest discretion; that, in the first place, it should appear, before an attempt is made to exercice that power, that the Government has the clearest possible right to exercise it; and then it should appear that there was an obvious necessity for its exercise. It is a serious matter to interfere with the deliberate will of a Local Legislature under any circumstances whatever—the clear and deliberate will of a Local Legislature. It is a more serious matter—for the gravity is vastly magnified—when the question upon which it is attempted to conteract their will and to nullify their legislation is one which touches the most sensitive feelings, the religious sympathies and convictions of the majority of the people in the Province which is to be affected. Now, there are certain things which we must recognize as existing facts. It is true that this order of the Jesuits was at one time suppressed; that is a historical fact. It is equally true—and that is a present and pregnant fact which we must recognize—that the order of the Jesuits has to-day, in the Province of Quebec, legal status, a status which is assured by the strongest legal sanctions of the Legislature, and which is assured by the highest sanction of the church and recognized by the whole body of the Roman Catholic Church. So that an attack upon the order of the Jesuits in the Province of Quebec is an attack upon the Roman Catholic Church, upon the entire body of the Roman Catholic Church, and there should be not misapprehension upon that point. We must not delude ourselves into the belief that we are assaulting an obnoxious and a friendless power or entity that is entitled to the execration of all mankind. We must recognize the fact—and I do not know how it has come about, whether by a change in their practices or a change in their reliefs or otherwise; I have not gone into an enquiry into that point—but we must recognize it as a positive fact that they are to-day under the ægis of the supreme Pontiff and of the church, and are fraternally recognized today by the entire body of the church. Consequently, we must realise that if we nullify this Act of the Provincial Legislature as is proposed, we have not only to override a sentiment in Quebec, which is stronger in that Province than in any other in this

Dominion, in favor of the maintenance of provincial rights, but we have to make up our minds to attack the solid sentiments of the majority of the people of that Province in their religious convictions, and in regard to that legislation which the majority believe to be their right and duty within the lines of the Constitution. I say, then, that we must carefully revise our position and see that we make no mistake. We must see that we have a clear, and positive, and undoubted right to do this thing ; then we must see that there is an obvious necessity for doing this thing, and then we must consider, in view of the integrity of our country, in view of the peace, the prosperity, the harmony and the contentment of our people, the full, the possible, the certain consequences of adopting the course which is now proposed. We have a Constitution, it is true, which binds our Provinces together in a Confederation but that is a paper bond. The moment you destroy mutuas good-will between the people of this country, the moment you array the people of this country in hostility —personal and religious hostility—one against another, you have destroyed the only bond which can permanently hold us happily together. Now, I am going to limit my argument within very narrow lines, and I maintain that if this House agrees with me in these premises, the right to disallow must be very clear and the duty obvious before we undertake this serious responsibility, before this House goes on a step further in the direction proposed. We had the deliberately and carefully considered opinions of the Minister of Justice, and all his colleagues in the Government, that the Act of the Quebec Legislature was wholly *intra vires*, and that there is no legal or constitutionnal power in the Dominion Government to disallow it. Does not that of itself create a doubt ? Have we not also the opinion of men of eminent ability in this House and in this country, of high authority on constitutional questions, differing from the Government in politics, differing from them on most every point, yet who are in agreement with them on this point, that we have no right to disallow this Act ? Then, I say, is there not sufficient ground to establish the only proposition I care to establish, that there is some doubt about it ? Then, I say, if it is a doubtful right, we should not face the certain consequences, the disastrous consequences of disallowance. Now, Mr. Speaker, we have in the records in this Parliament a closely parallel case to this, and in many respects a stronger case than this, in which Parliament has recorded its deliberate opinion ; I refer to the New Brunswick school question, which was precipitated upon Parliament within the memory of those of us who where members of the first Parliament of Canada, precipitated upon at a very inconvenient period, just on the eve of the general elections of 1872, a question which raised discussions of a most alarming character, and which created a degree of anxiety in the minds of every member of the House, which has never been equalled in the 21 years of my experience in Parliament. At that time a Catholic minority of one of the Provinces of this Dominion came before Parliament, not with any abstract proposition, but with a clear and positive grievance. They made out a case which aroused the sympathies of Parliament to an extent that I have never seen them aroused before. There was not in Parliament, as the records will show, an individual member of this House, on either side, Protestant or Catholic, or of any nationality, or from any Province, who did not record his vote of censure against the authorities of New-Brunswick by an expression of regret and a hope that the causes of discontent would be removed—I say not a single member of the House who did not record his vote in that sense except those wanted to go further and give a positive remedy. The Catholic minority of New-Brunswick came to us and said : " Before Confederation we had the right of enjoying our own separate schools ; we were receiving Government assistance in support of our own schools ; we were not compelled to send our children to the schools or to assist in maintaining the schools, which we thought dangerous to the morality and the religion of our pupils; we enjoyed that right long before Confederation ; Government assisted those schools ; we built the schoolhouses at our own expense, the Government made appropriations for the support of those schools ; we had, in fact, enjoyed a system of separate schools for many years before Confederation and from Confederation up the year 1871, when, contrary to the determined opposition of the Catholic minority, composing two-fifths of the population of New-Brunswick, contrary to their protestations, the Legislature of New-Brunswick, by a vote which was carried in the Upper Chamber by a majority of one, reversed that system, and compelled us to support schools to which we could not send our children, they withdrew all support from the schools which we must sustain as concentious men ; " and they came to this Parliament and asked a remedy. They said to us : "We think this is a case clearly within the 93rd section of the Constitutional Act, and we ask for remedial legislation under the 4th sub-section or for disallowance ; but if you are unwilling to apply either of these remedies, then we ask that you will memorialise the Imperial Parliament to revise the Constitution and place us where we ought to have been place us where we supposed we were at the time of Confederation, place us as the minorities in Ontario and Quebec are placed in respect to separate schools, we care not what remedy you apply, but relieve us from the situation. Those different propositions were brought before the House, and every one of them was refused. We refused to disallowed the Act. Why ? Not because we did not believe that if fairness and equity alone were to previal it ought to be disallowed; but because we had a doubt as to the right to exercise that veto. The Minister of Justice of the day expressed the opinion that we had no right to disallow it ; and an hon. learned gentleman of highest authority in this House at that time, and of highest authority in this House and in this country on those matters at the present time —I allude to the hon. member for West Durham (Mr. Blake) — expressed himself as having doubts on that question. On the other hand Hon. Mr. Dorion, now chief Justice of Quebec, Hon. Mr. Fournier, now a judge of the Supreme Court, Hon. Mr Holton, a high authority on constitutional law, and Hon. Mr. Joly, with thirty-four, voted to censure the Government for not having disallowed the Act. Parliament deliberately recorded its doubts by adopting the Mackenzie amendment, which asked the advice of the Judicial Committee of the Privy Council on that question. We felt it was a case where a remedy should be applied to remove an existing grievance, but we doubted our right to apply that remedy, and we expressed our doubt by adopting the Mackenzie amendment, and proposing a reference to the Judicial Committee of the Privy Council. We acknowledged the justice of their cause, they were coming to us for relief, the whole of the catholic portion of the Province was aroused on that question, their clergy and leading men came to us, bringing every influence they could to bear, and yet we refused that remedy to the Catholic minority of the Province of New Brunswick. To-day we are asked, in a case of doubtful authority, to do for the Protestant minority of the Province of Quebec that which we refused to do in a similarly doubtful case for the Catholic minority of New Brunswick. So this House is asked in regard to the Protestant minority in Quebec, which made no strenuous resistance to the passing of the obnoxious Act by the Legislature of that Province, to intervene upon doubtful grounds, while we refused to intervene in behalf of a Catholic minority whose claims we acknowledged to be just claims, who used every influence and power they possessed, who fought the question in the Local Legislature inch by inch and then came here resting on their rights and claiming them and urging them in the most emphatic manner upon us. Now, I think we can hardly be excepted to do that. If the former course was the right course, the course now proposed would be a glaringly wrong course. If we will not relieve actual grievances of the most serious character to persons aggrieved and who begged our intervention, shall we intervene in behalf of those who do not claim, who do not state they have any grievance; shall we step out of our way to do this, to voluntarily do it when our right to do so is doubtful ? I do not think, Mr. Speaker, that this House can deliberately come to any conclusion of that kind. When we remember the keen resentment which was expressed by all the organs of

Protestant sentiment in New Brunswick because this Parliament had presumed to express regret that discontent existed there, and a hope that the School Act might be so amended as to give reasonable satisfaction to the Catholics of New Brunswick which was the substance of the amendment which I had the honor to propose at that time, and which Parliament then adopted in order to alleviate the situation; when I say we call to mind the keen resentment with which this mind interference was received by the Protestants of New Brunswick, we may well imagine what an outbreak would occur in Quebec were the Protestant majority in this Parliament to cause the disallowance of an Act which was passed by the unanimous vote of the Legislature of Quebec ; that Legislature having acted, as is believed by a majority of the people, within the line of their strict rights. I believe, Sir, that the paramount duty of whatever Government controls the destiny of Canada is to preserve the integrity of the Union within the lines of the Constitution. I believe it is their duty to avoid, so far as they can do it, keeping within the lines of their constitutional duty, every cause of offence to the various Provinces, because any conflict between provincial authority and the central power is pregnant with danger. The Constitution has already stood several severe strains. We have seen, I will not say by whose fault, in one Province of the Dominion, that Province swept by a sentiment favorable to an entire separation from this Dominion. We have seen in another Province the Government of the day and all existing things swept away by a spirit of nationalism, that felt in some way injured by the action of the central Government. We have seen the Province of Ontario agitated on account of an alleged infringement of provincial rights, and so also the Province of Manitoba.

Mr. MILLS (Bothwell). A real infringement.

Mr. COLBY. A real or fancied—I am not discussing that question now. All these were serious blows and injurious to the Constitution and to the country, and are to be deeply regretted. Those who desire the perpetuity of our system of Confederation should never make use of such questions for party purposes, except constrained by necessity, because they are not fair party weapons, and they tend to disorganize the country. I say the constitution has stood several strains of a serious kind; but there is one strain it has not been subjected to, and I hope it may never be subjected to it, and it is that where religious strife and altercation, where animosities and feelings of the kind which grow out of exasperated religious sentiment are evoked. We know, and I will not comment upon it, and people outside of this House must realise that if we pass the resolution proposed it will precipitate a crisis the most dangerous that ever occurred in the history of this country, and the most dangerous that could possibly be imagined. I have no doubt, Mr. Speaker, from the manifestations of feeling which are being expressed in certain parts of the Dominion, that the very zealous Protestants of some sections must have felt that the Protestant minority in the Province of Quebec have been very apathetic in the matter of the passage of this Jesuit Settlement Act. I believe there is nowhere in this Dominion a body of Protestants more willing to vindicate their rights, more willing to make sacrifices for the preservation of their rights than are the Protestants of the Province of Quebec. I do not believe they are disloyal to Protestant ideas. But the Protestants of the Province of Quebec have lived for many years in close relation and in close contact with their fellow-citizens of a different religion, and many prejudices which the one might otherwise feel against the other have been worn away by contact. The Protestants and the Catholics ot the Province of Quebec, so far as I know their relations, live together happily upon mutually respecting terms, each respecting the other's rights, each respecting even the other's sensibilities and prejudices, and co-operating together, working together, for what they believe to be for the common interests, without jealousy, without friction, without over-sensitiveness, recognizing the good things in each other; if they differ, quietly differing, and not making themselves obnoxious to each other. These are the relations which have grown out of long years of personal contact, living together side by side, meeting and knowing each other. That is a happy condition of affairs, but it is an actual condition of affairs in those parts of the Province with which I am personally acquainted. That is not a condition of affairs that the Protestants of Quebec desire to have disturbed. The Protestants of Quebec, and I think I fairly voice their sentiments, acknowledge the fact—if they do not acknowledge it to be so, it is a fact—that there never was a minority in any country treated with more justice, with more generosity than the Protestant minority of the Province of Quebec have been treated, irrespective of political parties. They have always had the control of affairs that most concerned them, those matters connected with education and other matters concerning which the Protestants were most interested as Protestants, and they have had as much control over such questions as if they had an entire Legislature of Protestants; they have not been meddled with, they have simply been permitted to manage their own affairs and they have not felt that they were in a minority in any instance that I recollect. Look at the political sentiment also. The Liberal party of Quebec elected as its leader for many years that noble man whom we all respect, Mr. Joly, a Protestant. They were not jealous, they had no objection on account of his Protestantism to serving under a leader whom they recognized as an able man whose views were in political accord with their own. The Conservative Government were equally liberal. Why, during the Conservative regime in Quebec perhaps the most important office in the Cabinet had all along been held by a good old orthodox Presbyterian Treasurer, M. Robertson, and we were allowed during that regime, perhaps, an undue representation in the Government of the Province. We had two members, able and influential men, in a Cabinet of seven, which is certainly an undue proportion, and they were men of influence and men of character and ability. So that in all these respects we have nothing to complain of, and, perhaps, it is for that reason that we do not wish unnecessarily to provoke an issue which would result in the disturbance of those kindly relations. Then, again—and I know it influenced some men of high standing among the Protestants of that Province—we are finding Protestants and Catholics alike, Protestant and Catholic clergymen, standing on a common platform in the advocacy of matters which both think concern the well-being of the people. It is not very long ago, if I recollect aright, when His Eminence Cardinal Taschereau presided over a meeting held by Catholics and Protestants to consult with regard to the best legislation to be had on the subject of temperance. Leading men of both churches are working together to promote the best ends of the community as viewed from their common standpoint. That is a condition of affairs which had been recognized by many Protestants who are interested in the cause of temperance as one which should be perpetuated. I simply instance these things to illustrate the friendly sentiment, and to show the cordial relations existing between Protestants and Catholics in the Province of Quebec and the desirability from the point of view of either that those relations, friendly coperative relations as they are, should not be disturbed. Again, let us consider what would have been the result if we had precipitated an agitation, if we had made the attack, or if we had raised this issue in which we were sure to be defeated. I may say here, which is a fact, that there is hardly a constituency in the Province of Quebec in which either the Roman Catholic electors are not in an actual majority, or in which they do not hold the balance of power. It is attributed to an hon. member of this House—I do not know how truly—that he said the other day with regard to the French Roman Catholics that they considered first their religion, second their nationality, and third their party, and I believe that this is truly said of them. We saw in the great change that was made at the last elections in the Province of Quebec what the national feeling when appealed to would exhibit, I think it is true that the religious sentiment is the highest with the French Canadian people, and if it is above nationality, if it is above party, if that sentiment is prepared to ally itself with one party or another party and that the question of party is a minor consideration, then in almost every constituency of the Province of Quebec the Protestants would be deprived of their just representation in the Legislature of the Province. There was nothing to be gained by raising an issue in which the result was a forogone conclusion and which issue could not by any possibility have resulted favorably to the Protestants. For these reasons what course was pursued ? The Protestants of Quebec have never acknowledged that the Jesuit body had a legal claim to the restoration of those estates. The press has never acknowledged it, the public men have never acknowledged it, the pulpit has never acknowledged it. Further than that the Protestants of Quebec have never acknowledged that the Jesuits had a moral claim to the restoration of those estates, and they placed themselves deliberately on record by their speeches in the Legislature on that point. It was a most bitter and nauseous pill they had to swallow when the name of the Pope was foisted into the Act. But that objection was more a matter of sentiment than otherwise. Assuming that the thing was to be done, assuming that $400,000 was to be divided among certain Roman Catholic institutions, it certainly was desirable, from every standpoint, that that the distribution should be final; that it should not be an ever-recurring question and a reference to the highest authority of the church, the only one power which could make that a final settlement had its advantages. There is no doubt about that. If it was acknowledged that a sum of money should be distributed among the Catholic institutions it was desirable that it should be so distributed as to satisfy those who would receive it, and it was desirable that it should be recognized as a final settlement, so that from a practical standpoint, it might have been attended with certain wise and practical advantages if this reference were made; but I say that, as a matter of sentiment, it was not a pleasant thing to Protestants that the Pope should be consulted. Yet the Protestant did nothing more than to record their protests against it. I do not think that any one who knows the editor of the Montreal *Witness* will suspect him to be a man who would not proclaim his Protestant principles if assailed, or who would truckle to Roman Catholics; and yet, if I recollect aright, the Montreal *Witness*, which is the most outspoken and the most advanced Protestant newspaper in the Province of Quebec, had but two mild editorials while this thing was going on. It published the reports of proceedings as news items, but it simply quietly objected to the proposition that the Jesuits had either a moral or a legal right to what they asked. It did not say to its readers: " Your rights have been assailed—agitate! agitate! arouse yourselves! " It said nothing of the kind. The pulpit is usually outspoken when the pulpit feels that rights dear to it are inpaded; yet no man that I have heard of from the pulpit ever called upon his congregation or upon the people to agitate on this question. He expressed his views upon it; and there is no doubt as to the Protestant view on the subject; it is not the Catholic view on the question; and while the Protestants have never surrendered their views, they have placed them quietly on record, and they have contented themselves with that. I do not read all the newspapers of the country, but I do read that great organ of public opinion, the Montreal *Herald*, and I do not recollect that the Montreal *Herald* ever put in anything more than a mild protest. It did not called on the people to " agitate! agitate! " The Montreal *Gazette* was, perhaps, the most pronounced in its utterances on the question, but it merely expressed its views, and did not call upon the people to agitate the question. There were no petitions that I know of going up to the Legislature from any portion of the Protestant community, asking it not to pass that Bill. So, if the Protestants of Quebec may be fairly credited by the Protestants of Ontario and other Provinces as being men of equal ability with themselves, of equal fidelity to the principles of Christianity, of equal capacity to judge with regard to the utness of things and what was right or wrong, what was opportune or inopportune, if they may be fairly credited with equal opportunities of judging, I think they should be spared the animadversions which some are inclined to cast on them. I think they understood the situation better, and I think they were as true to the principles of Christianity as the blatant men here now who are trying to agitate the country after the thing is done, and when there is no good object to be served. I think they are equally true, equally intelligent, equally devoted to the cause of Protestantism, and I think they are in a better position to know what is best for them, from their individual standpoint. At all events, if the Government are censurable for not having disallowed this Act what opprobrium should not be cast on the Protestant minority of Quebec for not having protested against it, as the minority of New Brunswick did against the school law in that Province. It was because they felt and realised no actual grievance, and because they did not want, for a sentimental grievance, to fight in a hopeless cause, to arouse animosity, to disturb the relations which are beneficial and in the interest of the whole community. Now, Mr. Speaker, I do not care to protract my remarks longer. I am a Protestant. The Roman Catholic Church—I will not speak of it as a religious body—I look upon to-day, speaking of it from a political standpoint and a political standpoint only—as one of the strongest if not the strongest bulwark we have in our country against what I conceive to be the most dangerous element abroad in the earth to-day. The Roman Catholic Church recognizes the supremacy of authority; it teaches observance to law; it teaches respect for the good order and constituted authorities of society. It does that and there is need of such teaching; for the most dangerous enemy abroad to-day in this land and on this continent is a spirit of infidelity; is a spirit of anarchy, which has no respect for any institution, human or divine; which seeks to drag down all constituted authorities; emperors, kings, presidents from their seats; the Almighty from the throne of the universe, and lift up the goddess of Reason to the place of highest authority. This dangerous enemy, this insidious enemy, is infecting the popular mind, not so much in Canada—thanks, largely to the safeguards thrown about its people by the Roman Catholic Church—as in the neighboring Republic. If there is a danger in that country and in this more to be dreaded than all others it is to my mind that spirit of infidelity and anarchy, that destructive insidious spirit, and it can be best combated by that great spiritual power which upholds authority and law, whose very existence is dependant on the idea of authority, which cannot exist as a church or an institution of influence except upon the idea of authority and the observance of law, whose teaching are all in that direction. I do not believe it is the interest of this Dominion to alienate, by any undue or unnecessary attacks, any one of the great powers upon which we must depend for the maintenance of our most cherished principles and institutions. I believe, Sir, that we have a duty to perform to each other, and that duty I have indicated. I did not intend to trespass on the House so long as I have done,but I thought it was proper that some one should represent what he conceives, at all events, to be the sentiment of the Protestant community in the Province of Quebec. I think the time is near at hand when it will be recognized by the two great religions of this country, the Protestant and the Roman Catholic, that the time for bickering has passed, that they have a common interest, and that for the promotion of that common interest they should stand shoulder to shoulder, work confidingly and in a friendly way together for the preservation of a common Christianity and all that is more dear and sacred to both, and thus, I conceive, will the best interest of this Dominion, and the best interest of civilisation on this continent, be promoted.

Mr. MITCHELL. (NORTHUMBERLAND).

Mr. Speaker, I do not rise for the purpose of making a speech on this question, I rise for the purpose of simply giving a few brief explanations for the vote that I shall give. I may say at the outset that for once during the present Session and the last preceding one or two Sessions, I am going to support the administration. I do not do it because of any particular virtue in that Administration; nobody would believe me if I said I did; but I do it because I feel it to be to the interest of the smaller Provinces, a county in one of which I have the honor to represent. Sir, I am not going to enter into the merits of the question as to the whether the course Mr. Mercier pursued in dealing with the Jesuit's estates was a prudent course or not. Perhaps, if had been a member of the Legislature of Quebec, representing a Protestant element in that Province, I might have doubted the propriety of that measure, and, perhaps, have voted against its passage. I have heard it stated to-night by some gentlemen that it was an improper thing to first charter the Jesuit Society. I have heard it next stated that it was an improper thing to pass the Bill voting the money, and that it was giving to a foreign power to right to dictate how the money of the People of the Province of Quebec was to be administered. These questions, I taxe it, are within the Province of the Legislature of Quebec, and during the passage of that Jesuit Bill, occupying a public position as connected with a leading journal—I am proud to say it is recognized on the other side—I have taken somewhat of an interest in observing the effect it had amongst the Protestant element in that Province who are paying the money. Now, Sir, I may say this, and I think I will say it without fear of contradiction, that during the passage of the Bill incorporating the Jesuits' Society, there was scarcely a Protestant paper throughout the whole of the Province that raised one single objection against it. I will next say, when dealing with the financial feature of the question, that with the exception, so far as I can recollect, of two members out of the fifteen Protestant members in the Legislature of Quebec, not one of them raised their voices against the passage of the Bill, and those two did raise them in very moderate tones. And when it came to the question of dividing the House upon the point, these gentlemen called out, " carried on division." The Premier said : No, I will take the names upon it ; and when they found that the names were to be taken, if I recollect the facts aright, they said " unanimous," and it was carried unanimously. Was there any excitement or any agitation on the part of the Protestant element of the Province of Quebec during that time ? No. Months have elapsed, and it is only when some of the—shall I call them fanatics ?—I think it would be a good name to give them—in the Province of Ontario raised, for what purpose I do not know, this agitation, that this question comes up. A good many of them are friends of the right hon. the First Minister, and I fear he has often expressed the wish: " Save me from my friends." But whatever may have been their motive, it could have been no very good one, for there is no object to be gained by the agitation of this question, but to create trouble, dissension and bad feeling throughout the community. I re-echo the sentiments of the hon. gentleman who last spoke, that Christian charity should prevail, and that in place of sowing dissension broadcast throughout this land we ought to endeavour to harmonise in a community, so mixed at this, the different religious elements, in place of sowing discord among them and creating feelings such as have been by these men to-day. If there are any people aggrieved in relation to this matter, who are they ? Are they the Protestants of Ontario ? What right have they to dictate to us, the Protestants of the Province of Quebec, as to how we shall dispose of our own money ? I have heard the arguments they have used by those who sustained this motion, that this property was given for a special purpose. But how is this money voted ? For what purpose is it given ? It is not given for purpose of education, for that is the object for wich those who receive it intend to appropriate it ? Let any one come and reside in the Province of Quebec and become acquainted with the institutions which are to get this money, and he will find that they are promoting education among a large and the most numerous class of the people in the Province of Quebec in a manner that reflects credit upon their institutions. I am not a Roman Catholic, but I respect the Roman Catholics of the country. It will ever be my wish to live in harmony and peace with them, and whenever I can promote their interests fairly, giving due consideration to the interests of the Protestant community, they will always find, as they always have found during my past career, that I will do it. Our Provincial Legislature voted this money—and I will not say it was a wise thing to do, because it has raised to feeling which I regret has been raised, and which I will say now never ought to have been raised by the people of Ontario. It has raised that feeling, but as the money has been voted, I say it is the money of the people of the Province of Quebec, and the Protestants of the Province of Ontario have no excuse for their agitation. Years after the incorporation took place, and many months after the money was voted, they have no right to create that agitation, whatever may have been the motive for it. They have no right to interfere with the manner in which we, in the Province of Quebec, shall dispose of our own money. I represent and have some control over a leading organ of the Press in that Province. I have taken very little part, through that paper, in this discussion, but throughout the whole of it, while I did not approve of Mr. Mercier's course in voting the money, I justified the action of this Government to-day in refusing to veto this Bill. When one of these Provinces, coming within the limits of the power given them by the British North America Act, chooses to dispose of its money in the way this money has been disposed of, I justify this Government in not interfering with the operation of the Act; and if they had interfered, they would have met with any censure which I, in my place here and through the newspaper which I control, could have passed on them. I am glad to say the Government has pursued the course they have. I am glad to say they have done the right thing. From the standpoint of a Maritime Province man, coming from one of the two or three smallest Provinces of this Dominion, it would be a sacrifice of the dearest interests and the greatest security which the British North America Act gives to the smaller Provinces if the Government had been allowed to interfere within the limits of the powers of the Legislatures of these Provinces in the way some hon. gentlemen desire they should. I have simply risen to state these few facts, in order to justify by this explanation the vote which I shall give. I feel that outside of everything else, I am a Protectionist of my own Province. I desire to protect the rights of the smaller Provinces of this Dominion against the superior ones and I think that the people of the Province of Ontario, where this agitation has entirely arisen, have gone beyond their limits in this matter. The agitation has been created in the Province of Ontario; it has been swelled into importance by the agitation, the ministerial agitation—I do not mean governmental; I mean ministerial in another sense. And for what purpose? Ought it to be desire of any man who seeks to secure the future peace, harmony and prosperity of this country, to create dissensions between the Roman Catholics and Protestants, between the French Canadians and Ontarians ? No, Sir. We ought to promote harmony if we can ; we ought to endeavor to remove religious dissensions ; we ought to endeavor to keep within the bounds of the political rights which the British North America Act has established for the different Provinces of the Dominion, and we ought to be especially careful that the larger Provinces, or the Dominion, should not attempt to assume a jurisdiction they have no right to exercise, and to infringe upon the privileges and rights of the smaller Provinces. With these few remarks, I shall endeavor to bring to a conclusion anything I have to say upon this matter, and I should not have spoken upon it were it not that I did not wish to give a silent vote on an important motion like this. I wish to say one thing more, and I hope the right hon. the First Minister will receive it in the spirit in which I give it. I do not think it is good policy for my right hon. friend to put up his followers behind him to defend the course the Administration will pursue in relation to this matter ; and in place of protracting a discussion such as this, the right hon. gentleman or the gentleman in his Cabinet who occupies a prominent position in the Orange Association, which is largely at the bottom of this matter, or my respected friend the Minister of Justice, who is so able to do it, should rise and state the policy of the Government. I now call upon one or other of them, I do not care which—and I believe I have the right to do so, under the practice of the Imperial Parliament on such an occasion—to state what is the policy of the Administration on this matter. Let them come out frankly and state if they are prepared to stand by the course they have pursued of not touching the Bill, of not attempting to disallow it, but of letting it take its operation, emanating as it does from the power which had the constitutional right to pass it. I say, if one or other of those gentlemen will get up and make a declaration on this point, I believe they will squelch out the efforts which are being made to sow dissension throughout this land, and will put an end to this senseless debate which has been brought before this Parliament.

M. McCARTHY, (SIMCOE N. RIDING.)

At the close of the sitting last evening I rose somewhat reluctantly, and only because I thought if I did not seize that opportunity, you, Sir, would call in the members, and the opportunity of addressing the House would be lost. I thought then, and I think now, that considering the nature of the motion which is before the House, it would not have been unreasonable for the Government, or some member of the Government, to have defended their action in the past in allowing the Bill under discussion, and to have given those reasons to us which, perhaps, would have justified their course, and, at all events, would have enabled those who differ from them to show wherein that difference lies. My hon. friend from Muskoka (Mr. O'Brien) is entitled to the thanks of this House and country for bringing this matter before Parliament. It would have been, I think, an everlasting disgrace to us if, in this, a free Parliament and free country, there would be no member found out of the 200 odd who compose this House, to give voice to the opinions of a very large body of the people who have been aroused with regard to this measure. I say when my hon. friend from Muskoka (Mr. O'Brien) gave reasons why he thought this Bill should still be disallowed, notwithstanding the action of the Government, when he assailed the action of the Government upon constitutional grounds, and when to that was added the attack made by my hon. friend from West York (Mr. Wallace), and the more elaborate attack upon legal grounds, made by the hon. member for North Victoria (Mr. Barron), it does appear to me that it would have been ordinary courtesy to those hon. gentlemen, and to the House itself, that some defence should have been made from the Treasury benches. I hardly think that we can take seriously the defence which has been offered by the hon. member for Lincoln (Mr. Rykert). I do not for myself take it seriously. With regard to the hon. member for Stanstead (Mr. Colby), the case is different. His remarks require attention, and from me they shall receive serious consideration. But, although my hon. friend from Lincoln (Mr. Rykert) is a gentleman of long standing in the House, he frankly told us that he prayed, as I understood him, that he never again would have to present himself before his constituents to ask for a renewal of their confidence.

Mr. RYKERT. I did not say so.

Mr. McCARTHY. I must have misunderstood the hon. gentleman, and, of course, take that back. Then my hon. friend, the other gentleman to whom I have referred (Mr. Colby), who spoke so feelingly and so ably, whose voice we are always glad to listen to, whose wisdom we all recognize, is possibly a prospective Minister; but, although that be so, I think it would still have been perhaps better if we had heard from an actual Minister, and not a prospective Minister, on a question of this importance. It may be that before this debate closes the House will hear from the Treasury benches upon this subject. Their silence so far in the discussion is, I consider, hardly giving us fair play. Fortified by the leaders opposite, fortified by the great number of hon. gentlemen who are going to support them in this House, I do think they should have allowed the small band here who are opposed to their action any possible advantage that could be given by the debate, and not have remained silent, but have given the reasons why the course of the Government should be sustained. However that may be, we must take the situation, just as we find it, and I was not willing the discussion should close without giving the reasons why I am taking the course which I propose taking on this important matter, and in which I will have to separate myself from my political friends with whom it has been my pride and pleasure to act up to this time. The question must be considered in a two fold aspect. It has to be considered as to its constitutionality in the narrower sense of the term, and as to its constitutionality in the wider sense of term. If it is *ultra vires* the Legislature of Quebec, it ought to have been disallowed. If it is *intra vires*, if it is within the powers of the Legislature of that Province, then I still say it ought to have been disallowed. But the matters are so entirely separate and distinct—the one resting upon legal constitutional principles of one description, and the other depending upon consideration of a widely different character, that I have to ask the permission of the House to deal with these matters separately and distinctly. First, it is well we should clearly understand the character of the legislation which is assailed. It will not do to ignore the past; it will not do, as the hon. member for Stanstead (Mr. Colby) did, to say it is not necessary to consider fine spun legal arguments, or to deal with the question in that way. All these questions have first to be considered from the legal point of view. We have a very large volume, not down to the present time, of the cases which have been disallowed, most of them because they were beyond the power of the Provincial Legislatures to enact. Therefore, the first question which the Minister of Justice had to report upon was whether this Act was constitutional in that sense of the term. The first question was whether it was within the powers of the Legislature of the Province. Then the other question came before himself and colleagues—a matter more of great public policy than of law— as to whether on these grounds the measure ought to have been disallowed. It is well to look at the Act, and although I have no doubt that all of us have read the Act and pretty well understand it, yet I will ask the House to bear with me while I give shortly a summary of what I consider to be the salient features of this most extraordinary piece of legislation. It commenced by a letter from the Premier of Quebec, in which he addressed His Eminence the Cardinal, who, I suppose, occupies somewhat the position of the Prime Minister of His Holiness the Pope. In that letter Mr. Mercier, having recited the history of the case, says :

" Under these circumstances, I deem it my duty to ask Your Eminence if you see any serious objection to the Government selling the property, pending a final settlement of the question of the Jesuits' Estates."

Here we have the Premier of one of our Provinces asking of His Holiness, or of the Secretary of the Propaganda, occupying the position to which I have referred, for permission, it being his duty, as he says, so to do, to sell the property—asking him to see if there is any serious objection in the way of the Government selling the property, pending the final settlement of the Jesuits' Estates. It is sufficiently startling to find such a recital in a British Act of Parliament, and I venture to say it is unheard of, I venture to say that, in all the legislation passed by the Parliaments of Great Britain or the Legislatures of any of the Colonies, you will search in vain to find any so humiliating a statement as this very first paragraph of the Bill presents to you. But that does not seem to excite surprise in the power to which it was addressed, because the answer is in this form :

" I hasten to notify you that, having laid your request before the Holy Father at the audience yesterday, His Holiness was pleased to grant permission to sell the property which belonged to the Jesuit Fathers before they were suppressed,——"

So the permission is given—

"—upon the express condition, however,——"

So the condition is annexed—

"—that the sum to be deposited and left at the free disposal of the Holy See."

Thus the Province of Quebec is permitted to legislate. The first step has been gained in the settlement of this important question. The free Parliament of Quebec, entrusted under the British North America Act with important powers, and representing a mixed community, a community with which the Supreme Pontiff of Rome has no power to interfere as a temporal power, asks, and the Supreme Pontiff graciously grants permission to that Legislature, to deal with what, I think I will show to the satisfaction of every member of this House before I close, was recognized as a portion of the public domain. Mr. Mercier did not see his way to allow this condition to be imposed. It could not be at the disposal of the Holy See, but—and to my mind it is a distinction without a difference—it was to be retained as a special deposit to be disposed of hereafter with the sanction of the Holy See. I do not know whether there is very much difference between these two provisions. It is a difference in words, but not a difference in fact or in substance, as the sequel has shown. Practically, it has been a gift to the Holy See, and has been distributed as to His Holiness the Pope seemed best. Then, having obtained this consent, as a condition precedent to the legislation, we find that negotiations were entered upon, and the result of these negotiations is that the lands of the Jesuits' Estates are to be left intact. That is another concession granted by the representative of the Holy See; and, instead of that, compensation in money is to be made, and the claim is presented, which we find amounts to $2,000,000. As $1,000,000 of that is the property of this Dominion, I do not think we have got rid of that claim yet. I do not suppose that the Province of Quebec could do more than make an arrangement in regard to that property which belonged to that Province; but, in regard to that which belongs to this Parliament or to this Dominion, I suppose, by-and-bye, we will have our First Minister asking leave—because what can be assented to by the authorities here as right in the Province of Quebec would not be wrong in regard to the property, belonging to the Dominion—we may have the First Minister here asking that the portion of that property belonging to the Dominion shall be dealt with by permission of his Holiness at Rome. I find further in these documents the following:—

"I deem it my duty to ask your Eminence if you see any serious objection to the Government's selling the property, pending a final settlement of the question of the Jesuits' Estates."

There is no doubt at all about the meaning of this. There is no doubt about the understanding which is arrived at. Before the Government are put in full possession, and in order that they may be put in full possession of these estates, there is to be a compensation made, and, finally, the bargain is worked out, and the conditions of the bargain are, what? The conditions are that this arrangement is to be non-effective until it receives the sanction of His Holiness of Rome. It is to be ratified—that is the term use—but it means practically that it might be vetoed, and to make, no doubt, that there was no attempt at conciliation or at sparing the feelings of those who are known to entertain strong feelings on this subject, this matter was not submitted to His Holiness of Rome until it was brought before the Legislature of that Province. Whether that was by arrangement or not, I do not know. Whether it was paying proper respect or not to the Sovereign Pontiff to ask him to express his approval or disapproval, I do not pretend to judge, but the legislation of the Province is clearly made dependent upon the act of His Holiness the Pope of Rome.

Not only so—and then I have finished my summary of the Act—but the sum of money which is granted, the $400,000 granted which is payable out of any money of the public revenue is to be distributed, in effect, though perhaps not in the terms of the contract, under and with the sanction of His Holiness of Rome. Now, that is shortly the meaning of this legislation. I will have finished with the Act when I make a further observation, and I make it now, perhaps, a little out of place, but it must not be altogether lost sight of. This Act in effect does away with the purposes for which the Jesuits' Estates were appropriated, and I think that is a matter of such great importance that I can only feel astonished at the calmness with which my hon. friend from Stanstead (Mr. Colby) regards it, and the indifference with which it has been received among the Protestant portion of the Province of Quebec, as my hon. friend has stated. This Bill puts into the general fund the money which was granted for educational purposes. It misappropriates—I do not use the term in its technical sense, for I quite recognize the right of the Province to use the fund—but from a general standpoint it misappropriates this fund by providing that $400,000 may be paid thereout to a certain institution. Now, having said so much as to the Act, let me say a word or two as to the property, and that brings me to what might be a long history and a long statement, and I hope the House will not be impatient with me when I deal with this somewhat complicated matter, which I will endeavor to make as plain as I can. I do not accept the theory which I have seen put forward in some quarters, that the Jesuits held their estates in trust for educational purposes. As far as I have been able to examine the deeds—and I have examined the report made in the year 1824—these estates were given to them in fee simple for all time. So far as I can judge from the history of the body at that time, it was not an uncommon thing for the Jesuit Fathers to accumulate both lands and goods in very considerable quantities. I find that one of the accusations made against them was avarice; one of the causes of the suppression of their order shortly after that, was the complaint made by the other orders of the Church, that they were avaricious, and that they accumulated wealth unduly in their order, notwithstanding the vow of poverty which they had taken. But however that may be, I think it is quite plain that they did hold these estates for themselves. Now, then, just let me trace the story of events by which this country became subject to the British Crown. We must never forget—I am afraid that some of my friends from the Province of Quebec do sometimes forget—that this is a British country, that by the fortunes of war that event was decided and the greater half of North America passed under the British Crown; and that being so, effect had to be given to the laws to which the country then became subject. Now, what were those laws? Granting, Sir,—which is not quite accurate—that the Jesuits held these estates at the time of the Conquest —I spoke before of the manner in which they held them originally—but granting they held them at that date—which would not be accurate—when we have before us the decree of the Parliament of Paris, suppressing the Jesuit Order in the year 1762, taking from them their land; when we have that, it would not, I say, be strictly accurate to affirm, that at the time of the Definitive Treaty in 1763, these Jesuit Fathers held their estates as they certainly did aforetime. But even if they did, while admitting freely that this country, New France, having then a settled law, and passing under the British Crown as a conquered country, while I admit freely, that the British law did not, by virtue of the conquest, become the law of New France, I do say, it is beyond all doubt, that it was in the power of the conquering State to enact such laws as to the conquering State seemed proper, to change the civil law which then prevailed, and to introduce the common law of England. It is beyond all controversy that, the treaty having been agreed to on the 10th February, 1763, in the October following, the King did issue a proclamation that introduced at once into this country, the laws of Great Britain, and that those laws continued to be the laws of this country until, in 1774, the Quebec Act was passed, which restored to the French Canadian inhabitants, the civil law which they liked best, to

5

which they were accustomed, and for which they had petitioned to the King and to the British Parliament. The constitutionality of the proclamation, the power of the King to introduce English law, is not now open to controversy, because the very self-same treaty underwent consideration in the celebrated case with which all lawyers who have made any attempt to master this subject are perfectly familiar ; and it was upheld as constitutional, as a proper exercise of the prerogative power, and as being binding and efficacious to the full extent and limit of the command contained therein. Now, Sir, what was the effect of that ? It will not be denied that at that time the Jesuits were an organization which could not be tolerated, and were not tolerated, by the laws of England. I am not going now into any argument, any citation, to establish that point ; it is beyond controversy. It was laid down by the law officers of the day—I have their citations here to establish it—it was laid down by Blackstone in his Commentaries, the first edition of which was published shortly before that period, that the Jesuit organization was an illegal one, and then the moment British laws were introduced into this country, *ipso facto* the Jesuits' estates became forfeited to the Crown, and the title of the Crown to these estates has always been recognized from that period up, has always been considered as indefeasible. If sanction was wanted for it, we could find it by the action of the Parliaments of this country, upon petition of the French Canadian people of the country, who desired that the lands should be kept for educational purposes when it was proposed to give out of these lands, and perhaps the lands themselves, to General Amherst, who had been the general in command at the time of the cession. So not only have we, as I will prove, by the law that was enunciated by the law officers of the Crown, by the highest authorities of the day, but we have the action of our own Parliaments, the Parliament of the Province of Quebec before the Union, the Parliament of United Canada after the Union ; and yet, Sir, here, 100 years afterwards, we find the Premier of the Province suing humbly to the Pope of Rome for liberty to sell the Jesuits' estates. Can humiliation go much further, if we are indeed a free people.

Some hon. MEMBERS. Oh ! Oh !

Mr. McCARTHY. Some of my hon. friends laugh ; I do not see any laughing matter in it, I cannot see why they should laugh about it. If the property is in the condition that I have proved it to be, I think the conclusion that I have stated follows from it ; and if we are a free people, if the Act of Supremacy means anything, if we are not subject to his Holiness of Rome in temporal matters—I am not speaking of spiritual matters, I am speaking of the public domain of this country, I am talking about the temporal power, it was of that power that consent was asked to dispose of the estates—and so I say it is a humiliation to us as a free people to find that one of the Premiers of this Dominion has thought it necessary to obtain the sanction of any foreign authority to dispose of this property. It is argued that the Pope is no longer a foreign potentate ; I think he is. His temporal power was never feared, it was the spiritual power which was struck at by the Act of Supremacy, not the temporal power of the Pope. It was the power that he claimed to excommunicate Sovereigns, to absolve their subjects from their allegiance—these were what was struck at by the Act of Supremacy, not his guns or his men, for guns and men he never had in numbers to alarm or affect any of the great powers of Europe. Now, Sir, am I right or am I wrong, in what I have stated ?—because I desire to make no misstatement of this question. Let us see just what the law officers of the Crown stated at that time. We know how it was done. The law officers, I believe, at that time, were Mr. Thurlow, the Attorney General, and Mr. Wedderburn, Solicitor General, both distinguished lawyers, but neither of them perhaps, competent to give an opinion in matters of civil law. Sir James Marriott was skilled in civil law and in ecclesiastical law, and he was called upon for a report—merely for a report, because the responsibility still rested with the law officers of the Crown. Extracts of his report have been published, and we are more or less familiar with them, and his report established, and the law officers adopted his conclusion, that the Jesuit estates were at once forfeited to the Crown. That under the treaty there was no claim for either the Jesuits or for other religious communities; but, anxious as the Sovereign was—and, I say, if you will look back at the history of that period, no man with British blood will have cause to regret the conduct of the British authorities in those days or the manner of their disposition—the Sovereign said: The Jesuits are beyond the pale. We cannot listen, for one moment, to their holding their estates, but the other religious communities are to be permitted to remain in possession of their estates, and they are to remain there for the purpose of enabling us to judge whether it is necessary under the treaty (afterwards, under the Statute of 1774, they were continued in their possession), in order that effect might be given to that portion of the treaty, and that portion of the Act of Parliament, which guaranteed to the inhabitants of the conquered country their rights. I shall have to trouble the House with reference to the facts which govern the whole subsequent proceedings, and let me commence with the earliest date. On 13th August, 1763, in the instructions which were given by the Earl of Egremont to Governor Murray, we find these words:

"Though the King has, in the 4th article of the Definitive Treaty, agreed to grant the "Liberty of the Catholic religion to the inhabitants of Canada;" and though His Majesty is far from entertaining the most distant thoughts of restraining his new Roman Catholic subjects from professing the worship of their religion according to the rites of the Romish Church, yet the condition expressed in the same article must always be remembered, viz:—" As far as the laws of Great Britain permit:" which laws prohibit absolutely all popish hierarchy in any of the dominions belonging to the Crown of Great Britain, and can only admit of a toleration of the exercise of that religion. This matter was clearly understood in the negotiation of the Definitive Treaty. The French Ministers proposed to insert the words comme ci-devant in order that the Romish religion should continue to be exercised in the same manner as under their Government; and they did not given up the point till they were plainly told that it would be deceiving them to admit those words, for the King had not the power to tolerate that religion in any other manner than " as far as the laws of Great Britain permit." These laws must be your guide in any disputes that may arise on this subject; but at the same time that I point out to you the necessity of adhering to them, and of attending with the utmost vigilance to the behaviour of the Priests, the King relies on your acting with all proper caution and prudence in regard to a matter of so delicate a nature as this of religion; and that you will, as far as you can consistently with your duty in the execution of the laws and with the safety of the country, avoid every thing that can give the least unnecessary alarm or disgust to His Majesty's new subjects."

That is the foundation of all the subsequent proceedings. We find in 1765 these instructions further given, and they are found in the commission to the King's Receiver General, and read as follows:

" And whereas the lands of several religious societies in the said Province, particularly those of the Society of the Jesuits, are, or will become, part of His Majesty's revenue, you are therefore to endeavor, by agreements to be made with the persons interested for the present in any of the said estates, to take the said estates into your charge, giving unto them respectively such competent allowance thereon for their lives, as you may judge proper, taking care that these lands may not be sequestered or alienated from His Majesty."

Again, in letter from Lord Shelburne to Governor Carleton, November 14, 1767, we read:

" It has been represented to His Majesty that the Jesuits of Canada make large remittances to Italy, and that they imperceptibly diminish their effects for that purpose * * * Too much care cannot be taken that they do not embezzle an estate of which they enjoy only the life-rent and which must become on their demise a very considerable resource to the Province, in case His Majesty should be pleased to cede it for that purpose."

As to effect which is to be given to the treaty, although perhaps I have said enough on that point, I want to fortify my position. I do not expect hon. gentlemen will be willing to take my *ipse dixit* in a matter of this kind, and I desire to establish from the public records the doctines which were held by the law officers at the time: in order to make good my point. Sir James Marriott reported at great length, and the book is accessible to all, and no doubt many hon. members have taken advantage of it. He reports on this particular question, which hon. members can easily understand when we look at the terme of the treaty. Let me read from it :

" His Britannic Majesty agrees to grant the liberty of the Catholic religion to the inhabitants of Canada ; he will consequently give the most effectual orders that his new Roman Catholic subjects may profess the worship of their religion according to the rites of the Roman Church as far as the law of Great Britain permit."

Now, we all see the difficulty that at once arose. The laws of Great Britain at that time hardly permitted the exercise of the Roman Catholic religion. The law officers of the Crown, however, decided that this was not to be treated as a dead letter, but that full effect in every way must be given to the treaty. The difficulty was in reconciling the profession of the Roman Catholic religion which the laws of Great Britain, which pratically forbid the practice of that religion, and so the proposition is worked out. And how is it worked out ? Sir James Marriott gave an opinion on this point as follows :—

" Now, I consider that the laws and constitution of this Kingdom, permit perfect freedom o- the exercise of any religious worship in the colonies, but not of all sorts of doctrines, nor the mainf tenance of any foreign autho ity, civil or ecclesiastical, which doctrines and authority may affect the supremacy of the Crown or safety of Your Majesty and the realm ; for a very great and necessary distinction, as it appears to me, must be taken between the profession of the worship of the Romish religion, according to the rites of it, and its principles of church government. To use the French word, the *culte*, or forms of worhip or ritual are totally distinct from some of its doctrines. The first can, may and ought, in my opinion, in good policy and justice to be tolerated, though the second cannot be tolerated."

Mr. Wedderburn, afterwards Lord Loughborough, gave an opinion on the same subject. Speaking more especially in regard to the Jesuits, he said :

" The establishment of the first (the Jesuits) is not only incompatible with the constitution of an English province, but with every other possible form of civil society. By the rule of their order the Jesuits are aliens in every government. They are not owners of their estates but trusts for purposes dependent upon the pleasure of a foreigner, the General of their order. These great Catholic states have, upon grounds of policy, expelled them. It would be singular if the first Protestant state in Europe should protect an establishment that are now must have ceased in Canada had the French Government continued. * * * It is therefore, equally just and expedient, in this instance, to assert the sovereignty of the king and to declare the lands of th Jesuits are vested in His Majesty, allowing at the same time to the Jesuits now residing in Canada liberal pensions out of the incomes of their estates."

This opinion was reported by him to the law officers of the Crown, and the opinion of the law officers of the Crown framed upon it is the foundation of what was afterwards embodied in regard to this subject in the Quebec Act. Then we find in the Quebec Act that while the religion of the inhabitants of the country was specially protected, that the religious communities were excepted therefrom and that they were left to be dealt with by the Crown, thereby leaving those matters just as they stood —owing to the conquest, by virtue of that conquest and by virtue of that proclamation—leaving matters exactly as they stood with regard to the religious communities, and dealt whith the people of the country as distinct and separable from their religious communities. Then let me read what was the outcome of the Quebec Act. It was passed in 1774, and in 1775 express instructions are given to Guy Carleton, the Captain General and the Governor in Chief of the Province of Canada, and, these are the instructions :

" That the Society of Jesus be suppressed and dissolved, and no longer continued as a body corporate and politic, and all their rights, possessions, and property shall be vested in Us, for such purposes as we may hereafter think fit to direct or appoint; but we think fit to declare Our Royal intention to be, that the present members of the said Society as established at Quebec, shall be allowed sufficient stipends and provisions during their natural lives."

Now, can it be reasonably argued, that this estate of the Jesuits did not vest and pass to the Crown, and were not held by the Crown ? I have spoken of this simply as a lawyer, I have spoken of it simply upon the grounds and with reference to the authorities which I find I offer no opinion of my own about it, and I simply state facts as I find them. Let me follow up a little farther to see what becomes of these matters. Sir James Marriott's opinion is again invoked, but I will not trouble the House with this long exact. Sufficient to say that it substantially agrees with his former opinion. In a few words, just to summarise what he states, he says:

" In a few words the Society of Jesus had not and cannot have any estate in Canada legally and completely vested in them at any time, and therefore could not and cannot transfer the same before nor after the term of eighteen months so as to make a good title to purchasers, either with or without the powers or ratification of the Father General who, as he could not retire, so he cannot retain any possession in Canada, since the time limited for the sales of estates there agreeably to the terms of the treaty; because he is as incapable of becoming a British subject, as he was of being a French subject ; nor can the individuals of the communities of the Jesuits in Canada, take or transfer what the Father General cannot take or transfer ; nor can they, having but one common stock with all to other communities of their order in every part of the globe, hold immoveable possessions, to be applied for the joint benefit of those communities which are resident in foreign states; and which may become the enemies of His Majesty and his Government."

Mr. MILLS (Bothwell). That is the third opinion as to how the estates are consfiscated.

Mr. McCARTHY. It is the third opinion. It is in the same report to which I have referred, or rather it is the second opinion on this special question submitted to Sir James Marriott with regard to the Jesuits' properties. Now, in 1770, General Amherst, I believe, petitioned the Crown to be compensated for the services which he had rendered the country in the conquest of Canada out of these estates ; or rather he made a petition generally, and the King ordered and directed that the General should be compensated, and compensated out of the Jesuits' estates. I only state that to show that these estates were dealt with at that time beyond all peradventure as a part of the Crown lands. Now I would read an extract which shows the different manner in which the Jesuits were treated from the other religious communities; by-and-bye, perhaps, it may be my duty to point out why it was so, for I cannot very well, however much I would wish to avoid it, however much I would wish to do as my hon. friend behind me (Mr. Colby) did, ignore the past. I am afraid it will be impossible to treat this subject properly without some little reference to the historical facts we have relating to the Jesuit Order. But however that may be, we find that the Royal Instructions in 1772 were conveyed in this way :

" It was declared that for the present and until we can be fully informed of the true state of the religious communities, and how far they are or are not essential to the exercise of the religion of the Church of Rome as allowed in the said province, to permit those religious communities to remain in possession of their estates."

There, was a clear line of demarcation in dealing with the ordinary religious communities. I perhaps, am not familiar enough with the language to state what that difference was, but there was a clear distinction drawn between the ordinary religious communities, if I may so express it, and the particular body which is now more especially under discussion. Now we have come down very nearly to 1791 or 1792. We have got things down to the period in which the Province was granted a species of representative government which continued up to the Union of 1840 or

1841 ; and we find, if we consult history, that there was a loud protest against the King appropriating this property. It was no denial of his right, but it was against the wisdom and fairness and justice of his handing over this property to the General who had conquered the country ; the allegation being put up then, and then, so far as I know, for the first time, that this property had been really given to the Jesuits for the purpose, and in trust, for education. I think, Sir, that if you will consult Mr. Garneau's history, which I believe is the history most acceptable to my hon. friends from the Province of Quebec, that it will be found as early as 1800 that the matter was brought prominently before the Legislature, and from that time out the agitation in that view was kept up so briskly and so successfully, that in 1830 or in 1831 the Crown ceded and granted to the Province all these Jesuits' estates for the express purpose for which it had been asked, and that was for the purpose of education. The Province accepted the trust, the Province dealt with it on that footing ; and if I may read the first section of the Act, chapter 41, William IV, passed in 1832, we find that by an Act of that Province it was stated :

" That all moneys arising out of the estates of the late Order of Jesuits which now are in, or may, hereafter come in the hands of the Receiver General, shall be applied to the purposes of education exclusively."

Again, in 1849, 9 Victoria chapter 59, another legislative declaration, this time by the united Provinces, says :

" That the revenue and interests arising from the real or funded property forming part of the estates of the late Order of the Jesuits and now at the disposal of the Legislature for educational purposes in Lower Canada, shall be, and are hereby declared to be applicable to such purposes, and to no other."

And, finally in 1856, 19-20 Victoria chapter 54, the legislation on the matter says :

" The estates and property of the late Order of the Jesuits, whether in possession or reversive, including all sums funded or invested, or to be funded or invested as forming part thereof are hereby appropriated for the purposes of this Act and shall form a fund to be called the Lower Canada Superior Education Investment Fund."

I think, if there ever was a little to an estate or property recognized by legislative action, clear in its origin, made more certain and more definite at every stage in which we find it cropping up from time to time, it is the title to the Jesuits' estate. When we are asking His Excellency the Governor General to disallow this Act, when we are taking upon ourselves the responsibility of saying yea or nay on that question, it is impossible that we can deny to ourselves the opportunity of scrutinising every letter in it ; and I find here :

" The Act of the Legislature, 48 Victoria, chapter 10, notwithstanding section 5 of the said Act, and notwithstanding any other Act to the contrary, shall apply to the said estates, the proceeds whereof may be applied also, notwithstanding any Act to the contrary, for the above mentioned purposes, or for any other purposes approved by the Legislature.

So that this special property, set apart for education in the Province of Quebec—not the education of the majority, to whom my friend behind me pays such humble court, but all the people of the Province of Quebec, the minority as well as the majority—has been swept away by this enactment ; although, when the Premier was taxed in Quebec the other day with the question, his answer was by no means such as might have been expected, but was evasive, and not, I am afraid, altogether according to the record. If ever there was legislation which we could interfere with on such grounds it is this ;—property given by the Crown, for the express purpose of the education of the people of the Province; property which remained for that purpose from the year 1831, to the year 1888 ; property which a Parliament, elected under an excitement of race and revenge, has decided should be taken away from the minority, as well as the majority, and dedicated to other purposes, and other uses. Well, Sir, I say—and that is my first proposition—if I have satisfied this House, that this property was public domain—and, if I am not able to satisfy the House of that, I am incapable of making any statement—then the proposition with which I started, is made out, that this Act uses Her Most Gracious Majesty's name as enacting that, her own estates, or the estates she had surrendered to the Province of Quebec, for the purposes of education, were not hers, not the Province's. All this history of the past is to be blotted out; it is to be all child's play; the Crown did not own, the Crown did not get, the Crown did not take, the Crown did not grant a rod, but went through a farce, when it dedicate the property for educational purposes, at first to the Province of Quebec, and again, to the United Provinces of Upper and Lower Canada. All that was humbug, nonsense, child's play ; the property was all the time vested in either the Sovereign Pontiff, or in the Order of Jesuits ; and, as a result, the Pope is applied to, as the only authority which could authorise the disposal of this property, which, most people had thought belonged to the Crown, for permission to dispose of it. Let me do no injustice : let me read the words again :

"Under these circumstances, I deem it my duty to ask Your Eminence if you see any serious objection to the Government's selling the property, pending a final settlement of the question of the Jesuits' estates."

If the Supremacy Act is in force, and whether it is in force or not, I hold it to be, and I believe it can be established to be, a well settled principle of international law, that no foreign authority or power—I care not whether it be temporal or spiritual—can be allowed to interfere in the affairs of another country or another state : and if that be the rule of international law—as I think my hon. friends, if they choose to consult the authorities, will find in to be—how much more does that principle apply to the municipal law of the country, and to the law of Elizabeth, which has been handed down and made specially applicable to this country by the Quebec Act of 1774. How was it possible, I say, to tell that an Act of Parliament would be submitted to His Excellency the Governor General, that he was to pass upon it by the advice of his Minister of Justice, and that the Minister of Justice should send it back—how ? Why, Sir, with a dozen other Bills of no more consequence than an Act incorporating a joint stock company or a railway company—no explanation, no justification, no reasons given. I regret that I have not heard the argument of the hon. Minister of Justice. I may do him an injustice ; but I read here, that when an appeal was made from the Evangelical Alliance or some other body in Lower Canada—those people who my hon. friend says are willing that this legislation should stand—the hon. Minister of Justice reported this was a fiscal matter. Sir I do not understand the Queen's English if this can properly be described as a fiscal matter. But so it passed before His Excellency and upon that His Excellency has acted; and I trust the opportunity will be afforded to His Excellency to reconsider that question, and see whether Her Majesty's name is thus to be trailed in the dust, is thus to be dishonored, and whether this legislation should not disappear from our Statute-books, whether it be provincial or federal. Well, I assail this, not merely upon the ground. I assail it upon other grounds. I say that either this Act is unconstitutional, that it is *ultra vires* of the Province, that it ought to have been disallowed upon that ground, because it violates a fundamental principle of this country, that all religions are free and equal before the law ; or, if that be not so as a legal proposition, then, Sir, I claim that there should have been exercised that judgment, that discretion, that policy, which would at once stamp out in whatever Province it reared its head, the attempt which has been made he to establish a kind of State Church amongst us. Sir, is that law or it is not ? We find that in the good old days a Protestant Church had to be despoiled ; and for my part, Sir, I have never regretted that the Clergy Reserves were secularised, and I do not believe that anyone who belongs to that church can say that that measure has proved injurious to it. It placed it on a footing of equality with the other religious bodies throughout the Provinces; and I believe that church has grown and prospered far more as a church, holding no legal pretence of superiority over other religious bodies, than it would have done if it had continued to hold the Clergy Reserves, no matter how much wealth they might have added to its coffers. Now, what do we find in this Bill, enacted by the United Parliament of Canada—an Act referring to Upper Canada and to Lower Canada, and, so far as I know, to this very moment the law of the Province of Quebec? First, we do know that the law of the Provinces which were in force at the time of the British North America Act, remained in force until repealed. And what do we find?

"Whereas the recognition of legal equality among all religious denominations is an admitted principle of colonial legislation; and whereas, in the state and condition of this Province, to which such a principle is peculiarly applicable, it is desirable the same should receive the sanction of the direct legislative of authority, recognizing and declaring the same as a fundamental principle of civil policy."

Therefore the free exercise and enjoyment of religious profession, without discrimination or preference, so long as the same be not made an excuse for acts of maliciousness, or a justification of practices inconsistent with the peace and safety of the Provinces, is, by the constitution and laws of these Provinces, allowed to all Her Majesty's subjects therein. There is a legislative declaration of what every man who lives in this country has always understood to be the law. Does the enactment of the Province of Quebec violate that principle? Is the grant of $400,000, to be distributed under the sanction of His Holiness of Rome, not a grant of public money to a particular church. I am not saying whether the church may or may not be the correct church; I am simply speaking of the legal principle. I ask, how is that? Let me give you an answer from the books of the Legislature when the Clergy Reserves were secularised. What were those reserves? They were lands belonging to the Crown, held in trust for the support and maintenance of the Protestant faith, and held to apply to the Church of England and the Presbyterian Church of Scotland. When these lands were secularised, it was declared that the Act was for the purpose of sweeping away the last vestige of connection between Church and State. The holding of these lands by the Crown for this purpose formed a connecting link between Church and State, which Parliament stated should be swept away, which the representatives of the Province of Quebec joined with those from the other Province in saying should be swept away. Will any man of common sense tell me that this grant of $400,000, given as it is given, is not a recognytion of Church and State? How is it given?

"The aforesaid arrangements, entered into between the Premier and the Very Reverend Father Turgeon, are hereby ratified, and the Lieutenant Governor in Council is authorised to carry them out according to their form and tenor.

"The Lieutenant Governor in Council is authorised to pay, out of any public money at his disposal the sum of four hundred thousand dollars, in the manner and under the conditions mentioned in the documents above cited, and to make any deed that he may deem necessary for the full and entire execution of such agreement."

Then the document I have just cited declares that this $400,000 is to be distributed under the sanction of His Holiness the Pope of Rome. Now, I have heard it said—I rather think I heard the First Minister applauding the sentence—that this was given for the purpose of education. Surely the First Minister has not read the Act, or he would never assent to a statement of that kind. Education—why, if it is possible to draw a distinction in an Act of Parliament, it is drawn here. While the $60,000, which is the supposed compensation of the minority, is expressly given for education—expressly tied up, and is not to go to any sectarian purposes—the other is left subject to the disposition of His Holiness of Rome. There is but one condition annexed and that is that this money is to be spent within the Province of Quebec. That is the sole condition. We have had an indication in the press this morning that a bull or brief, whatever be the correct ecclesiastical term, either has been, or is to be issued, disposing of this money. Do you want any further evidence that the grant was made absolutely subject to the disposition of a particular religious body? If so, on what pretence, on what ground was it made. Was there a legal claim? Mr. Mercier says no. Was there a moral claim? I would like to know who will answer yes to this. Even my hon. friend behind me will not say that. He and his Protestant friends have always repudiated the idea of a moral claim. What pretence of a moral claim is there? Where is it? In whom is it? Why the Jesuits of those days, if they held it individually, are extinct. They left no heirs. If they held it as a community, and undoubtedly that was the opinion of the law officers of the Crown—an opinion which I humbly venture to think was right—it belonged to the whole body. That was held by the Parliament of Paris in the great Trading Case where the General Superior of the Order repudiated the liability contracted by one of the communities or one of the Jesuits. After full investigation, after an appeal to the highest tribunal, the tribunal of the Parliament of Paris—and hon. gentlemen, I am sure, from the Province of Quebec will not object to that—my hon. friend from Montreal (Mr. Curran) laughs. He is an Irishman and perhaps despises the Parliament of Paris. I confess I do not join with him, although I am an Irishman also: I rather think that must have been a very important appelate tribunal. At all events, if you will read the report of the Attorney General with regard to that, if you will read the proceedings, if you will remember that all the books of the order were for the first time brought into court in order that the order might espace liability, and repudiate responsibility, and make it appear that they were not bound to these merchants for the money that Father Lavalette owed—if you will look at all that, you will see the result was the court determined there was a solidarity amongst all the communities, and that the Jesuit property belonged to, and was at the disposal of the General of the Order and was vested to him alone. I have taken the trouble to examine into the authority of the General of the Order, and if it were not too tedious, I would give some extracts which would abundantly establish that. I, therefore, contend there can be no pretence of a good moral claim. Is the incorporated body of the other day the successors of these men of 1763? On what pretence? If I read the Act of Incorporation aright, I understand it to mean that the whole body of Jesuit throughout the world are incorporated by the Province of Quebec. The first clause of the Act is as follows:—

" The ' Society of Jesus' shall be a corporation, composed of the Reverend Fathers Henri Hudon, Adrien Turgeon, Léonard Lemire, George Kenny, Arthur Jones and all persons who now or may hereafter form part of the said Society, in accordance with its rules, by-laws and regulations. Under the above name it shall have perpetual succession."

So that the Act of Incorporation, which I venture to think is not worth the paper it is written upon—and I trust it may be found so—actually incorporates the whole body of Jesuits, and only in that sense. They pretend to represent the body of 1763 which was suppressed in 1774, but I place no reliance on that suppression. I admit we cannot take notice, standing in an English country, governed by English laws, paying regard, as we are bound, to the Act of Supremacy, of that suppression. The English law officers of the Crown could not notice the suppression by the Pope of the Order of the Jesuits. I affirm that beyond all fear of contradiction. I say it is impossible, in an English Community, to say that the Pope's bull or the Pope's brief dissolving a corporation could have the slightest possible effect. So that the matter stands in the way I have endeavored to point out, and I say, without fear of contradiction, that my hon. friend from Stanstead (Mr. Colby) was right, when he said, there was not the shadow of foundation, or even the pretence of a moral claim. Under these circumstances, is there any possible standing ground for this Act? Does it not violate the rules of the separation of Church and State in this country, and equality of all religions? I need not go through the second ground of this resolution, because I have sufficiently dealt with it; so I have now come, and I trust it without undue delay, to the other branch of the argument which I desire to present. In all fairness to my hon. friends, I must say that, if there is, in the legal proportions which I have undeavored, faintly to put forward, a reasonable doubt, I do not think that standing alone, it would be becoming on the part of a Minister of the Crown, to disallow the measure, because that would place it, as you will see, in the hands of the Government here, to disallow, on pretence of *ultra vires* of the Local Legislature, enactments which might be open to question, and which the parties ought to have the benefit of the ruling of a court upon. But I have endeavored to point out, upon the ground I have already stated, that this Act ought to have been disallowed as being beyond the power of a Local Legislature. I do not desire to be at all misunderstood. I do not pretend that the Crown of England, or the Crown of any other country, cannot submit matters to a foreign Power. We know it is done continually. We know that matters are settled by arbitration, and that generally, and almost always, it is done by calling in the arbitrament of a foreign Power; but I contend that, while the Sovereign Power can do that, the private subject cannot. There is a broad distinction. If I have a dispute with my hon. friend, I cannot submit that to the President of the United States, because the dispute would be between British subjects And I say that a Province cannot do that, because it does not represent the plenary power of the Crown; and I say that even this Parliament cannot do it, and, of course, it does not stand in the same position as the Parliament of Great Britain and Ireland. But on the grounds of policy, surely I am right. Surely there are not men enough in this House who will cast any doubt upon the clause of this resolution which declares that there should be a separation of Church and State, and absolute equality of all religions before the law. Surely, in this part of the nineteenth century, and in free Canada, we will not have to fight for a principle which we thought was determined for all time when the secularisation of the Clergy Reserves took place. Is it because this is a particular church? If it is right in the Province of Quebec to grant money to the Church of Rome, it would be equally right in the Province of Ontario to grant money for the maintenance of the Methodists or the Episcopalian body or Scotch Church; and, if we did that, there would be no hesitation—and properly so—in bringing before the House the complaint of the minority whose money would be spent in that way and for that purpose. We never find that, when the body to which I refer feels that its interests are at stake, and that injustice is being done, it has any hesitation or makes any delay at all in coming at once before the Parliament and proclaiming its grievances. These people never say: We are afraid we will be stirring up religious strife, causing hard feelings. or putting race against race and Catholic against Protestant. No, they come here—as they have a right to do—and boldly put their case before Parliament, no matter what it may be; and they always manage to get justice. at all events. If Parliament think any doubt is to be cast upon this measure, if they find that this money is dedicated for educational purposes, I think in that case the point I am attempting to make would fail; but when I observe the definiteness of the provision under which the $60,000 is granted. I cannot see that any such purpose is intended with regard to the $400,000. I, therefore, say that that part of the case is made out. Let me now come to a question which I would have willingly avoided. Let me invite the attention of the House to the greater question which is before it. These are technical matters that I have dealt with so far—matters perhaps of moment, matters of great importance, but still, after all, they are more or less purely legal in the narrow sense of the word. But I assail this legislation upon broader and higher grounds. I say that the incorporation of, and the grant of money to, the Jesuit body under any pretext or for any purpose, was an Act which should have at once been disallowed if it were passed by a Provincial Legislature. I put that upon the highest possible grounds. I think I have a right, and it is a right which I suppose to exercise, to speak with freedom on this subject. I will assail no man's religion. I will not utter a word, which, properly understood, will give offence to the most sensitive on this subject; but I deny the right of my hon. friend behind me or any one else to gag me. and to say. You must remember that the Jesuit body is under the protecting ægis of His Holiness of Rome, and you most not speak of it except with bated breath. I deny that any such rule can apply to this free Parliament. It is not a question of religion. It is not a question whether the religion of the Church of Rome is better than the religion which I was brought up in, and which I profess. I am not to sit in judgement on my fellow-members. They are quite right to worship their God in the manner they choose, as I am right in worshipping Him in the manner I choose, but I contend that the Church of Rome needs not the Jesuit body for its organisation or its support. It is true that, during the reign of certain Pontiffs, that order has received the support of the church. It is also true that, during the reign of other Pontiffs, it has been banned and sometimes dissolved. One case has been mentioned, and it was once before, if my hon. friend will go so far back. though it is perhaps unfair to bring it up here in judgment against them. The fact, however proves that the order, or company, or society of which we are speaking, is not in any sense essential to the free, perfect and full enjoyment of the Roman Catholic religion. And what is the society, what is the object of its founder? I will quote from what appears to be a very fair statement in the *Quarterly Review* of 1874, containing a summary of what appears to have been the object of the founder. It was:

" To effect an organisation which would result in a thoroughly disciplined and mobilised body of men, moved like a highly trained military unit at the word of command, and stating ever ready under the proclaimed chieftainship of Jesus, to war against and smite by superior dexterity in arms, the foes adverse to the absolute ascendancy of the Papal system."

Let any person who knows anything about their history quarrel with that definition of the Order of Jesus. I should be glad to know wherein that definition is incorrect. They take a vow of implicit obedience to their chief. He says go, and they go; come, and they come. They are educated so as to have no will, and, to use the language of the Spiritual Exercises of the founder of the order himself, they ought to be:

" Like a corpse who has neither will nor understanding, or like a small crucifix which is turned about at the will of him who holds it, or like a staff in the hands of an old man, who uses it as may best assist or please him."

I believe I am citing nothing which is not reliable. I take this from the authorised version of the constitutions, as they are called, and it is to be found among the Spiritual Exercises determined by the founder. Let me give one extract upon this subject:

" It is so complete and entire that while every member of the society is obliged to obey the General as implicitly and blindly as if he were Jesus-Christ, in all things whatsoever, without reserve, without exception, without question or examination, or ever mental hesitation, to carry into execution anything he may prescribe with the same fullness of consent and submission that they feel in the belief of the dogmas of the Catholic faith itself, to be in his hands as passive as a corpse, or as a staff in the hands of an old man, or as Abraham when under the command of God, he was ordered to sacrifice his son, he must pursued himself on principle that all that he has ordered to do is right, and above all personal feeling and volition."

I am quoting from the decree of the Parliament of Paris. Much more might be adduced to the same effect. Those who have thought of this subject, those who have given it any consideration, have, no doubt, made up their mind one way or the other on it. Nothing, perhaps, is more true than the statement that is made in, the report of the Attorney General of Paris, who was called upon to investigate the position of this body. Looking at them as one set of people are anxious to do, and they appear to be all right; look at them from the other side, and they hardly appear to the same advantage. I think it is only fair to say—I do not desire at all to be misunderstood—that the individual men are, perhaps, the *élite* of their order, highly educated, better men upon the whole, for their system of drill. The long probationary period they have to undergo, necessarily weeds out the weak ones and leaves only the strong and robust—intellectually as well as physically—and, I suppose, that amongst no equal number of men will the compeers of the Jesuits be found. I will read a note showing the view of the Attorney General of the Parliament of Paris, in his report:

"The constitutions have two faces—"

That reminds me of the shield of the hon. gentleman opposite, one side of which he presented on his visit to England to float our bonds, and the other side of which he shows to us when he comes back.

Sir RICHARD CARTWRIGHT. Both sides were perfectly correct.

Mr. McCARTHY. I accept that illustration also; that applies still more forcibly to what I am going to read—both sides here appear to be perfectly correct also:

"The constitutions have two faces, because they were formed into two intentions—on the one side, for the glory of God and the salvation of souls; and on the other side, for the glory of the society and its future extension. This causes the difference of opinion concerning them. Their admirers look only at the first aspect, and their detractors see only the second."

Now, I think that statement was one that I was bound to make, because I am not at all here as a protestant bigot. I do not pretend to make any statement here as a Protestant. I was astonished to hear the hon. member for Stanstead (Mr. Colby) speak as a Protestant. I do not speak as a Protestant, I speak as a representative of my constituency, entitled to discuss all subjects that are presented here, and without offence. as I trust I am doing on this occasion, to the feelings of any hon. member of this House. Now, let me give a slight idea of their organisation, of the vows which they take, of the obedience which their constitution inculcates, and which they are always willing to render. I will show wat is said of them in modern times, because I have been told, and I admit the fact, that it is not fair to judge any order or body of men by their history of two or three hundred years ago. But I think I will be able to show that, down to a very recent period, there is in this body no change nor shadow of turning, that it is their boast that they are, and will continue, as long as they exist, to be under the same rules that the founder of the order, now the sainted Ignatius, established for them. Now, let us see what is said of them by comparatively recent writers. I regret that our library does not afford a very full catalogue of works in regard to this subject, and I have been compelled to rely upon authorities written 20 or 25 years ago. I will read such as I have, and the House will be able to judge of their pertinence to the order at present. Garnier-Pagé says:

"They know but one law, one faith, and one morality. That law, faith, and morality, they call authority. To a superior they submit life and conscience. To their order they sacrifice individuality. They are neither Frenchmen, Italians, Germans, nor Spaniards. They are not citizens of any country. They are Jesuits only. They have but one family, one fortune and one end; and all these are included in the word community."

Mr. LANDERKIN. A regular Tory Order.

Mr. McCARTHY. Very much like that: that is the only reason you do not belong to them, I am afraid. I am now quoting from the *Quarterly Review*, and if hon. gentlemen will take the trouble to read that article, and it is a fair criticism, so far as I am capable of judging, of the works of the Jesuits and the Jesuits writings which were under review, I think they will be satisfied. In the *Quarterly Review* of 1874 I was very glad to find that the popular delusion as to the poisoning of the Pope who dissolved the order, was exploded by the writer. Down to a very recent period, indeed, this had been believed on the authority of a high and distinguished German doctor, who wrote in 1872, and stated on undoubted authority that Pope Clement the Thirteenth had been poisoned by that order.

Some hon. MEMBERS. Oh, oh.

Mr. McCARTHY. I say that a German doctor said so; and that this English authority in 1874 exploded that doctrine and showed that it did not rest on any solid foundation. I was very glad, and I am sure any hon. gentlemen will be glad to find that that is so. But the author who dealt with the Jesuits in that impartial spirit may be perhaps entitled to some credence when he depicts, as he does in the following year, some doctrines held by the order. He endeavors to establish, and, in my humble judgment, he does establish, that the three principles upon which the order is established are justified, a Probabalism, Mental reservation, and that the end justifies the means. To argue that, would involve an enquiry foreign perhaps to this discussion. I am merely stating the conclusion at which the writer arrived, and every hon. member can form his own opinion as to whether that opinion is well or ill-founded. But, in practical matters, let us see what this order lays down. First, as to the duties of a judge, the writer says:

"We are told, also, it is by no means decided that a judge is bound never to accept money gifts from a party to a suit before him. If the gift were proffered with the view of influencing a prospective judgment, contrary to justice, the judge should, indeed, sternly refuse acceptance; 'but, the sentence having been already pronounced, it is a matter of controversy' whether he may not retain what might then seem a mere offering of gratitude from one benefited by the delivered sentence, even when this had been contrary to justice. Decisions of this character subvert fundamental notions as to right and wrong. Let us take the case of a person knowing all about a theft and accepting hush-money from the guilty party. According to received ideas, the compact would be criminal. Father Gury, however, decides that, provided the person bribed be not *ex-officio* bound to give information, the bargain would be quite lawful, 'as without injustice he might keep silence about the thieft, in difference to his entreaties * * * therefore, *espari*, without injustice, silence might be observed in deference to gifts given or promised."

I need not tell hon. gentlemen who have paid any attention to the subject, that Father Gury is a comparatively modern writer, that his works were published under the Propaganda, and therefor under the highest authority, and his works are for morals, for teaching in the schools, and for the guidance of those who desire instruction of this kind. So far in regard to the judges. But there is also a law for witnesses, and the law for witnesses is even more dangerous than the law laid down for the judges. The writer says:

"The first point laid down is, that no obligation to make reparation can attach to any one who has given false witness from invincible ignorance, inadvertance, or delusion, a proposition which, though not wholly free from objections, we will not canvass. But Father Gury proceeds to consider the case of one who, with the view of supplying deeds that have been lost, and all promoting the success of indisputable right (the indisputableness of such right being left to the subjective test of individual appreciation), either reproduces, that is, forges, or tampers with a writing, a chirograph, or a deed of acknowledgment; and he concludes that, though a person acting thus, 'would, indeed, sin venially on the score of a lie, the document produced not being the authentic one, on the strength of which judgment should rest; and though he might possibly incur a grave sin against charity toward himself by exposing his person to imminent peril of very severe penalties in the likely event of detection; nevertheless, he would be wholly free from all sin against mutual justice, and would consequently stand absolved from all obligations to make restitution.'"

Mr. CURRAN. Will the hon. gentleman give the authority?

Mr. McCARTY. I am quoting from the *Quarterly Review* of 1875.

Mr. DESJARDINS. Who is the writer?

Mr. McCARTY. I cannot tell.

Mr. CURRAN. Has the hon. gentleman consulted Father Gury in the original?

Mr. McCARTHY. I leave that for the hon. gentleman to do. I do not suppose a writer in a great magazine like the *Quarterly review* misrepresents Father Gury; if the hon. gentleman thinks so, I rather imagine he will find himself mistaken. If he will take the trouble to read the article, which was not written in a spirit of hostility but rather of enquary for the truth, I shall be glad. I have now done with that part of the subject. But I think there are people in this country, the fair sex, who ought to be protected. It seems there is a rule, a law for them also, and that breach of promise is not en improper act in certain events and in certain cases. The writer says :

" In the matter of plighted troth we learn from Gury, 'that he who has sworn it to a girl, rich and healthy * * is not boun t by his oath should she h ippen to have become poor or fallen into ba l health.' Again we are informe l that a probible opinion, contenunced by St. Liguori, would allow an engagement to be broken off if a ' fat inheritance ' should accrue, seriously modifying the status as to fortune of either party, and the case is thus illustrated. ' Edmund had betrothed himself to Helen, a girl of the same station an l fortune as his own. As he was on the very point a deceased uncle. Wherefore, he repudiates Helen, that he may marry another with a fortune to match. It seems that Edmund should not be disturbed for this. Jilting is no unfrequent practice, but it is striking to find it justified in a handbook of morals, whenever 'faith could be kept only by the surren ler of a b'g advantag) which would be tantimount to great loss.' "

That is confortable doctrine for one side, but rather unconfortable for the other.

Mr. MITCHELL. It is hard on the girls.

Mr. McCARTHY. Yes, as my hon. freind says, it is hard on the girls. I will pass over the next extract in consideration sor the galleries. If this is anything like a proper statement of the moral teaching of the order, I hardly think it is one that ought not to be bonussed, to use a familiar term, by any of our Local Legislatures. But what as regards the history of this order? Is it dispited as an historical fact that they are responsible for the expulsion of the Huguenots? I trow not.

Mr. LANGELIER (Quebec). It is disputed.

Mr. McCARTHY. I am astonished to learn it; I thought it would not be disputed. Is it doubted that they brouth about the revocation of the Edict of Nantes? It is doubted that they were responsible for the causing the Thirty Years' War? It is seriously open to question that they had much to do with precipitating the Fraco-German war? Of course, those hon. gentlemen who will not believe anything against the Jesuits will not believe that, but there is weighty evidence to show that they were concerned in precipitating that war, which, as we all know, occurred in comparatively modern times.

Mr. BERGERON. In whose interest?

Mr. McCARTHY. In the interest of the order and body to which theybelong, in the interest of the church, of which they are the light horse—the Cossacks, the advanced guard. Now, I suppose Cardinal Manning's statement with regard to them will not be denied to be, at all events, an authentic statement; and Cardinal Manning, in his book of sermons published by Duffy of Paternoster Row, at page 187, says writing of the Jesuit order:

"That it embodies the character of its founder, the same energy, perseverance and endurance, it is his own presence still prolonged, the same perpetuated order, even in the spirit and manner of its working, fixed, uniform and changeless."

That is within the life of the distinguished prelate who speaks of them as being the same as they were 300 years ago.

Mr. BERGERON. We do not deny that.

Mr. McCARTHY. No person will deny that. Then, it is useless to continue the argument, it is useless to make citations; but I do think that their expulsion from France in 1880 would be of interest to my hon. friends, and that it would not have been altogether treated as of no consequence. It is strictly true that France is now a Republic, enjoying a free Government, but it is perfeclty clear that the Jesuits were expelled, and the gentleman who had charge of the educational department in France put forward those grounds for the reason for their expulsion. If I cite from past history I will be told : " Oh, the order may have changed ; " and if I cite from modern days I dare say that there will be some other answer, but I do say this, and I think we ought all to be willing to accept it, that everybody else cannot always have been in the wrong, and Jesuits always in the right. They have been expelled from every country time and time again.

Mr. BERGERON. But they are back again.

Mr. McCARTHY. Yes, they are back again.

Mr. AMYOT. They were not then expelled from Russia.

Mr. McCARTHY. They were, and I will give the hon. gentleman the date of their expulsion. Having been expelled from the Catholic countries, they found a harbor of refuge in Russia and Prussia, after being suppressed by the Sovereign Pontiff, and, having lived there under the protection of that Government, their education and training, of those whom they brought up were found incompatible, as they were found elsewhere, and must always be found, according to their teachings, incompatible to State Government or to any organised condition of society. These are the reasons which made not only the expulsion of the Jesuits from Russia necessary, but also brought about, as we find the putting an end to " the concordat " which, up to a certain time, had existed between the Court of St Petersburg and the Sovereign Pontiff at Rome. I will refer to what Mr. Ferry said in introducing this measure in France for the expulsion of the Jesuits, and I am not going to read it all but just one or two particulars, because I do not care to deal with what may be termed even remotely the religious aspect of the question. I want to treat this simply from the position of State : whether as a matter of statesmanship, as a matter of policy it was proper to have admitted this Act to remain in force, or whether it is not proper and right that this Act should still be vetoed. The measure in the French Chamber, as explained, is chiefly directed against the Jesuits on the ground that " they are the enemies of the state, that their teachings are in opposition to the principles of government, and would suppress all freedom of education." Many other reasons were given against the Jesuits by Mr. Ferry, and the following among the rest. He quoted the decree of the Parliament of 1826 which recites :

" That the edicts by wich Jesuits had been banished and dissolved, were founded upon the recognised incompatibility of their principles with the independence of every Government. "

Mr. BERGERON. What are you reading from ?

Mr. McCARTHY. I am reading from the published report of the debates that took place in Paris at the time of the expulsion of the Jesuits.

Mr. MULOCK. What report is it ?

Mr. McCARTHY. It is a condensation of the report of the debates. Mr. Ferry then goes on to say, from the statement of the Archbishop of Paris, Mgr. Darboy:

" That the Jesuits were neither subject to the jurisdiction of the diocesans, nor obedient to the laws of the State. "

And further :

" That the State is, in temporal matters, subordinate to the church, and has only the authority which an inferior tribunal possesses, for confirming the sentence of the superior ; that in question of marriage, burial, institutions for charitable purposes, liberty of conscience, and questions of the moral law, the spiritual power may intervene to correct or annul the civil laws. "

Further, Mr. Ferry quoted from some passages from public works, showing :

" A detestable hostility to all the laws and institutions of modern society. These works distinctly taught the divine right of kings, and advocated to carrying on of religious wars. They attacked the revolution, and glorified the revocation of the Edict of Nantes ; they calumniated Nicker and Turgot ; they rejected th- principle of the national sovereignty, and they taught that France was beaten in the late war because she had deserted the Pope. In these books universal suffrage and trial by jury were denounced as vexatious institutions, liberty of conscience and of worship were condemned, and the liberty of the press was asserted to be a principle that has never been admitted by a wise Government. "

Whether those are principles which ought to be endorsed by this Parliament it will be for the House to judge.

Mr. BERGERON. Were they expelled then ?

Mr. McCARTHY. Yes.

Mr. BERGERON. But they are there now.

Mr. McCARTHY. The hon. gentleman has perhaps more information than I have on that subject, but that they were expelled is beyond question. I told the hon. member for Bellechasse (Mr. Amyot) that they were expelled more than once from France. They were expelled from France in 1595, at the close of the War of the League. Now, I do think that in the stage of the debate it is not necessary to trouble the House by reading the decree of suppression of the Pope in 1773 ; but surely if the order has not changed, surely if they have remained as they were, there is ground for interference. I think that it was about the time of their expulsion from France, in 1762, when it was asked of them to change their mode of carrying on operations, and when the answer was : " We must continue to be as we are or cease to exist. " I say that when those things are considered ; this evidence of a statement made by the Pontiff with full knowledge of all the circumstances it is impossible to displace ; there is no way of getting rid of that evidence. It cannot be impugned by the members of the church of which the Pontiff referred to was a distinguished ornament. It cannot be impugned by any candid person, because the character of Pope Clement was of the very highest order and he stood conspicuously above his compeers. Now, a list was given—and therefore, I need not repeat it—of the expulsion of the Jesuits from various countries. It is not to be lost sight of that they were expelled from Germany in 1872. They had been admitted into Prussia by Frederick II, and why were they expelled ! It seems to me that the reason for their expulsion is particularly applicable to our position here, for there was in that country a mixed community of Protestants and Catholics. The Jesuits were admitted to this country, the corporation having been dissolved and their having been sent about their business by a decree to which I have referred. And having obtained a foothold in Prussia, what was the result ? Let me read :

" But in North Germany they became very powerful, owing to the footing Frederick II had given them in Prussia, especially in the Rhine Provinces ; and, gradually moulding the younger generation of clergy after the War of Liberation, succeeded in spreading ultramontane views amongst them, and so leading up to the difficulties of the civil government which issued in the Falk laws and their own expulsion. "

Now, Sir, I have done with the extracts which I propose to make upon that subject, and I come to the more important part of the subject under consideration. It may be that all I have said is true, and that yet if this matter—I am arguing it now, of course, upon that theory—was in the legislative competence of the Province, it ought still to remain as law. I venture, Sir, to ask the House seriously to consider the position in which we stand. The worship of what is called local autonomy, which some gentlemen have become addicted to, is fraught, I venture to say, with great evil to this Dominion. Our allegiance is due to the Dominion of Canada. The separation into Provinces, the right of local self-government which we possess, is not to make us less citizens of the Dominion, is not to make us less anxious for the promotion of the welfare of the Dominion ; and it is no argument to say that because a certain piece of legislation is within the power of a local Parliament, therefore that legislation is not to be disturbed. By the same Act of Parliament, by which power is conferred upon the Local Legislature, the duty and power—because where there is a power there is a correspouding duty—are cast upon the Governor in Council to revise and review the acts of the legislative bodies. The Legislatures are not to be at liberty to run in indifferent directions, to promote in one Province one nationnality and one church, and in another Province another nationality and another church, or in any other way to run counter, because such courses must inevitably bring about the dissolution of Confederation. It is not because a Province is kept in check, it is not because its legislation is vetoed, that there is danger to our system. We can impose no law upon a Province; it is merely a negative power which the central Government possesses—a power to prevent evil laws, in the sense which I speak, in the wider field of the Dominion, viewed here from the centre—and this power ought to be, of course, prudently, wisely, but duly exercised when occasion may require. It must be exercised by Ministers who are responsible to this House. To my hon. friend from West Durham (Mr. Blake), we are indebted for the clear recognition of the principle that His Excellency the Governor General, in every act of allowance or disallowance, must find Ministers in this Parliament who have the confidence of this Parliament, and who are willing to accept the responsibility for that act. And that is the safeguard which will always make it impossible for any Minister here to advise His Excellency to disallow measures which ought to be permitted to go into operation. But if the other system is set up, if the alternative presented by my hon. friend from Stanstead (Mr. Colby) is to be adopted ; if you are to say that because a law has been passed within the legislative authority of the Province, therefore it must remain ; we can easily see, Sir, that before long these Provinces, instead of coming nearer together, will go further and further apart. We can see that the only way of making a united Canada and building up a national life and national sentiment, in the Dominion, is by seeing that the laws of one Province are not offensive to the laws and institutions, and, it may be, to the feelings of another—I will go so far as to say that they must be to some extent taken into consideration. Not be any means that those considerations are always to govern, but they are matters worthy of the consideration of statesmen. If the Provinces were sovereign powers, if they owed no local allegiance, if they were not subject to the control of a Governor who enjoyed the confidence of this House, the hostile legislation of one Province would be a fit subject of remonstrance from a friendly power. It may not be a very apt illustration, but at the moment it occurs to me that Napoleon III remonstrated during the time of Lord Palmerston, because he said that under the law of England persons who were known to intend his assassination were harbored in England. We know what the result of that was that the English people rebelled against the interference of a foreign power. I do not know whether the same spirit dwells in their descendants here or not. This illustration shows what I mean. Under our system, no matter what the law may be, no matter how hostile the people of the adjoining Province of Ontario may consider this law to be, the answer which is given as the final and conclusive answer, without appeal or resort, is that it is passed by the Province of Quebec in the legislative power of that Province, and therefore it must go into operation. Now, take this particular Bill. If the view which I venture to hold is correct—and, Sir, I hold it after careful consideration—the view which is held by a large body of the people of the Province, men distinguished for learning, men distinguished for piety, men distinguished in all the walks of life, as to the character of this order ; the view which is held, with the record before us of the expulsion of the order from every Christian state in Europe ; I say is it possible to imagine that the establishment of such an order as that is not a matter of concern to the people of the Province of Ontario and the rest of the Dominion ? Putting the question on the lowest ground, is this order, thus subsidised, going to confine its operations within the limits of the Province of Quebec ? True, the money is to be spent there, although I do not know how that is to be guaranteed. I find no machinery for ascertaining how the money is to be expended ; but, assuming that the money is to be spent there in good faith, it only strengthens the order for incursions beyond the border. We know that some of its members—some of the very same gentlemen, I believe, who have been incorporated—do sometimes visit the Province of Ontario. It is idle, therefore, to say that you can establish such an order as that, and claim it is not a matter of common concern to the rest of the Dominion.

  Mr. AMYOT. Do you object to that ?

  Mr. McCARTHY. I decidedly object to them, or I would not be standing here.

  Mr. BERGERON. They are British subjects.

  Mr. McCARTHY. Yes, I believe those at present in this country are ; but, as I have already pointed out, the whole body, numbering perhaps 20,000 men, is incorporated by this little Bill of the Province of Quebec. The very words of the Bill are : " All who now are or may be of that order." I have heard it said : Oh, you are too late. Where were you when the incorporation Act was under consideration ? Why did you not raise your voice then ? Why did not the Protestants then strike at the root of the evil ? I do not know, though I am pretty familar with what is called the doctrine of estoppel, that any such doctrine can be applied to a people. I am not aware that the laches of a Government I have supported, or that the laches of hon. gentlemen on either side, are going to prevent the people from objecting, even if it be too late to object to the Act of Incorporation, to the Act of Endowment, honored by the official seal of the Legislature of the Province of Quebec. In my judgment the Act of Incorporation amounted to very little. The

Jesuit body claimed to be incorporated before, and they did not car of incorporation, except for the purpose of holding lands in the Province. They claimed to be incorporated under the revival of the order by the Pope in 1814, and the only object of their incorporation by the Act was to enable them to hold real estate, which is a matter not particularly concerning the rest of the Dominion. What does strike me, what has roused the people of the Province from which I have the honor to come, as they have never been aroused in my time, is that one of the Provinces has thought fit to recognise by its legislation and its grant of public money, the order which they have been brought up to oppose, their reading as to which in later years has strengthened their early training in that respect. Is it the work of politicians ? I think in that it is unique in its character. I believe on no platform, in no place has the voice of any public man in the Province been raised in promoting this agitation. It has come from the people. It is promoted, not by the so called professional politician or any politician, but by the people. By the people it is supported, by the people it is maintained and by the people it is bound to succeed, be it sooner or later. This is not going to end the controversy which as it is said, has come to stay. The principle which this Bill involves and which this measure has drawn attention to, is perhaps the one which excites naturally the greatest indignation, and has called forth the greatest agitation. It is impossible to believe that the men who are at the bottom of this agitation are moved by any particular purpose, or particular view, or desiring aggrandissement. I was astonished to hear the hon. member for Lincoln (Mr. Rykert) denounce these men. They were, he said, mere ministers. Principal Cavan, a teacher of the Presbyterian body, a man with whom I have not the honor of personal acquaintance, a man who, so far as I know, in politics differs from me, but a man who, so far as I have heard, is entitled to the respect of every citizen where he lives and is known. Dr. Stafford, who ministered in this city for many years—men of that description are not thus lightly to be spoken of and to be sneered at because they have stepped out from the ordinary walk of their calling, and gone on the platform to uphold what they believe to be the rights of the citizens. I submit instead of that being a subject for sneering, instead of its being a subject which would call for the condemnation of my hon. friend from Lincoln (Mr. Rykert), it is the best tribute to their sincerity. This spontaneous exhibition on the part of the people is genuine and heartfelt, because it is really intended and really meant. Now, these are the reasons why the Government should disallow this measure. I have but one other, which I spoke of before, and it is the question of religious equality. I listened with rapt attention to the—will I call it plaintive—appeal made by my hon. friend behind me. There is no censure, he said, which you can make upon this occasion, which will not fall with tenfold force upon the Protestant minority of the Province of Quebec. Nothing that you can say here can remedy the laches which the Protestant minority displayed in not opposing the majority. I am not here to explain the cause of these laches. I do think we need not go very far for the reason, and I dare say before this debate closes we will learn it; and I call upon hon. members who represent the Protestant constituencies in Quebec, to tell us whether they accept the doctrine of my hon. friend behind me. I ask the hon. member for Huntingdon (Mr. Scriver), I call on the hon. member for Brome (Mr. Fisher), I call on the hon. member for Argenteuil (Mr. Wilson) to let us in Ontario understand whether there is the turtle dove, peacefulness, existing between the Protestant minority and the Catholic majority in the Province of Quebec which the hon. member for Stanstead (Mr. Colby) depicted last night. I call on them to state here whether there is nothing but billing and cooing between these separate and distinctive parts into which that Province is divided. My hon. friend's language would seem to imply that. The Protestants enjoyed every Protestant liberty—really, they were allowed to manage their own little Protestant affairs as if there was no majority at all. They were in no way thwarted, interfered with, or troubled by this majority, and this majority, and the instances he cited to us of this spirit of toleration on the part of the majority were, to my mind unfortunate and unhappy. Mr. Joly was one. He was, I believe, the leader of the Liberal party, as my hon. friend has stated, but has my hon. friend forgotten modern history? Has he forgotten that Mr. Joly was deposed from his position, or resigned, because of the impossibility of acting? Has he forgotten that Mr. Joly actually resigned his seat, and that practically he was driven out of public life?

Mr. LAURIER. He was always opposed by the minority.

Mr. McCARTHY. Well, so much the worse for that minority. I say that minority has no reason to plume itself upon Mr. Joly's successor. Those who opposed him in former times must certainly now look back with regret.

Mr. MITCHEL. You mean Chapleau, Ross and the others. You cannot mean Mercier also.

Mr. McCARTHY. I do not mean you, and that ought to be quite sufficient for my hon. friend from Northumberland (Mr. Mitchell), nor do I even mean his organ, the *Herald*. Another example cited was the Protestant paper, the *Witness*. The *Witness* had never said anything. I do not know how that may be. But it is true that the *Witness* was excommunicated, and remains still under the ban of the Church? Is it not true that the people of a certain religion cannot buy the *Witness* newspaper, under the pains and penalties that may follow thereon? That did not seem a very happy way of manifesting the toleration of the majority of the Province of Quebec. At last my hon. friend's argument culminated—will he pardon the world—in what appeared to me the acme of absurdity, when he said the Protestants recognized no right in the Jesuits of a legal kind. The Protestants disclaimed that there is any moral claim. The Protestants were opposed to the introduction of the name of His Holiness the Pope as—did he use the word pestiferous? or what was the word almost as strong—a bitter pill for them to swallow. But they did not do anything. The Act took away from them their education fund. By one short clause it is declared that the education fund hitherto belonging to Protestants and Catholics alike shall become a part of the general revenue of the country, and that out of the general revenue of the country $60,000 might be paid to the Protestant minority of the Province of Quebec; and not one word was raised against this Act of spoliation.

Mr. LANGELIER (Quebec). Where is that to be found?

Mr. McCARTHY. In the latter part of the Act, if the hon. gentleman will read it.

Mr. LANGELIER (Quebec). I have not seen it.

Mr. McCARTHY. I cannot make the hon. gentleman read it. And there is not one word from the Protestant minority. It is easy to understand how they get on, as he says, if they submit to all that injustice without a word of remonstrance. It is easy to understand how happy they can be if the Protestant minority are willing simply to take what they can get, a seat here occupied by my hon. friend from Stanstead (Mr. Colby), with a seat in the other House given to the representative of the majority. My hon. friend tells us that no Protestant can be elected in the Province if the majority chose. If the Protestants come here from that Province only to carry out the behests of the other side, they are a deception. We do not realise their position, because we understand that they are representing the minority, but it appears that they are truly the representatives of the majority, and we are told that, if this cry is raised, if this body is assailed, if we venture to raise our voices in this Parliament, we are going to raise such a cry that the Protestant representatives from the Province of Quebec will lose their seats. I cannot believe that that is possible. I cannot believe that my hon. friend is right in thinking so ; but even at that expense, even at the expense of the loss of my hon. friend from this House, which together with that of other members, would be a calamity to the country, though I cannot believe that that would be the result of a fair, full, frank and calm discussion of this subject, although it is one which trenches upon feelings which are guarded most sensitively, still that would have to be borne. For these reasons, I venture to think, it will not be found that my hon. friend's statements are correct. As he made the statement, my eye caught the report in a newspaper petitions were being in the city of Montreal, that already 3,000 names had been obtained to those petitions, and that more were coming in—petitions to the Governor General, calling upon him to disallow this measure. Does this look as if the Protestants of the Province of Quebec were desirous, and willing, and anxious that this legislation should remain unchanged, or does it not look as if the Protestant minority in that Province were given reasonable encouragement, that they would get justice—and no more than justice are they entitled to, and no more than justice I hope they will ever ask for—from the Parliament of this country ? Then they will be up and doing, to do their share of this legislation. But in the Legislature of that Province, composed as it is now, they cannot expect it. There was no Protestant representative in the Cabinet of that Province until recently, and, when one was chosen, he had to be elected in spite of the vote of the Protestant minority. I can understand that, if there were a fighting man in that House like the hon. member who leads the Third party here, there might be a chance of obtaining someting like justice, but men with that skill and ability, with parliamentary knowledge to back it, are not to be found every day, and we are not to judge the Protestant representatives of the Province of Quebec on that high standard. We were told that the *Herald* had not said anything about this iniquitous scheme, though the hon. gentleman (Mr. Mitchell) said that, if he had been there, he would not have approved of it. I have not heard anyone approve of it. It has gone without defence. The hon. member for Stanstead (Mr. Colby) does not approve of it. Perhaps my hon. friend from Lincoln (Mr. Rykert) does approve of it, in his great desire to have perfect religious liberty, and not to drive the French out of Ontario. My hon. friend candidly told us that he would not have approved of it. Then, what muzzled the great organ of public opinion ? Was it because it was the organ of the Government ? At one time that was the organ of the Protestants of the Province of Quebec.

Mr. MITCHELL. I will tell the hon. gentleman, if he wishes to know.

Mr. McCARTHY. I will let the hon. gentleman tell me when I get through. Perhaps then you will allow me to ask you a question or two.

Mr. MITCHELL. I will give you perfect liberty.

Mr. McCARTHY. I think we are encouraged to persevere in the course we have pursued, and the course we have taken, by the ebullition of popular feeling which we now see is aroused and is manifesting itself in the Province of Quebec. It cannot now be said that it is only the members from Ontario who have raised this cry and who are seeking for this disallowance.

Mr. MITCHELL. That is all it is.

Mr. McCARTHY. Then the petitions are very extraordinary, and I can hardly accept the contradiction of my hon. friend in the face of those petitions. I cannot do better than close in the language of Principal Cavan. I adopte every word which that distinguished gentleman uttered the other evening in reference to the question of disallowance. Speaking on this question, he says :

" He was quite willing to admit that within their own distinct limits the autonomy of the Provinces ought to be respected. Under the Act of Federation certain subjects were designated as belonging to the Dominion, and certain subjects were named as within the jurisdiction of the several Provinces, and while he had never committed himself to the principle, as a universal principle, that the central authority could not revise the Acts of the Provinces that were within their own limits ; while he distinctly desired not to be committed to that principle ; while he did hold that as a general thing it was a safe and wise principle, as long as the Province has kept fairly and difinitly within its own limits, even though its action is not the wisest action, that the central authority should be very careful about revising it—he believed that occasions did arise when it was not simply permitted to the central authority, but that it was the bounded duty of the central authority to revise provincial legislation, legislation lying distinctly within the limits of the Provinces. He supposed on most subjects he would be regarded as thinking with the Liberal party, but if the Liberal party had even taken ground in opposition to that he must beg to be excused from following the Liberal party. He supposed that was a bold thing for a man who was neither lawyer nor politician to say, but was prepared to take the ground that the Jesuits' Estates Act was not within the limits of the Province of Quebec. So far as it dealt with education it was within those limits, so far as it dealt with money it was within those limits, but he thought he could show that it was marked by features which took it out of those limits, and making it a matter that the Dominion ought to deal with."

Sir JOHN THOMPSON. (Antigonish.)

I feel that in addressing the House upon this question and in presenting to it, at this stage of the debate, the reasons which, I believe, justified the Government in advising His Excellency not to exercise the power of disallowance as to the Jesuits' Estate Act of Quebec, I must ask more than the usual indulgence of the House. I shall be compelled, in the first place, to dwell at considerable length, on details which the House has already heard discussed; and I shall have to speak under a sense of the fact that with one large portion of the people of Canada nothing that I can say will be satisfactory, and that with another, and I hope the greater portion of the people of Canada, no defence of the Government is necessary. Nevertheless, considering the arraignment which the policy of the Government on this question has had, considering the interest which the measures has excited in all quarters of Canada, it is only becoming that I should ask the indulgence of the House in order that I may make a plain statement of the reasons which have induced us to give to His Excellency the advice for which we are to be held responsible to-night. I desire, before beginning a statement of these reasons, to take exception to a remark which was made by the hon. member for Simcoe (M. McCarthy), at the outset of his address, with reference to the position which members of the Government occupy in this debate. The hon. gentleman, in complaining that no member on the Treasury benches had risen to take part in the debate down to this stage, spoke of it almost as an act of decourtesy. He seemed to think that the mode in which the discussion should be carried on was a mere matter of politeness and a mere matter of fence. I do not so regard it. I understand the position of the Government to be this : The case on behalf of the amendement was first presented forcibly and ably last night by the hon. member for Muskoka (Mr. O'Brien,)sustained by an hon. gentleman on the opposite side of the House (Mr. Barron); but I leave it to the sense of the House, whether, when the debate was adjourned at near midnight, any argument remained unanswered which called for an answer from the Treasury benches. But with regard to the hon. member's complaint on the ground of discourtesy. I have to appeal to the sense of fairness of the House in this particular. No member on either side of the House was unaware from the commencement of this debate, that the main argument on which the conduct of the Government would be assailed, would be presented by the hon. member for Simcoe (Mr. McCarthy). I was the Minister, who, if there be a difference between colleagues as to the extent to which responsability is heard, was primarily responsible, and I submit it to the sense of fairness of every member, whether, before giving the reasons upon which I must stand or fall as regards the correctness of the advice which I gave to His Excellency it was not my right to bear my accuser? The hon. gentleman thinks otherwise, and the position he takes is this: That courtesy to him and to the gentleman who will divide with him on this question to-night require that his arraignment of my report, his arraignment of the Government with regard to every subject of this discussion, should have been made after my mouth had been closed, and I ceased to have a right to defend myself. If there is any fairness or courtesy in that position, I am willing to submit that I was wrong in reserving the remarks which I have to make until the hon. member for Simcoe had been heard. Now, in presenting the case which I have to present on behalf of the Government, I must ask your attention for a few moments again to the wearisome narration of the position which these lands occupied in the Province of Quebec. Not that that matter has not been discussed in every detail, but because in almost every detail I have essentially different opinions from those of my hon. friend from Simcoe (Mr. McCarthy), and because, in some respects, the points upon which the merits of this case depend were lost sight of by the hon. member in the admirable address he made this afternoon. Why, I venture to say, without the slightest disrespect for the hon. member for whose talents no one in this House has a higher respect than I, and I would be the last person to disparage any observations which he might address to us—I venture to say that the reason why this House ought not to ask His Excellency now to dissallow that Act, if we had no better reason, is that the hon. member for Simcoe (Mr. McCarthy)—a master of legal argument—addressed the House for nearly three hours this afternoon, and presented a case in which, for one whole hour, the hon. gentleman went from detail to detail, from step to step, for the purpose of proving —what? for the purpose of proving that the Jesuits of Quebec lost their title to the estates in question—a fact which is admitted in the preamble to the Act. He spent an hour more in discussing theological questions, and questions connected with the ecclesiastical history of England, which, in England itself and in every one of her colonies, have been kept asleep for the last two hundred years by the spirit of toleration on which alone a British country can be governed. Now, let me call the attention of the House to a brief statement with regard to the position of these estates, not for the purpose of showing that this society in the Province of Quebec, whatever its character and merits may have been, had a legal title to the property, but for the purpose of showing that this is not a question which we can decide, but is one which must and ought to have been left to that authority which the Constitution makes not only competent to deal with such questions but omnipotent in dealing with them, subject only to control in so far as the rights of the whole Dominion or the policy of the Empire may be involved. Now, Sir, the House will remember that, long before the cession of Canada to the Crown of Great Britain, the Jesuits had labored in the wilderness, and in the schools of Canada, and in the churches of Canada, and that, as a reward for their missionary zeal, for their talent as teachers, and for their services to this, one of the great colonies of France, that order had been erected into an incorporated body, under the most solemn acts which the King of France could pass under his hand, had been endowed with these estates by the King of France, and by private donors, who wished to place in their hands the means by which the work of Christianity and civilisation amongst the savages could be carried on, and by which the work of education amongst the youth of the Province of Quebec could be carried on. These were the terms on which they held their lands when the battle was fought on the Plains of Abraham, and the conqueror took possession of Canada under terms which are in the first place set forth in the capitulation of the city of Quebec, and afterwards in the capitulation of the city of Montreal, and under terms which are plainly defined by the law of nations, recognized by every civilised country in the world. What were these terms? By the law of nations, recognized, as I have said, in every civilised country in the world, the conquering power took possession of all the rights, privileges and property of the conquered monarch in the country, but he took no more. He took the sovereignty of the country, he took the King's fortications in the country, he took the King's stores of arms and ammunition in the country, he took the King's lands at the country, he took the King's treasures in the country, but he had no right by the law of nations to lay his hands on the property, movable or immovable, of the humblest subject in the country. If he had despoiled private property it would have been an outrage which would have disgraced the British arms, and he would have committed an act, let me tell the House, which, irrespective of the law of nations, begun at Quebec, repeated at Montreal, he would not do. It has been said in this debate that, by the Terms of Capitulation, the Jesuits of the Province of Quebec, and all their property, were placed at the mercy of the conqueror. I do not so read the Terms of Capitulation. Let me see article 34 of the Terms of Capitulation of Montreal :

" All the communities—"

And at that time the Jesuits were in community in the Province of Quebec——

"——and all the priests shall preserve their movables, the property and revenues of the seignories and other estates which they possess in the colony, of what nature soever they be, and the same estates shall be preserved in their privileges, rights, honors and exemptions."

That was the request made, and the answer given to that request was unequivocal —"Granted." And yet we are told that these estates, which came within the exact words of that provision as to the seignories and property, movable and immovable, of the priests and religious orders in the Province of Quebec, were reserved to the King's mercy. It is true that the preceding section 33 was refused until the King's pleasure should be known, and in that there was a distinct reference to the Jesuits, but that article referred, not to the property only of the Jesuits, but asked in addition to the provisions as to their property in section 34, that they should have all their constitutions and privileges, that their monasteries should not be entered by troops, and that safeguards should be given to them from military intrusion, and that they should preserve their rights to nominate to certain curacies and missions as theretofore. Those privileges, vague and undefined by the terms of the article, were met by the words: " Reserved until the King's pleasure be known," although the response to the article, dealing with the properties of these people, was the unequivocal one—" Granted." The conquering arms of England were used against the soldiers of France, but not against individuals, either in France or in Canada. Now, we go a step further, and we read the Treaty of Peace. The war had gone on, and the treaty was not made until 1763, and let me read to the House a passage from the treaty, because the Terms of Capitulation are liable to be qualified by the final and definitive treaty at the close of the war. This provision was made by the treaty :

" His Most Christian Majesty cedes and guarantees to His Britannic Majesty in full right, Canada with all its dependencies, as well as the Island of Cape Breton, and all the other islands and coasts in the Gulf and River St. Lawrence, and, in general, everything that depends on the said countries, lands, islands, and coasts, with the sovereignty, property, possession, and all rights, acquired by treaty or otherwise, which the Most Christian King and the Crown of France have had till now over the said countries, islands, lands, places, coasts, and their inhabitants, so that the Most Christian King cedes and makes over the whole to the said King and to the Crown of Great Britain, and that in the most ample manner and form, without restriction, and without any liberty to depart from the said cession and guaranty under any pretence, or to disturb Great Britain in the possessions above mentioned."

Now, in return for that cession of Canada and Cape Breton and all the islands of the St. Lawrence, this solemn compact was made by His Britannic Majesty:

"His Britannic Majesty on his side agrees to grant the liberty of the Catholic religion to the inhabitants of Canada. He will consequently give the most precise and most effectual orders that his new Roman Catholic subjects may profess the worship of their religion, according to the rites of the Romish Church, as far as the laws of Great Britain permit. His Britannic Majesty further agrees that the French inhabitants, or others who had been subjects of the Most Christian King in Canada, may retire with all safety and freedom wherever they shall think proper, and may sell their estates, provided it be to subjects of His Britannic Majesty."

This House has been told that the essence of the whole clause is in the qualification, "as far as the laws of Great Britain permit," and we are told that that of itself introduced all the laws of England relating to public worship, the Supremacy Act, and everything of that kind which could be invoked.

Mr. McCARTHY. Not by me.

Sir JOHN THOMPSON. The hon. member for Simcoe did not assert that it introduced the Supremacy Act, but the argument was made before he spoke in the debate, that that introduced all the restrictions on the exercise of religion; and we were told that it even introduced the Supremacy Act, under which, let me tell the House plainly, if it had been introduced in the Province of Quebec, no man could have exercised the Catholic religion at all. The very essence of the Supremacy Act is that no person—I am stripping the Act of all its verbiage, I am giving its essence, and at the same time quoting its exact words when I say, that the gist of the whole Act is this: That no person outside the realm of England shall have or exercise within the Queen's dominions—even spiritual superiority. If no spiritual superiority in Rome then no bishop in Canada; if no bishop in Canada, no priest in Canada; if no priest in Canada then no sacrament for the living or the dying in Canada. Every altar in Canada would have been thrown down by the very terms of a treaty in which His Britannic Majesty, in return for the cession of half the continent, solemnly promised not only that the people should have the right to exercise their religion, as they had been accustomed to do, but that he would give the most precise orders that freedom of worship be carried out in every particular. Now, Sir, obviously the treaty meant no such thing; obviously His Britannic Majesty did not take with one hand the cession of this country, and hold out a false promise with the other. Obviously he meant that there should be perfect freedom of worship in Canada, the newly ceded country subject only to the legislation which might be made upon this subject from time to time by the Parliament of Great Britain, certainly not that it was subject then to the laws as regards freedom of worship in Great Britain; for, let me remind the House, that instead of there being any freedom of worship in Great Britain at that time, the exercise of the Roman Catholic religion then amounted to the crime of high treason; and no dissenter, under the risk of long imprisonment, could enter a conventicle or a meeting-house; so that obviously it did not mean to introduce into the country ceded, the laws of Great Britain with regard to public worship or even with regard to supremacy at that time. But let me suggest to the House what the obvious meaning was, as quoted from the words of the Attorney General and the Solicitor General of England, and of the Prime Minister of England, in discussing this treaty stipulation, and what, upon its face, every sensible and unprejudiced man will say its meaning was; and that was this: "In so far as the laws of Great Britain permit freedom of worship in her colonies"—and the laws of Great Britain at that time did permit freedom of worship in her colonies —and likewise "in so far as the laws of Great Britain passed in future years might permit." Well, Sir, we pass on to the Quebec Act of a few years later, in 1774, and I come now certainly to a branch of the argument against us which my hon. friend from Simcoe did press upon us this afternoon, namely, that by the express term of that statute, the provisions of the Statute of Elizabeth with regard to the supremacy of the Queen, was enacted with regard to the Province of Quebec. Now, let me ask the House, for the purpose of considering how far passion has guided and swerved the reason of some of those who have spoken upon this question, to look at that statute, and they will find that the rights of the people of Canada and their freedom of religious worship are as fully guaranteed by the terms of the Quebec Act as they were by the terms of the Treaty of Paris itself. While it is true that one of the provisions of that Act declares that the statute made in the first year of the reign of Queen Elizabeth should apply over all the countries which then did, or thereafter should belong to the Imperial Crown of this realm, and should apply to the Province of Quebec, this is subject to a limited construction, because if it is to be read in its literal sense, it was an absolute prohibition of the practice of the Roman Catholic religion in the Province, an absolute prohibition under the penalties of high treason itself. But the Act left no such ambiguity to be dealt with by mere construction, because it goes on to limit the operation of the Statute relating to Royal Supremacy, by declaring that instead of the oath of abjuration which, by the terms of the statute of Elizabeth, all people professing the Catholic religion were to take, not only to abjure all foreign jurisdiction in relation to temporal matters, but all foreign jurisdiction in relation to spiritual matters as well : there is to be a new form of oath and a new statutory provision for the people of the Province, whereby they shall no longer be bound to abjure foreign jurisdiction in matters spiritual, and shall be entitled to all the privileges of British subjects, and all privileges of worship on taking an oath of allegiance merely, which applies only to the temporal affairs of the reigning sovereign. Therefore, instead of its being in any sense true that by the terms of the Quebec Act the restrictions of the Supremacy Act were imposed upon the Province by the express terms of that statute, the people of Quebec were relieved from the most odious provision of the Supremacy Act—the provision by which they were bound to swear against conscience, and in abnegation of their faith, that they would recognize the power of no foreign priest, even in spiritual matters. So much then for the Quebec Act of 1774, by which, I think, I have shown that there was a toleration extended in regard to the Province of Quebec which did not exist in the mother country, and which was utterly inconsistent with those old statutes, which, forsooth, 115 years afterwards, we are asked to advise His Excellency to apply to the Province of Quebec. Now, Sir, in 1791, 30 years after the conquest of Canada, the King of Great Britain issued a proclamation suppressing the Order of Jesuits in the colony. As history has told us, the estates which are even now in question, were looked upon with a covetous eye by Lord Amherst who had taken an active part in directing the armies of Great Britain. On this subject I need not go into details. This covetous attempt was frustrated, but suffice it to say, at this stage of the controversy, that the King of England, and I submit it to the legal sense of the House, the King of England had no power to revoke the terms of the charter of incorporation which the Jesuits of Canada had received from the King of France. I admit that the Parliament of Great Britain could have brought in the whole body of the common law, and could have applied to the colony all the penal statutes which the bigotry of that age might choose to invoke. But the King of England had probably no such prerogative. If the King grants a charter, the King himself, with all his power, cannot revoke it. It is only Parliament who can do that, and, in this instance, by the attempt, I venture to think, of the King to suppress that order, and to revoke that charter, he exceeded the authority which he possessed. But, Sir, we were told that by a royal proclamation all the common law of England was introduced into Canada. I doubt that that could be done. By the law of nations, recognized at every stage and period of English law, the laws of a conquered country prevail until the paramount authority of the conquering country imposes new laws upon it. But the monarch of a conquering country probably cannot of himself change those laws, cannot of himself do it under the constitution of Great Britain. But if there is a doubt upon that subject as to the general rule, I say this, that the King of England could not introduce the common law by his proclamation in violation of the treaty which he had made in 1763, and by the terms of the treaty he had reserved all those rights which touch this question, even in the remotest degree. Therefore, it is idle for us to discuss how far he might have made other branches of the common law applicable to this country. In the year 1800 the last Jesuit died, and I think that by the law of England, applicable, perhaps, at that time to this property in Canada, on the death of the last surviving member of the corporation the property escheated to the Crown, and the Crown could have taken possession of it as escheated lands. Steps were taken to assert his right on the part of the Crown ; but the question has been complicated in the meantime by the fact that the Pope had suppressed the Company of Jesus nearly all over the world. By the terms of that suppression and by the terms of the civil law, which, it is contended still prevailed in the Province of Quebec, the properties, instead of reverting to the Crown, passed to the ordinaries of the dioceses in which they were situated. I do not mean to say that that is so: I present that to the House as one of the questions which has been raised, and which tends to make this case anything but a plain one. I will do more. I will admit the hon. member for Simcoe's contention, that the common law had in the meantime been introduced, that the civil law had been superseded, and that by the terms of the common law these estates had become escheated to the Crown. One of the questions, however, which has been constantly agitated ever since in the Province of Quebec is this—that if you are to subject this property to the rigor of the common law, you at least ought to give the benefit of that principle of the common law, which declares that whenever property of any kind has been escheated to the Crown some consideration should be shown to the persons who are morally entitled to it, and regard should be had to the use to which it was intended to be applied. By this rule of practice the escheat does not wholly result as an emolument to the Crown or as an augmentation of the revenue, but a liberal proportion is appropriated to the intention of the donors or to those who morally may be considered entitled to it. If that consideration were to prevail to any extent, the clergy, and it may be the Jesuits, on the reinstatement of the order, would have some kind of moral right to compensation respecting these estates. But let me call the attention of the House to this fact, which I think has been kept out of view, and which certainly the hon. member for Victoria (Mr. Barron) who addressed the House last night, overlooked in his argument, that the very brief by which these properties were taken possession of on the part of the Crown, when they were eventually seized, does not allege the right of escheat, but declares the right by which the Crown intended to claim the properties to be the right of conquest—a right which, as I have said, is repudiated by the law of nations, was repudiated by the Crown officers of Great Britain at the time, and which, after all that has been said in this debate, has not had one word said in favor of it. That was the only title by which Great Britain claimed she had a right to these estates. Now, it is true likewise that subsequent statutes vested the title in the Province of Canada, and ultimately in due course of law, and as the result of statutes, the title to those lands became vested in the Province of Quebec. As to the conclusion which the hon. member for Simcoe drew, that the Province had a good title to them, a perfect title under the law, I have not one word to say ; and if this Act had come before us as legislation in recognition of a legal title, I would have felt bound to call the attention of my colleagues to the fact that a very great mistake had been committed, on which, perhaps, it might have been necessary to have advised the Provincial Legislature to reconsider its conclusions. But it is admitted by the Legislature of Quebec that a good title existed in the Province, and all that is said on the face of this Act or in the arguments in support of it, is this: That there existed a moral claim to some degree of compensation, little or much, which, to a greater or less extent, was binding upon the conscience of the Legislature of that Province. Now, Sir, the result of the existence of that claim—the result of the assertion of that moral right, whatever it may have been worth, was that, from year to year, when the Province went on to assert its right to those estates, and as the Province ventured to place piece after piece of the property on the market, it was met by a protest from the united hierarchy of Quebec, demanding that such properties should not be sold, should not be diverted from the original charitable and religious purposes for which they were intended, and so every step by which those estates were sought to be made useful to the revenues of the Province was contested in the most formal and solemn manner. It is recited in part of the preamble of this Act, that not many years ago, one of the most valuable parts of the property, being situate opposite the Basilica in the city of Quebec, was brought to market, and there was met by solemn protest of all the hierarchy of the Province. In face of that protest, casting as it did, a cloud upon the title of the Province, involving as it seemed to do a dispute as to the right of the Government, and as to the title of the purchaser, that property had to be withdrawn from sale. Let me assure this House again that in presenting our case I am endeavoring to do so, not from my individual point of view at all, but simply from the point of view in which we may be asked to withhold or to give advice with respect to the great power of disallowing a provincial statute. Let me call attention then to all these details, and let me ask the House to keep in mind that state of affairs with respect to the property itself, with respect to the assertion of this claim, good or bad; with respect to the assertion of this moral right, worth little or much, and to remember the difficulty of marketing the property in the Province of Quebec under those circumstances. If the House will bear all this in mind, and then will read with me the statute which we are asked to disallow, I say that the provisions of that statute will cease to be obnoxious to any reasonable man, that they cannot be misunderstood and that they can hardly be misrepresented even by the most violent prejudice. The sale, as I have said, was forbidden. I am not driven at all to defend the policy of the Government of the Province, as to the propriety of opening up that question; as to the propriety of not insisting that these properties should be sold even if they should be sacrificed in the face of that formidable protest. That was for the Legislature of Quebec to say. The constitution has charged me with no duties and with no responsibilities, as to the weight of any legal or of any moral claim which the Legislature has thought proper to recognize. I may concur with gentlemen who have spoken this afternoon that it was unwise not to insist on the strict statutory title based on confiscation, severe though it may have been, but in this case the constitution has not made me the judge. It has not made me or my colleagues the arbiters between the two sets of opinions in the Province of Quebec; it has not clothed His Excellency with the power to step in and consider every question which arises among the people of the Province: it has vested that authority in the Provincial Legislature, which by a unanimous vote, as was pointed out by the hon. member for Northumberland (Mr. Mitchell) last night declared that this was the true and proper solution of the question. Under those circumstances have I any right to exercise a superior and overruling judgment over the Province? Is that the theory upon which our constitution is to be worked out? This moral claim, as they choose to call it, may have been as weak as air, but it was considered weighty by the conscience and the judgment of those whom the constitution solemnly appointed to decide and after that it is not for us to say : " The Legislature arrived at a wrong conclusion." I can state the matter no more forcibly than in the very words of one of our opponents on this question, who declares that the authority given to the Provincial Legislatures over certain classes of subjects carries with it, like all authority, a liberty to error which must be respected so long as the legal power is not exceeded, and the error is not manifestly subversive legally or morally of the principles of the constitution or of the great objects of the state. As far, therefore, as we have to consider the power of the Legislature to recognize a moral obligation—

leaving out of sight for a moment the theological questions which my hon. friend from Simcoe (Mr. McCarthy) and I are to join issue on, with a view to the House passing judgment, as to which is the better theologian forsooth, and as to whose advice on the question of theology His Excellency the Governor General as the supreme theologian is to act—I contend that the Legislature had supreme authority to decide, and had a perfect right to decide, without veto or controlling authority at Ottawa, even though we thought they decided erroneously. Now, Sir, having asked the House to bear in mind the situation in which these properties stood in the Province of Quebec, the way in which an attempted sale was met by a protest which completely frustrated the sale, let me call the attention of the House to another state of facts as regards the various claimants upon this property. There were the Bishops of the Province who said: "As a result of the suppression of the Society of Jesus in this Province we were vested with all the estates as the ordinaries of the various dioceses in which these properties were situated." Nay, more, they said: "We have inherited their moral claim too, because when the means were striken from their hands of carrying on the missionary work and the work of education, we took it up and, by the sacrifice of our people's labors and treasures, we built up institutions of education all over this country." The Society of the Jesuits had in the meantime been re-instated and re-organized in the Province, and upon this point let me call the attention of the House to the argument of my hon. friend from Simcoe (Mr. McCarthy) which was that by the decree of suppression in France the order became extinct in Canada. He cited to prove that the decision of the Parliament of Paris, which merely decided that the Jesuits in France were liable for the debts of the Jesuits in Paraguay, because the properties of the two sets of men were held in solidarity. That decision has not the remotest effect upon the statute of the Jesuits in Canada, who, themselves, were a body corporate under the most solemn instrument which the King of France could give them to indicate his will in that regard. I have mentioned that the bishops claimed that they represented the moral right, which, as I have said, the Legislature thought was worthy of compensation, and the Jesuits claimed it likewise. Look at this as a business matter. Look at this matter simply as relating to a piece of land in the city of Quebec, and tell me how, under these circumstances, the title was ever to be cleared of this dispute. Obviously not by compensating first one party and then the other, because under those circumstances the Legislature would have had to pay twice the value of the claim. It could be only settled by getting the two parties to arbitrate and to leave it to some person to settle their mutual dispute, or by saying : " You must conform to the decision of some person who has authority over you both." Let me argue this question throughout, if we can, without feeling that we belong to different religious persuasions, without feeling that a religious question is mixed up with it at all; and, therefore, let us leave out for the moment any name which might excite the prejudices of some portions of the community. The Bishop of Quebec and the other contesting parties who struggled for compensation for this moral claim were all members of the same church, and by their membership recognized supreme authority in the head of that church to settle their disputes, even though the settlement should be against their will. The head of their church had that authority—not by any provision of the law of Quebec mind, not by any provision recognized by English law mind, but by the consent of the parties who were free to belong to that church and free to leave it, and while they did belong to it were subject to a spiritual superior. He had that power by their choice; he had the right to say to one or the other, no matter how small or how great the proportion might be that was divided between them : " You must submit; it is a fair settlement between you, and I, as your supreme arbiter bind you by my decision." The Government of Quebec, therefore, having made up its mind to recognize the moral claim, if for no other purpose, for purposes of public policy, found that they could not arrive at a solution of the question without some person to act between the claimants and to bind them both. It was only by a method like that that they could reach a solution—paying once, and once only, the value of this moral claim. Now, that being so, let me see what was done in pursuance of that method of settlement. The head of that church, so possessed with power to preclude the Jesuits from making any further claim, so possessed with power to preclude the bishops from making any further claim, authorised, in 1884—and this is an important fact, as the House will see when I proceed a little with the argument—authorised the Archbishop of Quebec to act as his attorney in the negotiations for the settlement. On the 7th of May, 1887, a document appears which has been one of the means of exciting hostility to this Act. On the 7th of May, 1887, the head of the church *reserved to himself* the right to settle the question with regard to the value of that moral claim and the division of the proceeds—reserved it to himself in virtue of his prerogatives as a potentate? Not at all. Reserved it to himself simply in the withdrawal of the authority which he had given to the Archbishop of Quebec, and left himself unreprensented in the Province by any attorney whomsoever. And, therefore, when it is said that the Pope reserved to himself the right to settle the question, he was not by any means claiming to reserve any right in the public domain in the Province, or any right to the appropriation of money of the Province. He was simply withdrawing the power which he had given to another person to settle the question, and saying : " Until a new authority is given, you will negotiate with me." The next step, Sir, was on the 17th of May, 1888, and that was in a letter which was written by Mr. Mercier, the First Minister of Quebec, and which, without an undue desire to defend the propriety of these negotiations, the policy of the Act, or any other step of the transaction, I think has been very much misunderstood in this discussion. That letter recites, among other things, that the Holy Father by reserving to himself the settlement of that question, virtually had cancelled the authority, the only authority, which existed in the Province of Quebec, to negotiate with the Government. The First Minister said :

" My predecessors in the Government deemed it their duty, in 1876, believe, to order the demolition of the college and the division of the property into buildings lots, in view of an immediate sale, which, however, did not take place, owing to certain representations from exalted personages at the time.

" To avoid further difficulties, as I supposed, my predecessors let the matter lie and allowed the property to be so neglected that it has become a grazing ground and a receptacle for filth, so much so that it is openly said in Quebec that the matter has become a public scandal.

" Under these circumstances, I deem it my duty to ask Your Eminence if you see any serious objection to the Government's selling the property, pending a final settlement of the question of the Jesuits' estates."

My hon. friends so far misconceived that request as to represent it be a petition on the part of the Government of the Province to a foreign potentate for permission to sell the property—a permission which they did not need, because by the law of the Province they had the power to sell it, and they had from year to year sold portions of it, and put the proceeds in the public Treasury. But in asking his consent to the sale of the property, they were asking that, when they brought it to the market again, they should not be met by the protests of the bishops whom he had the power to control; and, therefore, when the First Minister said : " Will you permit this property to be sold, pending a final settlement of the Jesuits' estates ? "—he was simply asking that that protest should no longer be made, and that there should be a consent to the sale on the part of all who asserted any claim whatever, even though it were only the shadow of a moral claim. He said : " This is a receptacle for filth, so much so that it has become a public scandal; let us all agree that it shall be sold, pending a settlement of the Jesuits' estates." Surely that is only the ordinary transaction of every day life, when a man has possession of real estate to which another sets up even an unfounded claim. He will say : " Rather than that this property should go to waste and be a public nuisance, better that we should all consent to sell it." Yet we are told that the First Minister went to the feet of a foreign potentate to enable him to exercise power which he ought to have found in the statutes of his own Province. He was not denying his legal title or power; but he was simply saying : " Give me your consent so that this claim, whether little or much, shall no longer stand in the way of a sale for the benefit of all concerned." He said :

" The Government would look on the proceeds of the sale as a special deposit to be disposed of hereafter, in accordance with the agreements to be entered into between the parties interested, with the sanction of the Holy See. "

Simply this, that all parties claiming the property, or any rights in respect of it, shall agree that the property shall be sold and the proceeds shall be kept inviolate, so that anybody having any claim against the property shall not be prejudiced, but shall have the same claim as before—precisely the same arrangement as any business man having property to sell would make with his adversary. The letter goes on to say :

" As it will perhaps be necessary, upon this matter, to consult the Legislature of our Province, which is to be convened very shortly, I respectfully solicit an immediate reply. "

We were told in sarcastic tones to-day that it was *absolutely necessary* to go to the feet of the Sovereign Pontiff, but it might only *perhaps* be necessary to consult the Legislature of the Province of Quebec. I say when we know the facts with regard to that property, criticism becomes unfair. The Government of the Province had already power to sell the estates by law, and therefore, unless it were agreed upon with the head of the church that the property should be sold under these conditions, and an agreement were made to value this very claim, and to put aside the funds to meet it, there was no necessity to consult the Legislature at all. If the personage to whom that letter was addressed had declined the negotiations, it would not have been necessary to consult the Legislature, because the Provincial Government had all the legal authority the Legislature could give them. It was only in the event of a compromise being arrived at and the payment of money being involved, that it was necessary to consult the Legislature. And yet this letter has been put to the House, as if, forsooth, the fair and true meaning of it was that it was only *perhaps* necessary to consult the Legislature, but at all events it is necessary to consult the Holy See. Now, the answer to that letter was in these words :

" I hasten to notify you that, having laid your request before the Holy Father at the audience yesterday, His Holiness was pleased to grant permission to sell the property which belonged to the Jesuits Fathers before they were suppressed, upon the express condition, however, that the sum to be received be deposited and left at the free disposal of the Holy See."

The claimant representing this moral claim says : " I agree that you shall sell that lot in the city of Quebec, but if you sell it, place the fund to my credit in order that we may know where it is when we arrive at a satisfactory conclusion as to what shall be done with it." The answer of the First Minister was that he declined to accede to that, but he proposed a reasonable alternative, that the Government retain the proceeds untill this dispute should be settled. Thus what is declared to be an assumption of authority on the part of the Pope, actually in contravention of the Supremacy Act, and what we are told actually trails the Queen's honor in the dust, is that the Pope consents to the Quebec Government retaining the proceeds of the sale of the Jesuits' estates, subject to a future settlement of the dispute. The Government of Quebec, pending the settlement of the claims of these two litigants, which were to be held in suspense to be settled, not before the sale of the property but afterwards, retained custody of this fund ; and when the authority representing these rival claimants agrees to this proposition, it is asserted, forsooth, that because he use the word "allows" meaning evidently "consents," he has encroached on the prerogative of the Queen. In agreeing to the Government retaining the proceeds of the sale of the Jesuits' estates, he acted simply as the arbiter between the two contesting claimants. He allows this simply as the person who, as the head of the church to which the claimants belong, has, by their own choice, a right to give this consent ; and yet when he consents to that, it is actually declared that he is asserting the prerogative of a foreign potentate in derogation of the prerogative of the Queen. I repeat that when we know the facts with regard to the situation of this property, and with regard to the position of the two rival claimants, it is impossible to misunderstand, and almost impossible for ingenuity to misrepresent, the preamble of this Act, as unfortunately it has been misrepresenting during the long discussion which has taken place, since the Act was passed, in various parts of the country. The letter of Cardinal Simeoni, of the 27th March 1888, contain this passage with regard to the conclusion arrived at :

" Affirmatively in favor of the Fathers of the Society of Jesus and in accordance with the method prescribed in other places, that is to say, that the Fathers of the Society of Jesus treat in their own name with the Civil Government, in such a manner, however, as to leave full liberty to the Holy See to dispose of the property as it deems advisable, and consequently that they should be very careful that no condition or clause should be inserted in the official deed of the concession of such property which could in any manner affect the liberty of the Holy See."

As I have said, down to that time, the power of the attorney which enabled any one to negotiate with regard to this question had been withdrawn, and then there has simply a new authority given to a new attorney, namely, the fathers of the society, to treat with the Government of Quebec, and the stipulation, not that the property of the Province should be subject to any conditions, but that if there should be a conveyance made of it to any parties—to the Jesuits on the one side or the hierarchy on the other—in settlement of the claim, these parties should not take a deed which would preclude the Pope from giving a final decision as to the way in which the proceeds should be devided between them. Then, in his letter dated 1st May, 1888, the First Minister of the Province of Quebec distinctly stipulates that he is not recognizing any civil or, as we would call it, any legal obligation, but merely the moral obligation in this respect. He says :

" 6 That you will grant to the Government of the Province of Quebec a full, complete and perpetual concession of all the property which may have belonged in Canada, under whatever title, to the Fathers of the old society, and that you will renounce to all rights generally whatsoever upon such property and the revenues therefrom in favor of our Province, the whole, as well as in the name of the old Order of Jesuits, and of your present corporation as the name of the Pope, of the Sacred College of the Propaganda and of the Roman Catholic Church in general."

Then follows the clause to which above all others, exception is taken, and to which I shall ask the special attention of the House :

" 7. That any agreement made between you and the Government of the Province will be binding only in so far as it shall be ratified by the Pope and the Legislature of this Province."

Now, when we look at the Act itself, when we see what the Government of Quebec asked the Legislature to do, when we see them ask the Legislature to vote, in extinction of this moral claim, whatever it was worth, the sum of $400,000, we cease to be surprised and to be deceived as regards the effect of that provision of the statute. The Ministry of Quebec were dealing with two rival claimants—the hierarchy and the Jesuit Society. They are dealing also with a third party, the Pope, who accupied the position of mediator by consent between these two, and the First Minister of Quebec stipulated that before the Province should be asked to pay one dollar of the money, it should have a conveyance, in the first place, from the fathers of the society, in the second place from the Pope himself, and, in the third place, from the Sacred College of the propaganda and the Roman Catholic Church in general. He stipulated that before he should be bound to pay a dollar of that money, nay, even before he should ask the Legislature of Quebec to autorise him to pay a dollar, he should be in a position to say : " I have obtained a complete release from all the parties who forever after can assert the slightest right or title or the slightest claim, legally or morally in regard to these estates." Why could he not do this ? Could he have said : " I ask the Legislature of the Province of Quebec for authority to pay this money on obtaining a conveyance from the fathers of the society ? " Would he not have left outstanding the rights of the hierarchy, who contested, every inch of the way, the rights of the fathers of the society to the proceeds of the settlement? Would he not have left outstanding still the possible claim of the authority superior to them all ? I assert it, without fear, that the contention will not commend itself to the good sense of the House, that that provision No 7, which is taken such great exception to, is a distinct provision *against* the authority of the Pope and not in favor of the authority of the Pope. In fact by that provision, the substance of the agreement was this : " While I am willing to offer to you $400,000, I am not willing to be bound by my offer until your master ratifies your agreement to accept it. I will not only not pay you a dollar of that $400,000 until every one of you gives me your conveyance, but until the greatest superior you have on earth gives me his deed ; and until I get all that, I will not ask the Legislature of Quebec to give me authority to pay you a single dollar." And yet, because the Legislature of Quebec demanded, before it should put that money even at the disposition of the Governor in Council, that they should have everybody's rights foreclosed, and that the highest authority the claimants recognized on earth should give his deed also, and more, that the College of the Propaganda should also give its release, and that every step down to that point should be without prejudice to the rights of the Province of Quebec, we are told that this is an assertion of the prerogative of a foreign potentate. I am dealing with no merely legal theory upon this question. I am not devising any excuse for the legislation of Quebec. I say that the Legislature of Quebec so understood it. It was so explained to them. I hold before me a statement which the First Minister who introduced that Bill into the Legislature made to that Legislature, and upon which they passed the Bill. He says :

" In the first place we must not mistake the bearing of this declaration nor forget that it was inserted as a protection."

The Legislature of Quebec passed it as a protection on the statement of their First Minister. They passed that provision unanimously as protection, and yet months after we are to put a different interpretation upon what their intention was, and to ask that His Excellency, a stranger to that Legislature, a stranger to their motives, should decide that that was not their true motive at all, that it was not a protection but a distinct challenge of the supremacy of Her Majesty Queen Victoria. Mr. Mercier said :

" Any serious objection to it, however slight, may disappear, for it is we, the Ministers, who insisted on it, in order not to give effect to the transaction, unless it was sanctioned by the religious authority, in the person of the Pope. And it is easy to understand why. In all important treaties made by mandatories (agents as we understand) ratification must be made by the principal, *i. e.*, the mandator. Thus, for example, take what concerns me personally, what concerns Ministers,—what is it usual to state in resolutions and letters ?—that the transaction will not avail unless sanctioned by the Legislature. Well, the Rev. Father Turgeon, who was charged by the Holy See to settle this question with us, is only an agent, a mandatory, an attorney. And so that there may be no misunderstanding, so that the transaction may be final, so that the settlement may no longer be open to discussion by the religious authorities, we insist that the Pope shall ratify the arrangement. There is no question of having the law sanctioned by the Pope. Let us not play upon words. The law will be sanctionned by the Lieutenant Governor, and it will take effect in the terms of the agreement. That is to say, Sir, that if the Pope does not ratify the arrangement there will be neither interest nor principal paid, but we shall then say to the religious authorities : " You appointed an agent to settle this question ; we came to an understanding, and if you do not ratify the act of your mandatory it is your own fault, for we, the inhabitants of the Province of Quebec, though the constituted authorities, have done our part, have kept our promise." I am pleased to believe that the importance of the precaution taken by us will be understood. But once more, if there is any serious objection to that part (of the matter) it is very easy to come to an understanding. But in that case we must substitute something equivalent. What shall we put? We must, after all, put something to express that the transaction will not avail till the Pope ratifies it. Well, Sir, we said " the Pope " intentionally. We did not say the Congregation of the Propaganda. We did not say the Secretary of State. We said the Pope. We desire that the ratification be given by the head of the church, in order that all those interested may be bound."

When we know that that was the intention of the Legislature of the Province, when we know it from the statutes, from the correspondence, and from all that we know of the facts regarding these estates, and when we know it also from the declaration of the First Minister of the Province in which the Act was passed—an explanation which was accepted by both sides of the House, for be it remembered, as the hon. member for Northumberland (Mr. Mitchell) said last night, the Act was afterwards passed unanimously, and the First Minister was not asked, after his explanation, to substitute anything for that provision—we ar now actually ask to advise His Excellency that all this had a different and an occult meaning, and that the Legislature of Quebec did not mean what the First Minister of that Province said it did in passing this Act. Then, in the letter of the 1st May, 1888, he goes on to say :

" That the amount of the compensation fixed shall remain in the possession of the Government of the Province as a special deposit until the Pope has ratified the said settlement, and made known his wishes respecting the distribution of such amount in this country."

Before I leave this stage of the transaction, I repeat that this was distinct legislation against any possible rights or claims on the part of the Pope, and that any Protestant Legislature in this country—I say more—the Parliament of the United Kingdom, if it had been called upon to pass a statute effecting property in regard to which there were foreign claimants, high or low, would have passed provision to that effect, and achivieving the result. I admit that the words which give offence to persons of various other persuations throughout Canada and make distinct reference to the Pope, might not have appeared in the preamble of an Act of the United Kingdom I admit that it would have been in better taste, in view of the great difference of opinion which exists in this country on matters of that kind, if that language had not appeared in the Act, and if the same result had been obtained, as the First Minister of Quebec says it might have been, in a different way ; but the result, whatever may be the form of words used, is a proper result, guarding all the rights of the Province until everyone else had given up his claim. And, when it comes to a question of disallowance, we are here to advise disallowance or allowance, not upon the form of words, not upon the question of the drafts man's taste, but according to what we believe was the true meaning and intent of the Act itself. Now, let me again before I leave the subject of the Act, call the attention of the House to the fact that all the argument which has been made with regard to the necessity for disallowance is based on objections to the preamble of the Act. In the history of disallowance in this country, in the history of disallowance of our own statutes in the mother country—and we know that scores of them were disallowed—the records will be searched in vain to find on which was disallowed because the preamble was not agreeable to anybody. I do not pretend to dispute the statement of my hon. friend from Muskoka, (Mr. O'Brien ) that the preamble is a part of the Act. So it is title a part of the Act, and so are the head-notes of sections ; but has anyone ever heard of a Government being ask to disallow an Act because they did not like the wording of the title or of the head notes ? The preamble is understood to be a part of the Act, for the purpose of interpreting the Act, but there is nothing in this Act for which interpretation is needed, and I distinguish, in referring to this, the most trivial and technical objection which could be taken to a statute, between those parts of the preamble which assert that certain correspondence has passed, such as this between the Premier and the cardinal at Rome, and those preambles which recite certain agreements which the statute validates. Who can doubt that nine-tenths of the agitation, and nine-tenths of the trouble, in reference to this measure have arisen from the fact that in March, 1888, there came from Rome a telegram stating that the Pope allowed the Government to retain the proceeds of the sale of the Jesuits' estates as a special deposit, forgetting that this was a part of other negotiations, which gave it an inoffensive meaning. Yes, nine-tenths of the agitation for disallowance has arisen from the Act that that telegram came from Rome and that this Act asserts that such a telegram did come, although within the four corners of the Act there is not a word based upon that telegram; and although all the statute does is to ratify and confirm an agreement between Father Turgeon and the Government of Quebec—the terms of which were that $400,000 should be paid as between the two litigants, and that, before any money should be within the power of the Lieutenant Governor of Quebec to dispose of, the two litigants should give up any claim whatsoever on the estates— I assert, without fear of contradiction among people who will consider this matter in a calm and business-like way, that that part of the preamble, which is the only part relevant to the purpose of the Act itself, is utterly harmless entirely business-like, free from the slightest suspicion of derogating from any right of Her Majesty, and from the slightest suspicion of infringement of the Constitution. Now, it is said, and the House will remember with what gravity, and force, and eloquence it was urged upon the House this afternoon, that this statute denies the supremacy of the Queen. I have read to you all the passages which refer in the slightest degree to any person outside of Her Majesty's dominions. I have stated the facts, in regard to the position of this property, the negotiations which were had in regard to it, and I will leave it to the dispassionate judgment of the House, or of any man, Catholic or Protestant, in this country whether the Act, in the slightest degree, considered in the light of the surrounding circumstances, affects in any way the authority or the supremacy of Her Majesty spiritual or temporal. Let me ask : What rights Her Majesty had in this property— as the spiritual or as the temporal sovereign ? Absolutely none whatever—absolutely none whatever, excepting that she stood as the trustee for the Province of Quebec; Her own personal rights were not affected, her sovereign rights were not affected. These were no part of Her Majesty's domain, they were no part of Her Majesty's revenue. If they were, under this Act all sold and turned into money to-morrow, not one dollar will ever pass into Her Majesty's Treasury, public or private, not one dollar will ever be disposed of under the advice of Her Majesty's Ministers. Her Majesty, with regard to those lands, had not interest, either as the spiritual or the temporal sovereign. Let me ask then in what particular that Act derogates from the authority of Her Majesty as head of her church, or as head of any religion in the British Empire ? None whatever. It is purely a question of temporal concern, purely of the public domain of the Province of Quebec. My hon. friend from Victoria (Mr. Barron) said last night that it derogated from her authority, inasmuch as it placed a portion of the public money in Quebec at the disposal of a foreigner. It does not, I submit, place the public money of the Province of Quebec at the disposal of a foreigner ; it sets aside a sum of money for the extinguishment of a claim upon the public property of Quebec, and then calls upon those which are litigants in regard to it to abide by the decision of their arbitrator in the matter. When that $400,000 shall have been paid from the Treasury of the Province of Quebec, Her Majesty has not the slightest right or interest with regard to the distribution of it In the ordinary course it would be paid to one of the claimants on the property ; but as there happen to be two it is paid into the hands, or held subject to the order of the person who has to settle the disputes between them. By what right can it be claimed that Her Majesty, or that her Government, either in England or the Province of Quebec, has a right to distribute a single dollar of that money ? Surely the rights of the Crown and of the Province end when the Government there is able to say : " We have received the deed of all these outstanding claims for which we consent to pay the money," and to contend after that there is any royal or legislative right to control the subdivision of the money, would be like saying that after a grant of public lands had passed under the great seal, the Province had a right to say who should have interest in the land for all time to come. Now, I would be content if so much had not been said upon this subject as to mislead the judgment of hundreds of persons in this country, whose judgment upon any public question is well worth having—I would be content to rest the case there, and to say that no right of Her Majesty either as a temporal or a spiritual power, is in the least degree involved ; but when we are taken so far afield upon the question as to go back into the legislation of 300 years ago, when we are asked to apply to the question the Supremacy Act, which could not have the slightest bearing upon it, even if it be in force in the Province of Quebec, I feel bound to follow out that argument to some extent for the purpose of showing how unreasonable the demand is that, under the British North America Act, and in this day of colonial rights and of self government the federal authority in Canada, should undertake to control the legislation of one of its Provinces, according to the coercive legislation which used to exist in the mother country 300 years ago. I have reminded the House what privileges were, even as regards the Act of Supremacy, ceded to the people of Quebec by the Terms of Capitulation, by the terms of the treaty and by the terms of the Quebec Act. I have shown that absolute freedom of worship was extended by the Treaty of Paris and by the Quebec Act ; I have shown the House, I think, what is the meaning of the reservation as to the law of Great Britain as regards religion. Sir, in the year 1765, the law officers of the Crown made this statement on their responsibility to the Government :

"Her Majesty's Roman Catholic subjects residing in the countries in America ceded to Her Majesty by the Treaty of Paris are not subject, in the colonies, to the incapacities, deprivation of rights and penalties to which the Roman Catholic subjects in the Kingdom are subject."

The First Minister of that country, Lord North, then said the same thing in debate, a brief extract of which I will read to you :

"It has been the opinion of very many able lawyers that the best way to establish the happiness of the inhabitants is to give them their own laws, as far as relates to their own possessions. Their possessions were marked out to them at the time of the treaty; to give them those possessions without giving them laws to maintain those possessions would not be very wise. As to the free exercise of their religion, it likewise is no more than what is confirmed to them by treaty, as far as the laws of Great Britain can confirm it. Now, there is no doubt that the laws of Great Britain do permit the very full and free exercise of any religion different from that to the Church of England, in any of the colonies; therefore, I apprehend that we ought not to extend them to Canada."

Well, Sir, let us not, in dealing with this question of supremacy, be more restrictive on the people of our own country in favor of the authority of the souvereign, whom we all revere and whose powers and prerogatives we all wish to maintain, than the sovereigns of Great Britain have been themselves. What has been their action in respect to this question of the supremacy ? Let me read to you a passage in Lord Thurlow's statement in the debates of 1774 :

"I stated in the beginning that it did not affect to relate to Canada ; but I said that the capitulation did reserve all their effects, movable and immovable. But even if it were otherwise, is it to be supposed that the tithes would accrue to the King ? The tithe is collateral to the land, not sunk in it. To give the right to it is giving to the secular body as well as the regular clergy all they were in possession of before. It was always in my opinion an established fact, that the clergy (in Canada) were entitled to tithes though they might not have use for them." (Debates, 1774, page 71).

So that the people in the Province of Quebec, who are said to-day to be under the provisions of a Supremacy Act so severe, that they cannot recognize the superiority of a foreign bishop, were, in 1774, by Her Majesty's Attorney General, declared to be subject to their own laws so far that their clergy were entitled to collect tithes from the people, although perhaps not by authority of law. Well, seventy-six years ago, by a solemn Act of State, the Roman Catholic Bishop of Quebec was recognized by the Governor of the Province under royal instructions. We are told that the Act of Supremacy was in force; and yet that man was a bishop simply by the superiority of the first bishop of is church. He was a bishop because he had received from Rome the bulls which, under the statutes of Queen Elizabeth, it was high treason to bring into the country at all. That was the way in which the religious restrictions of the people of this country were treated upwards of seventy-five years ago by the Imperial authorities; but after the lapse of three-quarters of a century we are to be wiser and we are to enforce against a great section of our free people legislation reserving rights to the Crown which the Crown deliberately chose to ignore seventy-six years ago. In 1817 the Roman Catholic Bishop of Quebec received a mandamus, calling him as a bishop to the Legislative Council of the Province. He held his see by the will and under the bull of his superior bishop, and he was called by virtue of his office to be one of the rulers of the Province of Quebec. In 1839 Governor Colborne issued letters patent to incorparate the Roman Catholic Bishop of Quebec and all his successors, whomsoever they might be, appointed by the foreign superior and under bulls, which according to the legislation that these hon. gentlemen ask us to apply to Quebec to-day, it would be high treason to introduce into the country. In 1838 a Roman Catholic college was incorporated in the Province of Prince Edward Island, and the question was submitted to the law officers of the Crown fifty years ago, whether it was a violation of the supremacy of the Crown. It was a violation of the supremacy of the Crown fifty times over if anything within this Act of Quebec is a violation of that supremacy. But the law officers of the Crown advised that it was within the competency of the local powers as they then existed, and that it was no derogation of the Act of Supremacy, if that Act could be held to apply to that Province. But since that period, since the period when the officers in this country charged with the maintenance of the right of the Crown began to be infinitely less restrictive than we are asked to be to-day, three-quarters of a century later, what a change as taken place in the colonies of British North America. We have been placed upon a different footing. We have received free institutions, we have received legislative powers, and by the voice of our Sovereign, by the voice of Her Parliament, by the policy of Her Ministers, as expressed in every act of State, it has been declared that, subject only to those matters which are of Imperial concern, we shall be as fully clothed with the rights of self-governing freemen in every part of Canada as are the subjects in the heart of England. Yet we are told now that we are under, not only the restrictive legislation of 300 years ago, but that no Legislature of Canada has power to repeal any such restrictive legislation, and that any restrictive legislation of that kind is beyond the competency of a Provincial Legislature. Why, we heard last night the singular statement that a Provincial Legislature has only a derived or delegated authority. I deny that statement as explicitly as it is courteous to deny any statement made by any hon. member of this House. I go further and I say that, within the limits of its authority and subject only to the power of disallowance, a Provincial Legislature is as absolute as is the Imperial Parliament itself. The Imperial Parliament is not restricted as to the subjects over which it can legislate, the Provincial Legislatures are restricted in regard to the subjects on which they can legislate, but in legislating upon these subjects a Provincial Legislature has all the rights which it is possible for the Imperial Parliament to confer. I say more : I say that a Provincial Legislature, legislating upon subjects which are given to it by the British North America Act, has the power to repeal an Imperial statute prior to the British North America Act affecting those subjects. It has been urged upon the House these two days that we had no power, and that the Act of 28 and 29 Victoria, called the Colonial Enactments Act, provided that no statute of a colony should have force as against an Imperial statute. But after the statute of 28 and 29 Victoria, the British North America Act was passed, and it gives us, as I have said, a division of powers between the two bodies, but it gives the two bodies in legislating in their respective spheres all the powers that the Imperial Legislature possessed. The hon. member for Victoria (Mr. Barron) was misled, I think, last night in his reference to the British North America Act. It is true that the British North America Act seems to contain in the 129th section a reservation in that behalf; it reads :

"Except as otherwise by this Act all law in force in Canada, Nova Scotia and New Brunswick at the union and all courts of civil and criminal jurisdiction and all legal commissions, powers and authorities and all officers, judicial, administrative and ministerial existing therein at the Union, shall continue in Ontario, Quebec, Nova Scotia and New Brunswick respectively, as if the Union had not been made ; subject nevertheless (except with respect to such as are enacted by or exist under Acts of the Parliament of Great Britain or of the Parliament of the United Kingdom of Great Britain and Ireland) to be repealed, abolished or altered by the Parliament of Canada or by the Legislature of the respective Provinces according to the authority of the Parliament or of that Legislature under this Act."

The hon gentleman read it as being a restriction by the British North America Act against our repealing or modifying an Imperial statute relating to any subject under our control. I do not so regard it. I regard it as containing neither a grant of power nor a restriction as to our legislating upon Imperial statutes. But since that Act was passed, in which the Imperial Parliament virtually said : "We say nothing as to Imperial statutes ;" we have had three distinct decisions of the Judicial Committee of the Privy Council in regard to legislation by a Province upon a subject within its control, and declaring that the Provincial Legislature has power to repeal a statute of the Imperial Parliament. The first is the case of Harris against Davies, page 279, which was an appeal from New South Wales, and in which this was held with reference to a statute of James I, which had distinct force in that colony :

"Held that the Legislature of New South Wales had power to repeal the statute of James I, which according to its true construction placed an action for slander for words spoken, upon the same footing, as regards costs and other matters, as an action for written slander."

The statute of James I made distinct provision as to the amount of costs which the litigant could recover when he only obtained a verdict for a certain amount for slander ; the Legislature passed an Act repugnant to that and the provisions of the Colonial Enactment Act were cited. The judgment of their Lordships was delivered by Sir Barnes Peacock, who said :

"Their Lordships are of opinion that there are no sufficient grounds for reversing the judgment of the court below. Their Lordships are of opinion that the Colonial Legislature had the power to repeal the statute of James I if they thought fit, and they are also of opinion that looking at the first section of 11 Victoria, No. 13, it was the intention of the Legislature to place an action for words spoken, upon the same footing as regards costs and other matters as an action for written slander."

Mr. BARRON. Have they a statute in that colony corresponding with the British North America Act ?

Sir JOHN THOMPSON. Yes. I have examined that, and it conveys no larger grant of legislative powers than the British North America Act does to us. If the hon. gentleman will look in the same volume to the case of Powell vs. Apollo Candle Company, Limited, in which the law of New South Wales came up likewise, he will find that the conclusion which he urged as to the Colonial Legislature being a mere delegate of the Imperial Parliament was fully considered and discussed, and principally on reference to the case from Canada of Hodge vs. The Queen. The Judicial Committee said :

"Two cases have come before this board in which the powers of Colonial Legislatures have been a good deal considered, but these cases are of too late a date to have been known to the Supreme Court when their judgment was delivered. The first was the case of Regina vs. Burah (1), in which the question was whether a section of an Indian Act conferring upon the Lieutenant Governor of Bengal the power to determine whether the Act, or any part of it, should be applied to a certain district, was or was not *ultra vires*. In the judgment of this board, given by the Lord Chancellor, the legislation is declared to be *intra vires*, and the Lord Chancellor lays down the general law in these terms : 'The Indian Legislature has powers expressly limited 'by the Act of the Imperial Parliament which created it, and it can of course do nothing beyond the limits which circumscribe these powers. But when acting within those limits, it is not in any sense an agent or delegate of the Imperial Parliament, but has, and was intended to have, plenary powers of legislation as large, and of the same nature, as those of Parliament itself.' The same doctrine has been laid down in a later case of Hodge *vs*. The Queen (2) where the question arose whether the Legislature of Ontario had or had not the power of entrusting to a local authority — board of commissioners—the power of enacting regulations with respect to their Liquor License Act of 1877, of creating offences for the breach of those regulations,and annexing penalties thereto.Their lordships held that they had that power. It was argued then, as it has been argued to-day, that the Local Legislature is in the nature of an agent or delegate, and, on the principle *delegatus non potest delegare*, the Local Legislature must exercise all its functions itself, and can delegate or entrust none of them to other persons or parties. But the judgment, after reciting that such had been the contention, goes on to say : ' It appears to their lordships, however, that the objection thus raised by the appellants is founded on an entire misconception of the true character and position of the Provincial Legislatures. They are 'in no sense delegates of or acting under any mandate from the Imperial Parliament. When the British North America Act enacted that there should be a Legislature for Ontario, and that its Legislative Assembly should have exclusive authority to make laws for the Province and for provincial purposes in relation to the matters enumerated in section 92, it conferred powers, not in any sense to be exercised by delegation from or as agents of the Imperial Parliament, but authority as plenary and as ample within the limits prescribed by section 92, as the Imperial Parliament in the plenitude of its power possessed or could bestow. Within these limits of subjects and areas the Local Legislature is supreme and has the same authority as the Imperial Parliament."

(1) 3 App. Cas., 889. (2) 9 App. Cases, 117.

Well, Sir, later on we had the not forgotten case of the Queen against Riel before the Privy Council in which this state of affairs was shown. There had been three Imperial statutes passed expressly for the regulation of the trial of offences in Rupert's Land, now known as the North-West Territories. The statutes of Canada contained provisions repugnant to those, and on the appeal to the Privy Council it was decided that the Parliament of Canada had the power to pass legislation changing those statutes and repealing them if necessary. I infer from this that in touching on a question of religious liberty, which is surely a civil right of the people of the Province, the Provincial Legislature is untrammelled in the exercise of its power by the Imperial legislation of centuries ago. I say, therefore, that, even though it can be contended that this statute was in any degree a derogation from the restriction of the Supremacy Act—from the oppressive restrictions of the Supremacy Act and if it should be seriously decided that the Supremacy Act— prevails in British North America, that we have no freedom of religion, that no man has a right to dissent from the Church of England, that no man has a right to exercise the Catholic religion, that no man has a right to exercise submission to a superior,whether that superior be the president of a conference, the moderator of an assembly, or the first bishop of his church, then, I say, the first duty of this House, the first duty of every Legislature in the Provinces of Canada, would be to declare that we have in this 19th century the rights of freemen and the rights of religious liberty according to our consciences, and to say that that Act, 300 years old, and for 200 years and upwards ignored in the United Kingdom, shall not restrict the people of these Provinces in their right of belief, and freedom of worship and their right under the British North America Act to have a constitution similar in form to that which our fellow subjects in the United Kingdom enjoy. Let me see how far the Provinces, from time to time, in the exercise of their right of self-government conferred upon them, have insisted on that policy, and have insisted upon that right with the full recognition of the Imperial authorities, for let it be remembered that before 1867 our statutes had to go home and be revised by the Office under the advice of the Crown officers. Why, Sir, in the year 1850 the Roman Catholic bishops in the Province of Upper Canada were incorporated, and their successors from time to time canonically appointed. "Their successors." our friend from Simcoe will tell us, " oh, yes, but not successors recognising any authority from a foreign superior." Read the statute, and I will give up the argument if it does not say:

"In communion with the Church of Rome."

Therefore, in 1850, the Legislature of Upper Canada incorporated those bishops and gave them corporate powers, on the one condition which, according to the hon. member for Simcoe, it is unconstitutional we should allow in this country at all, namely, that they should be in communion with the See of Rome. In 1854, Sir, the same thing was done for all the bishops for all time to come in Lower Canada; and an Act for the division of the parishes of that Province for the purposes of public worship, under the supervision of those bishops, was authorized by the Province. In 1862 all the bishops of the Province of New Brunswick for all time to come were incorporated. You can look at the statutes of every Parliament in British America, and you will find precisely the same legislation ; and the main of those corporate powers is that those who are to exercise them shall be bishops in communion with the Church of Rome. We have heard to-night, and we heard last night, about the laches of the people, who we are told, were not to be procluded, not having objected to the Jesuit's Incorporation Act of 1887, from objecting to it now. Perhaps not. We were told that a great evil had been done, that a great class of public sinners in the country had been given powers of incorporation in 1887, and that it was not too late to rise in indignant protest. We were told that a people does not lose its right to object to provisions which are repugnant to an English statute of 300 years ago, which they contend and we deny, has any force, or ought to have any force, in this country, in regard to people of other religious beliefs at any rate. It is perhaps not too late. But they are not only a year behind the time ; they are 37 years behind the time, because 37 years ago the Parliament of Canada incorporated a body of these Jesuits, for the actuel purpose of teaching what the hon. member for North Simcoe calls their wicked tenets, in the Province of Quebec. In 1852, Sir, St. Mary's College, in the city of Montreal, to be taught by Jesuits, and the corporators of which were Jesuits, was incorporated by the Legislature of Canada; and in turning to the division list on that Act, as one of my hon. colleagues did last night, he showed me that 29 Protestants and 27 Catholics voted for it, and only 7 voted against it altogether in that whole Legislature. We had, Sir, 37 years ago religious toleration which would have frowned down the argument which was presented to this House this afternoon, if it had been clothed in ten times the ability and force with which we saw it paraded before the House to day. Then, in 1868, a college for the same purpose at Sault au Recollet, in the Province of Quebec, was incorporated ; and I ask members on both sides of this question, whether, down to a few weeks ago we have ever heard any remonstrance againts the powers which were conferred on those bodies, or whether any section of the people of this country, or any one, high or low, of one denomination or another—and I speak of those who have been appealing to public opinion on this question from the pulpits with the profoundest respect—has ever objected to the teachings of those institutions, or uttered any reproach with regard to their conduct in this country, with regard to their loyalty, or with regard to the effects of their instruction or example on the youth of this country. Again addressing myself to the argument that it is not necessary for us in British North America to be more restrictive as regards the rights and powers of the Crown than the Crown has been in England, let me call the attention of the House to the fact that 80 years ago, in the heart of England, a magnificent institution of learning was placed under the control of this same order, in which they have been carrying on, every year since, the education of hundreds of English youths, and that that institution at Stoneyhurst has had added to it other like institutions all over England. Are we to say that the Act in Great Britain, or that the prohibitory legislation with regard to the Jesuit Order, which is not to be applied in Great Britain, must be applied to one section of the people in British North America, and applied under our federal system by the arbitrary power of disallowance with which His Excellency is entrusted? I might well reiterate, but I will not do further than refer to the eloquent and forcible argument which you, Sir (Mr. Colby), addressed to the House last night, in which you pointed out that we had lived to too late an age for any section of the people of this country to be willing to live under a government by which that kind of legislation would be applied. In the exercise of the immense powers, limited though the range of subjects may be, which are given to the Provincial Legislatures, there is no Provincial Legislature in Canada, which, legislating upon the subject of the civil and religious liberties of its people, would consent to have its powers curtailed by the Federal Government taking from the wall a rusty weapon which had hung idly there for 200 years. I will spare the patience of the House and not do what I intended to do, namely, quote legislation still in force with regard to all Her Majesty's domain, but a dead letter for scores of years—legislation which, if it were in force would put one-third of the people of this city into prison to morrow, for the offence of heresy, the offence of nonconformity, the offence of not taking the sacrament, or for daring to profess the belief of Unitarians, some of these statutes being still actually unrepealed. But what is the use? The greatest writer on the subject of criminal law which the century has produced, Sir Fitzjames Stephens, has put the story well in two paragraphs, and his authority upon it will not be denied; the acceptability of his sentiments with regard to the United Kingdom will not be questioned; and he says this:

"For 200 years Government has been carried on—"

And he is speaking of government in the United Kingdom—

—"without prejudice to differences of opinon which in previous times were regarded as altogether fundamental."

For the last 200 years in England, I venture to say, government could not have been carried on if it had not been by practically ignoring legislation which previously was levelled at differences of opinion which were considered altogether fundamental. At that time a man who did not conform to the religion of his neighbors and the religion of the law was put out of the pale of the law altogether and treated as a public criminal. A great body of that legislation has never been repealed to this day; a great body of it is just as much in force in the Dominion of Canada against our freedom of opinion, against our freedom of worships, as the statutes which have been invoked yesterday and to-day; and yet when we read this lesson that for 200 years it has only been possible to carry on government in England by ignoring those differences of opinion which used to be aimed at by the criminal law and were considered as fundamental, we are, in this country, to look still at the old fundamental differences and curtail our liberties by the strong arm of the federal authority; and, in the exercise of federal power, we are to curtail the rights of our Legislatures to infringe upon, impugn, or make any enactment repugnant to this legislation which has been buried under the weight of public opinion for upward of two centuries. Well, I forgot to say, and I will digress from my argument to mention it, that, in 1871, by a statute of the Province of Quebec, there was an Act passed incorporating the whole Society of Jesus in the Province. The order was precisely the same society which was incorporated by the Act of 1887, and the only difference is the difference of legislative provisions as to the method of working their incorporation. From 1871 to 1887, no word of objection was raised in any part of the country to that incorporation, as to its constitutionality or effect, but because in 1889 we did not advise disallowance of an Act of precisely the same kind, we are to fall under the censure of this House. I have referred to the statement of Sir Fitzjames Stephens as to the value of this legislation to England, and I will cite another passage which, for its terseness and its force, is worthy the attention of hon. gentlemen. He says, referring to the legislation against the Jesuits in the year of George IV:

" These powers, I believe have been considered, ever since they were passed, as an absolutely dead letter."

Before I close my argument, I must address myself for a moment to a view which was put forward by the hon. member for Simcoe (Mr. McCarthy) as regard the effect of the statute on the fund for higher education in the Province of Quebec. He put forward as a reason why this Act should be disallowed, if no other reason existed, that it was a breach of trust, and that it misapplied, or, to use his own words, misappropriated the property which it related to. I think the hon. member for Quebec (Mr. Langelier) was quite right in challenging him to read any part of the Act which sustained his argument, and the House observed that he did not respond to the challenge. Let me remind the House at the outset that, in regard to the sale of the property, the statute gives the Province no greater power than it had before. It is a statute as its title implies, for the settlement of the Jesuit claims. But the Province of Quebec, before that, had, under its existing legislation, ample power of sale, and the Act makes no provision different from that which did exist as to what is to be done with the property or the money. One would suppose, listening to the argument of the hon. member for Simcoe (Mr. McCarthy) although he did not state it in so many words, there was a provision in the Act which declared that that trust should no longer apply to the property, that it might go into the consolidated revenue and be disposed of as the Government pleased. Not so. The last clause of the Act provides that when these properties are sold, they are to be subject to the disposition of the Legislature. Are we to infer and to advise disallowance on the ground of that inference, that the Legislature of the Province is going to betray its trust with regard to any property, when it has never made that declaration or never sought power to desert the trust ? I will tell the House what is the absolute fact on this point: That the minority in the Province of Quebec, that those interested in higher education, that those interested in any way in the execution of the trust, have not suffered one whit or jot by the passage of the Act. The fact has been that the revenue from those estates has been paid from year to year into the consolidated revenue fund and not into the fund for higher education. The fact is likewise that the proceeds of large portions of that property which have already been sold have, from year to year, been placed to the credit of the consolidated revenue, and spent for the general purpose of the Province. From year to year, the Provincial Legislature, not out of the revenues of the Jesuits' estates or the proceeds of the Jesuits' estates, which were too small for that purpose, but out of its consolidated revenue, has made ample provision for the higher education of the Province; and after the argument made this afternoon about the way in which the minority would be prejudiced, and the supineness of the minority in submitting, as it was said they would be willing to submit, to this legislation, and the breach of trust, which was apparent on the Act itself, in the division of the only fund that exists for the higher education of the Province, the House will be surprised to learn that from year to year I speak in general terms —the allowance in the Province of Quebec for the higher education made out of the consolidated revenue fund has been, on an average, more than three times the annual proceeds of the Jesuits' estates. Not a single school, high or low, in the Province of Quebec, has been sustained from those estates so far, because the fund was utterly insufficient. Ample provision was made out of the consolidated revenue fund, and yet we are told that when these estates disappear and go into the market, they go free from any trust, and that neither the majority nor the minority will have any security for higher education in the Province. It is sufficient for me to have shown the House that the Act purports to do nothing of the kind, that it sanctions nothing of the kind; but I think the argument has irresistible force when I show that these properties have not been considered a security for these purposes at all. The hon. member for Simcoe (Mr. McCarthy) challenged the propriety of my report upon this Act, when, after favoring the House with his long and interesting theological discourse, and after having excited to some extent the feelings and sympathy of the House, he declared that I had presented that statute to His Excellency as of no more importance than the eleven others accompanying it, which I had recommended should be left to their operation. Now, upon the importance or unimportance of the statutes it is not necessary for me to advise His Excellency, but I take the responsibility of having advised His Excellency that that Act was no less within the powers of the Legislature of Quebec than the other eleven which accompanied it. And when I have reminded the hon. gentleman that it is not a question of trust, that there is no diversion of trust by the authority of that Act, and that these estates have not been the source from which higher education has been supported, I think he will be almost inclined to agree with me that I was right after all in saying this was a fiscal matter within the control of the Province. But this is not the first time, although it is the first time this excitement has been raised with regard to it, that this society, who have been spoken of so severely in this debate, have been dealt with by the Province of Quebec. I have in my possession a list extending back over fifteen years of appropriations in the Supply Bills made by the Legislature of Quebec to support the higher education carried on by this society within that Province, and, according to the statement we have heard this afternoon, all that has been unconstitutional, and every one of these Supply Bills ought to have been disallowed, because, forsooth, they were ignoring the distinction between Church and State. I think it is rater late to treat this question as anything other than a fiscal question, and that the difference between the Supply Bills in all those fifteen years, and the Act which is now being discussed is simply a question of degree and of amount. The principle of supporting the higher education carried on by that society in that Province has been recognized, as I have said, every year in the Supply Bill, and, yet, for the first time, because this is a larger sum which is being dealt with, and larger because it deals with the rights or claims of that society to lands, we are asked to assert a principle which we were never asked before to assert in regard to them. Now, I desire to call the attention of the House for a moment to two other branches of the argument which were presented to it this afternoon. We were told that there was a restriction in the Act as regards the expenditure of the $60,000, but that there was no restriction as regards the expenditure of the $400,000. The $60,000 has been appropriated to a body which had no claim, legally or morally, and had never asserted any as regards the title to the Jesuits' estates. They have claimed to be interested in the appropriations which are made from time to time for higher education, and rightly so, and those claims have always been considered. I am not prepared to say, whether the proportion allotted to them in this Act is right or not. That is a question upon which the hon. member for North Simcoe (Mr. McCarthy), if he had a seat in the Legislature of the Province of Quebec, might have adressed the House with great force, but for us here to discuss the appropriation of money, and the proportions in which it is appropriated by a Province would be as absurd as for us to take the Supply Bill of the Province every year, and enter into a discussion of its different appropriations. The reason why, as I presume, the restriction has been imposed in regard to the $60,000, and not in regard to the $400,000, is that the $60,000 is voted for educational purposes purely and simply, and, while the $400,000 has every prospect of being so applied, because it is voted to a body whose business it is to teach, still it is paid to them in extinction of a claim which they had made to a part of the public domain of the Province. But we were told, and this is almost the last argument used by my hon. friend from North Simcoe (Mr. McCarthy) but one to which I must advert, that the grant of money to this corporation was a church endowment which violated the principles of the separation of Church and State in this country. I pass by at this moment the position which any church occupies in this country. I do not intend to discuss how far, in any portion of the country, any church may be considered as now established; but I do say that it passes the power of ingenuity to show that the grant of money to a corporation of teachers and preachers is the endowment of a church in Canada. It is true that a church may be in part a society of preachers and teachers, but this society is not a church, and in the most illogical way in which a fallacy could be put on paper, this resolution asks the House to come to the conclusion that, because a society incorporated under a statute of the Province and employed in preaching and teaching the tenets of a certain religion receives a grant of money, that is the endowment of a church within the Province. I venture to say that there is no one in this country, who knows the facts upon which that resolution is based, and who reads that resolution, but must be surprised that it should receive the support, as it has done, of able and intelligent men in this House. Let me say to my hon. friend from Simcoe (Mr. McCarthy) that this is no more the endowment of a church, and that it is no more an interference with the separation of Church and State in this country than would be the endowment of a hospital or an orphanage er an asylum which was under the care of a religious organisation. We all cherish the principle that there should be no Church control over the State in any part of this country, but my hon. friend proposes something worse than that control. He proposes that we shall step into the domain of a Provincial Legislature, and shall say that no Provincial Legislature shall have the power to vote any money to any institution if it partakes of a religious character. It may profess any other kind of principle. It may profess any objectionable principle, and it is lawful to endow it, but, if it professes the Christian character, it is, forsooth, unconstitutional to allow such an Act to go into operation. I listened to the remarks which the hon. member for Simcoe (Mr. McCarthy) addressed to the House on the third branch of his argument, as to the objectionable teachings of this society with some surprise, though I do not intend to-night to challenge his ample liberty to differ from me as to the correctness and propriety of those observations. I hoped that, in this discussion, he and those who will vote with him will not prove themselves any less friends of religious liberty then they have professed to be in the past, but I assume—I think I have a right to assume—that, when the case of the gentlemen who are opposed to the allowance of this Act is placed in the hands of an hon. member who is so able and so skilled in argument as he, we are not to be condemned for not asking His Excellency to disallow this Act, unless the reasons which he urged with such great force this afternoon are reasons which I could use in addressing His Excellency on the subject. Surely I have a right to assume that the hon. gentleman has put forward the best case he could, and I am not to be condemned unless I could avail myself of his reasons in asking His Excellency to disallow the Act. If I could picture myself going to His Excellency and asking for the disallowance of this Act, for the reasons which the hon. gentleman (Mr. McCarthy) presented in the latter part of his address, I would imagine myself just fit to be expelled from His Excellency's presence as quickly as possible. What would be the reasons which I should urge ? I am not finding fault now with the strictures that the hon. gentleman made in regard to the society, but, forsooth, I am to go to His Excellency and ask him to disallow this Act because, in the year 1874, a *Quarterly Review* published an article denouncing the Jesuit Society and its teachings. Am I not right in taking the argument and the evidence which he produces to-day as the argument and the evidence which I should produce to His Excellency ? If I were to go to His Excellency and say that the *Quarterly Review*, published in 1874, denounced in language as strong as could be the tenets and teachings of these people, His Excellency might ask me a number of perplexing questions, one of which was levelled at the hon. member for North Simcoe this afternoon without much profit to him. Let me suppose that His Excellency asked me : " Mr. Minister of Justice, who is the author ? " My answer would have to be—surely I cannot do better than take the answer of the hon. member for Simcoe—my answer would have to be: " I really do not know who is the author; but, your Excellency, I am sure that nothing would be published in the *Review* which would not stand criticism." I am afraid that His Excellency might not be satisfied with that answer, and that he might put me another rather more puzzling question: " Mr. Minister of Justice, are you aware that these able and eloquent, but anonymous, publications in that *Review* have been refuted time and again until the slanderers have been worn threadbare ? " I would ask my hon. friend from Simcoe what I should answer to that question ?

MR. McCARTHY. Refuted where ?

Sir JOHN THOMPSON. I would like to ask him, has he ever read the answers to them ? I would like to ask him, has he ever sought the answers to them ? Because these are questions which His Excellency may ask me when I go to him with this advice. The hon. member asks me, where ? Well, I tell him, in the first place, in publications so voluminous that I shall have to give him a catalogue of them ; but in order to be precise, and not to be suspected of evading the question, I will tell him that in an English publication called the *Month*, step by step, as every one of these articles came out, the answer and the refutation came out, and that in the opinion of a great many people, these men were able to refute the articles triumphantly. I am not to pass judgment as to whether they were successful or othe wise, I have no right to speak my own opinions here, I am speaking for those with whom I am acting in concert. His Excellency might ask me whether having read these articles what conclusion I had come to as to the balance of arguments *pro* and *con*. If he did so, I should be unable to find, in the course of that admirable three hours interesting theological discussion which we had to-day, a single hint as to my reply, and having read the attack in the *Review*, and the replies which were made, answer as I have done. I should have to tell His Excellency that unless he were to be guided by the opinion of a partisan on one side or the other, the best thing he could do would be to leave it either to his own conscience or to that conscience which the Constitution has provided for dealing with the subject—the conscience of the Legislature of the Province which had to deal with it. If His Excellency were to ask me : " Sir, in advising disallowance on the authority of the *Quarterly Review*,"— which I am afraid to the Colonial Office would not be a sound authority, would not be a satisfactory constitutional authority—" have you verified the quotations for yourself ? " I ask the hon. member for Simcoe what I should answer then ? What answer could he give to the House if I asked him now, whether he has verified a single one of those quotations—and I tell him that on the verity of the quotations half the controversy has turned. I tell him that it is claimed by those who have undertaken—I do not say they have succeeded—to refute them, that the tenets which they are accuse of teaching, they have not taught; that the passages put forward as proofs were problems—doubtful cases, cases to distinguish between that which is the sin, which the confessor has to deal with, and that which, though against public morals or public propriety, the confessor has not to deal with. In dealing with casuistry, and when dealing with moral theology, some of the old writers quoted have suggested difficulties, and problems, and questions. and have given advice to confessors upon such subjects; but they have not put forward the tenets as to be taught to the youth of the country. I might be told by His Excellency that I might find in the studies of my own profession a similar case; that I might find the leading writers in my own profession, eminent men, stating that things which we recognize from day to day as hideous wrongs, are not offences against the criminal law of the country—some of them I could name, but which it would be almost indecent to name in a mixed assembly. And, Sir, could it be said of these writers who declared that such was the law, that these things, however abominable they may be, however contrary to public morals, are not against the law—could it be said that these eminent writers like Sir Fitzjames Stephens and others are teaching that such things are lawful and ought to be done in the country, and are putting them before the youth of the country as things that are right? Is there not a broad distinction between the two ideas? If the hon. member for North Simcoe had read the answers which have been made to the publications, which he quoted he would not have dared, as he is an honorable man, to have presented to the House the argument that he made this afternoon, without, at least, presented the other side of it. If I were to advise His Excellency to disallow this Bill because of the objectionable teachings of this body, His Excellency might fairly say to me: "The Legislature of the united Provinces of Canada, 37 years ago, erected the society into a corporation to hold lands and to teach the youth of the country. Now, in looking over that 37 years of record, can you point me to one of the teachers or one of the taught who has been disloyal to his country? Has anyone been able to say: "This or that father has taught me immorality, this or that man is guilty of immorality in his teaching, this or that tenet was objectionable?" What reply should I have to give him? Well, Sir, if His Excellency went on and reminded me that the rules and constitutions of that order have been published for 45 years, and that before giving him advice of that kind I ought to be able to put my hand upon the passages of the rules and constitutions of that order which are objectionable on the grounds of public policy, I am afraid I should be unable to do so to an extent to justify the disallowance of this Act, and I am afraid I should not find in the speech of the hon. member for Simcoe much comfort in that respect. If I were to advise His Excellency to disallow the Act on the ground of the expulsion of the Huguenots, the Revocation of the Edict of Nantes, the Franco-German war, the expulsion from France in 1818, the expulsion from other countries, I am afraid His Excellency might tell me that all the statements of fact were disputed,and that he might read me a lesson in ancient and modern history of which one of the deductions could be that in some of these countries, to say that the court was opposed to the Protestant reformers, was no discredit to either the Protestant reformers or to the Jesuits. I do not think, Sir, that I need dwell on that bra.ch of the subject any longer. I think that whenever we touch these delicate and difficult questions which are in any way connected with the sentiments of religion, or of race, or of education, there are two principles which it is absolutely necessary to maintain, for the sake of the living together of the different members of this Confederation, for the sake of the preservation of the federal power, for the sake of the good-will, and kindly charity of all our people towards each other and for the sake of the prospects of making a nation, as we can only do by living in harmony and ignoring those differences which used to be considered fundamental—these two principles surely must prevail, that as regards theological questions the State must have nothing to do with them, and that as regards the control which the federal power can exercise over Provincial Legislatures in matter touching the freedom of its people, the religion of its people, the appropriations of its people or the sentiments of its people, no section of this country, whether it be the great Province of Quebec or the humblest and smallest Province of this country, can be governed on the fashion of 300 years ago.

Mr. McNEILL. (Bruce N. Riding.)

I am very reluctant to prolong this debate, but I feel that it would not be right if I did not say a word in explanation of the vote which I shall give. I repeat that I do not wish to prolong this debate, and have but a very few words to say, and in what I do say I hope I shall endeavor to say not one word that can add bitterness to the debate. We are here differing in race and differing in religion. We cannot see eye to eye in all things; we must differ and differ widely in our views upon many subjects: that is inevitable. But if we mean to make this country, this Canada of ours, a great and prosperous nation we must first endeavor as far as in us lies to bear and forbear with one another and endeavor to act together as an united people. And, therefore, it was that I listened with a great deal of gratification to the speech of the hon. member for Stanstead (Mr. Colby) last night when he assured us of the kindly consideration with which our Roman Catholic friends, in the Province of Quebec, treated our Protestant friends there. I believe that speech going abroad in this country will do an immense amount of good. I believe it will remove a great many misconceptions, I believe it will cause a warmer feeling ot friendship to exist between our Protestant friends and our Roman Catholic friends throughout this Dominion, and that, I think, will be a matter of incalculable benefit to this Dominion. We have no quarrel with our Roman Catholic friends, and, therefore, I was, I must say, surprised at the extraordinary statement made by the hon. member for Lincoln (Mr. Rykert) last night when he said that those members who were discharging in this House a very onerous and painful duty desired to prevent their Roman Catholic fellow-countrymen exercising their religion in this country, and in point of fact that they almost desired to drive them out of the land. That statement was not altogether what I would have expected from my hon. friend, and I think it was a statement hardly worthy of him.

Mr. RYKERT. I made no such statement, you cannot show it.

Mr. McNEILL. I am glad to find from what the hon. gentleman says that I misconceived him. I listened with a great deal of attention and I understood that was what he said, but I am only too glad to learn that that is not what he intended to say.

Mr. RYKERT. I did not say it.

Mr. McNEILL. If the opposition on our part to the endowment of the Jesuit Order be of any such character, if it be an attack upon the Roman Catholic faith and an attack upon our Roman Catholic friends in any shape and form, as I certainly think my hon. friend will admit he said it was, I would suppose that opposition to the incorporation of that body would be equally an attack upon the Roman Catholic religion and upon our Roman Catholic friends. But if that be the case, what are we to say of the conduct of His Eminence Cardinal Taschereau and the six bishops and archbishops of the Province of Quebec, who joined with him only the other day so to speak, in 1887, in petitioning the Legislature against the incorporation of this body. They, surely, are not to be looked upon as enemies of the Roman Catholic religion; they, surely, are not to be looked upon as persons outside of the pale of the Church and as persons who desired to prevent the Roman Catholic people of this country from the due exercise of their rights and privileges. But we find that Cardinal Taschereau and six bishops and archbishops of the Roman Catholic Church did petition the Legislature of Quebec not to incorporate the Jesuit Order. If that be the case, and it is a fact which cannot be gain-said, I think these statements which have been made with respect to the course of my hon. friends who have felt it necessary to support the amendment, these accusations of intolerance against them, because they object to the further strengthening of the power of that body in this country, are somewhat far fetched. I do think that when the Minister of Justice, in the very able, the magnificent speech which he has just addressed to the House was dealing with this question, it would have been a little more seemly had he refrained from the statements in which he indulged in the latter part of his speech, and in which he seemed to assert that those who objected to the endowment of the Jesuit Order desired to have recourse to the prosecutions of the middle ages. The argument which my hon. friend the member for North Simcoe (Mr. McCarthy), addressed with regard to the propriety of disallowing this Act, I do not speak of the legal argument, but I refer to the arguments which he presented in reference to the effect which the endowment of this body inflicted on the Dominion, and which were not founded on a reference to an article in the *Quarterly Review*, but included the statement that this was a society which had been found by almost every civilised state to be incompatible with the proper government of the country in which it existed—I think that this argument is one which should be met seriously, and not merely by the assertion or the implication that in every case in which those governments, Roman Catholic as well as Protestant, had found it necessary to suppress this society, the society was right and the government was wrong. I think the argument requires to be met more seriously. Now, Sir, the agitation and the excitement which has arisen in the Province of Ontario in reference to this matter is very natural. The people of Ontario have begun to feel in that Province of late years the ever increasing power of Jesuit pressure and influence. We have begun to experience in that Province some effects of the unceasing aggression which history shows to be one of the leading characteristics of those trained spiritual warriors of which we have heard so much during this debate. I give them all credit for their ability, I give them all credit for their many deeds of self sacrifice and heroism and for their learning and culture, but I beg to say that the Dominion of Canada is a Protestant country, and I think that while we give to all and desire to give to all who differ from us, the fullest rights and liberty for the exercise of their religious opinions, we have a right to remember that the Protestant majority in this country have some few rights and privileges also. I think that we have a right to expect that if the Jesuit Order find an asylum here in Canada which has been denied to them in many Catholic States, they should have at least some consideration for the religious sentiments of those who have extended this kindness towards them. But, Sir, I wish to ask what has been our experience in reference to this matter in the Province of Ontario. You cannot deal with this as a purely local question, for it is not a local question. The Jesuit Order is not confined to the Province of Quebec and because you endow the headquarters of the order there that does not make it a local matter. You cannot limit the operations of this order to the Province of Quebec, there is nothing local about it. What has been our experience in the Province of Ontario, which is not the Province of Quebec. What has been the conduct of this order of Jesuits in that Province ? We have every reason to believe that they have not scrupuled in that Province to attack our Protestant institutions and to dictate as to the education of our Protestant children. Only a few years ago we were startled to learn that a work which is one of the best known, one of the most generally admired, and one of the most beautiful compositions in the English language, a work, too, by an author who is preeminent for the purity and morality of his writings—had been, as we believe at least, at their instance, struck from the curriculum of our high schools. Only so recently as the year 1886 we find that the same influence was at work in our common public schools and that an attempt was being made and successfully made to banish from those schools that which is the very sign and symbol of the Protestant faith, the Protestant bible ; and to substitute for the book itself a collection of attenuated and mutilated extracts from it. We find, in fact, that an astute and subtle attack was being made against the very character of that book and that an attempt was being made to poison the minds of our children against it, and to represent it as a book unfitted to be placed in their hands. Now, Mr. Speaker, I would ask my Roman Catholic friends in this House and in this country, to place themselves in our position and to ask themselves whether they would not have resented such an attempt to interfere with the educational system in the Province of Quebec, and whether they would not have resented such an insidious attack upon their own religion ? I would ask them to put themselves in the place of the Protestants of Ontario, and to tell me if they would not have viewed with alarm any action on the part of the state which was calculated to strengthen the hands of a society which they believed had been in this way interfering with the education of their childere and endeavoring to subvert their religious faith. Now, Mr. Speaker, I do not wish to take up the time of the House longer. I will only say that I intend to record my vote in favor of the resolution of the hon. member for Muskoka (Mr. O'Brien), and I will do so not so much as an expression of censure upon the conduct of the Government whose general policy I support with so much pleasure and whose conduct in reference to this particular matter has been circumscribed by conditions of such deep importance to the Dominion ; but rather because I disapprove altogether of the kind of legislation which we have had under our consideration. I believe it to be improper and dangerous legislation. I believe, in the first place — and as this debate has proceeded my opinion in that regard has been strengthened —that there has been a deliberate setting aside, with pomp and parade, of the principle that His Holiness the Pope of Rome should not interfere in our affairs of state. I think this is dangerous legislation for another reason. I think that in these days of party Government no more dangerous precedent could very well be laid down than that a political party should be enabled—it may be for purely party reasons—to endow a religious body with large sums of public money. It seems to me that if we admit such a principle as that, we open a door which it will be difficult to close ; and it seems to me that the dangers against which the Act of Mortmain was levelled were insignificant as compared with the dangers which may be incurred if we admit such a principle as that—the principle that a political party shall be permitted at any moment that it pleases to endeavor to secure the assistance of a religious body by conferring upon it large sums of public money. I say that is a dangerous principle, and that is a principle which is involved in the legislation we are discussing. I shall support this resolution also as a solemn protest by a humble member of this House against consolidating the power in this Dominion of a society which, however able and however devoted its members may be, is yet a society which throughout all Christendom has proved to be unscrupulous and aggressive, a fomentor of discord, and a stirrer up of strife, and which I am afraid, from what we have already experienced in the Province of Ontario, is prepared to pursue here in Canada those self-same tactics which rendered necessary its suppression in almost every European state.

## MR. MILLS (BOTHWELL).

I have watched with attention the proceedings in this debate, not with more attention to what has been said by hon. gentlemen who have taken part in the debate then to the manner in which it has so far been conducted. Since I have had a seat in Parliament, I do not remember any subject which has come before the House that has exhibited the tactical skill of the hon. the First Minister to greater advantage than this discussion. The hon. gentleman finds himself face to face with what may become a dangerous agitation, involving the Administration of which he is the head. That agitation was begun by a journal conducted with more than ordinary ability, and characterised by what may be called a spirit of aggressive Protestantism ; and it has gradually drawn to its side a large portion of the press of this country, and a very great deal of discussion adverse to the conduct of the Government has taken place in public meetings at several places in the Province of Ontario. Well, the hon. gentleman, in order to meet the dangers of the position, seems to have divided his forces that he may be in a position to control both sides. He has appointed his lieutenants—the hon. the Minister of Justice to lead one section of the hon. gentleman's forces, and the hon. member for North Simcoe (Mr. McCarthy) to lead another section of those forces. So the hon. gentleman has made such arrangements as to bring back to the support of the Government any that might be inclined to go astray. If they are dissatisfied with the conduct of the First Minister, they are at all events not dissatisfied with the position taken by his ardent and faithful supporter, the hon. member for North Simcoe (Mr. McCarthy). Now, the business of each of these two distinguished lieutenants is to look carefully after his own division of the grand Conservative army, and I have no doubt that those two hon. gentlemen have, in the estimation of their friends, discharged the duties assigned to them by their cheif with a great deal of ability and a great deal of skill ; and I am sure that the hon. gentleman must feel equally grateful to his colleague, the Minister of Justice, and to his supporter, the hon. member for North Simcoe. This is not the only feature of this discussion worthy of notice. There is the hon. member for Muskoka (Mr. O'Brien), who moves this resolution, and makes a very ardent and somewhat unreasonable Protestant speech, and there is another hon. gentleman, who, so far as I know since I have been in Parliament, has never been found voting against the Administration, the hon. member for Lincoln (Mr. Rykert). who is put up to answer the other ardent supporter of the Government, the hon. member for Muskoka. Then, the hon. member for North Simcoe (Mr. McCarthy), speaking after these hon. gentlemen, and after the hon. the Deputy Speaker (Mr. Colby), tells the House that he will not take the trouble to answer the arguments which were addressed to the House by the hon. member for Lincoln (Mr. Rykert). He tells us that that hon. member does not fear his constituents, because he never expects to return to them, that he is soon to go to his reward, that he has in this House no abiding-place, that his labors as a supporter of the Administration, in this House, are drawing to a close, and that every day he is pitching his tent a day's march nearer the place where he expects to be. The hon. gentleman expects, according to the information afforded to the House by the hon. member for North Simcoe, soon to be gathered, not to his fathers, but to the fathers, where scrap books will be no longer required, and where all anxiety, as to the future of an election, will be dispensed with. That is the position presented to the House by the hon. member for North Simcoe (Mr. McCarthy) in regard to the hon. member for Lincoln. Then the hon. member for North Simcoe told us of the position of another supporter of the Government, the Deputy Speaker of this House (Mr. Colby). He told us that the roseate speech of the Deputy Speaker, in regard to the perfect harmony existing between the two sections of the population in the Province of Quebec, was due to thankfulness either for favors received or for those which were to come. The hon. member said the Deputy Speaker was expectant of future promotion, but the hon. gentleman did not wish to hear from a Minister *in futuro*, but from one who was actually in possession of the Treasury benches.

Sir JOHN A. MACDONALD. He did hear it.

Mr. MILLS (Bothwell). In fact, the hon. member for North Simcoe (Mr. McCarthy) gives a representation of the Deputy Speaker which reminds me of a statement in Lord Beaconfield's " Endymion." In describing one of the characters in that book, the author says he had a feeling in his bosom which he was not very sure whether it was gratitude or indigestion ; and so the hon. member for North Simcoe says that the able speech made by the Deputy Speaker was the outcome of some motive, either of favor already received or of favor to be received from the Government, but he was not very sure which. Now, the hon. member for North Simcoe, while he described the motives which actuated those with whom he is associated on that side, and the feeling which induced them to speak in support of the position of the Government, failed to give us any information as to the motives by which he was actuated himself. I do not say that the hon. gentleman was looking forward to a seat upon the Treasury benches. I do not know that such a position would have any attractions for him. It is quite possible that it might not have; but I remember very well the support which that hon. gentleman has given the Government in past Sessions. I remember that Railway Commission Bill which was introduced and supported by one who stood so near the Prime Minister, year by year, by which the Grand Trunk was paralysed and the interests of the Canadian Pacific Railway were promoted, and I cannot bring myself to believe that the hon. gentleman would have taken the position he has in support of the amendment of the hon. member for Muskoka (Mr. O'Brien) if he thought the Government had any serious objection to the amendment. The hon. gentleman not only failed to give us any information with regard to his own motives of action, but he failed to make any allusion to the speech of an hon. gentleman who supported the amendment—the hon. member for West York (Mr. Wallace.) Now, that hon. gentleman has been in this House a very ardent supporter of the Administration. How is it that the hon. gentleman on this question arrays himself, along with the hon. member for Muskoka (Mr. O'Brien) and the hon. member for North Simcoe (Mr. McCarthy), in opposition to the course that the Government has seen proper to pursue upon this Bill? Sir, rumor has gone abroad that the hon. gentleman is not without aspirations for a seat upon the Treasury benches ; rumor has gone abroad that a round robin has been sent along the back benches, on that side of this House, in the hon. gentleman's interests, asking the Government to find a place for him upon the Treasury benches. It is said that the scarlet robe of the Minister of Customs has become somewhat faded by his long sitting upon the Treasury benches, and that he is no longer a fitting representative of a very large section of the Protestant population of the Province of Ontario ; and so it is proposed— at all events, such is the rumor—to recuperate that section of the Government by adding the hon. member for West York (Mr. Wallace). Well, Sir, the hon. member for West York is opposing the Administration of which so many of his friends desire that he should become a member. The hon. member shakes his head. I have no doubt that he is sincere in that shake. I do not think the hon. gentleman feels that he is opposing the Administration ; I do not think he feels that by giving the vote he intends to give in support of the motion of the hon. member for Muskoka, he is doing any detriment to the Government of which he wishes to become an important member. The hon. gentleman, no doubt, feels that, as it is said all roads lead to Rome, so all lines of action upon this motion, on that side of the House, will lead towards the Treasury benches, because they are alike intended to protect and strengthen the right hon. gentleman and those associated with him in the Government of this country. I think the hon. member for West York is quite right, and perhaps quite consistent, in his support of the Administration by supporting the motion of the hon. member for Muskoka rather than the motion of the Minister of Finance. We have had the two sides of the Government presented on this question. The hon. member for North Simcoe talked of the two sides of the shield, and I never saw an instance in which there were two sides to a political shield more manifest; and, I may say, more admirably presented, than they have been on this occasion. Although we may admire the hon. Minister of Justice for the very able speech he made on one side, and the hon. member for North Simcoe, for the very ardent speech he made on the other, I think we must after all give credit to the skill and generalship of the Von Moltke who leads the Government, and who leads this House. This, Mr. Speaker, is a sort of introduction to the new plan of campaign——

Sir JOHN A. MACDONALD. The preamble is not part of the Bill.

Mr. MILLS—which the Government have presented. The introduction is not without interest. Of course when, in a novel play, the actor is introduced to an audience, it is always interesting to those who understand it, and who are looking on, and who are anxious to see how it will end. Sir, the Minister of Justice last night made a very exhaustive speech in defence of the action of the Government, a speech in almost every word of which I cordially concur. When the hon. gentleman had completed that speech the hon. Premier was ready for a division. He did not see any necessity for any further discussion upon the subject. It had been fully and exhaustively discussed. Both sides of the Government shield had been presented to the House. The Government had made their defence before the country, and they say to the electors: You can follow the Minister of Justice and support the Government, or you can take the other side, and follow the hon. member for North Simcoe, and support the Government; and so, whichever way the matter may be arranged, it comes to supporting the Government after all. It is like the trade between the hunter and the Indian. It is: you take the owl and I will take the turkey; or, I will take the turkey and you take the owl. It goes to the Government, no matter what the choice may be. Well, Sir, the Prime Minister was no doubt ready for a division, but we were not, and is it to be wondered at? I expect, at all events, and no doubt the vast majority on this side of the House expect, to support the Government. But when one is in questionable company he always feels obliged to make some defence or explanation of his conduct; and I feel it necessary, in view of the political character of the gentlemen with whom I am to be associated in this vote, to give some account and some justification to the public for the course I intend to pursue. Now, we, on this side of the House, feel that this is a very important question. It is one which is calculated to arouse religious feeling, and religious prejudice; it is one in respect of which men, if they once become permeated with it, are likely to throw reason to the winds; and, therefore, in this incipient stage—if the incipient stage of the excitement and controversy is not passed—it is important that the Opposition, as well as the members and supporters of the Government, should have an opportunity of assigning to the public what is a sufficient reason for their own justification, and which I think will be regarded as a sufficient reason by the great mass of those who support them, for the course which they intend to adopt on this occasion. We have had most of the speaking so far done on one side. Our business in this discussion, Mr. Speaker, is to stand up for the right, to allay, so far as we can. the popular excitement, to correct the popular misapprehension as to the nature of the question put in issue by this Bill—not to become mere weathercocks which will indicate the strength of the gale which may be blowing from this or that particular direction. I have, and I have no doubt that every gentleman on this side of the House has too much respect for the good sense and the good intentions of the people to undertake to convert this Jesuits' Estates Bill into a sort of " Ginx's Baby " for the purpose of creating religious excitement and for arousing religious animosities throughout the country. So, for these reasons, we propose fully to discuss this question, and I think the time occupied in such a discussion is not wasted. There is one advantage amongst the many disadvantages of popular excitement, that under it people are more likely to listen, with attention to what is said, and you have an opportunity of imparting to them information upon a subject which they would not be likely to receive under other circumstances. That being the case, I think we are justified, notwithstanding our anxiety to bring this Session to a close, in taking whatever time may be necessary, to enter fully into the discussion of this subject, and to give to the people who sent us here all the information necessary to enable them to form an intelligent conclusion on the merits of the question in issue. Sir, this is a most important question. The motion that has been placed in your hands by the hon. member for Muskoka (Mr. O'Brien) is, in some respects, one of the most important that has ever been brought before Parliament. We have in this motion, in the name of toleration, a demand for intolerance, and we have, under the pretext of resisting encroachments upon constituted authority and the maintaining of the Supremacy of the Crown, a motion asking for a violation of the Constitution. This motion is, in my opinion laden with mischief, because it mingles religious prejudices and religious animosities with the consideration of the question. It mingles up stories of wrongs done and wrongs endured, as narrated in history, with fables and romances, I did not know when I heard the speech especially the latter portion of the speech of the hon. member for North Simcoe (Mr. McCarthy) and the speech of the hon. member for Muskoka (Mr. O'Brien), whether they had derived their information from history or romance. I thought that the hon. gentleman who moved the amendment had studied the "Wandering Jew" more carefully than anything else, and that in all probability the political portion of his speech was derived from "Henry Esmond." In a country where you have 2,000,000 of Roman Catholics, and something less than 3,000,000 of Protestants, it is in the last degree mischievous to invade the political arena with religious discussions, and to endeavor to convert Parliament itself into an ecclesiastical council for the purpose of deciding what religious opinions ought to be encouraged, and what religious opinions ought to be suppressed. We must continue to be one people, or at all events a people of one country, and it is not desirable to make the people of Canada, like the Jews and Samaritans, the two sections of which would have no dealing with each other. There may be questions involving principles so vital to human progress, that the evils arising from undertaking to evade the question, the evils arising from acquiescence, would be greater than those which would flow from converting the country into two hostile camps; but it seems to me, Mr. Speaker, that this is not one of those occasions. In this case no such disagreeable choice is forced upon us. We have in this motion simply the question of the right of local self-government on the one side, and the assertion of a meddlesome interference and oversight on the other. We have in this motion a proposition to set aside the judgment of a Province upon a question within its own jurisdiction, and to replace that judgment with that of a majority of the people, or a section of the people, in another Province. I do not think we can permit any such course to be adopted. If we were to do so, it would be practically an end to the system of federal government. The hon. member for Muskoka and the hon. member for North Simcoe have quoted history upon this question. But the history or the controversial papers written by men of strong polemical tendencies, the more they are studied the more the readers are likely to be led astray, and especially is history misleading when it relates to a remote period and when the surrounding circumstances and the environing influences of our own day are altogether different from that of the age about which they were writing. The past never repeats itself. The hon. gentleman assumes that it does; his speech was based on that assumption. I say the present is always being taken up into the past in the form of permanent results and the future will differ from the present by all the influences that are to be found in the events of the age immediately preceding. Were it not so you might take a thousand years out of the history of a people, without any change in its subsequent history. The thousand years before and a thousand years afterwards would fit together, for the intervening period would be of no account. That is not the course of historical events, and when an hon. gentleman undertakes to tell us what this and that party believed or did 100 years or 500 years ago, without taking into consideration the circumstances under which those doctrines were laid down, or those principles enunciated or undertaken to be applied, he is giving information which is calculated to mislead rather than to enlighten the people of the present day. I have no doubt that this question also is dangerous to public tranquility, from the consideration that it is a religious question. Men always feel they can go a long way when they think they are supporting their religious dogmas, or the religious dogmas of somebody else, and they will employ in the defence and in the promotion of those views, and those religious opinions and preferences, means which they would altogether set aside in the affairs of civil life. In order to consider with profit some of the legal and constitutional features of this question, and some of the legislation to which the hon. member for North Simcoe (Mr. McCarthy) has referred, we have to take into account the limits of government in former periods. We must remember we have largely circumscribed the field of government. There was an age when the Government undertook to control the whole domain of human action, when private domestic relations, the religious and political affairs, were all brought under the control of Government, and when the affairs of life, whether private or public, were regulated by the united authority of Church and State. Sir, in order to fully understand the legislation to which the hon. member for Muskoka (Mr. O'Brien) referred, we must remember that in the rise of the Teutonic kingdoms on the ruins of the Roman Empire, provincial churches were superseded by national churches, ecclesiastical persons were included in the government, and while men came there with spears and shields, there came also bishops and leading men of the church, and they sat in council together, and legislated together, and dealt with ecclesiastical and religious, as well as with civil matters; and so the legislation in a large degree covered everything relating to questions of religion and conscience, as well as to political affairs. Under the circumstances it was as much an act of wrong-doing and as much a violation of the law of the land to dissent from the rites and the polity, the doctrine and the discipline, established by the laws relating to the church, as it was to disregard matters of civil authority. And so every case of dissent was regarded as a case of sedition. Men and churches, whether they were Protestants or whether they were Roman Catholics, under those circumstances, were intolerant. It was a necessary condition of the state of society then; they could not well be otherwise. If a man sought to set up a separate church establishment, it was as much against the law as if he had undertaken to set up a separate political tribunal, or a separate judicial institution; and so, as I have said already, the domain of government was extended over almost the entire field of political and religious opinion and action. This was the condition of things during the Tudor period in England, and it was the condition of things, in a large degree, though not to so great an extent, in the period of the Stuarts. Now, let me call the attention of hon. gentlemen on the opposite side, who have dealt with the Jesuits question to some facts of history—and I am not going to say anything in defence of this order, I am not going to enter upon any such discussion, but I wish to call the attention of the hon. gentlemen to the past, and I would like to ask them, would they be willing that their rights should be governed, and their action controlled and circumscribed, by the intolerant acts of the church or of a religious society of that day, with which they are now connected. Take the reign of Queen Elizabeth, and in her reign there were upwards of 200 Roman Catholics executed for sedition of treason. The charges against them were political charges. I am speaking now of those who were put upon trial, and the records of whose trials exist, and we find that fifteen were executed for denying the Queen's supremacy in ecclesiastical matters, that one hundred and twenty-six of those were executed for undertaking to exercise priestly functions, and that eleven were put to death for the pretended plot of Rheims. Every one of those parties were tried, as Sydney Smith points out, for a political offence; but what was the political offence ? There was the established church; the Queen's advisers had stated what the doctrines and discipline of that church ought to be, and those men, by remaining members of another communion, set the law in regard to that establishment at defiance. But they were not the only ones who acted in this way.

We find that the Nonconformists, Joan of Kent, and Peterson, and Turwort and others, were executed on precisely the same principle, for holding opinions different from Elizabeth and her advisers. If hon. gentlemen will refer to some of the histories of that period they find these parties are spoken of as conspiring againts the Government, and as parties guilty of treason; both Nonconformists and Roman Catholics. But what was that offence? It was that they declined to accept the rites and discipline of the establishment that had been created by law. Cambden, in his Annals, mentions that, in his day, there were fifty gentlemen imprisoned in the Castle of York, the most of whom died of vermin, famine, hunger, thirst, dirt, damp, fever, whipping, and broken hearts, and that the only offence of those victims was, that they dissented from the religion of the Statute-book, and that of Her Majesty's spiritual advisers. Now, hon. gentlemen would not like to have the intolerance of that age quoted as a reason why they should not now be granted the rights of ordinary citizens. They would not like to have the religion of that period, and its enforcement by those who were of the same religious persuasion as they are, quoted as an evidence of their intolerance. It was the necessary outcome to the age in which those people lived, for when you undertake to extend the authority of government over the religious and ecclesiastical, as well as over the civil affairs of life, when you insist upon conformity to the one, as well as the other, it was a necessary consequence, that those who dissented in their views from the establishment, should be in a very uncomfortable position. Now, one of those who was executed at that period for opposition, was the Jesuit Campion, and he, at his trial, said, that his only offence against the Government was that he had been guilty of holding a faith different from that held by the State. We would, no doubt, be ignoring history altogether if we did not see that many members of the Jesuit Order took an active part in the restoration of the Stuarts, and why was that? Because the Stuarts favored their religion, and the Stuarts would establish it. The universal opinion was that some religion or other must be established, and they did what was perfectly natural for anybody to do—they sought to establish their own religion. When James II became an avowed Roman Catholic, and when he was using his sovereign position for the purpose of the restoration of the Roman Catholic faith and for overturning that of the great majority of the nation, there were protestants who were then as active as ever the Jesuits were in endeavoring to bring in King William and in affecting a change of Government, giving to the country a parliamentary sovereignty instead of one based on the nation of Divine Right. So you find the Jesuits were in treaty again on the death of Queen Anne, or to the closing years of her life, to bring back the Pretender, because the dynasty was at an end, a new family was to be established on the throne, and the question was as to whether it was to be the Pretender or some member of the House of Hanover. If you take the history of the Stuart periode in Scotland, and if you consider the relations of Mary, Queen of Scots with Knox, or of James VI with Knox, you will see that that great Reformer's opinion of duty of the sovereign and of the connection between the Church and State are wholly different to anything what we entertain to day. No Presbyterian to-day would care to have his political views measured by the political standard of John Knox. He knows that society has undergone great changes, and that what was regarded as right and proper at that period would be a wholly improper thing to-day. Toleration is of later growth; toleration grew as the state authority was contracted. There is no place where we hear so little with regard to religious interference in the affairs of state as in the republic beside us. Why is that? It is because the Government is extremely limited, and because every subject of that sort is excluded from the domain of political authority. So, to-day, we have a far greater amount of religious toleration, we have a more tolerant spirit abroad amongst every religious community, than existed in the former period, simply because we more fully appreciate the importance of confining the sphere of Government operation within narrower limits than did our forefathers. Now let us look at some of the political views of that question. I regard it as extremely dangerous to our constitutional system. The hon. gentleman has put forward, as the first branch of this amendment, a proposition which I do not see how any hon. gentleman who favors a Federal Government can uphold. He says that this House regards the power of disallowing the Acts of Legislative Assemblies of the Provinces, vasted in His Excellency in Council, as a prerogative essential of the national existence of the Dominion. Why, Sir, the United States has a national existence; it as lived for the past 113 years, and the President has no power of disallowing a State law, or in any way interfering with the authority of a State Legislature. Every measure is left to its operation. If it is *ultra vires*, the courts, and the courts only, can say so. But the hon. gentleman asks this House to declare that the whole machine of Government in Canada would go to pieces unless the Government exercised this veto. But, Sir, there is no doubt whatever that it would be a gross abuse of the trust committed to them by our Constitution if they were to exercise it on the present occasion. Our constitutional system is similar in principle to that of the United Kingdom. What is the meaning of that? The United Kingdom has no federal organisation. Why, Sir, these words refer to the relation between the Executive and the Legislature. Our Constitution is similar in principle to that of the United Kingdom, in giving us responsible government; it gives us a Cabinet controlled by a majority of the House; and it gives us a House subject to an appeal to the country at any moment that the Crown thinks necessary. There is a certain sphere of exclusive action assigned to the Local Legislature, and a certain sphere assigned to this Parliament. Let us suppose that a Local Legislature, within its own sphere, had certain important question coming before it; suppose this question were one; suppose Mr. Mercier had said the Jesuits have a moral claim upon the Jesuits' estates, and that he had been beaten in the Local Legislature; that he had gone to the country on the question, and that a majority had been returned with him to the Legislature to carry out that particular measure; how long would your system of parliamentary government endure, if the Government here should, after that measure was carried, take sides with minority and disallow it? Sir, the Local Government have a right to go to the country upon a public question, if the country is the proper tribunal to decide whether they are right or wrong, it is perfectly clear that it cannot be the constitutional rule that this House is the proper tribunal to decide. How long could parliamentary government endure if the Administration here were to exercise that species of supervision over the Legislatures upon whom responsible Government has been conferred. If we should act the part of ancient Downing street, and undertake to decide what is wise or unwise, why, Sir, your Government would be at an end. If you have local self-government conferred upon the people of the different Provinces, it is clear that the electors of those Provinces, within their constitutional authority, are the ultimate court of appeal for the purpose of deciding whether the political course of their Government is what it should be. They are the proper parties, and they alone. It is not to the hon. gentleman on the Treasury benches, but it is to the electors that the Local Legislatures are responsible for their acts within constitutional limits; and while they keep themselves within those constitutional limits, I hold that we have not, according to the spirit of our Constitution, a whit more right to interfere—to use this prerogative for the purpose of disallowing their acts—than we would have to interfere with the acts of the Legislature of the State of New York. They are a distinct political entity for all the purposes for which exclusive power is given to them; they are constitutionally beyond the control of this Government and this Parliament; if they have acted wisely, their own electors will sustain them; if, in the judgment of the electors, they have acted unwisely, they will condemn them, and will send to Parliament representatives who will repeal the law. By the judgment of their own masters they must stand or fall. But, Sir, it was hinted by the hon. member for North Simcoe, that these people were not fit to be trusted fully, and, therefore, this meddlesome oversight is necessary. If you take that position, your whole system of government is at an end. That system is based on the theory that the people of each Province are fit to be trusted, that they are competent, and that if the Government do wrong, the people will set them right. I see statements in the press and elsewhere, that this Government ought to exercise this power given to the Government here, by which they may act absolutely and upon the theory that they never err, that the Local Legislatures are not to be trusted, and that this power is to be frequently exercised, in order to keep them right ? What would we say in this House, if the Imperial Government were to interfere on any question wholly within the purview of our authority ? Would we submit to that interference ? You would have the whole country aroused; you would have it declared, that we would not submit to the meddlesome interference of Downing street; you would have the old question about parliamentary government revived again. I say, that what would be improper to be done by the Imperial Parliament against us would be improper to be done by us against the Local Legislatures. Now, we never can proceed upon the assumption that this Parliament is wiser, in matters within the purview of the Local Legislatures, than the Local Legislature or the Local Government are. The assumption in our Constitution is that authority is vested in those who are most competent to exercise it. Certain general matters are entrusted to us, because it was believed—in the public interest—that we could do better for the whole community than each section of the community could do for itself. It is upon that ground that the Union is established; but it is also assumed, in the reservation of certain powers to the Local Legislatures, that they are the most competent to discharge the duties connected with those powers. If they are the most competent, upon what ground can we interfere ? What right would we have to interfere ? Why, the very ground on which interference is asked in this case would, if it had been put forward when the Constitution was framed, have been sufficient to have kept the Province of Quebec out of the Union. Are you going to entrap them into a union by a form of constitution which seemingly gives them exclusive control over certain subjects, and then, after they have become members of the union exercise a meddlesome oversight over their domestic affairs ? That is what is proposed. I say that is an improper thing, and I repeat that you never can safely undertake, even where a Local Legislature goes wrong, to correct their errors, instead of leaving the correction of those mistakes to the electors where it constitutionally belongs. Now let me call your attention to a precedent or two on this subject. When this question was raised in connection whith the New Brunswick School Bill, Lord Carnarvon said :

"That the Constitution of Canada does not contemplate any interference with provincial legislation, on a subject within the competence of the Local Legislature, by the Dominion Parliament, or, as a consequence, by the Dominion Government."

There is the limit Lord Carnarvon sets for that authority to disallow. He asks : Is the question one competent for the Local Legislature to deal with ? If it is, your jurisdiction is excluded, your right to interfere is excluded. The Act may be unwise, but that is for them to judge, and not for you. You are not made a sort of second body to represent the people of a particular Province in provincial matters. In that same case, the law officers of the Crown, Sir J. D. Coleridge, the present Lord Chief Justice, and Sir George Jessell, afterwards the Master of the Rolls, one of the most distinguished judges of his century, said :

" Of course it is quite possible that the new statute of the Province may work in practice unfavorably to this or that denomination, and, therefore, to the Roman Catholics, but we did not think that such a state of things is enough to bring into operation or restrict the power of appeal to the Governor General."

Now, here was an Act which he said, might work unfairly and injure a particular class of the people who were complaining, but with which, as it was within the exclusive jurisdiction of the Province, although injustice might be worked, it was not the business of the federal authority to interfere. That is the doctrine clearly laid down in this case. In 1875, when the then hon. member for Terrebonne (Mr. Masson) brought this matter before the House, we refused to comply with his wishes, we refused to seek to set aside the provincial legislation upon the subject; and when Bishop MacIntyre, of Prince Edward Island, asked the Government of my hon. friend from East York (Mr. Mackenzie) to disallow the school Bill of that Province, which, he complained, was unfair to his people, we refused to interfere because we believed the matter to be wholly within the jurisdiction of the Legislature and Government of Prince Edward Island. What we then declined to do for the Roman Catholics we now decline to do against them. We are acting consistently; we are seeking to uphold on this, as on that occasion, the principle of provincial rights. The first Minister, in discussing the report of the school Bill of New Brunswick, laid down this proposition, that there were only two cases, in his opinion in which the Government of the Dominion was justified in advising the disallowance of a local Act. The first was that the Act was unconstitutional and *ultra vires*, and, the second, that it was injurious to the interests of the whole Dominion. Now, there is no doubt whatever about the soundness of the hon. gentleman's first proposition, and there is no doubt about the soundness of the second proposition, if there is no possibility of disputing the facts. The Government of the Dominion could not act, and they would have been guilty of a violent breach of the constitution if, because they held a different opinion from the Local Legislature, they should set up their judgment against the solemn decision of the Province in a matter entirely within the control of that Province. That was the position of the hon. gentleman on that important question, and with that position we never quarrelled; to the principle laid down on that occasion we unreservedly suscribed, and to that we have ever since adhered. Let us look for a moment at the federal principle. If the Government were completely federal, there would be no power of disallowance, and I have always been of opinion that the power to disallow was an unfortunate provision of our Constitution. I have always been of opinion that it would have been on the whole, very much better to have left the question, as in the neighboring republic, entirely to the courts, rather than take the risk of the pressure which may be brought on Administration, from time to time, to interfere in a way detrimental to the rights of the Provinces. The first question to be asked is : Is the Act in controversy within the exclusive jurisdiction of the Province ? If it is, upon what grounds can its disallowance be called for ? Where the Minister of Justice thinks an Act is *ultra vires*, and that serious wrong might be done by allowing it to come into operation, he may make it a subject of correspondence with the law officer of the Province, and if after full discussion with that law officer, he is still of opinion that the Act is *ultra vires* he may disallow the Act, instead of leaving it go into operation until pronounced void by the courts. Now, what the hon. gentleman who has made this motion proposes is to convert Parliament into a Court of Appeal. He proposes to make this House a court for the purposes of diciding the limits of local and federal jurisdiction. Well, this Parliament may have a question of that sort, when it undertakes itself to legislate, forced upon it, and it must, for its own purpose, decide whether the question is *ultra vires* or *intra vires*. The House, it seems to me, is a body ill suited to exercise judicial functions, and to undertake to say, in any question or proposition of this sort, what is the exclusive jurisdiction of the Province, and the exclusive jurisdiction of the Dominion. Now when we look at the Constitution, we find that everything relating to property and civil rights is under the control of the Local Legislature, except in so far as the control of property and civil rights is specifically given to the Dominion in the provisions of section 91. I am inclined to think that we often forget how comprehensive those words are : " property and civil rights. " Civil rights, barbarians of course have none. The civil right is a right regulated by the State. It is the exercise of a right, that belongs to the individual, in a way consistent with the rights and liberties of another individual. It may embrace religious as well as political creeds. The relations between parent and child, between guardian and ward, between master and servant, are all civil rights. The relations between the Churches and the State are civil rights. It is possible for a Local Legislature to say this religious body may be endowed by the State, and another shall not be endowed. There is nothing in the Constitution to prevent a Local Legislature endowing a church, if it sees proper to do so. In the exercise of those powers over property and civil rights, it may do so. It may regulate the observance of the Sabbath and the observance of holidays. It may make our school system secular or denominational, in so far as it is not prevented by a specific provision of the Constitution. It may make the school system wholly religious. The Province of Ontario to-morrow might make a provision doing away with public schools and adopting a system of denominational schools in its stead. I do not know any ground upon which we could interfere on the subject of the relations between Church and State in a Province, except it would be in saying that a person belonging to one denomination may have the elective franchise and another not. The hon. gentleman told us yesterday that the connection between Church and State was entirely abolished by the Act of 1854. The hon. gentleman sought to leave the impression on the House that that Act was a finality, that the Provinces were restrained in some way by that Act. Why the Province of old Canada, which passed that Act, might the next year have repealed it, and have established the old Church of Scotland as the Established Church of Canada,or the Church of England,or the Methodists, or some other body. Of course, in my opinion, as an opponent of the connection of Church and State, it would be unfortunate to do any one of these things, but the power is not taken away simply because it would be unwise, or inexpedient to use it. Now, the Local Legislature in any Province may very widely depart from the order of things which existed at Confederation. Everyone who knows the history of this Union knows right well that, at the period of Confederation, there was a disposition on the part of Ontario to take one view of public policy, and on the part of Quebec to take another view. There were a number of questions upon which there was friction; and what was one of the objects of the dissolution of the old Legislative Union, and the establishment of the Federal Union in its place? It was to get rid of those difficulties, by allowing each Province to take its own course. Whether that was wise or unwise, whether it was the best in the interests of civilisation, or whether it would lead to a different result, each Legislature was free to decide for itself, within the limits fixed by the Constitution, what course it would adopt. The hon. member for North Simcoe (Mr. McCarthy) yesterday concluded his speech by a quotation from a speech of Prof. Caven. I have not the pleasure of knowing Prof. Caven personally, but everything I have heard in regard to him has led me to the conclusion that he is one of the ablest thinkers in the Dominion, and that he is not a gentleman likely to form an erroneous conclusion when all facts are properly before him; but he lays down in that speech three propositions. One was that the appropriation of these funds in the Province of Quebec was a malversation of public funds. Now, that is not so. That is a total misapprehension of the state of the question. Quebec may have acted very unwisely in dealing with the funds as she did, but the Legislature of Quebec was as free to deal with the funds under the control of that Province as this Legislature is, or a private party is to deal with the moneys and property belonging to him. Whether Quebec has used the moneys wisely or unwisely it is not necessary here to discuss. The fact is that the money was her own to do as she pleased with. It was under her sovereign control—for, for this purpose, she is sovereign—and it was no more a misappropriation of her money than it would be if we were to take moneys which we have been in the habit of devoting to one purpose, and were to withdraw them from that purpose, and to use them for some other and different purpose. We have had discussed here these three questions: To whom did this property belong? how was it acquired? how was the ownership lost? In part it is said to have been granted by the King of France, in part it consisted of private benefactions, and in part it was property purchased by the society with its own money. Now, as to the first two classes of property, they were given to the society to propagate the Roman Catholic religion. The society itself was not an end. It was not for the advantage of the society, as a society, that it was given to the society as a means to an end, and that end was the propagation of the Roman Catholic faith, the society forming a part of that church. If the views of that society were in any respect at variance with the views of the church, then the property was not given for the promotion of those views. The hon. member for Simcoe (Mr. McCarthy) said that the church to which he belonged had been despoiled of its estates when the Clergy Reserves were secularised. Why, the Clergy Reserves never belonged to the church. They were reserves, not grants. They belonged to the State. The State held them during its pleasure for a particular purpose, and, while that pleasure continued, the State applied the proceeds to that purpose. But there were 57 rectories, and those were grants, and, when the connection between Church and State by the Act of 1854 was declared to be abolished those 57 rectories were not taken from the church. The church retained those rectories because they were its private property at the time this Act of 1854 was passed. Let me state some of the analogies which I think may be fairly used to illustrate the position of the Jesuit Society. That society had very much the same relation to the Roman Catholic Church in New France as the trustees of Queen's College have to the Presbyterian Church, or Victoria College to Methodists, or the trustees of McMaster Hall to the Baptists. Now, if any of these corporations failed, and the Crown took possession of the property which belonged to the extinct corporation, would any one of these denominations be quite satisfied with the result? For instance, if Queen's College was taken possession of by the Crown and its property sold, and the moneys put into the Consolidated Revenues of Ontario, would not the Presbyterian body assert a moral claim, in spite of the legal right which might belong to the Crown in respect of those properties? That is very much the position which the Jesuits and the Roman Catholic Church in Lower Canada took towards the Crown when the Crown appropriated these estates. It is said by the hon. gentleman that these are very improper people, that they have been intriguers, political intriguers, in every country in Europe, and that they are not to be trusted. Well, speaking from the ethical point of view, that reminds me very much of the position of a man who owes another and does not want to pay what he owes, and he says: I will not pay the man I owe because he is a drunken rascal and beats his wife, and, if I paid him the money, he would get drunk and would beat her again, and, as I am a moral man, I prefer to keep the money. The hon. member for North Simcoe (Mr. McCarthy) yesterday went on to state the origin of the title of the Crown to this property. I do not attach any importance to this, for this reason, that the legal title of the Crown is not disputed by the Prime Minister of Quebec, although, historically, it is an interesting question as to how the Crown came into possession of these estates. The hon. gentleman yesterday stated four theories, three of which must be erroneous, as to the way in which the Crown acquired possession. He cites two of these from two separate reports of the Judge Advocate General, Marriott. The one was that the property had been confiscated by the King of France before the Conquest, and was part of the public domain belonging to the King of France at the time of the Conquest. The law officers of the Crown, the Attorney and Solicitor Generals, did not concur in that opinion, and did not act upon it. Then Mr. Marriott gave another opinion that these estates belonged to the General of the Order, and that as proprietor there was no provision made for his selling or disposing of them, that the only parties who had a right to hold estates in Canada were those who were British subjects, that the General of the Order was not a British subject, that no provision was made for selling except by those who wished to leave the country, and as the General of the Order had never been in the country, he could not sell, and so the property necessarily belonged to the Crown. This may be ingenious but it is not sound. Then there was also the title set up based on the Conquest, and there is the title set up by the extinguishment of the corporation by the Pope's bull. When we look at the papers we find a proclamation, dated in 1774, in which the Crown declares its intention to take possession of these estates in consequence of the dissolution of the order, and the proclamation seems to have been repeated again in the Royal Instructions given in 1791. It is said in the Royal Instructions :

"It is our will and pleasure that the Society of Jesus be suppressed and dissolved, and no longer continued as a body corporate or politic, and all their possessions and property shall be vested in us for such purposes as we may hereafter think fit to appoint, and direct and appoint."

That was in 1791, 30 years or more after the conquest. Now, I do not see myself on what legal principle the King could, at that time, or at any time after he had established a government in the country, assert any such title as that to the estates. He did not assert it at the conquest. There was no formal possession claimed or taken. I find at a still later period, the next year, another and different ground is put forward as the ground of the King's title. It is in the fiat issued by the Governor of that day, and he says :

"Whereas all and every of the estates and property, movable or immovable, situated in Canada, which did heretofore belong to the late Order of Jesuits, have, since the year of our Lord 1760, been and are now by law vested in us."

So we find in that fiat the title is dated back to 1760, although in the Royal Instructions it is dated in 1791. But there is no doubt that the Crown went into possession in some way or other, and if the title was not a legal title, it in the first instance became a title by prescription against the order. I don't see any ground for asserting a title in the Crown, except by prescription. Mr. Mercier does not admit any legal title in the Order of Jesuits, but their moral claim he admits to exist. Now, let me call the attention of hon. gentlemen to certain articles in the capitulation of Montreal. I think it is clear, from these Articles of Capitulation, that the King was precluded from asserting any legal title as conqueror :

"Art. XXXII. The communities of Nuns shall be preserved in their constitution and privileges. They shall be exempted from lodging any military, and it shall be forbidden to trouble them in their religious exercises, or to enter their monasteries; safeguard shall even be given them if they desire them.
"Answer.—Granted.
"Art. XXXIII. The preceding article shall likewise be executed with regard to the communities of Jesuits and Recollets, and to the house of the priests of St. Sulpice at Montreal. This last, and the Jesuits, shall preserve their rights to nominate to certain curacies and missions as heretofore.
"Answer.—Refused till the King's pleasure be known.
"Art. XXXIV. All the communities, and all the priests shall preserve their movables, the property and revenues of the seignories and other estates which they possess in the colony of what nature soever they be, and the same estates shall be preserved in their privileges, rights, honors and exemptions.
"Answer.—Granted."

Now, I ask the attention of hon. gentlemen to this, that all the communities spoken of are the Nuns, the Jesuits, the Recollets, and the priests of St. Sulpice. These are the four orders, and it is said in this article that all the communities and all the priests shall preserve their movable properties and revenues, seignories, &c., on this ground. Then this construction of this article is further confirmed by article 35 :

"Art. XXXV. If the canons, priests, missionaries, the priests of the Seminary of the Foreign Mission, and of St. Sulpice, as well as the Jesuits and the Recollets, choose to go to France, passage shall be granted them in His Britannic Majesty's ships, and they shall all have leave to sell, in whole or in part, the estates and the movables which they possess in the colonies."

Now, there were two things allowed to these orders : To remain in the country and to remain in possession of the property under the 34th article, or to leave the country and sell the property before they left under article 35. If the property had been confiscated to the Crown, or had been taken possession of by the Crown, by the virtue of the Conquest, no such article as this would have been granted. But in both these cases there is a provision in the Articles of Capitulation preserving to these parties their rights, which made it impossible for the Crown to acquire a legal title to their estates any more than to the estates of any other portion of the community of the Province of Quebec. It is true the Crown did come into possession. That was largely due to the undue influence of General Amherst, who desired to get possession of these estates as a personal endowment for his services during the war. Now, it may be the Crown acquired a legal title to these estates by holding them, and if it did so, and the right of the Jesuits to assert their title was gone then their remains only, as Mr. Mercier has spoken, a moral right to any interest in the property. I think that is a very proper question to consider in the Legislature of Quebec, it is not a question, it seems to me, with which we are called upon to deal, and I would not have referred to it if the member for North Simcoe had not denied altogether any moral right in the matter, and treated this as an act of spoliation which justified our interference. Sir, if it were an act of spoliation, still I do not think that we have anything to do with it. From my point of view, from my interpretation of constitutional rights, from my notion of the use of this prerogative, it does seem to me that if it were a Protestant community, if it were an English Church, or a Presbyterian, or a Methodist, or a Baptist Church, that was in exactly in the same position, I do not think any Protestant member of this House would be disposed to deny that there was a moral right to some compensation for property which had been once owned and which had thus been taken away. The hon. gentleman has also pointed out that, we, he says, declared in favor of the absolute separation of Church and State. And if you pay a church anything, no matter if it is only a claim rightfully due, you have connection between Church and State. If the hon. gentleman will look at the Act of 1854, he will see that if that rule were admitted, the very Act which declares that it is desirable to disestablish or put an end to the connection between Church and State does the very thing he says should not be done. There was provision made for existing life interests of parties in the fund, and the present First Minister was the member of the Government who introduced that Bill and carried it through the Legislature. There was a proposition at that time that, in order to secure the immediate separation of Church and State so far as that question was concerned, there should be a commutation of the salaries or compensation due to the different parties, and this proposition was submitted ; and the right hon. gentleman, so for as I can recollect, in the discussion said this in reply : If you pay those Ministers the amount to which they are entitled, computed upon their probability of life, they might take the money and go to Australia and South Africa, and might cease to perform those duties which entitle them to receive this money, and you pay over the money upon which the church has a moral claim by its claim to their services. You must take some means of securing the performance of those duties in behalf of which the money is voted. That was the position taken by the right hon. gentleman, and I think, he entered into a correspondence—he will remember the matter better than I do, as he was the active party in the case—with the bishop of the Church of England, and with the moderator, or somebody else, on behalf of the Presbyterians, and arranged the commutation of those sums due to the clergy, and paid the money over to the church and not to the individuals.

Sir JOHN A. MACDONALD. Yes, that is so.

Mr. MILLS (Bothwell). I think the sum was $400,000 or more.

Sir JOHN A. MACDONALD. More.

Mr. MILLS (Bothwell). Very much more, I think. And that very Act, under which the money was paid and which was declared to be for the purpose of putting an end to the connection between Church and State, upon the theory of the member for North Simcoe, actually established connection between Church and State. Then there is another consideration. So far as I remember the provisions of that Act, the right hon. gentleman made its provisions depend upon the successful carrying out of the arrangement by those parties who were interested in the matter. If it was treason for Mr. Mercier, and contrary to the Act of Supremacy, to enter into discussions with any outside person as to the settlement of the disputes in regard to the Jesuit matter, was it not equally improper to enter into a commutation arrangement with a party who was not a member of Parliament, who had not a seat in Parliament, and was not in any sense a representative? The right hon. gentleman entered into correspondence with the bishop and with other parties, and it was for the purpose of deciding—what? It was for the purpose of deciding whether commutation should be had with the church or not. The Legislature confirmed in advance what was done. Now, so far as this case is concerned, my point is this: No one pretends that the bishop or any other church dignitary was made a party to the enactment because he was a party to the terms of settlement. No more is the Pope a party in this Bill, but a party to a contract, which this Act subsequently brought forward was intended to carry out. Let me take another case. Supposing, in the case of the Canadian Pacific Railway, the Government had entered into a contract with Sir George Stephen, Sir Donald Smith, Mr. McIntyre, and Mr. Kennedy of New-York, and certain parties in Paris. The right hon. gentleman might have set out the correspondence in the Bill, and then we would have a Bill in exactly similar terms to the provincial Act respecting the Jesuits' estates, and the right hon. gentleman would have had in that contract and Act the names of parties who were non-residents of this country. He might have had in it the name of some party at Frankfort.

Sir JOHN A. MACDONALD. Mr. Reinhardt.

Mr. MILLS (Bothwell). Yes, and the parties in Paris. The right hon. gentleman might have had all those names in the Act and according to the view of the hon. member for Muskoka (Mr. O'Brien), if it had not been a violation of the Act of Supremacy to have dealt with foreign parties who might be regarded as capitalists, the right hon. gentleman might have been open to the suspicion of legislating for Canada not simply by the Queen and the two Houses, but by the aid of German, French and New-York bankers. It is said by a writer in the "Law Journal" that this Act is "ultra vires." The writer says:

" It is *ultra vires* the constitutional power of a Colonial Legislature to confer on or delegate to any fo eign Sovereign or Tribunal lawful jurisdiction or authority to determine or ratify the distribution of the moneys or properties of the Crown, or how money grants to the subjects of the Crown within its Colonial jurisdiction are to be distributed."

This, I have no doubt, is intended as a legal proposition, embracing this particular case or Act before us. Let me say that it is wholly beside it. There is here no foreign potentate; there is a foreign party interested. The foreign party is claiming a property, and that foreign party negotiated with Mr. Mercier prior to legislative action. Those negotiations were simply a contract with the Crown, prior to any legislation, and prior to the meeting of the Legislature. He did just what the bankers in Paris did in regard to the Canadian Pacific Railway, with the difference, that the Pope, as the head of the church, acting not personally, claimed the right, the moral right at all events, to this property. Mr. Mercier said: You have no legal right; I can on' recognize a moral right. So there was no question of sovereign right, and there was in no way a violation of the Queen's supremacy by Mr. Mercier who entered into negotiations and dealt with the Pope in the same way as he would deal with any other party having a claim against the Government, whether foreign or native, and Mr. Mercier, after an agreement was arrived at, went to the Legislature and sought to give effect to it. The Legislature, with its sovereign authority over the question, confirmed the agreement which thus had been entered into. Let me call the attention of the House to an opinion given by Lord Selborne on this point. In the case of Brown vs. Curé, &c., de Montreal, 6. Privy Council Appeals, 173, counsel said appeals to the Pope were in contravention of I Elizabeth. Lord Selborne observed:

"That statute is not understood to make it an offence at law for Roman Catholics, in this country or in Ireland, to carry appeals to the Pope. The Pope is a sort of arbitrator, taking a legal view of their position, whom they may consult upon the question."

That is the position, and the Roman Catholic in Canada do not violate the Supremacy Act in appealing to the Pope for the purpose of settling any ecclesiastical or spiritual question in which they are interested. I will place the dictum of Lord Selborne against the authority of the Toronto "Law Journal", and I think those hon. gentlemen who were converted to that side by the powerful argument of the Toronto "Law Journal", may be converted back again by the still higher authority of Lord Selborne. The "Law Journal" says:

"But the statutes of Elizabeth, the express words, abolish the usurped jurisdiction of the Bishop of Rome, heretofore unlawfully claimed and usurped within the realm and other the dominions to the Queen belonging."

I ask the indulgence of the House for a moment while I call its attention to the position of this question. It is necessary to look to some extent to the history of the question in order thoroughly to understand the pretentions of the Pope, and his relation to the church in questions of this sort. I will refer to the views that are expressed by Lord Selborne in his book on the English Establishment. He says it was the practice in various times, in order to maintain the ancient privileges of the church, not to permit of appeals to Rome, that it is shown by the constitution of Clarendon, and by earlier provisions of the law, that this was then the practice; but that when Stephen came to the Throne, and his brother, who was the Pope's Legate, was also the Bishop of Winchester, he introduced another practise and they permitted, and in fact authorized appeals to Rome, which were at fitful intervals continued down to the time of Henry VIII. The statutes that are found in the period of Henry VIII (and wich were repealed under Mary), which put an end to the appeals to Rome, were re-enacted by this statute of Elizabeth. Let me call your attention just for a moment to indicate in a brief summary the provisions of these Acts. Henry the Eighth legislated in favor of ecclesiastical emancipation in this particular. Before his day, and up to the middle of his reign, appeals were taken to the Pope in testamentary acts, and on the questions of matrimony, divorce, tithes and oblations and by the statute of the 24th year of Henry VIII, chap. 12, those appeals were abolished, and it was declared that hereafter they were all to be adjudicated by the King's temporal and spiritual courts. It will be seen that in every one of these cases there was involved some material interest. They were not purely spiritual cases, they grew up because the ecclesiastical law was applied to parties who made their wills, and so on, at the period of their deaths; and as the ecclesiastical law was not understood by the English lawyers, appeals were frequently taken on civil cases from England to Rome. By an Act of the 25th year of Henry VIII, cap. 19, it provided for the settlement of all those cases by the King's Majesty. It forbade the clergy, under penalty of fine and imprisonment, to make a constitution without the King's assent, and it forbade appeals to Rome other than those that were permitted by cap. 12 of an Act passed in the 24th year of Henry VIII. By an Act passed in the 25th year of his reign, cap. 20, he prevented the payment of annates, and the first fruits that were allowed still to continue after the former statute ; that is, that the persons entering into an ecclesiastical office, to which a salary was attached, were obliged to pay the first year's salary to the Pope as a part of his revenue. After that it was declared that the archbishops and bishops were to be elected, presented, and consecrated within the realm of England. In the 25th of Henry VIII, cap. 21, exoneration from exactions by the See of Rome was secured, and they were declared to be independent of all foreign interference. The same statute forbade the payment of Peter's pence, and declared that neither the King, nor his subjects, shall sue to Rome for any dispensation or license. The Archbishop of Canterbury was to grant such in future, but he was never to do so unless he obtained the approval of the King in Council. The 5th and 6th of Edward VI, cap. 1, enacted the principle of uniformity, the use of the Book of Common Prayer, and enforced attendance at church on Sundays. All these statutes were repealed in the reign of Mary, and they were all re-enacted by this Act. The 1st of Elizabeth, cap. 1, declared that " All foreign jurisdiction is abolished, and all spiritual jurisdiction united to the Crown. " All these measures amount simply to this, that as the Church was connected with the State, the administration of the affairs of the State, executive and judicial, were declared to belong to the Sovereign. They were vested in the Sovereign, and not one of them was to be invested in any other tribunal. As long as the power of the Sovereign extended over the religious community, and as long as strict observance of the laws of the establishment were enforced, those Acts of Supremacy, and all those other Acts, were rigidly enforced against the Roman Catholics. But, when it was once admitted, that dissent might be recognized as possible, without treason, sedition, revolution or disloyal intent, variation in divine services, in church polity, and in church rites, were overlooked, and were ultimately tolerated, and they were admitted not to fall within the penal provision of this statute of Elizabeth. It was so held by Lord Selborne, in the case I have mentioned. It is true, that the judgment of the Pope has not, in England, nor in Ireland to-day, so far as the Roman Catholics are concerned, the force of a judgment of an ordinary civil tribunal. There are no means, except those which belong to him, as the moral head, to enforce his conclusion ; there are no means of enforcing obedience to his judgments, except excommunication or exclusion from the church's privileges, but that he may (as Lord Selborne said) be appealed to, and that he is a moral arbitrator acting according to certain judicial principles, and that he has the right so to act, and that the Roman Catholics of the United Kingdom have a right so to appeal to him, is beyond all question. We have here submitted to us in this amendment, and in the speeches which have been delivered in its defence, a proposition as to whether the law is in that respect the same in this country, or whether the Roman Catholics of the Province of Quebec are more restricted in their rights than the Roman Catholics in the United Kingdom. Let me say, Mr. Speaker, that the rule which I have quoted from Lord Selborne came into being after the statute of Elizabeth was relaxed, when the dissent from the Establishment was permitted, and when a large portion of the population of the United Kingdom were privileged to worship in some other form or way than according to the Establishment without having their civil rights impaired or their liberties interfered with. Now, Quebec received its law from the King, subject to the terms granted in the capitulation. There was no statute of Elizabeth in force and that statute was not carried to any one of the colonies. I might quote the view of Lord Mansfield, whose authority is unquestioned both in judicial decisions and in a letter addressed to Mr. Grenville, the Prime Minister, in 1764, in which he says that the penal laws of the United Kingdom are never carried to a colony as part of the common law they take with them. If that is so in a colony settled by the people of England, it is much more so

9

in the case of a colony that is secured by conquest. Such a law cannot operate, as the hon. the Minister of Justice pointed out last evening, unless it would be by the abrogation of all those rights that were ceded by capitulation and contained in the Treaty of 1763. Now, we have in the Act 14 George III, chapter 83, this provision :

" For the more perfect security and ease of the minds of the inhabitants of the said Province, it is hereby declared, that His Majesty's subjects professing the religion of the Church of Rome, of and in the said Province of Quebec, may have, hold, and enjoy the free exercise of the religion of the Church of Rome, subject to the King's supremacy, declared and established by an Act made in the first year of the reign of Queen Elizabeth, over all the dominions and countries which then did, or thereafter should belong to the Imperial Crown of this realm ; and that the clergy of the said church may hold, receive and enjoy their accustomed dues and rights with respect to such persons only as shall profess the said religion."

The whole Act of Elizabeth is not introduced by this, but only those provisions. I think sections 7 and 8, which relate solely to the question of the Sovereign's supremacy, and that supremacy is not affected, as Lord Selborne points out, by an appeal to the Pope as the spiritual head of the Roman Catholic Church, who, in deciding questions relating to the church over which he has jurisdiction not incompatible with the civil law, acts as a moral arbitrator. Of course, the position of the Roman Catholic Church in the Province of Quebec is not altogether that of a voluntary association ; it has certain connections with the State. It is not true that we have an entire separation between Church and State in all the Provinces of this Dominion. The Roman Catholic Church in the Province of Quebec occupies a somewhat anomalous position. Under the Quebec Act and ever since, that church has been allowed to collect tithes from its members, but not from members of other religious persuasions. The collection of those tithes, for the purposes mentioned, imposes on the church certain obligations. For instance, a case has been decided in the Quebec courts in which a resident of a parish who had paid his church rates, insisted on the curé, with whom he had some difference, baptising his child, and the curé refused ; and a judgment was given enforcing the rights of the parishioner as against his ecclesiastical superior. And so with regard to other matters, in so far as the church enjoys certain special advantages, the civil authorities have a right to see that the corresponding obligations are properly enforced whenever the question is raised. It was on this ground that judgment was given for the burying of Guibord within the ground usually regarded as consecrated. In discussing this question the court said :

" Nor do their Lordships think it necessary to pronounce any opinion upon the difficult questions which were raised in the argument before them touching the precise *status* at the present time of the Roman Catholic Church in Canada. It has, on the one hand, undoubtedly, since the cession, wanted some of the characteristics of an established church ; whilst, on the other hand, it differs materially in several important particulars from such voluntary religious societies as the Anglican Church in the Colonies or the Roman Catholic Church in England. The payment of *dimes* to the clergy of the Roman Catholic Church by its lay members, and the ratability of the latter to the maintenance of parochial cemeteries, are secured by law and statutes. These rights of the church must beget corresponding obligations, and it is obvious that this state of things may give rise to questions between the laity and the clergy which can only be determined by the municipal courts. It seems, however, to their Lordships to be unnecessary to pursue this question, because, even if this church were to be regarded merely as a private and voluntary religious society, resting only upon a concensical basis, Courts of Justice are still bound, when due complaint is made that a member of the society has been injured as to his rights, in any matter of a mixed spiritual and temporal character, to enquire into the laws or rules of the tribunal or authority which has inflicted the alleged injury.—207-208. Their Lordships conceive that if the Act be questioned in a Court of Justice, that Court has a right to enquire, and is bound to enquire, whether that Act was in accordance with the law and rules of discipline of the Roman Catholic Church which obtain in Lower Canada, and whether the sentence, if any, by which it is sought to be justified was regularly pronounced by any authority competent to pronounce it."

And so far, on account of its special rights, making it to a limited extent a State

Church, it has imposed upon it certain obligations, and so far those may be brought before ordinary civil tribunals for the purpose of their enforcement. But beyond this, there is no connection; beyond this, it is purely a voluntary association, and it has the same right of appeal to the Pope as the spiritual head of the church that any other church would have to appeal to the constituted authority of that church. It is not a national, it is a Catholic Church, that is, its authority extends, regardless of political boundaries, over all those who profess its faith. Now, to deny that right, so far as Lord Selborne lays it down—and that is as far as it is asserted in this particular case—would be to say to those of the Roman Catholic persuasion: Although you may have your notions of church polity, which are not the same as ours, yet you are not at liberty to assert them; because you believe that a church may have boundaries wider than those of other churches, you are to be limited by political considerations to the limits of a particular state. I say that would be an intolerable rule. If the Presbyterian Church of Canada to-day chose to connect itself with that of the United States, I do not know any law that would prevent it establishing its ecclesiastical courts to which both bodies would be subject; and, in so far as the civil tribunal might be called on to adjudicate on questions relating to those courts, those questions might be disposed of in so far as they might be connected with the material affairs of either country. Now, let me call the attention of the hon. member for North Simcoe to this. The Government of England has legislated upon this subject. At the time of the American Revolution there was no Episcopal bishop in the colonies now the United States. After the revolution the Episcopal churches of the independant colonies required spiritual heads; they required bishops in the Episcopal churches of the United States. How were they to get them? They were separated from England, and the English Parliament had no longer any jurisdiction over them? The result was that, after a good deal of hesitation, Parliament legislated, and passed the Act 26 George III, chapter 84, authorizing the Archbishop of Canterbury to ordain bishops for the Episcopal churches within the Independent Republic of the United States. There was Parliament itself, on account of the connection between Church and State, undertaking to exercise what might be regarded as a legislative and spiritual jurisdiction in a foreign country; and they hesitated so long, if I recollect rightly, that the Scotch bishops ordained the first bishops before the Act of Parliament came into operation. The United States never took any offence, so far as I know, at that Act, and never claimed that it was a usurpation of supremacy or an interference with their sovereignty. The Archbishop of Canterbury, in this respect, did everything that the Pope has done throughout Christendom in the ordination of bishops in the Roman Catholic Church. Now let me take another case. There was the appointment of a bishop at Jerusalem, for Syria and the countries of the east, by the English Church. Parliament authorized that appointment. It was the exercise, according to the hon. gentleman's view, of sovereign authority within the dominion of the Sultan of Turkey; and the only ground of embarrassment with them was whether the Greek Church, as well as the Church of England, being part of the general Catholic Church, would be offensed and think that the English Church were interfering with their jurisdiction; and so the Archbishop of Canterbury addressed a letter to the Bishop of Jerusalem, warning him that he was to cultivate a spirit of Christian charity and of good understanding with the authorities of the Greek Church in that particular section of the country. But to set up the doctrine laid down by the hon. gentleman here, based on the Act of the Queen's supremacy, would be to deny to all churches having a particular form of church polity, the privilege of entending their views of Christianity over the habitable world. I would like to know, according to his view, how it would be possible to obey the Divine command to go into all the world and preach the gospel to every creature. The hon. gentleman would arrest every minister of the Gospel under that theory, who would undertake to preach beyond the limits of the country to which he belonged. I dare say some hon. gentleman will remember when the Methodist Episcopal body in this country formed a part of the Methodist body of the United States, when they had no bishop in Canada, when their conference was held in the State of New York—

Sir JOHN A. MACDONALD. I remember that well.

Mr. MILLS (Bothwell)—when their minister were sent to the Province of Ontario, and when, on account of the sympathies of those ministers with liberal views and their opposition to the connection between Church and State, they were charged with being American emissaries in this country. But I never knew any one who pretended to say it was an act of sedition on their part to come into this country for the purpose of preaching the Gospel. If there had been a State Church in the United States, and had they been sent here by the President, the hon. gentleman might, perhaps, argue as he has on this question, but where are the estates of the church ? Where are the possessions of the Pope that give him anything like temporal dominion ? His authority rests solely upon the implicit acceptance of his teaching and his views by those who profess to be members of the society of which he is the head, and to say that the Roman Catholics in this country may not make him their arbitrator to decide questions of difference, to decide how property, which the only party competent to decide says rightly belongs to them, shall be distributed, would be to place Roman Catholics not on a footing of equality, but on a footing of inferiority to those who are members of other churches. The hon. gentleman argued, from opinions expressed by a writer in the *Quarterly*, that the views entertained by the Jesuit Order were such as they are represented to be. Now, I do not know what their views may be. I do not care. I am not a keeper of their consciences, and so I do not interest myself in them ; but I deny altogether that this Parliament has a right to constitute itself an ecclesiastical tribunal or council for the purpose of seeing whether their views are right or wrong. We may decide for ourselves in our individual capacities, but we are not endowed with any power of that sort, and I do not think any Protestant would care to be judged by any such rule. I was interested, in looking over the speeches made many years ago in the House of Common (England), when it was said that certain members of the Church of England were adopting Armenian views, and one speaker, Mr. Rouse, declared that these persons were emissaries of the Church of Rome. He said :

" I desire it may be considered how the See of Rome doth eat into our religion, and fret into the very banks and walls of it, the laws and statutes of this realm. I desire we may consider the increase of Armenianism, an error that makes the grace of God lackey after the will of man. I desire that we may look into the belly and bowels of this Trojan horse, to see if there be no men in it ready to open the gates to Romish tyranny, for an Armenian is the spawn of a papist, and if the warmth of favor come upon him, you shall see him turn into one of those frogs, that rose out of the bottomless pit : these men having kindled a fire in our neighbor country are now endeavoring to set this kingdom in a flame."

Now, we know that a large portion of the Protestant community in this country are Armenians ; and if we are to judge by the public meetings and the discussions which have taken place on this question, they are as far from Roman Catholicism as any other section of the community. Anyone who remembers something of the history of Holland, will remember how Grotius, because he was an Armenian, was carried out of the country in a cask ; and how John Barnaveldt was carried into another world on a scaffold because he was an Armenian, and for the very reasons given by Mr. Rouse that the doctrines they were teaching would necessarily lead to the restoration of Roman Catholicism. There is nothing, in my judgment, more mischievous than to undertake to pass judgment upon the religious opinions of any portion of the community in a popular assembly and make those opinions the pretext for withholding rights and for imposing disabilities. We have, irrespective of religious opinion in this House, occasionally given aid to Mission Schools. We have aided the Presbyterian Mission Schools, the Methodist Mission Schools, the English Church Mission Schools, the Roman Catholic Mission Schools, and I have never heard any one say that because we did so, as a matter of expediency for the present, and because it was better to establish these schools among the Indians for the time being, than public schools, that this Government was connected with a church or in favor of any particular church on that account. I am not the least afraid that, if we have an open field and fair play, Protestantism is likely to suffer in this country, in consequence of the aggressions, or attributed aggressions of the Roman Catholic Church. I have no doubt whatever, that in a fair field Protestantism will be able to hold its own, and it will succeed just in proportion as it is actuated by the spirit of toleration and fairness, which will serve rather to draw men towards it and secure a favorable consideration for those religious views that it seeks to enunciate, rather than the spirit of intolerance which will repel men from it. How can we secure a fair hearing for our dogmas from our Roman Catholic friends if we do that which they think is unfair to them, and if we undertake to deny to them privileges that we maintain for ourselves? I am not disposed to confer upon any Roman Catholic institution in this country privileges that I would withhold from any Protestant institution of a similar character. I believe that the more clearly the line of separation is drawn between Church and State, the better it will be for all classes in this country, but I admit that I am unable to interfere or to assist in drawing that line in any Province except in the Province of which I am a member. I have the right to exercise my privileges as an elector, and if the policy that has been carried out is one that I think detrimental to the public interest I may, in that capacity, oppose it; but I have no right, from my place in this House, to undertake to do for the people of another Province what I can only do legitimately in my own Province, as an elector of that Province. And so, the more clearly we have impressed upon our minds the fact that each Province must take care of itself, that it must entirely separate the Church from the State for itself, that with that we have nothing to do, that except by usurpation, we cannot interfere, the sooner we can have clearly impressed upon our minds this line of action and the more steadily we adhere to it the better it will be for all parties concerned. The early founders of our Christian religion were men in rather poor circumstances, and occupying very humble social positions. Their influence, at the beginning was with the humbler classes, with Jewish hucksters and with slaves of the Roman Empire. They gradually, in the course of three centuries, worked their way up through every grade of society until the Emperor himself became a convert to the Christian system. At first they had the best organized Government the world has ever seen, hostile to them. If they were able, by their industry, their zeal, their self-denial and their devotion, to what they believed to be the cause of religious truth, to overcome such obstacles and conquer such difficulties, there is no danger that Protestantism in this country, if its ministers are true to the profession of their faith—and, remember, that they are to know nothing else except Christ, and Him crucified—if they are true to their faith and their high calling, and preach the Gospel instead of politics, I am perfectly satisfied that Protestantism will have nothing to fear. I am as ready as any member of this House to resist encroachment. Why should it be otherwise? If I, as many others here are doing at this moment, take a position which many of our friends may not concur in, because they have been misinformed, if I would not be disposed to do wrong to serve the interest of my own friends, and those with whom I sympathise, why should I endanger my political position to promote the religion of a portion of the community which I believe to be, in many respects, erroneous? Let those answer who accuse us of pandering to the Roman Catholics. I do not pretend to judge for them I judge for myself. I accord to them the same freedom I claim for myself, and I would rather, a hundred-fold, be the victim of the wrongful judgment of others, than myself become the instrument of wrong to any portion of my fellow-countrymen.

Mr. CHARLTON. (NORFOLK, N. RIDING.)

I feel called upon, before recording the vote I shall give upon the motion now in your hands, to explain the reasons that will actuate me in voting for that motion I feel that, in doing this, I am separating myself from the majority of my friends in this House, that I am acting with a minority, and probably with a very small minority, of its members; and, were I to look at this question purely from the standpoint of its value in votes, I should no doubt feel perfectly content to give a silent vote, and a vote with the majority. My convictions, however, forbid my voting in this way. I realize that the position I take is an unpopular one in this House. I realize, also, that the position I take will quite possibly send me to private life after the expiration of this Parliament but I feel bound from conviction of duty to take the course I propose to take in reference to this matter. Many of the gentlemen who have addressed the House upon this question have professed to be able to do so entirely independent of all feeling of a religious character. They have professed to be able to divest themselves of all prejudices or bias resulting from their religious belief. I do not know that I will claim to be able to do this. I presume that I am swayed and influenced in the course I take in this matter by my education, by my religious belief, and I approach the consideration of this question, I am free to admit, from the standpoint and influenced by the belief of a Protestant; and, although I shall endeavor to be, and I believe I shall succeed in being impartial in this matter, I do not, I repeat, believe I shall be able to divest myself entirely of all influences that religious training and religious belief may be calculated to exert in reference to it. I feel that this is a question of very great importance, and one of far reaching consequence, and I feel that it is a question upon which men should act from conviction, upon which men should act in the way they believe they are required to act in the best interests of their country and for the purpose of securing the best results as to the future welfare and the future well being of that country. This question has been discussed from a legal standpoint fully and ably. The views of those who are opposed to the action of the Government in this matter, the views of those who will support the motion of my hon. friend from Muskoka (Mr. O'Brien), were most ably presented to the House and to the country by the hon. member for North Simcoe (Mr. McCarthy). The defence of the Government was made in a brilliant and able effort by the Minister of Justice, and the effort of the Minister of Justice was ably seconded by the scholarly and profound argument of the hon. member for Bothwell (Mr. Mills). I shall not attempt to traverse the ground traversed by these gentlemen. My education perhaps does not fit me for an exhaustive disquisition upon the character of this measure from a legal standpoint, and I shall endeavor to present the case from a layman's standpoint, and to present the reasons which influence me in the course which I shall take upon this great question.

There is one feature of this case that has not yet been dwelt upon, at least, to any considerable extent—I refer to the peculiar ethnologic conditions of this Dominion. When the younger Pitt, in 1791, erected the two Provinces in Canada, granting to one Province the use of the French language, French laws, French customs and institutions, giving to the other Province the English language, English laws, and English institutions, avowedly for the purpose of creating two rival, jealous, and, in a sense, hostile Provinces, that the catastrophe that had occurred a few years before, when the thirteen colonies revolted from the British Crown, might not recur again; when, I say, that he erected these two Provinces upon these divergent lines for this avowed purpose, he certainly succeeded most admirably in creating two Provinces with mutual contrasts in language and in the essential characteristics of nationality. These Provinces are not only diverse in race and in language, but also in religion, and the dominant church in the Province of Quebec is a political factor of the very highest importance in this Dominion. It naturally exercises its power and its great influence for the purpose of forwarding its own interests and designs. It does this, Sir, with sleepless vigilance, it does it with consummate ability, and it has been enabled to exercise a most powerful influence upon the destinies and upon the politics of the Dominion of Canada. Now, Sir, as I say, this power is exerted for the furtherance of its purposes, as is most natural. I do not complain of this, I do not say that it is to be expected that any other course would be taken by the French Catholic Church of Canada, I would not say that it was in the interest of Canada, but it is not unnatural that the church should do this. The Minister of Justice last night, in the course of his speech on this question, in defending Mr. Mercier in the course he has taken in regard to the Jesuit estates, alluded to one fact which exemplifies, in the most vivid light imaginable, the great influence and power of that church in the Province of Quebec. He told us that the Jesuit estates held by the Government of Quebec to be Government property, held by them to be a property in which the Jesuits' fraternity had no legal right, to which they had no legal claim, notwithstanding the position of the Government in regard to these estates, the Government was unable to sell this property, that it had been offered for sale and no purchasers could be procured. Why, Sir? Because the power of this church was so great that men did not dare, or would not, as they were deterred by the influence of the church, purchase this property; the power of this church was so great that estates held by the Government to be the property of the Crown, to be a property to which the church and the Jesuit fraternity had no legal claims, could not be sold in consequence of the opposition of the church to their sale. Well, nothing could exemplify more vividly the great influence of this society than this fact referred to by the Minister of Justice.

Sir, I referred, a moment ago, to the peculiar ethnologic conditions of this Dominion. Now, no man, I presume, in this House or in this country, would for a moment assert that it was not in the interest of the country that homogeneity, that assimilation, should be promoted. But the question is, how can this result be obtained? How can the diverse races of this Dominion be made homogeneous, how can they be made to assimilate? It is desirable that such should be done. Every man who wishes to see the Dominion of Canada become a great nation, must desire to see the races occupying this country acting in concert, acting in harmony, and to a much greater extent than at present made homogeneous. I hold, Mr. Speaker, that any measure that will retard the realization of this desire for the assimilation of these races, that any measure that will, on the contrary, have a tendency to set them wider asunder, that will have a tendency to create and foster animosities and the jealousies that are natural to the existence of two such races, is a measure that should be deprecated, is a measure that should be opposed by every lover of his country in this Dominion. Now, events as they are developed have hitherto had a tendency, in some respects, to put these two races wider apart, and this very tendency, in face of the desire of those who wish to see a homogeneous people and a great nation, this very tendency to drive these two races apart, awakens alarm in the breasts of tens of thousands of people in this country; and the desire to avert this tendency, the desire to bring the races nearer together, to secure greater harmony and action between them, is a patriotic desire, by whomsoever it may be entertained.

Mr. MILLS (Bothwell). As in Ireland.

Mr. CHARLTON. Not as in Ireland, but as in Canada, with the hopes of the future before us, with the desire to create a great nation, with a desire to have a nation, not inhabited by two races pulling in different directions, jealous of each other, and seeking, the one to crowd the other out of the race, not as in Ireland, but as we hope to see it in Canada, with every influence set aside that would work against the realization of this dream. Now, Sir, there are, in the agitation that exists to-day, great forces beneath the surface; there are undercurrents that we do not see, the power of which, perhaps, we do not realize; there is an undercurrent that is proceeding from this very desire that this should be a homogeneous people, a desire to lift this nation up to a higher plane with a common purpose, to create a great free state. The question that agitates the mind of the people, that creates the interest in this matter which we are discussing here to-day, is, shall the Dominion of Canada be Saxon or shall it be Celtic? Or shall it be both Saxon and Celtic for all time to come? Shall the two races live together in harmony, or shall they live apart? Shall this be one country, or shall there be a disruption? The question is one of great magnitude, the question is one the importance of which cannot be over estimated, and the issue, Sir, is one that cannot be shirked. Now, these are British Provinces. The design was that these should be Anglo-Saxon common wealths, and the tendency to foster an intense spirit of French nationality, a tendency made more pronounced by the fact that that nationality has a national church which naturally fosters that feeling in the promotion of its own interests, is a tendency that we must all deprecate, is a tendency that we do not wish to see aggravated, is a tendency that those who have the good of their country at heart would rather see mitigated if not removed.

Mr. AMYOT. Oh! Oh!

Mr. CHARLTON. My hon. friend on my left laughs. Well, perhaps he would not wish to see it removed, perhaps he would rather see the difficulties intensified. I would rather see them removed ; I would rather see these two races live in harmony, I would rather see them drawing closer together. I have every respect for the institutions of Quebec; I realize that the character of its institutions, the nature of its laws, and the cast of its society is, in some respects, mediæval rather than modern, but I have every sympathy for Quebec, and I have no desire to interfere with that Province in the least.

Mr. CURRAN. You do it all the same.

Mr. CHARLTON. Sir, I do not propose to do it all the same. I feel that if we desire to promote harmony between these races, the introduction of a society that sedulously fosters the seeds of discord, the history of which in every state of Christendom has shown that it is in its nature an organisation against constituted authority is a great misfortune—Sir, as a lover of this country, as a man desiring to see harmony in this country, I deprecate the introduction of that society into the political circles of Canada. It is for that reason that I, and thousands in this Dominion, deprecate the introduction of that society, deprecate the action of the Government in permitting the incorporation of that society and in permitting its endowment, foreseeing, as they believe they do foresee, in those actions future mischief and future disaster to this country. This is my belief.

Now, Sir, it is true that the Protestants of this country have been supine and nerveless for many years past as regards public questions. They have been for many years past without organisation to guard their own interests and liberties, and until quite recently there has been no distinctive and pronounced Protestant organ. Both the great political parties in this country have sought to obtain French Catholic support. The solidarity of the Catholic French party has enabled them to hold the balance of power; they have held it, they have exercised it for the advantage of their race and for the advantage of their religion, to some extent at least; and in the manipulation of this element, and in the influence wielded by this element, it reminds me at every turn of the history of the United States when the slave power —I make the comparison in no other sense except that they were a minority, and acted for their common interest—controlled the United States for 40 years, although they possessed only about one-third of the votes in the House of Representatives.

controlled the United States because they acted in their own interests at every turn, and supported first one party and then the other as circumstances incident to their own requirement made it necessary to do. We have had the Protestants, as I have said, without an organ, without an organisation, and not awake to their interests, and it is only of recent days that the people are awakening to the danger which, in the estimation of many Protestants, threaten them in this country. I make no apology for being an Anglo-Saxon. I do not consider it a disgrace. I do not consider it even a disadvantage. I look back to the history of the race with pride, I look back to the history of that mother of nations—England—and I think it is a glorious history. I think her institutions are good institutions and that she has been a blessing to the world, and I have no apology to make for saying that I believe it. I make no apology for saying that, so far as my own Province is concerned, I would resist the introduction of that system which is peculiar to your Province, Mr. Speaker. I make no apology for saying that, in my belief, civil and religious liberty should be carefully guarded, and any encroachment upon that civil and religious liberty should be resisted, resisted strongly. resisted vigorously, resisted with courage and resisted without compromise. As regards Quebec, of course there are certain things there that I would not select as a matter of choice. I do not,for instance, think it a very great advantage to pay tithes ; I am unable to see any advantage in fabrique assessments, in a church absorbing the wealth of the country and in its property being exempted from taxation ; but it is none of my business. I do not propose to interfere with it.

An hon. MEMBER. Hear, hear.

Mr. CHARLTON. If the hon. gentleman can see any blessing in that, he is at liberty to enjoy it. But I would interfere and resist any attempt to impose it upon a country where it was not in existence at the time ; I would feel that to be my duty. Now, Mr. Speaker, I do not say this in any offensive sense. Men disagree, men have different opinions, men differ in politics, and in religion, and in what they believe to be for the public interest, and they have a right to do so, and they will continue to do so until the end of time.

The Minister of Justice, last night, in referring to old English law, dwelt at very great length on the subject of obsolete laws. I almost imagined before he had concluded that there was scarcely a law in existence that was not obsolete, and that we were scarcely bound by anything on the Statute-book of England. But I think the Great Charter is not obsolete, that charter upon which we have built our liberties, upon which we have constructed British institutions, that charter under which we have responsible government and parliamentary representation, with the people, through their representatives, controlling the expenditure of the country. The Bill of Rights is not obsolete ; it is in force yet. The supremacy of the Crown, as the embodiment of the power and majesty of the people, is not obsolete. The safeguards of liberty designed by our forefathers to preserve us from encroachments are not obsolete, and the spirit of liberty is not obsolete among the English-speaking race. And it is for this reason, that the spirit of liberty exists, that the safeguards of liberty are in force, that tens of thousands of men have risen in Canada within the last two months to oppose the endowment of that order, whose interests and character we are discussing in this debate, and whose character and record I hold it proper and necessary to discuss and examine in the broadest sense possible. I hold that the incorporation of this order lies at the root of all this trouble. And it is owing to the fact to which I called attention a few moments ago, that there existed among the Protestants a great degree of supineness, and nervelessness, and of blindness to their own interests and the interests of their country, that the incorporation of that order was not resented at the time and was not prevented. Why, a few years ago, in 1873, the Orange Order was incorporated by the Legislature of Ontario. The

Lieutenant Governor of that Province, who was appointed by the right hon. gentleman opposite, withheld that Bill from assent; I am unable to say whether by private advices he was intructed to do so or not, but he withheld it. But we had here the incorporation of the Order of Jesuits two years ago without any withholding of the Bill from assent, without any interference on the part of the Government, and it seems to me a monstrous thing that so loyal an order as the Orange Order, for it is unquestionably loyal, should be denied incorporation and the Jesuits should be permitted incorporation. It reminds me of a story, to the effect that an Irishman, on landing in New-York, was attacked by a dog, and endeavored to pick up one of the paving stones, whereupon, on failing to do so, he said : It is a queer free country this, where the dogs are let loose and the stones are chained down. This is a queer sort of justice that incorporates the Jesuit Order and denies incorporation to the Orangemen ; and I think, while I opposed at the time the incorporation of the Orangemen, on the ground that it would produce dissensions and troubles, the same reasons should have held good in the case of the Jesuit Order as well. The Minister of Justice, last night, held that the Jesuit Order had, in effect, already been incorporated. He instanced the case of the incorporation of the St. Mary's College, which had Jesuit professors, and he contended that because the clergy, forsooth, were Jesuits, this was incorporation, in point of fact, of the Jesuit Order. If a college happened to have three or four infidel professors, would it be the incorporation of the infidel order, or if the college had a few Presbyterian professors, would it be the incorporation of the Presbyterian order ? The assumption was preposterous. The Minister of Justice also said that the order had previously been incorporated. If the society was incorporated in a surreptitious manner it affords me reason for saying that it should not have been done, whether it was done or not.

Now, Mr. Speaker, the character of the Jesuit Order is a matter, in my opinion, which should receive the attention of this House, and the attention of this country. My hon. friend, the Minister of Justice, last night spoke somewhat sneeringly of Parliament resolving itself into a committee for the examination of theological questions, and my hon. friend, the member for Bothwell (Mr. Mills), asserted that Parliament had not the right to constitute itself an ecclesiastical council, to judge the Jesuits. Well, Sir, Parliament, in this matter, is neither constituting itself into a committee for the trial of a theological question, nor into an ecclesiastical council for the trial of the Jesuit Order, but Parliament is called upon, under the circumstances, to examine into the moral and the political tendencies of the order that is on trial before the people of this country. It has the right to do so, it has more than the right to do it; it is the bounden duty of Parliament to enquire as to the character of this organisation, to enquire as to whether those various charges made against this organisation in history for more than 300 years are true, or if any of these charges are true, whether it has proved to be an organisation detrimental to the interests of liberty, in every generation and in every age, or not, and if its antecedents are such as they are represented to be, it should be the duty of Parliament to examine thoroughly the question of whether that order is now what it was before. It is a question of the utmost importance; it is not a theological question; it is not an ecclesiastical question, but it is a question of the highest moment to the State. It is a question which should engage the attention of every statesman in the country; it is a question that has an intimate bearing upon the welfare of this country, and I propose, Sir, to examine that question. I propose to examine it, not that I think I am making myself a member of a committee to examine into theological tenets, not that I propose to make myself a member of an ecclesiastical committee to try a religious order, but I propose to look into the antecedents and character of this order, in order to see whether I believe that their establishment in Canada would be detrimental to the political interests of this country. I propose to examine the question in its political bearing, and in its political bearing alone. Now, Sir, this order had been in existence for nearly 250 years, when it was suppressed by the authority to which it professed to owe allegiance. I suppose the Pope was infallible then, and if Pope Clement XIV was infallible, and if he suppressed the order of the Jesuits he probably had good reasons for doing so, and I think he had. I do not propose to call into question his infallibility. I do not propose to look into the question of the propriety of the step he took in dissolving that order, but I do propose to ask the attention of this House to some portions of the celebrated brief which Pope Clement XIV issued, and by which this order was disbanded. After declaring in his brief the purposes for which the order was instituted, and the various privileges granted by Paul III, and subsequent Popes, the brief of suppression goes on to say :

"Notwithstanding so many and so great favors, it appears from the Apostolical Constitutions that almost at the very moment of its institution there arose in the bosom of this society, divers seeds of discord and dissention, not only among the companions themselves, but with other irregular orders, the secular clergy, the academies, the universities, the public schools, and lastly, even with the princes of the states in which the society was received. These dissensions and disputes arose sometimes concerning the nature of their views, the time of admission to them, the power of expulsion, the right of admission to holy orders without a title, and without having taken the solemn vows, contrary to the tenor of the decrees of the Council of Trent, and of Pius V, our predecessor; sometimes concerning the absolute authority assumed by the General of the said order, and about matters relating to the good government and discipline of the order: sometimes concerning different points of doctrine, concerning their schools, or concerning such of their exemption privileges, as the ordinaries and other ecclesiastical or civil officers declared to be contrary to their rights and jurisdictions. In short, accusations of the gravest nature, and very detrimental to the peace and tranquility of a Christian commonwealth have been continually brought against the said order. Hence arose that infinity of appeals and protests against this society, which so many sovereigns have laid at the foot of the Throne of our predecessors, Paul IV, Pius V, and Sixtus V.

"After so many storms, troubles and divisions, every good man looked forward with impatience to the happy day which was to restore peace and tranquility. But under the reign of this same Cl-ment XIII, the times became more full of difficulty and storm: complaints and quarrels were multiplied on every side; in some places dangerous seditions arose, tumults, discords, scandals which, weakening or entirely breaking the bounds of Christian charity, excited the faithful to all the rage of party hatred and enmities. Desolation and danger grew to such a height, that the very sovereigns, whose piety and liberality towards the society were so well known as to be looked upon as hereditary in their families—we mean our dearly beloved sons in Christ, the Kings of France, Spain, Portugal and Sicily—found themselves reduced to the necessity of expelling, and driving from their states, kingdoms, and provinces, these very companions of Jesus; persuaded that there remained no other remedy to so great evils ; and, this step was necessary, in order to prevent Christians from rising one against another, and from massacreing each other in the very bosom of our common mother, the Holy Church. They said, our dear sons in Jesus Christ having since considered, that even this remedy was not sufficient for reconciling the whole Christian world, unless that society was absolutely abolished and suppressed, made known their demands and wishes in this matter to our said predecessor, Clement XIII. They united their common prayers and authority, to obtain that this last method might be put in practice, as the only one capable of assuring the constant repose of their subjects, and the good of the Catholic Church in general. But the unexpected death of the aforesaid Pontiff, rendered this project abortive.

"As soon as by the Divine mercy and Providence we were raised to the chair of St. Peter, the same prayers, demands, and wishes were laid before us, and strengthened by the pressing solicitations of many bishops, and other persons of distinguished rank, learning, and piety. But, that we might choose the wisest course, in a matter of so much moment we determined not to be so precipitate, but to take due time ; not only to examine attentively, weigh carefully, and take counsel wisely, but also by unceasing prayers to ask of the Father of lights His particular assistance; exhorting the faithful to co-operate with us by their prayers and good works in obtaining this needful succor."

After remarking on what the Council of Trent had decided, with respect to the clergy who were members of this society, the brief proceeds:

"Actuated by so many and important considerations, and, as we hope, aided by the presence and inspiration of the Holy Spirit ; compelled also by the necessity of our office, which strictly obliges us to conciliate, maintain and confirm the peace and tranquility of the Christian Commonwealth, and remove every obstacle which may tend to trouble it ; having further considered that the said Society of Jesus can no longer produce these abundant fruits and those great advantages, with a view to which it was instituted, approved by so many of our predecessors, and endowed with so many and extensive privileges : that, on the contrary, it was difficult, or to say impossible, that the church could recover a firm and lasting peace so long as the said society subsisted ; in consequence hereof, and determined by the particular reasons we have alleged, and forced by other motives which prudence and the good government of the church have dictated it, the knowledge of which we keep to ourselves, conforming ourselves to the example of our predecessors, and particularly to that of Gregory X, in the General Council of Lyons; the rather as in the present case we are determining upon the fate of a society classed among the mendicant orders, both its constitution and privileges; after a mature deliberation, we do, out of our certain knowledge and the fulness of our apostolical power, suppress and abolish the said society ; we deprive it of all power of action whatever, of its houses, schools, colleges, hospitals, lands, and in short, every other place whatever, in whatever kingdom or Province they may be situated ; we abrogate and annul its statutes, rules, customs, decrees and constitutions, even though confirmed by oath and approved by the Holy See, or otherwise ; in like manner we annul all and every its privileges, favors general or particular, the tenor whereof is, and is taken to be as fully and as amply expressed in this present brief, as if the same were inserted, word for word in whatever clauses, form or decree, or under whatever sanction, their privileges may have been conceived. We declare every authority of all kinds, the General, the Provincials, and Visitors and other superiors of the said society, to be forever annulled and extinguished, of what nature soever the said authority may be, whether relating to things spiritual or temporal."

This, Sir, is a portion of the brief of Pope Clement XIV suppressing this order. Now, Sir, I want to enquire whether it will be asserted that His Holiness the Pope of Rome, in thus suppressing this order, and in using the language he did with regard to it, was acting in ignorance—whether in his infallibility he was mistaken as to the character of this order.

Some hon. MEMBERS. Oh.

Mr. CHARLTON. Well, I am not very well posted as to the tenets of the church, if the Pope is not held to be infallible there is a popular misapprehension upon that point. If any one in this House wishes to cast discredit on his judgment or on the motives which actuated him in issuing this brief, I have nothing to say; but I believe the Pope, in suppressing this order, acted from reason and knowledge in sying what he did in this brief, and that, in issuing it, he acted in accordance with the desire of every king and every statesman in Europe. This order has been arraigned at the bar of history, and has been condemned; I believe it deserved suppression; and I believe that Pope Clement XIV, acting at the solicitation of the various kings of Europe, suppressed it for good and sufficient reasons. Now, my hon. friend from Lincoln (Mr. Rykert),the other night,read an extract from Macaulay regarding this order, and, as in the case of a good many other extracts, stopped just where he should have gone on. I will take up the thread of the hon. gentleman's discourse, and proceed from where he left off. At that point Lord Macaulay proceeded to say:

" But with the admirable energy, disinterestedness, and self devotion, which were characteristic of the society, great voices were mingled. It was alleged, and not without foundation, that the ardent public spirit, which made the Jesuit regardless of his case, of his liberty and of his life, made him also regardless of truth and of mercy ; that no means which could promote the interest of his religion seemed to him unlawful, and that by the interest of his religion he too often meant the interest of his society. It was alleged that, in the most atrocious plots recorded in history, his agency could be distinctly traced ; that, constant only in attachment to the fraternity to which he belonged, he was in some countries the most dangerous enemy of freedom, and in others the most dangerous enemy of order. The mighty victories which he boasted that he had achieved in the cause of the church were, in the judgment of many illustrious members of that church, rather apparent than real. He had indeed labored with a wonderful show of success to reduce the world under her laws ; but he had done so by relaxing her laws to suit the temper of the word. Instead of toiling to elevate human nature to the noble standard fixed by Divine precept and example, he had lowered the standard till it was beneath the average level of human nature. He gloried in multitude of converts who had been baptised in the remote regions of the East ; but it was reported that from some of those converts, the facts on which the whole theology of the

Gospel depends had been cunningly concealed, and that others were permitted to avoid persecution by bowing down before the images of false gods, while internally repeating paters and aves. Nor was it only in heathen countries that such arts were said to be practiced. It was not strange that people of all ranks, and especially of the highest ranks, crowded to the confessionals in the Jesuit temples ; for from these confessionals none went discontented away. There the priest was all things to all men. He showed just so much rigor as might not drive those who knelt at his spiritual tribunal to the Dominican or the Franciscan Church. If he had to deal with a mind truly devout, he spoke in the saintly tones of the primitive Fathers; but with that very large part of mankind who have religion enough to make them uneasy when they do wrong, and not religion enough to keep them from doing wrong, he followed a very different system. Since he could not reclaim them from guilt, it was his business to save them from remorce. He had at his command an immense dispensary of anodynes for wounded consciences. In the books of casuistry which had been written by his brethren, and printed with the approbation of his superiors, were to be found doctrines consolatory to transgressors of every class. There the bankrupt was taught how he might, without sin, secrete his goods from his creditors. The servant was taught how he might, without sin, run off with his master's plate. The pander was assured that a Christian man might innocently earn his living by carrying letters and messages between married women and their gallants. The high-spirited and punctilious gentlemen of France were gratified by a decision in favor of duelling. The Italians, accustomed to darker and baser modes of vengeance, were glad to learn that they might, without any crime, shoot at their enemies from behind hedges. To deceit was given a license sufficient to destroy the whole value of human contracts and of human testimony. In truth, if society continued to hold together, if life and property enjoyed any security, it was because common sense and common humanity restrained men from doing what the Society of Jesus assured them that they might with a safe conscience do, so strangely were good and evil intermixed in the character of these celebrated brethren ; and the intermixture was the secret of their gigantic power. That power could never have belonged to mere hypocrites. It could never have belonged to rigid moralists. It was to be attained only by men sincerely enthusiastic in the pursuit of a great end, and, at the same time, unscrupulous as to the choice of means."

Now, Sir, I spoke of this order having been banished from various countries. It was banished from England in 1579, again in 1581, again in 1586, again in 1601, again in 1604, and again in 1791; and, Sir, in view of the character of British legislation with regard to the Society of Jesuits, its existence and its presence in any part of the British realm is a contempt of law. By the Chatolic Emancipation Act, 10 George IV, chapter 7, certain political disabilities were removed from the Catholics of Great Britain. The Act recites the oath which Catholics were required to take before being invested with the rights of citizenship and the right to hold office ; and this Act of 1829, which is not an obsolete law, but a law still in force, which is a law paramount over all colonial laws, contains an enactment with regard to the Jesuits; and I shall take the liberty of reading sections 28, 29, 30, 31, 33 and 34. I shall read them because they have an important bearing upon the case under discussion, because these articles, of this Emancipation Act, clearly prove that the incorporation of the Society of Jesuits is an unconstitutional Act in this country or in any other part of the British realm :

" Section 28. And whereas Jesuits and members of other religious orders, communities or societies of the Church of Rome bound by monastic or religious vows, are resident within the United Kingdom, and it is expedient to make provision for the gradual suppression and final prohibition of the same, therein, therefore be it enacted that every Jesuit and every member of any other religious order, community, or society of the Church of Rome, bound by monastic or religious vows, who, at the time of the commencement of this Act shall be within the United Kingdom shall, within six calendar months after the commencement of this Act, deliver to the clerk of peace of the county or place where such person shall reside or to his deputy, a notice or statement in the form and containing the particulars required to be set forth in the schedule to this Act annexed ; which notice or statement such clerk of the peace, or his deputy, shall preserve and register amongst the records of such county or place without any fee, and shall forthwith transmit a copy of such notice or statement to the Chief Secretary of the Lord Lieutenant or other Chief Governor or Governors of Ireland, if such person shall reside in Ireland, or if, in Great Britain, to one of His Majesty's Principal Secretaries of State, and in case any person shall offend in the premises, he shall forfeit and pay to His Majesty, for every calendar month during which he shall remain in the United Kingdom without having delivered such notice or statement as is hereinbefore required, the sum of fifty pounds.

" Section 29. And be it further enacted, that if any Jesuit, or member of any such religious order, community or society as aforesaid, shall, after the commencement of this Act, come into this realm, he shall be deemed and taken to be guilty of a misdemeanor and being thereof lawfully convicted shall be sentenced and ordered to be banished from the United Kingdom for the term of his natural life.

" Section 30. Provided always, and be it further enacted, that in case any natural born subject of this realm, being at the time of the commencement of this Act a Jesuit, or other member of any such religious order, community or society as aforesaid, shall, at the time of the commencement of this Act be out of the realm, it shall be lawful for such person to return or come into this realm : and upon his return or coming into the realm, he is hereby required, within the space of six calendar months, to deliver such notice or statement to the clerk of the peace of the county or place where he shall reside, or his deputy, for the purpose of being so registered and transmitted as hereinbefore directed ; and in case any such person shall neglect or refuse so to do, he shall for such offence forfeit and pay to His Majesty for every calendar month during which he shall remain in the United Kingdom without having delivered such notice or statement, the sum of fifty pounds.

" Section 31. Provided also, and be it further enacted, that notwithstanding anything hereinbefore contained, it shall be lawful for any one of His Majesty's Principal Secretaries of State, being a Protestant, by a license in writing, signed by him, to grant permission to any Jesuit or member of any such religious order, community or society as aforesaid, to come into the United Kingdom, and to remain therein for such period as the said Secretary of State shall think proper, nor exceeding, in any case, the space of six calendar months, and it shall also be lawful for any one of His Majesty's Principal Secretaries of State to revoke any license granted before the expiration of the time mentioned therein, if he shall so think fit ; and if any such person to whom such license shall have been granted shall not depart from the United Kingdom within twenty days after the expiration of the time mentioned in such license, or if such license shall have been revoked, then within twenty days after notice of such revocation shall have been given to him, every person so offending shall be deemed guilty of a misdemeanor, and being thereof lawfully convicted, shall be sentenced and ordered to banished from the United Kingdom for the term of his natural life.

" Section 33. And be it further enacted that, in case any Jesuit, or member of any such religious order, community or society, as aforesaid, shall, after the commencement of this Act, within any part of the United Kingdom, admit any person to become a regular ecclesiastic, or brother, or member of any such religious order, community, or society, or be aiding or consenting thereto, or shall administer, or cause to be administered, or be aiding or assisting in the administering or taking any oath, vow, or engagements, purporting, or intended to bind the person taking the same to the rules, ordinances, or ceremonies of such religious order, community, or society, every person offending in the premises, in England, or Ireland, shall be deemed guilty of a misdemeanor, and in Scotland shall be punished by fine and imprisonment,

" Section 34. And be it further enacted that, in case any person shall, after the commencement of this Act, within any part of this United Kingdom, be admitted, or become a Jesuit or brother, or member of any other such religious order, community, or society, as aforesaid, such person shall be deemed and taken to be guilty of a misdemeanor, and being thereof lawfully convicted shall be sentenced and ordered to be banished from the United Kingdom for the term of his natural life."

Now, that is the statute which imposes penalties and a fine upon any foreigner who is a Jesuit for coming into the United Kingdom, and which imposes penalties and a fine upon any person who inducts a person into the order, and upon any person who becomes a member of the order. That is taken from the Catholic Emancipation Act of 1829. Now, I am unable to see, in the face of the provisions of that Act, how the incorporation of this order can be legal or constitutional either in Canada or in any other part of Her Majesty's realm. This case was referred to, some years ago, in a debate in the House of Commons. Mr. Disraeli who was then the First Minister of the Crown, stated, on the 10th of July, 1875, that :

" Although no proceedings had been taken against the Jesuits under the Act of 1829, he begged it to be understood that the provisions under the Act are not obsolete, but on the contrary are reserving powers of the law of which the government will be prepared to avail themselves if necessary."

And Mr. Gladstone, who was asked his opinion upon this matter, as to the legality of the residence of the Jesuits in England, referred his correspondents to this Act of Parliament, the provisions of which with regard to the Jesuits I have read. And the *Law Journal* of England, which contains an account of this matter, then adds:

" This Act, while it carried out the well known reform commemorated by its name, imposes restrictions on 'Jesuits and members of other religious orders, communities or societies of the Church of Rome bound by monastic or religious vows,' of which it recites it is 'expedient to provide for the gradual suppression and final prohibition.' Any of these persons, not including nuns, coming into the realm without a license which can last only six months, are, by section 29, declared guilty of a misdemeanor and may be sentenced to be banished for life. Similarly, any persons admitted within the kingdom to membership in any of the orders in question may, by section 34, be sentenced to banishment for life. If, although banished they do not go out of the country, the Sovereign in Council may have them conveyed to some place abroad. Moreover, if they are found in the country at the end of three months they may be convicted again and transported. Will this law be now enforced ? Or will a charitable reserve be shown, entailing, as it naturally will do, further lawlessness."

Now, the treaty ceding Canada in 1763, provided for the freedom of the Catholic religion in the country, so far as the laws of Great Britain permitted the exercise of that religion, and the Act 14 George III, chapter 83, provided that the French Catholics in this country may exercise the religion of the Church of Rome subject to the King's supremacy. The right to exercise this provision is thus subject to the provisions of the law, and one of the provision of that law I have called the attention of the House to with regard to the Jesuit organisation, contained in the Emancipation Act of 1829. It was claimed last night by the Minister of Justice that, at the time of the Conquest, the property of individuals was not forfeited or confiscated. It was claimed that the property of the Jesuits was not subject to forfeiture or confiscation under the terms of the Treaty of Paris ceding Canada to Great Britain. But I think it must be held that the Jesuit organisation would not be treated upon the basis of individuals, but as corporation, and I find that Act says :

" And be it further enacted, by the authority aforesaid, that all His Majesty's Canadian subjects within the Province of Quebec, the religious orders and communities only excepted——"

Are to have these privileges. So that the religious orders and communities were, by the terms of the cession, expressly excepted from the privileges granted to the inhabitants of the Province of Quebec, or the Province of Canada.

Mr. MILLS (Bothwell). What are you reading from ?

Mr. CHARLTON. I am reading from 14 George III, chapter 83, the Quebec Act. All the rights possessed by the citizens of the Province of Quebec, or of old Canada, were rights delegated by the British Crown, rights expressly granted, rights, in every case, subordinate to the supremacy of the Crown, and subordinate to the supremacy of Imperial law ; and, if that Catholic Emancipation Act of 1829 contains, as I have shown, express provisions, making it a misdemeanor for a foreign Jesuit to come into England, making it a misdemeanor to induce a British subject into the Jesuit Order, making it a misdemeanor on the part of the person who inducts him and on the part of the person who is inducted, in face of the provisions of that law, I hold that it is simply preposterous to say that the incorporation of the Order of Jesuits in British America, is a constitutional Act. If the incorporation of this order is unconstitutional, it follows, as a matter of course, that all the Acts based upon that incorporation, are unconstitutional. If the incorporation is unconstitutional, the endowment is unconstitutional, and the Jesuits' Estates Act is an unconstitutional Act, if the Incorporation Act is so.

It has been made by British law, upon more occasions than one, an unconstitutional Act to procure judgments or determinations, &c., from the See of Rome, of any foreign potentate. This legislation was first initiated under Edward III, it was continued under Richard II, again under Henry VIII. By 24 Henry VIII, chapter 21, penalties are imposed for procuring inhibitions, judgments and other processes from the See of Rome within the King's dominions—not alone in England, Ireland and Scotland, but in any part of the King's dominions. The 24 Henry VIII, chapter

21, prohibits the King, his heirs and successors, kings of the realm, and all subjects of the realm or of the Crown, for suing for licenses, dispensations, compositions, faculties, grants, rescripts, delegations, or any other instruments in writing from the Bishop of Rome, called the Pope, or from any person or persons having or pretending to have any authority by the same. " The King, his heirs and successors," being expressly named in the Act, the reigning sovereign is bound by the prohibition; and it is not within the constitutional power of a Colonial Legislature or Governor to absolve the Crown from its provisions, or to enact or assent to any Bill violating this or any other Imperial statute in force in the colony. The Crown can only be relieved from the prohibitions of the Act by the power that imposed them, namely, the Imperial Parliament. And in 13 Elizabeth, chapter 2, and 1 Elizabeth, chapter 1, it is provided in more express terms that:

" The usurped power and jurisdiction of the Bishop of Rome, heretofore unlawfully claimed and usurped within this realm, and other the dominions to the Queen's Majesty belonging. "

Shall not be exercised. Neither the Treaty of Surrender, nor the Act of 1774 did more than to grant the free exercise of the Catholic religion in Canada, so far as the laws of Great Britain permit. But we are told by the Minister of Justice that a Provincial Parliament can repeal Imperial statutes as concerns itself, if I understood him aright. I do not accept this definition of the law. I do not hold that the thing formed can say to that which formed it: what doest thou? and can set aside the mandate of the power which formed it. I find in the British North America Act a provision which is antagonistic to the statement of my hon. friend the Minister of Justice. The 129th section of that Act contains the following :—

" Except as otherwise provided by this Act, all laws in force in Canada, Nova Scotia or New Brunswick at the Union, and all courts of civil and criminal jurisdiction, and all legal commissions, powers and authorities, and all officers judicial, administrative and ministerial, existing therein at the Union, shall continue in Ontario, Quebec, Nova Scotia and New Brunswick respectively, as if the Union had not been made: subject, nevertheless (except with respect to such as are enacted by or exist under Acts of the Parliament of Great Britain, or of the Parliament of the United Kingdom of Great Britain and Ireland) to be repealed, abolish or altered by the Parliament of Canada ; or by the Legislature of the respective Provinces, according to the authority of the Parliament or of that Legislature under this Act. "

So that by this Constitution of British North America, by section 129, special exception is made as to this power in regard to such Act as existed by the authority of the Parliament of Great Britain or the Parliament of Great Britain and Ireland. I have here a case, if it is necessary to quote it, *ex parte* Renaud, which bears out this view. The judgment is too long to read unless it is desired, but I can send it to the Minister of Justice if he desires. I have laid down the premises, and I think they cannot be controverted that the recognition of any foreign potentate, prince or ecclesiastical, in any statute enacted within the dominions of the Crown of Great Britain, which recognizes that power or its inhibitions, decrees or processes, is an unconstitutional act. Now, the Estates Bill which we have under consideration does recognize His Holiness the Pope as a potentate. It treats with that potentate as to the terms of the settlement of a domestic matter in a Province of the Dominion. The Bill is passed subject to the approval of that potentate, as is shown by the language in this return of correspondence in connection whih this matter. I find in the letter of Mr. Mercier to Father Turgeon, dated the 1st May, 1888, in the seventh paragraph, the following language used :

" That any agreement made between you and the Government of the Province will be binding only in so far as it shall be ratified by the Pope and the Legislature of this Province."

" By the Pope and Legislature of this Province". Sir, the Legislature not only passes a Bill subject to the Pope's approval, but this Act places public money at the disposal of His Holiness the Pope, as is shown in the same letter, in paragraph 8, which reads as follows:

"That the amount of the compensation fixed shall remain in possession of the Government of the Province as a special deposit until the Pope has ratified said settlement, and made known his wishes respecting the distribution of such amount in this country."

Now, Sir, the hon. member for Stanstead (Mr. Colby) told us the other night that this provision was a very bitter pill for the Protestants of Quebec. I do not wonder that is the case. A pill that treats with His Holiness as to the terms of a domestic matter, that passes a Bill subject to the approval of His Holiness, that places public money at the disposal of His Holiness, must have been a bitter pill, as the hon. gentleman expressed it, for the Protestants of Quebec to swallow. But not only is the Bill open to these objections, but it distinctly submits the legislation of the Province of Quebec to the ratification of the Pope, as is shown by this return on page 13:

"It is also one way of commemorating, in the political history of the country, that glorious concordat, the effecting whereof would be associated with the name of your Government, as soon as the Holy Father has ratified it; that is, that the establishments of the Jesuit Fathers in this Province are always allowed, in accordance with their deserts, and if they ask for it, to participate in the grants which the Government of this Province allows to other institutions to encourage teaching, education, industries, arts and colonisation."

Now, Mr. Speaker, any law which is open to these objections, any law which calls in a foreign potentate to dictate with reference of the settlement of a domestic matter, which places moneys at his disposal, which submits legislation to his ratification, leaving him to accept or reject it—any Bill, I say, subject to these conditions, liable to these objections, is a Bill which, under the law I have quoted bearing upon the question of the Queen's supremacy in the British realms, is clearly unconstitutional and clearly contrary to the spirit and to the letter of the English law. The Minister of Justice told us last night that the only objections to this Bill were contained in the preamble. He did not deny that these were some objectionable features in the preamble of this Bill, but the preamble, he said, was not really a portion of the Bill, and consequently the Bill was not subject to that objection. But I find, Sir, that the Bill itself refers to this preamble, and if the hon. gentleman will turn to sections 1 and 2 of that Bill, he will find that those sections read as follows:—

"1. The aforesaid arrangements entered into between the Premier and the Reverend Father Turgeon are hereby ratified, and the Lieutenant Governor in Council is authorized to carry them out according to their forms and tenor."

Section 2 says:

"2. The Lieutenant Governor in Council is authorized to pay out of any public moneys at his disposal, the sum of $400,000 in the manner and under the conditions mentioned in the documents above cited, and to make any deeds that he may deem necessary for the full and entire execution of such agreement."

So the objectionable features contained in the preamble are embodied in the Bill, specially referred to in the Bill, confirmed in the Bill, and form in point of fact a portion of the Bill itself. Now, Mr. Speaker, it is asserted by Mr. Mercier, it is admitted, I believe, by my hon. friend the Minister of Justice, it is not disputed, so far as I am aware, by anyone, that the Jesuits had not legal right to those estates. My hon. friend the member for Bothwell sought to break the force of the arguments with reference to the want of any legal claim on the part of the Jesuit Society, sought to break the force of the payment of money to the order of the Pope, by referring to the Clergy Reserve case, by speaking of the commutation of the Clergy Reserves having been paid by the Government of Canada to certain ecclesiastical bodies,

Well, Sir, the cases are not parallel. No claim was set up in that instance that these ecclesiastical bodies had not a legal claim. On the contrary that claim was admitted there was a commutation of the claim, and the money was paid to them under that commutation. But that is not a parallel claim to this present case, where there was no legal claim, where no legal demand could possibly be made on the part of the Jesuit organisation for the payment of money. Now, I have referred before to the fact of these estates being the property of the Crown. I have referred to the Act of 1774, which specially exempted the ecclesiastical corporations from participation in the rights and annuities that pertained to individuals, and the property of the corporations was undoubtedly the property of the Crown. Foreign corporations could not hold property then, they could not hold property in Canada till a very recent period. The fact that this was a religious order that had been endowed with its lands by the King of France, places this corporation in such a position that its rights were forfeited when the conquest took place, and the forfeiture was completed when the order was expelled. We have an instance recorded, a case brought to trial within recent years, where it was decided that a foreign corporation could not hold property in the Province of Quebec except by virtue of special legislative action, the case of the Chaudière Gold Mining Co. vs. George Desbarats which was before the Privy Council in 1873. It was held :

"That, by the law of the Province of Quebec, corporations are under a disability to acquire lands without the permission of the Crown or the authority of the Legislature, that a foreign corporation could not purchase lands in said Province without such permission or authority, and had no action for damages against the vendor."

There can be no question about the loss of title by the Jesuit Order. In 1841, when this property was dealt with, it was the property of the Crown, and there can be no doubt that between 1841 and 1867, when the Provinces entered into confederation, this particular property was appropriated to the schools of the Province of Quebec, and there can be no doubt that this property having been appropriated to the school funds of the Province, it was unconstitutional to divert it to other sources and use it for other purposes.

Now, there is another objection to this settlement which leads me to believe that it cannot be a final settlement. Other demands may be made. Subsequent events may show that the lands were sold for more than was anticipated. The Jesuits may fall back on the estimation of the value made at one time which was about $400,000 and may claim more if the property sells for more. The correspondence, if carefully scrutinised, will lead one to the conclusion that we are not by any means in a position where we can be sure that this case is finally closed. There is one piece of property which is considered as part of the Jesuits' estates, the Champ de Mars, which is Dominion property. There is Laprairie Common, which has been passed over to the Jesuits but held to be Dominion property. It has been occupied by the Dominion Government as a parade ground for many years, and they have the right of possession at least. I assert my belief that the common of Laprairie is Dominion property, which has been granted to the Order of the Jesuits by the Province of Quebec. The correspondence with regard to this matter, if it is carefully scrutinised, will lead us to the opinion that it is far from being settled. I find in the letter from the Premier of Quebec to Father Turgeon, dated 1st May, the following clause :—

"That you will grant to the Government of the Province of Quebec in full, complete and perpetual concession of all the property which may have belonged in Canada, under whatever title, to the fathers of the old society, and that you will renounce to all rights generally whatsoever upon such property and the revenues therefrom in favor of our Province, the whole, as well in the name of the Order of Jesuits, and of your present corporation as in the name of the Pope, of the Sacred College of the Propaganda and of the Roman Catholic Church in general."

To this letter the Rev. Father replied on 8th of May as follows :—

" The Government of the Province of Quebec will receive a full, complete and perpetual concession of all the property which may have belonged in Canada, by whatever title, to the fathers of the old society, and the Jesuit fathers will renounce all rights generally whatsoever upon such property and the revenues therefrom in favor of the Province, the whole, in the name of the Pope, of the Sacred College of the Propaganda and of the Roman Catholic Church in general."

What does that amount to ? The Society of Jesus gives a quit claim for all its property to the province of Quebec. Part of that property, the Champ de Mars, valued at $1,024,000 is the property of the Dominion ; and we shall have in due time, perhaps, Mr. Mercier coming to Ottawa with a demand for the settlement of his claim against the Dominion Government for the value of the Champ de Mars because of this transaction, and because a quit claim was given by His Holiness the Pope in behalf of the Jesuits. If the argument of the Minister of Justice is correct, if the Jesuits have a title to this property that claim would be good ; and if this Bill becomes law we are exposing ourselves to the possible contingency of having the Province of Quebec make a claim on the Dominion for the value of that portion of the Jesuits' estates known as the Champ de Mars. And then we have the other possibility of the Society of Jesus coming to the Dominion and demanding the value of the Laprairie Common, which has been granted it by the Province of Quebec, but which is probably the actual property of the Dominion of Canada. We are leaving ourselves open to further demands with respect to this matter ; and I believe for this consideration, if there were not others, it would be proper and prudent to disallow this Bill. The other objection I have to this Bill is, that I hold it to be in the highest degree dangerous and improper to make grants to religious bodies. If you once open the door, if once you permit that species operation to be commenced in this country, there is no human wisdom that can tell where it eventually will end. Can any one believe that this grant made to the Society of the Jesuits by the Province of Quebec has no connection whatever with political exigencies ? Can anyone doubt that seeking political influence has something to do with this matter, and if it has been the motive in one case, may it not be the motive in another ? Are we not opening the door to great evils that will be introduced if we permit an arrangement made between the Premier of the Province of Quebec and the Society of Jesus, by which the Jesuits are endowed with $400,000 upon a most doubtful claim—what may be the next thing ? I believe upon the ground that this Bill paves the way to further demands for religious grants that may be successfully pressed when votes and influence are badly needed by some political party that it endangers the interests of this country, and for this, if for no other reason, this Act should be disallowed.

I have now concluded with the constitutional aspect of this case. I hold that the incorporation of the Society of Jesus is unconstitutional because the existence of that society is prohibited by English law. In England the Jesuits' society is an illegal body ; the initiation into the Society of Jesus of a member is illegal, it is illegal on the part of the man who does it, and it is illegal for the one initiated. They are under pains and penalties, it is an unconstitutional society, it is under the ban of English law ; that being the case, it is not an order that can be constitutionally incorporated in any part of the British realm. Then I hold that the Jesuits' Estates Act, being predicated upon, that Act is itself necessarily unconstitutional. It is unconstitutional further in the fact that it calls in a foreign potentate, recognizes him, places money at its disposal, place a piece of legislation at his disposal to ratify or to set aside, and in that respect it is clear that it is in contravention of British law and British supremacy. For these reasons I hold that the measure is clearly unconstitutional, and as such should be without delay disallowed by the Government of this Dominion,

But even if it was constitutional, even if the whole argument I have constructed so far was baseless and was swept away, and if this measure was shown to be constitutional, constitutional as regards the Bill, constitutional in being founded on a constitutional Act, permitting the incorporation of the Society of Jesus, yet I hold that, as a question of public policy, the measure should be disallowed. The position which the Liberals of this country occupy in this case is briefly this : They take high ground in defence of provincial rights ; they take high ground upon the question of the Dominion Government interfering with provincial legislation. And I suppose with there views upon this case, with their record, even though they did not approuve of this Bill, even if they considered it was an improper Bill, they would not counsel and support the proposition to disallow the Bill, on the ground that it was interfering with provincial rights. But whether it is desirable that the Government should be debarred from the exercise of the prerogative of this disallowance, is an abstract question : whether it would be a good thing to reconstruct our constitution and to bar the Government from the exercise of that privilege or not, I do not venture to say, but I do say that the right exists and is clearly conferred on the Government. And further, the right has been repeatedly exercised. The hon. member for Bothwell (Mr. Mills), in the course of his argument said that the prerogative of disallowance was not essential to the maintenance of our constitution, and he said that in the United States no such prerogative of disallowance was permitted on the part of the Central Government, that the remedy there lay in an appeal to the Supreme Court of the United States. That is perfectly true. But the hon. gentleman is aware that there is a vast difference between the structure of the Dominion constitution and that of the United States. The principle of the United States Government I believe is that the State is souvereign, within its own proper sphere, and all the powers exercised by the Government of the United States are powers delegated by the States, which in there individual capacity as States ratified the original constitution, and must ratify all amendments to the same, and every power not thus specially delegated to the Central Government by the constitution is reserved to the States. What is the case in the Dominion of Canada ? All powers not specially granted to the several Provinces by the British North American Act, are reserved to the Dominion and any Act passed by a Provincial Legislature may be disallowed by the Privy Council. That is the difference between the two. We had in this country a Legislative Union and we parted with that and entered into Confederation, and whether it was unwise to invest the Government at Ottawa with the power of disallowance or not, this Government can exercise the power, it has exercised the power, and it has in repeated instances put that power into operation. It has done it in the case of railway legislation in Manitoba,and it has done it in the case of the Streams Bill, and numerous other cases. I am willing to admit that this power should be exercised with the utmost caution ; I am willing to admit that the plainest and most palpable reasons should exist for the exercise of this power, but I am ready to assert, Sir, there has never been a case in the history of the Dominion of Canada where, upon broad constitutional grounds, and having due regard to the general interests of the great mass of the people of this country, it was more proper to disallow a Bill, than in this particular instance ; and that the settlement of the Jesuits' Estates Act was, above all other measures that have ever come under the cognisance of this Government, a measure that should be disallowed. My hon. friend the member for Bothwell (Mr. Mills) says that there are two classes of case where disallowance is warrantable, and one is the case where the Bill is clearly unconstitutional. This is a case of that kind ; this Bill is clearly unconstitutional in my opinion. He says the other case is where a Bill is not in the interest of the entire Dominion. Well, this case covers this Bill also. The Bill is clearly unconstitutional and it is clearly not in the interest of the Dominion, and so, by the hon. gentleman's own logic, this Bill should be disallowed. This power of veto is clearly a constitutional power which may be exercised by the Government, which the Government has the right to exercise, which the Government has exercised in former cases, and which, in my opinion, in view of the character of the Bill, and of the probable future consequences of allowing this Bill to become law, the Government ought, upon the highest ground of public interest, to disallow.

Now, as I said some time ago in considering this question of disallowance, in considering as to whether is proper to do so or not, the Government were warranted in investigating the character of the Jesuits. I have a list here of the countries from which this order had been expelled before its suppression by Clement XIV. They were expelled from the following countries at the date mentioned :

| | |
|---|---|
| Saragossa .................1555 | Moravia........................1619 |
| Palestine....................1556 | Naples and Netherlands.....1622 |
| Venice........................1568 | China and India................1623 |
| Avignon......................1570 | Malta.............................1634 |
| Portugal and Segovia....1578 | Russia............................1723 |
| England......................1579 | Savoy............................1729 |
| England......................1581 | Paraguay.........................1733 |
| England......................1586 | Portugal..........................1759 |
| Japan.........................1587 | France............................1764 |
| Hungary and Transylvania..1588 | Spain...............................1767 |
| Bordeaux....................1589 | The Two Sicilies................1767 |
| France........................1594 | Parma and Malta................1768 |
| Holland.......................1596 | All Christendom by the Bull of Clement |
| Tournon and Berne.......1597 | XIV.————— |
| England......................1601 | Russia.............................1776 |
| England......................1604 | France.............................1804 |
| Denmark.....................1606 | Grisons, Swiss Canton.........1804 |
| Venice........................1612 | Naples.............................1806 |
| Japan.........................1613 | France............................1810 |
| Bohemia.....................1618 | |

The order was restored Pius VII on 7th August, 1814, and since that date this self same order has been expelled from the following countries :—

| | |
|---|---|
| Belgium......................1816 | Switzerland......................1847 |
| French towns..............1819 | Bavaria............................1848 |
| Russia........................1820 | Naples and Papal States,Parma,Arch ⎫ |
| Colleges in France.......1826 | Duchy of Austria, Galica, Sardinia, ⎬ 1848 |
| France........................1831 | Sicily............................. ⎭ |
| Portugal.....................1834 | Paraguay.........................1858 |
| Spain.........................1835 | Italian towns....................1859 |
| France........................1845 | |

Now, we are told that the character of this order has changed, forsooth ; that it is not the order it was when Clement XIV suppressed it; that it is not the order it was when nearly all the potentates of Europe agreed in demanding that it should be suppressed. " Oh, no," they say, " it is not the same order." How is it, then, that the States I have mentioned have expelled this order since it was restored in 1814 ? and be it remembered that fifteen of these States were Catholic States or communities. I think that is a significant fact. I doubt very much, whether, in view of that fact the argument can be made successfully, that the character of this order has been changed. What was the opinion of Cardinal Taschereau with regard to this order, when it was proposed to incorporate it two years ago ? What was the opinion of Mr. Gladstone in regard to this order, so late as 1876 ? I find in the *Contemporary Review*, of June, 1876, that Mr. Gladstone has indicted the principles of which they are the professional exponents on these counts :

" (1) Its hostility to mental freedom at large ; (2) its incompatibility with the thought and movement of modern civilisation ; (3) its pretensions against the State; (4) its pretensions against parental and conjugal rights ; (5) its jealousy, abated in some quarters, of the free circulation and use of the Holy Scripture ; (6) the *de facto* alienation of the educated mind of the country in which it prevails; (7) its detrimental effects on the comparative strength and morality of the States in which it has sway; (8) its tendency to sap veracity in the individual mind."

Now, that is an arraignment by Mr. Gladstone of this order, the character of which we are considering to-day. In 1879 a discussion took place upon the character of this order in the French Chamber, and that discussion was referred to by my hon. friend from North Simcoe (Mr. McCarthy) last night. Now, Sir, I do not intend to detain the House with the speech of Mr. Ferry and M. Bert (since Minister of Education), Mr. du Bodan, M. le Prevost and others, but the substance of it amounted to this: that the Minister of Education sent and examined the character of the Jesuits' text books, and the character of their teachings in their schools and colleges, and the investigation made in regard to the character of that order was such as to satisfy the French Assembly, and the Department of Education in France, that the Jesuits were an order that ought not to be allowed to have anything whatever to do with education in that republic. Their principles were recognized to be incompatible with the independence of every government. They were proved to hold the same doctrines that they had held during the last 300 years. They taught the Divine right of Kings; they taught that the liberty of the press was a dangerous thing; they advocated religious wars; they attacked the Revolution and glorified the Revocation of the Edict of Nantes; they calumniated Necker and Turgot; they rejected the principles of national sovereignty; trial by jury was denounced, and liberty of conscience and worship was condemned. In one of these works, by Charles Barthelemy, the following passage, in the chapter dealing with Protestant people, disposes of English morality:—

"In London and all over England, the holiness of marriage is destroyed, bigamy is frequent, the wife is not the companion but the slave of her husband; the conjugal tie is dissolved; the children are poisoned or sold."

The subjects treated in Father Humbert's work, published in 1840, "Instructions chretiennes pour les jeunes gens et les jeunes filles," were found to be so monstrous and filthy, according to Mr. Bert, that though the work was put into the hands of young girls—objectionable passages could not be read in the French Assembly with ladies in the gallery. Without detaining the House with the evidence placed before the Legislative Assembly in France, by the Minister of Education and others, suffice it to say that upon that evidence the Jesuits were expelled from the educational institutions of that republic. I think, Sir, I am warranted in saying that we will consult the interest of this country, present and future, if we do not permit to be established in this Dominion that organisation whose whole history is a history of turmoil, of intrigue, of mischief and of attempts to pull down and destroy constitutional authority wherever they have been placed. Sir, we do not want an organisation in this country that will widen the breach that exists between the two great races in Canada; we do not want an organisation in this country, the influence exerted by which will be so detrimental to the best interests of this country present and future.

I have been requested, Mr. Speaker, before closing to read this resolution placed in my hands; a resolution adopted at a special meeting of the Protestant Ministerial Association in Montreal held this morning, it says:

"At a special meeting of the Protestant Ministerial Association of Montreal, held this morning, attention was drawn to certain statements made on the floor of the House of Commons, during the debate on the Jesuits' Estates Act, by the hon. member for Stanstead (C. C. Colby), who is reported to have stated that he represents the feelings of the Protestants of Quebec, that they have made no complaint; presented no petition and sought no redress from supposed wrongs, that, in fact, the Protestants have no grievances, but are treated with more justice, liberality and generosity than any minority in the world.
"Therefore be it resolved—
"That the Ministerial Association repudiate the hon. member's claim to represent the feelings

of the Protestant community of the Province of Quebec. That it is entirely incorrect to say that no petitions have been presented against the measure in favor of the Jesuits, inasmuch as this Association presented a petition against the incorporation of the Jesuits in 1887, to the Legislature of Quebec, and petitions to the Governor General in Council for the disallowance of the Jesuits' Estates Act, have been presented from this Association, from the Rev. the Presbytery of Montreal, from the Dominion Evangelical Alliance, and by some 6,000 citizens from the city of Montreal and other parts of the Province of Quebec. The matter also engaging the earnest attention of the Evangelical Alliance at its Conference in Montreal in October last, and strong resolutions in protest were adopted.

" And so par from having no grievances, the Protestant minority has serious cause of complaint in relation to many matters, among which the following are specified : The division of taxes for educational purposes; the recent unsettling of the foundation of the Superior Education Fund; in the degradation of degrees conferred by Protestant Universities; in the matter of the marriage laws; in the law of compulsory tithing, and the erection of parishes for civil purposes, both creating motives for the removal of Protestants, and generally in the virtual establishment of one church to the disadvantage of all other churches.

" Furthermore, we declare that the Protestant community of the Province of Quebec are unwilling to be indebted to the generosity or liberality of their Roman Catholic fellow-countrymen, but demand simple justice and their equal rights as subjects to the Queen.

" It was resolved to transmit the foregoing statement to the hon. member for North Simcoe (Col. O'Brien), with the request that it be read to the House of Commons by himself, or some other member he may select.

" J. COOPER ANTLIFF, D.D.,
" *President of the Montreal Protestant Association.*
" WM. SMYTH,
" *Secretary-Treasurer.*"

This is the communication, Sir, of the Protestant Ministerial Association of Montreal, duly signed by its officers.

Now, Mr. Speaker, I have but few words to say in conclusion. I wish, Sir, to refer to a statement made by my hon. friend the member for Bothwell (Mr. Mills), that if ministers would preach the gospel instead of preaching politics, it would be very much more in the line of their duty, and more conducive to the public interests. I have heard this charge brought against ministers before—the charge of preaching politics. I remember, Sir, in the great struggle in the United States, when the life of the nation was at stake, and when the slave power was making gigantic efforts to strangle liberty in that country, that the ministers of the country who stood up in defence of righteousness and right, were accused of preaching politics, one of the charges brought against them was that they were stepping outside of their legitimate province. When they were preaching opposition to slavery and exhorting men to patriotism, whether they were preaching politics or not, they were performing a good work. I hold that, in every emergency, when the liberties of a country are at stake, the minister is a dumb dog who does not raise his voice, warning his fellow citizens, and seeking by every influence he possesses to promote the right and combat the wrong; and if ministers in this country to-day see it to be their duty to warn the country of dangers impending, to warn it of the crisis threatened to be precipitated upon it, I say let them do so; if they do not do so, they are recreant to their trust and duty.

Sir, I conclude what I have to say to-night by asserting that I believe this Jesuits' Estates Act is an unconstitutional Act, because the society is under the ban of British law; I believe further that it is an unconstitutional Act by reason of the reference contained in the Bill to His Holiness the Pope; I believe further that it is unconstitutional by reason of the diversion of school funds in the Province of Quebec from their legitimate and proper purpose. And in addition to these three counts of unconstitutionality, I believe that upon the highest grounds of public interest and public good, upon the ground of due consideration of the public weal, present and future, in this Dominion, that this Act should have been disallowed in conformity with the possessed by the Government of this country.

Mr. MULOCK. (YORK, N. RIDING).

I admit, Mr. Speaker, that it is with some hesitation that I venture to address this House, as I will but very briefly, upon a subject so grave and important as that now receiving our attention. I cannot conceive of any question that might be fraught with more serious consequences to the welfare of Canada than the question which is now agitating the country, and which ought to receive the best consideration of the people's representatives. When I think that the solution of this problem may, according to the determination of this House, have such different results, I have been amazed to find that hon. gentlemen, who I believe in their calmer moments are as true patriots as are to be found, should for the moment allow themselves to be carried away by bigotry or fanatical zeal and should suggest to this Parliament the adoption of a course that would in my judgment destroy the Union of the Provinces that now constitute Canada. What proposition has the hon. member for Muskoka laid before this House and with what arguments and with what evidence has he sustained that proposition? Have his arguments and those of his friends justified them, and would they justify this House, in adopting the conclusion which he asks by this motion to adopt? Sir, the motion that has been placed in your hands by the hon. member for Muskoka (Mr. O'Brien) alleges that the Bill under discussion, for the settlement of the Jesuits' estates, passed by the Legislature of Quebec, was beyond the jurisdiction of that Legislature, and the motion goes on to give reasons in support of that proposition of law. So we have the hon. member alleging, and undertaking to prove conclusively to the House and the country, that this Bill is *ultra vires*, and on that ground he ask us to recommend to His Excellency the Governor General to wipe it off the Statute-book. Now, Sir, has he proved beyond all reasonable doubt the premises on the truth of which, Parliament would be justified in coming to the conclusion which he asks? His able chieftain, the hon. member for North Simcoe (Mr. McCarthy) laid down this doctrine for our guidance. He said : I admit that Parliament should not on this occasion ask the Governor to disallow this Bill if there is a shadow of a doubt that it is not *ultra vires*. The hon. member for Muskoka says it is *ultra vires*. Now, I ask hon. gentlemen who call on Parliament to adopt this resolution, is it admitted beyond doubt that the Act is *ultra vires*? We listened last night to the able address of the Minister of Justice. Will anyone say that he did not do more than establish a doubt? Will anyone say that he did not cite authorities which convinced the vast majority of this House that the position taken by the hon. member for Muskoka and the hon. member for North Simcoe (Mr. Carthy) is an untenable one, both in regard to the law of the case and in regard to the alleged facts on which they founded their charges. Taking the advice of the hon. member for North Simcoe (Mr. McCarthy), and applying it to what we have heard in this House, and without, and to what we know, of our own knowledge, of the law as well, I think we can fairly conclude that it has not been established beyond all doubt that the Bill is *Ultra vires*. Even if it had been established beyond doubt that the Bill is *ultra vires* there would, in this particular case, have been the very strongest possible reason why Parliament should not intervene and take the case out of the proper tribunals of the land. Is Parliament, a body of 215 men, representing widely different views, depending more or less upon the fickle populace; is this Parliament composed of persons more or less prejudiced upon a question of this kind—and no 215 men could be gathered together in any country in the world among whom there would not be found prejudiced men when a question of religion is concerned—is this Parliament, I say, a fit tribunal to find on the law and the facts clearly and unmistakably in order to arrive at an absolute conclusion on a question such as this? Is there a man in Canada who would assert that it would be fair and just to submit such a question as this to the arbitrament of even my hon. friend from Muskoka (Mr. O'Brien), for whose honesty of purpose no one has a higher opinion than I? I might say, also, that the hon. member for North

Simcoe (Mr. McCarthy) indicated a bias which would hardly qualify him to be selected as an independent juryman to deal with this question. I might run over the list and point out many of the members who have expressed a strong bias on this question and therefore, I doubt whether Parliament would be safe in following their views and in determining how it should find on questions of fact and law. For these reasons I am of opinion that under no circumstances should Parliament determine this question, unless there is no other tribunal in the land that can deal with it. Could there be a tribunal more unfit to deal with such a question than an assembly such as this? I would ask the hon. member for Muskoka (Mr. O'Brien) if he has thought of the consequence which would follow the adoption of this motion should it be carried. Suppose to-night the majority of the House should decide to carry this motion, that would be a withdrawal of the confidence of the country from the Government. What would then have to be the next step? The Government have taken a certain position upon this question, which I am glad to be able to endorse. They would have to tender their resignations to His Excellency, and either they would go to the country or the hon. member for Muskoka (Mr. O'Brien) would be called upon to form a Cabinet. In either case there would have to be an appeal to the country upon the new issue. Has the hon. gentleman thought of what the issue would be which would be presented to the country on that occasion? Is any man in this House prepared to present to the people such an issue, and to say that it is in the interests of the people that there should be an issue raised of race and religion to determine who shall and who shall not prevail in this House? It cannot be denied that that would be the very next step if this motion was carried, and that step would mean the dividing of this country into two great camps. Who would be found in these camps? Our Roman Catholic brethren, as a whole, would take their place in one camp, and our Protestant friends in another. This is the inevitable issue if this proposition be carried. My hon. friend may pretend that he is but attacking a community of the Roman Catholic Church; but if he appreciates the true sentiment of the people of Canada to-day, he will find that it is not a question of the hon. member for Muskoka (Mr. O'Brien) and his little band against the Order of Jesuits, who perhaps may enjoy some degree of unpopularity, but it will be a question of Roman Catholics against Protestants. Could any one conceive an issue more disastrous to the country than that? I cannot. It would destroy Canada. And are we to precipitate such a condition of affairs when there is relief at our hands, when there is a fit tribunal to deal with this case, whose judgment will be accepted loyally by all classes and creeds. Does the hon. member for Muskoka (Mr. O'Brien) suppose that by the carrying of this motion he would accomplish the suppression of the Jesuits, if that is what he seeks? It would mean the defeat of this particular Bill, but what would follow? Do you not think, Sir, that the Legislature of the Province of Quebec, which enacted that measure nine months ago, if it were disallowed under the circumstances, would not be called together again, under the inspiring influence of this racial and religious war or at least religious war? Would they not, the Quebec Legislature, be assembled together again as quickly as the constitution admitted, and would not the first Act they would pass be a re-enactment of the Jesuit Bill? Then the hon. member for Muskoka (Mr. O'Brien), if he carried the country, would rally his forces here, and would not his first duty, in obedience to the mandate of the majority of the people, be to call upon the Governor General to disallow the Bill again. So the repetition would go on, the public mind being more and more inflamed, and what the end would be no one can tell. Is that statesmanship? Is that patriotism? Is that in the interest of British institutions in Canada, or in any country on God's earth? I have heard the hon. gentleman speak of his love for the British flag and intitutions. I know he is honest in every sentiment he expresses in that regard, but I grieve to think that he has forgotten he is living in the 19th century. He has forgotten that he has come to free Canada, he has forgotten that the greater Ireland is on this side of the water, and he thinks he still lives in old

Ireland, where a minority wielded the power and where a minority was able to exercise its sway. Could he not have been generous enough to have told us at least one little consoling feature in connection with Roman Catholic Institutions? Sir, I am no Roman Catholic, but I think the truth should be told, I think the whole truth should be told in discussing a question like this, and yet it did not occur to him to utter one word of justification on behalf of any of the Catholic Church, but he, and those who are with him, declared in all their aguments that the Catholic Church endangered every representative institution.

Mr. O'BRIEN. If the hon. gentleman will allow me for a moment, I defy him, from any word which I have uttered in this debate, to justify the statement he has just made.

Mr. MULOCK. I am only too glad to think that I misunderstood the hon. gentleman. If I have not correctly interpreted his arguments, I would be only too glad humbly to apologize to him, and I wish I could say of all who have discussed this question that they have shown the same liberality as, in intent at all events, existed in the mind of my hon. friend from Muskoka (Mr. O'Brien); but I think we must all admit that those who have advocated the measure he asks us to adopt, and even the last hon. member who spoke, my hon. friend from North Norfolk (Mr. Charlton), asserted that the Roman Catholic Church endangered civil liberty. If that is the case, could not one man among them all have given credit to the church for having at times been, as I submit, perhaps even too loyal to institutions, the *de facto* governments of the day, in times gone by? We have only to look back to the history of England in the last few months, and we find that His Holiness the Pope, who has no friend amongst them to-day here, found the Marquis of Salisbury, or the Conservative Administration, only too glad to receive assistance from him in the form of the rescript he issued to the people of Ireland in order to induce them to submit to the constituted authority of the land. When His Holiness did that, he did an act which did not commend itself to his own clergy and his own flock in Ireland. He did it against the interest of the church itself in Ireland. He weakened his influence in that island, but he did it, as I understand, according to the well understood doctrine of the Roman Catholic Church, to be true and loyal in the support of the *de facto* Government of the day. I am no apologist for the Roman Catholic Church, but, when I hear a charge like this made, some little circumstance comes to my mind, and as a matter of justice I take the liberty of reminding those hon. gentlemen of doubtful memories of such a redeeming feature. Would our loyal friends who propose to set the heather on fire, to add to the inflammatory condition of the public mind to-day, who instead of meeting here in a judicial frame of mind and temperately telling the people what is best, be good enough for one moment to think of the grave trust cast upon them when Her Majesty placed in the hands of the people of Canada the British North America Act. Does not that Act—I ignore clauses and technicalities—does not a broad minded, a liberal and a fair interpretation of that Act say that whatever we do and whatever we legislate, we shall do all things to promote the peace, the order and the government of the people of Canada? When Her Majesty gave us that constitution, she expected us to work out that constitution, and not to exercise our majority powers on the floor of Parliament to destroy peace, to destroy order, to destroy good government in Canada, and to destroy Canada. Under these circumstances, I say in conclusion what I said in the beginning, that I am amazed that, when there is one simple possible solution of this question, an appeal to the proper courts of the land, anyone should seek to solve it in this unfortunate way, in a way that would not be a solution but only an aggravation of the evil complained of. For a moment, look at the consequences of the other course. An appeal to the courts takes place, and, if anyone is dissatisfied with the result of that appeal, he can carry that appeal to the foot of the Throne, and there get the advice of Her Majesty, the fountain of wisdom, of justice and of truth. A judgment is then delivered which will be accepted with satisfaction and resignation by all classes and all creeds; a finality will be given to this question, and then peace, order and good government will prevail in the land. Therefore my voice and my vote are in that direction. Without sacrificing a bit of my Protestant sentiment, without sacrificing peace, order or good government in Canada, but assisting to place Canada on a sure, stable and sound foundation, I shall vote against the motion of my hon. friend from Muskoka (Mr. O'Brien), and I ask him and all those who desire the permanent peace of the country to transfer this case to the proper tribunals, the duly constituted courts of the land.

Mr. SCRIVER. (Huntingdon.)

After the very able and exhaustive discussion which has taken place in the House upon this very important question, and feeling my own unfitness to deal with it from a constitutional or legal point of view, I should not have presumed to say one word upon the subject, but for one fact. I should have contented myself with giving a silent vote, but for the fact that the evening before last my hon. friend from Stanstead (Mr. Colby), in the very admirable and eloquent speech he made to this House, gave utterance to some sentiments with which I could not altogether agree, and which I consider it my bounden duty, as one of the representatives of the minority, which he also has the honor to represent, to controvert or to attempt to controvert. That hon. gentleman, not without due reason, spoke for the Protestant minority of the Province of Quebec—I say not without due reason, considering the distinguished position which he occupies in this House, considering the fact that he has long and honorably represented the County of Stanstead, considering his high character for candor, for honesty, for integrity, for intelligence, and the opportunity he has had to acquaint himself, not only with the minds of his constituents upon public questions generally, but with the minds of the people in that part of the Province—I say considering these things, the hon. gentleman spoke with an assumed authority, and an authority which he had a right to assume. More than that, his words were clothed in such beautiful language, and the sentiments which he uttered were so admirable, that I have no doubt they carried weight with them in this House, as they would in the country at large. With some things with which the member for Stanstead said the night before last, I can cordially agree. I agree with him in his statements that the relations between the two elements of population in the Province of Quebec, have been very cordial and pleasant. They are so still, and I would fain wish them to continue so. I think, perhaps, he painted the picture in somewhat roseate hues; the entire cordiality of which he spoke may not prevail in all parts of the Province, but certainly in the constituency which I have the honor to represent, and I believe in the constituencies known as the Eastern Townships, this cordial and friendly state of feeling prevails. I have the honor to represent a constituency divided almost equally between Protestants and Catholics, and they do not live in separate communities, Protestants in one section and Catholics in another, but with the exception of the western part of the county, they are very largely intermingled and in close neighborhood, and they are able to live in the friendly and cordial relations of which my hon. friend so eloquently spoke. If I might be permitted to say one word of a personal character, I would refer to the fact that although I am known, I think, as a good Protestant, I have had the honor to represent that constituency without interruption almost since Confederation, and I have enjoyed the almost unique honor, during that time, of having been elected five times by acclamation, which fact, I think, is a good evidence that the Catholics in my constituency are not governed by sectarian prejudices. I would agree further with my hon. friend from Stanstead that upon the whole the Protestant minority in the Province of Quebec have no reason to complain of their rights being invaded by any legislation resulting from the action of the majority in that Province. During two years from 1867 to 1869 I had the honor of representing the county which I now represent, in the Legislature of the Province of Quebec. Certainly during that time nothing transpired, either in the character of legislation or in the utterances of the members of that body, of which the most rigid and sincere Protestant could complain. Since that time until at least very recently, the same state of affairs has continued. But I regret to say that during the last two years events have transpired in the Province, perhaps not so much actual legislation on the part of the governing body, but at all events there have been utterances by representative men in that Province, disquieting to Protestants, and a disposition, as Protestants think, to give to the clerical authority an influence and almost a direction in the legislation of that Province, which has led to an uneasy feeling on the part of the Protestants generally, and a feeling that if they had not already been exposed to some trespass on their rights, there was danger in the future of a violation of some of the principles which they hold dear. They think they have seen in the character of some of the legislation, of some of the proceedings of the leading men of the Province of Quebec, a disposition, as I said, to give to the clerical power an influence which could only lead to one result and that is a closer union between Church and State than has hitherto existed or ought to exist in a colony of the British Empire. This feeling, I may say, has been intensified by something which has transpired in my own county. Municipal government has been interfered with in the county in which I live, in a manner which gives not only offence to the Protestants residing in that county, but causes them to fear their rights of municipal self-government are in danger of being seriously interfered with. Under the law of the Province of Quebec (at all events in the French speaking counties of the Province) a Roman Catholic Bishop has the right to erect territory into a parish in contradistinction from townships, and in consequence of that action, municipal division follows. This right was never attempted to be exercised in English speaking Protestant counties until very recently. But not very long ago this power was exercised in the county which I represent. The parish of St. Anicet was a part, originally, of the township of Godmanchester; it was erected, by ecclesiastical authority, into a parish, and following that, it was constituted a parish by the Legislature of the Province of Quebec. Until that time, at all events, this clerical authority that I speak of had not been exercised in the Townships with the result that followed, in that particular instance. But more recently a portion of this parish of St. Anicet was erected into a parish and the electors of that parish, called St. Barbe, proceeded upon the supposition that it had, by the Act, been constituted a separate municipal organisation. They elected their mayor. Their mayor was refused a seat in the county council of the Province. He appealed to the courts, and his right to sit in that council as the representative of this new constituency was sustained by the courts. This fact has given rise to a great deal of dissatisfaction and uneasiness among my constituents at all events. So far as I can learn, that power has not been exercised in the Eastern Township counties proper, but, in every instance where an ecclesiastical parish has been erected in a Township an Act of the Legislature of Quebec has been secured to constitute it into a municipal parish. And then we cannot conceal from ourselves that, during the past two or three years, there have been utterances on the part of some of the public men in the Province of Quebec, which were not in the direction of supporting the rights of the minority, and which we were of a character to lead them to feel a great deal of uneasiness; utterances of this kind have been made over and over again which have led the Protestants of these counties, at all events of my county (and I think the same is true, though not to so great an extent, perhaps, of the other townships and counties), to entertain feelings of uneasiness and disquiet. And following upon this has been the legislation which we have been considering during two or three days past. There is a general feeling, an almost universal feeling, on the part of the Protestants I represent that this legislation is not only unwise, not only in some of its features exceedingly offensive to their feelings as Protestants, but that it is for several causes, which have been set forth by those who have discussed the question and which I need not therefore repeat, unconstitutional. It is true, as the hon. member for Stanstead (Mr. Colby) said, that remonstrances against this legislation were not sent to the Legislature of Quebec at the time the Bill was under discussion. But it is to be remembered, that large bodies proverbially move slowly. The Bill was introduced rather suddenly and carried through the House very quickly, and there was hardly time for anything like united action. Indeed the people seemed not to have awakened to the character and possible results of the legislation until some-time after it became law. But my hon. friend was mistaken in saying no remonstrance against this legislation had been made to the authorities here or to the authorities of the Province of Quebec.

Mr. COLBY. I did not say that; I think I did not intend to say that. My statement was simply this, and if you will allow me I will take the opportunity to interject a remark The resolution which was read by the hon. gentleman just now from the Ministerial Association of Montreal put into my mouth words I never said, and passes strictures upon some sayings which they suppose I uttered. I made no statement with respect to representations being made or not being made to any Legislature at any time except during the pendency of the discussion of this Settlement Act in the Province of Quebec. I did not state, as they said I stated, that no representations were made against the Jesuit's Incorporation Bill. I did not state as those Ministers say I stated, that no reprentations had been made to this House in favor of dissallowance. I simply did state that no representations that I was aware of, that no petitions and no representations had gone to the Legislature against the particular act of legislation which we are now here considering.

Mr. SCRIVER. I think in that statement the hon. gentleman was perfectly correct. So far as I know, no petitions or remonstrances were sent to the Legislature of Quebec when the Act was under discussion. The hon. member for Stanstead (Mr. Colby), alluded as a proof of the disposition of the Protestant minority to accept this legislation, which he himself has characterised as a very bitter pill for them to swallow, and with that statement I fully agree, and I am afraid this bitterness will stay there for some time—that there was no general disposition on the part of the Protestant minority of the Province of Quebec not to be accept this legislation, as at all events something not to be prevented or helped, to the fact that no vote was taken in the Legislature when the Bill was under discussion, that not a voice was raised against it, except the voices of two members of the House who spoke briefly on the question from the constitutional and legal point. Well, Mr. Speaker, I do not consider it my place to criticise the conduct of those members of the Legislature of the Province of Quebec representing the same class of people as I represent with respect to that Bill or any other Bill, and whatever their motives were and whatever their views were, it is not my place here to pronounce any opinion with respect to them further than to say this: that I think they would have much better expressed the sentiments of the people who sent them there as their representatives if they had at all events raised their voices in remonstrance against the passage of such a law. But I do not propose to prolong my remarks on this occasion. I rose mainly, as I said at the outset, because I thought it my duty to state what is the fact, in opposition to what might have been inferred from the statement of the hon. member for Stanstead (Mr. Colby,) that there is not a disposition on the part of the Protestants of the Province of Quebec generally—I think I may say that much—to accept this legislation as satisfactory or as a finality. I think there is a general disposition to consider it not only unwise but wrong, as in some sense an invasion of their rights, and as fraught with danger to their position as a minority in the Province. But I am quite sure of one thing, that they will not agitate the question of disallowing or nullifying this law in any other way than in a strictly constitutional manner, and if it does become a finality by reason of the failure of the Federal Government to disallow the Act, or by a decision of the highest legal tribunals of the land, should they be appealed to, as I trust they will be, to test its constitutionality, I say I have no doubt they will as good, loyal, peaceful subjects accept the law, and make the best of the situation. I would have preferred, had I had my choice in the matter, that the motion of the hon. member for Muskoka (Mr. O'Brien) had been couched in somewhat different language : indeed, I would have preferred that such a motion as he has made should not have been made at all. I would have greatly preferred that the motion should have assumed the character of advising this House, or moving that this House should express the opinion that the question should be submitted to the proper legal tribunal to decide as to its constitutionality or otherwise. I should have preferred voting for such a motion to voting for the motion which the hon. gentleman has submitted, not that I do not agree mainly with its provisions, but because I think it was inexpedient, and that it cannot possibly result in anything practical, fated, as I believe it to be, to defeat in this House by a large majority. But holding the view which I do with regard to the legislation aimed at by the motion, I cannot see it to be anything else than my duty to vote for the resolution of the hon. member for Muskoka (Mr. O'Brien).

Mr. SUTHERLAND, (OXFORD, N. RIDING).

It is not my intention to detain the House longer than a few moments with an explanation of the vote which I intend to give on this question. With the member for Huntingdon (Mr. Scriver) I regret the manner in which this question has been brought before the House, and I would much rather that it had come in the shape in which that member has stated he would like to have seen it brought up. While I may say that I do not agree with portions of the resolution. I do not believe that differing from some of the recitals in it, is any reason why I should not vote for the main portion. I also regret the manner in which it has been brought before the House, because I cannot see that possibly any good effect or result can come of it, and if the suggestion made by the member for Huntingdon had been the substance of this resolution or if the subject had been treated in the manner he indicated, I think that the unfortunate turn of religious discussion which has apparently been brought around in this House and in the country by this question being brought up as it is at the present moment, would have been avoided. Now, Sir, I do not intend as I said to discuss this question at any length. We have heard the ablest legal minds in the House speak as to the constitutionality of the Act, and we all must see from the different opinions laid before the House by those able legal gentlemen that there is room for a layman to doubt whether or not this is a constitutional Act on the part of the Quebec Legislature. While I agree personally with the substance of most of the remarks made by the Minister of Justice, with regard to the treatment of Acts passed by the Provincial Legislatures, in the able speech that he delivered to this House last evening, there is one very material point to my mind, on which I do not agree with him and that is with reference to that portion of this Act appropriating the money, as he says, for educational purposes. That portion of his statement and argument I do not agree with. It does appear to my mind, from reading the Act and from the explanations that have been given, that this money has been given to a religious body and it is not stated in the Act to be for educational purposes. Then, as I understand it, the main portion of the resolution brought before the House is announcing the principle of religious equality and the complete separation of Church and State. That is a principle that I feel is necessary to be carried out to the fullest extent in this country for the material welfare and best interests of the people. Settled as it is by people of all nationalities and religious denominations of all kinds, I think it is very desirable that this principle should be carefully adhered to. As I cannot agree with the Minister of Justice in his statement with regard to that, I certainly feel called upon to vote for the motion now before the House. I regret, as I say, the religious aspect that this discussion has taken. I feel that it is unfortunate because throughout this country, for many years at least, we have had very little experience of religious cries or differences. In the section of the country in which I live, the Roman Catholics, Presbyterians, Episcopalians, and members of all religious denominations, live together in the greatest harmony. I do not see why this aspect of the question should be introduced here. It would make no difference to me, if this grant of money had been to an Episcopalian, Presbyterian, Methodist or Baptist body, I would fell compelled to take the same position on it if it was brought before the House. It is not because the money is granted by the Local Government to the Catholic Church that I object, but it is against the principle of granting money for any sectarian purposes that I wish to protest. That is the chief and almost the only reason why I cannot support the Government, but have to support the resolution of the hon. member for Muskoka (Mr. O'Brien).

Mr. McMULLEN, (WELLINGTON, N. RIDING).

It was not my intention to address the House, but I have listened with a great deal of interest to the discussion so far as it has gone, and I may say that I fully endorse the remarks of the hon. member from North York (Mr. Mulock). I regret exceedingly that the discussion has partaken of a character which is likely to cause very serious division between two great classes in the Dominion. Had the motion of the hon. member for Muskoka (Mr. O'Brien) been one that did not embody objectionable features from a Reform standpoint, I would have much preferred it. In the shape it is in now it is undoubtedly objectionable to those who sit upon this side of the House. As far as I am personally concerned I am just as strongly opposed to some of the doctrinal views of the Jesuit Order as any man that sits within this Chamber. I have no sympathy for them owing to their traditional record, which I believe is not very good. At the same time, Mr. Speaker, we live under a written constitution in this Dominion, and while I have sat and listened with a good deal of attention to the arguments that have been presented on both sides, I have failed to that it has been clearly proved to the satisfaction of my mind that the Bill which we have under consideration is unconstitutional. Of course I am not a lawyer, I am but a layman; but when I consider that I have on one side the hon. the First Minister who, I have reason to believe, says that this Act is constitutional, that we have the Minister of Justice who declares that it is constitutional, and that we have also other legal gentlemen supporting the Government who have declared that it is constitutional;—I come to my own side of the House, and I find that I have the hon. the leader of the Opposition who, I believe, says that the Bill is a constitutional Bill, and within the power of the Province of Quebec to pass, I also have the ex-leader of the Reform Party who says he believes it is a constitutional Bill (I believe he is of that opinion), and I think I am correct in saying that the hon. the leader of the former Government, the member for East York (Mr. Mackenzie), is prepared to say it is a constitutional Bill. I also have the statement of the hon. member for Bothwell (Mr. Mills) who declares that the Bill is a constitutional Bill and within the powers of the Provincial Government to pass; I have the opinion of the hon. member for St. John (Mr. Weldon) a man of extended experience and a cultured legal mind who says the Bill is constitutional, and I think that I am also correct in stating that the hon. member for Queen's (Mr. Davies) considers it a constitutional Bill. I find all these legal gentlemen who have seats in this House, some of the best legal minds this Dominion contains, saying on the one hand that this is a constitutional Bill within the powers of the Legislature of Quebec, and, on the other hand, I find the hon. member for North Simcoe (Mr. McCarthy) saying that it is not a constitutional Bill. But when I look over the legal history of that hon. gentleman I find that in almost every case in which he has argued upon constitutional principles he has failed, and I am bound to accept the opinions of the men who say it is within the powers of the Legislature of Quebec to pass that Act. Now, as I said, I have no sympathy with the Jesuits, but at the same time, if the Legislature of Quebec has the right and the power to pass that Bill, I claim to be a loyal British subject, I c aim to live under the written constitution that we have got, which permits the passage of an Act by the Local Legislature, even if it is an objectionable Act. I am perfectly willing to agitate for a revision of our Constitution, so that it would not permit the passage of Acts of that kind, but that is the only constitutional way to go to work. With regard to the effects of disallowance I agree heartily with the hon. member for North York (Mr. Mulock). I can easily see that if the Government were forced to reconsider their Order in Council allowing the Bill we would not then reach the end of the trouble. The probabilities are that the Legislature of Quebec, if they are acting within their constitutional rights, would re-enact the Bill next year. Are we to have all this agitation again next year? Are we to meet and have the important time of this House spent in discussing whether the next Bill is within the power of the Quebec Legislature, or whether we should disallow it or not? I think it is better, under the circumstances, that we should settle this question as quickly as possible, and I believe the best and the constitutional way of settling it is to relegate the whole question to the courts, and let them decide whether the Act is constitutional or not. Some say there may be a difficulty whatever in doing so. I understand that the *Mail* new-paper of Toronto has had an action brought against it by the Jesuit Order for certain statements which it has made with regard to that order there. The *Mail* news-paper, if it chooses, can carry that action to the Privy Council in England; it can force the Jesuit Order there and test the whole question in that very action. I must say I sympathise a great deal with its course myself; I am just as strong an advocate of religions liberty as any other member in this House; and if it is found that the Act is unconstitutional, that is an end of the whole difficulty. If the hon. member for North Simcoe, who is a man of extended legal knowledge, will show me that we can reach the object of our ambition in disallowing this Bill by the course he proposes to take in this House, I would not hesitate a moment to support him; but I cannot see that we can reach that point, because disallowance now means re-enacting in the Province of Quebec, which would bring disallowance again, and where would that stop? Are we to go with this, like the Streams Bill, which was enacted and disallowed, enacted and dissallowed, enacted and dissallowed, three times. The result was that it had to go to the Supreme Court before it was settled after all. This is a question which would cause a tremendous amount of trouble in this country if it were carried on in that way. I must say, although I have no confidence in the Government—I say, in the interest of the country, not in the interest of the Government at all—the best course is to sent this Bill where it will receive judicious handling at the hands of the Privy Council, which will settle the whole question at once, and relieve this House year after year from the discussion of a question, which is certainly a very awkward one for the House to deal with, and which we should not be called on to deal with. We make laws in this House, we do not administer them. This law has been made in the Province of Quebec; and if it is within the constitutional rights of that Province, much as we may deplore its results and its peculiar characteristics, it is not for us to say that the Province shall not have it. If it improperly imports the name of the Pope into this provincial exactment, or if anything else in it makes it unconstitutional, the courts will decide, and will rid the House of the question, and settle all the difficulty in the country. Under these circumstances, I shall not vote for the amendment of the hon. member for Muskoka unless before this debate is closed I can be convinced that by passing that motion we will be settling the whole difficulty. If I cannot be convinced of that, I cannot take the responsibility of what I see will inevitably follow, a condition of things such as has been pointed out by the hon. member for North York, and also by myself.

Mr. LAURIER, (QUEBEC, EAST.)

Mr. Speaker, it is not often that we on this side of the House can have the privilege of supporting the policy of the Government. In this instance, when the action of the Government is assailed by a number of their supporters, when their action has already caused an agitation which unfortunately is not unmixed with religious bitterness, not one word certainly will fall from my lips which would tend to fan those religious flames; and I may say at once, repeating what was said this afternoon by my hon. friend from Bothwell (Mr. Mills), in the admirable speech he delivered, that the course of the Government receives, with a few exceptions which I respect, the entire support of the Liberal party. No other course, Mr. Speaker, than the course which we intend to take on this side of the House, would be consistent with the policy which we have been advocating for the last fifteen or twenty years—nay, ever since Confederation has been in existence. And, Sir, I hasten at once to congratulate the Government upon the fact that at last they have come to the true policy which they have often fought against, that the only basis upon which we can successfully carry on this Confederation is to recognize the principle of provincial rights. And I cannot but say also that if the Government to-day have to face this trouble in their own camp, if they have to meet this agitation which is now going on in the Province of Ontario, and of which the hon. member for North Simcoe (Mr. McCarthy) said yesterday, we have not seen the last, it is due altogether to the vicious policy which has been followed by the Administration, and before the consequences of which they have at last to recede; it is due altogether to the manner in which they have governed this country, and to the means they have used to obtain a majority to support them. Sir, this is not a party question; it is at most a family quarrel; it is simply a domestic disturbance in the ranks of the Conservative party. A section of the Conservative party now required the Government to stand up or to stand down, whichever it may be, to the exigencies of the doctrine of disallowance, such as the Government has taught it, and such as the Government more than once called upon them to act upon. Well, there must always be a day of retribution, and that day I think is coming for the Government. The two chief Provinces of which this Confederation is composed are vastly dissimilar. One is French in origin; the other British. One is Catholic in religion; the other is Protestant. And in each are to be found the prejudices peculiar to the creed and race of each. I say prejudices, and I use the word advisedly, nor do I use it in any contemptuous sense, for everybody must recognize the fact that wherever you find strong convictions, you generally find an exaggeration of feeling very apt to carry men beyond the legitimate consequence of their convictions. Now, over since the year 1854, I charge against the Government and against the Conservative party that they have been able to retain power, almost without interruption, largely by pandering to the prejudices of the one Province and the prejudices of the other Province. In the good Catholic Province of Quebec, to which I belong, the party supporting the Administration have always represented themselves as the champions of the Roman Catholic cause. They have always denounced their opponents, the Liberals of French origin like myself, as men of dangerous doctrine and tendencies. They have always represented the Liberals of Ontario as men actuated in all their actions and inspirations by a hatred of everything French and Catholic. At the same time, in the good Protestant Province of Ontario, the same party has always been held up to the front as the party of unbending and uncompromising Protestantism and the Conservative press to-day represent hon. gentlemen on this side as basely pandering to the influence of the French people and of the Catholic persuasion. Now this game has been for a long time successful, but, perhaps, before going further, I may recall this fact, known by all those who are now listening to me, that the attitude of the Conservative party of Ontario has always been just what I represent it to be. It may not be so well known that, at the same time, the Liberals of Ontario are charged by the Conservatives of

11

the Province of Quebec, not with pandering to the Catholic influence but with being hostile to Catholic influence—and so the charges work both ways. In one Province the Liberals are charged with one offence, and in the other with another. I could quote columns upon columns of the press which supports the right hon. gentleman to prove what I say, but I shall limit myself to one short paragraph. The school question in Ontario is a burning question. The hon. member for Bruce (Mr. McNeil) yesterday spoke almost of nothing else. A few days ago there was in the Legislature of Ontario a debate upon this very question. The Government of Mr. Mowat were charged by the Conservative party with unduly favoring the teaching of the French language in the schools of Ontario. The debate was commented upon in the Province of Quebec, *La Minerve*, one of the papers which support the Administration, an organ of the Conservative party, referred as follows to this very debate:—

" The motion of the hon. member for East Durham (Mr. Craig) was followed by a most brilliant reply strongly conceived, broad in view and conclusive from the Hon. G. W. Ross, Minister of Public Instruction. Mr. Ross is a Grit of the clearest water, but we are too much accustomed to the gallophobic denunciation of that party and to the intemperance of their language, when the Province of Quebec is in question, not to rejoice at anything which remotely or approximately can look like a conversion.

You see the gist of this statement. It was charged that the language of Mr. Ross was an exception whereas the charge made by the Conservative party in Ontario against the Administration for which Mr. Ross spoke, was the very thing which is given him here as an exception. So it has always been. The party has always had two faces—a rigid Protestant face turning towards the west, and a devout Catholic face turning towards the east. In the Province of Ontario, the rallying cry of the party has always been: " Protestants, beware! these Grits are weak Protestants!"

Some hon. MEMBERS. No, never.

Mr. LAURIER. Among the Protestants of Quebec, their cry has always been: "Catholics, beware, the Liberals are weak and bad Catholics!" This game has been successful for a long time, but it cannot always be successful, and I say the day of retribution is now coming. I say that this motion which we now have is in many senses much to be deprecated, and I endorse every word which fell the other day from the hon. member for Northumberland (Mr. Mitchell). It seems to me that all he said then were words of wisdom, but at the same time I cannot resist the conviction that the Government of to-day are only reaping what they have been sowing. They have allowed a large class of the Protestant population of Ontario to look upon them as the champions of Protestantism. They have affirmed the doctrine of disallowance among that section of the party and now that section cries out : We have always looked upon you as the champions of Protestantism; here is legislation which we deem offensive to the Protestant interests and to the interest of the country at large, and we call upon you to exercise those powers of disallowance which you have so often exercised in the past. Well, as far as the Liberal party is concerned, their attitude upon this question was known before it was explained in this debate. The Liberal party always endeavors to meet those questions, not from the point of view that would include all different religious interests. Among the many questions which divided the two parties, there is no one upon which the policy of the two parties has been so clearly cut as upon this. The Conservative party, led by the right hon. gentleman, have always held the doctrine that they have the right to review the legislation of any Local Legislature. We, on the other hand, have always pretended that the only way to carry out this Confederation is to admit the principle that within its sphere, within the sphere allotted to it by the Constitution, each Province is quite as independent of the control of the Dominion Parliament, as the Dominion Parliament is independent of the control of the Local Legislatures.

On the contrary, the hon. gentleman has maintained again and again upon the floor of this House and by administrative acts that he claimed the power to review local legislation, to see whether it was right or wrong, and, if he found it clashing with his ideas of right, to set it aside. We all remember the famous Streams Bill. What was the language used on that occasion by the hon. gentleman? He claimed that it was a question of purely provincial character, that it was one which was clearly within the competence of the Legislature of Ontario, and yet the hon. gentleman took it upon himself to disallow it, and for what reason? For no other reason than that the Act clashed with his own opinions of what was right and what was wrong? He spoke as follows in regard to it :—

"But here, where we are one country and all together, and we go from one Province to another as we do from one country to another and from one town to another, it is to be borne that laws which bind civilised society together, which distinguish civilisation from barbarism, protect life, reputation and property, should be dissimilar ; that what should be a merit in one Province should be a crime in another, and that different laws should prevail."

Upon that occasion the hon. gentleman took upon himself to review the law of the Province, and, finding it was not consistent with what he believed to be right, he disallowed it. It chocked the tenderness of the right hon. gentleman's conscience that the Legislature of Ontario provided that Mr. Caldwell could not pass his logs through Mr. McLaren's improvements without paying toll, though the Privy Council afterwards decided that, without the law, Mr. Caldwell could have use those improvements without paying any tolls at all. The hon. gentleman now comes to the doctrine which has been very many times advocated on this side of the House, that he has not to consider whether this provincial legislation is good, bad or indifferent ; it is altogether within the competence of the Local Legislature of Quebec, and therefore, says he, let it pass. Let us read the report of the Minister of Justice of the day on the Streams Bill and compare it with the report of the Minister of Justice upon the present occasion. The Minister of Justice then said :

" I think the power of the Local Legislature to take away the rights of one man and vest them in another as is done by this Act, is exceedingly doubtful, but, assuming that such right does, in strictness, exist, I think it devolves upon this Government to see that such power is not exercised, in flagrant violation of private rights and natural justice, especially when, as in this case, in addition to interfering with private rights in the way alluded to, the Act overrides a decision of a court of competent jurisdiction, by declaring retrospectively that the law always was, and is, different from that laid down by the court."

Now, let us look at the report of the Minister of Justice in the present case. It is extremely short and sweet. The Minister of Justice simply says, referring to some petitions asking for disallowance:

" Before the petition in question came before him for his consideration the undersigned had already recommended to Your Excellency, that the Act in question should be left to its operation. The memorials referred to have not convinced the undersigned that that recommendation should be changed. The subject-matter of the Act is one of provincial concern only, having relation to a fiscal matter entirely within the control of the Legislature of Quebec.

Well, Mr. Speaker, this is sound Liberal doctrine. This is the very doctrine which has been always maintained and supported on this side of the House, and once more I beg to tender my thanks and my congratulations to the hon. gentleman on having at last come to the true and only basis upon which this constitution of ours can be satisfactorily maintained and supported. It takes a long time, however, for a true principle to penetrate the perverted minds, as I might say, of the hon. gentlemen opposite. No, I beg their pardon, it does not always take so long a time ; sometimes the operation is as fast as at others it is slow. Only three weeks ago, we tendered advice to the Administration as to the manner in which they should treat our friends to the South in reference to the *modus vivendi*. Our advice was treated with contempt, and it was stated by hon. gentlemen opposite that the proposal would be received with scorn by the people of this country; and yet, within three weeks, they have changed their minds and accepted the policy which we suggested. I can only say that, as long as the Administration continue to act in that way, first to reject the policy of the Opposition and then to steal our clothes and dress themselves in them, the country would not be the loser. I had hesitated, before I resolved to speak on his question, whether I should confine myself to this statement and then sit down, but I cannot ignore, no one who has at heart the interests of this country, the peace and harmony of this country, can ignore the agitation which is now going on in the Province of Ontario. Coming as I do, from the Province of Quebec, being a member of the Catholic persuasion and a supporter of the Government which passed this legislation, I cannot but view with deep concern the attempt which is now being made to arouse our Protestants fellow-citizens in the Province of Ontario against that legislation. Let me say this, which must be obvious to every hon. member, that, if we approach this question, or any question, from the point of view of the religious opinions which any of us profess, we are apt to stand upon very narrow, very unsafe, and very dangerous ground. I say dangerous ground because it is a matter of history, that it is always in the sacred name of religion that the most savage passions of mankind have been excited and some of the most shocking crimes have been committed. In this matter, I cannot forget the fact, as I have stated that an attempt has been made to arouse the feelings of the Province of Ontario, but I hope that that attempt will not carry, and that a better sentiment will prevail; I hope that the temperate language of which we have heard to-day, will be understood, and, though this legislation may be objectionable to some people, yet that every one will understand that in these subjects we must make allowance for the feelings of others. What is the cause of the agitation which is now going on? What is the cause of the legislation which has been the source of so much turmoil? Sir. it is simply this: It is a matter of regret that the European nations, France and England, when they came to this continent brought with them not only their laws and institutions, not only their civilisation, but brought also their hatreds. At this moment, and for more than seventy years past, France and England have been at peace, and it has given to our generation to witness a spectacle which would have seemed almost improbable, not to say impossible, a few years before. We have seen France and England arrayed together against a common foe; and to us British subjects of French origin, British subjects who have learned to love England, who appreciate her benevolent rule, who would not go back to the allegiance of France, but who still ever cherish in our hearts the love of the land of our ancestors, no spectacle could be more consoling than to see the banners of France and England waving together on the banks of the Alma, on the heights of Inkermann and amid the ashes of Sebastopool. Such is the case to-day. Such was not the case, however, at the time of the discovery of America at the time of the establishment of English and French posts upon this continent. On the contrary, at that time French and English had been arrayed for generations and centuries in deadly feuds. They brought over these feuds with them, they brought over with them the enmity which had divided them in Europe, and here on this continent they sought each other across lakes and rivers, mountains and forests, and endeavored to inflict upon each other all the injury they possibly could. They had before them the boundless space of this virgin continent, but they entered into a deadly war for the possession of the miserable huts which constituted their first establishments. Well, the long duel, as we know, was settled on the plains of Abraham. The war, however, was carried on for a year longer by the Chevalier de Lévis, and the continuation of the war had no material effect except to extract from the victor most generous terms of capitulation. These terms have been referred to, I need not refer to them again. The religious communities were granted all their possessions as freely as if they had remained under the domain of the French King. It was stated by the hon. member for Muskoka (Mr. O'Brien) when he opened this debate, that the Terms of Capitulation had been modified by the Treaty of Paris. For my part I am not able to see the difference, but if difference there be, I am quite willing to admit the interpretation of it which was given by the British Government itself. Respecting the treatment by the British Government of those communities which were promised special immunity, I can see no difference between their position under the French regime and their condition under the English regime. The British Government treated those communities and the whole population, for that matter, in religious concerns with the greatest generosity. All the generous communities, with the single exception of the Jesuits, were maintained in possession of their estates. There was an exception made of the Jesuits. What was the cause of it ? Was it by the right of Conquest as asserted by the hon. member for Simcoe (Mr. McCarthy).

Mr. McCARTHY. Will the hon. gentleman excuse me. I did not make that assertion. It was by the introduction of the law at the Conquest, not by virtue of the Conquest at all—the introduction of the English law whereby the estates became forfeited to the Crown.

Mr. LAURIER. So be it; I accept the correction. I do not intend to discuss the legal aspects of the question, because, in my judgment, the legal aspect does not come here. But even if, as stated by the hon. gentleman, the British Government took possession of these estates by virtue of the introduction of the English law into this country, still that might have applied as well to the other communities as to the Jesuit estates. Why was that exception made ? Why were these other religious communities maintained in possession of their estates, and the Jesuits excepted ? I think that the Minister of Justice yesterday gave the real key of the difficulty when he stated that it was the covetousness of Lord Amherst, who, in 1770, obtained from the King an actual promise of the grant of these estates. Had it not been afterwards for the abolition of the order by the Pope, I firmly believe the Jesuits would have continued in the enjoyment of their estates in the same manner as the other religious communities. But the order was abolished, and after the last Jesuit had departed this life the British Government took possession of the estates. Then, as we know, the heirs of Lord Amherst claimed these estates in virtue of the promise which had been made in 1770 by the King. But the protests were so strong, not only from the old inhabitants but from the new inhabitants as well, not only from the old subjects of the King, but from the new subjects of the King, that the Government could not carry out its intentions of making a grant of these estates to the heirs of Lord Amherst. On the other hand, though the Government had taken possession of these estates, and though they were promised to General Amherst, the Government could not put them into the general fund, and they erected into a special fund. But there is this to be remembered, whether the laws of England were introduced into the colony or not, whether the old laws continued to be in force or not, the old French laws continued to prevail in the country just as before. And there is this also to be remembered, that under the laws of Quebec as they existed under the French regime, property of the nature of the Jesuits estates, when the order had been abolished, would have reverted to the Ordinary of the Diocese, property of that kind would have gone to the Bishop of Quebec or to the Bishop of Montreal. Such was the contention of the church at that time, and from that day up to this, the ecclesiastical authorities of the Province of Quebec have never ceased to claim that property as rightly belonging to them. There has been a continuation of the protests from that moment to the present. Protests were made in these dates :

" 1. 4th February, 1793, by the citizens of Quebec. 2. 18th November, 1799, by His Grace Jean François Hubert, Bishop of Quebec. 3. About the year 1835, by His Grace Joseph Signay Bishop of Quebec; His Grace Pierre Flavien Turgeon, Bishop of Sydime, Coadjutor of Quebec; His Grace Jean Jacques Lartigue, Bishop Telmasse, Grand Vicar of the district of Montreal. 4. January, 1845, by His Grace Joseph Signay Archbishop of Quebec, and by the Bishops of Montreal, Kingston and Toronto. 5. June, 1847, by the clergy of the dioceses of Montreal and Quebec. 6. January, 1874, by the Rev. Father Théophile Chavaux, Superior General of the Jesuits' Mission in Canada. 7. 9th October, 1878, by the Archbishop of Quebec and Bishops of Three Rivers, Rimouski, Montreal, Sherbrooke, Ottawa, St. Hyacinthe and Chicoutimi. 8. 2nd January, 1885, by the Archbishop of Quebec."

So you see that from the moment the British Government took possession of these estates, the church authorities of the Province of Quebec never ceased to claim them as their own. Now, could that matter have remained in that condition? Could it be said in a Catholic country like the Province of Quebec, that such protests would remain unheeded? Time and again, as you are aware, the Government of Quebec attempted to dispose of these estates and to settle the question. Mr. Mercier is not the first man in office who attempted to deal with this question. Time and again his predecessors attempted to do the same thing. There was a reason for that. Those estates are valued to-day by Mr. Rivard, superintendent of the estates, at the sum of $1,200,000. They yield a revenue of only $22,000, less than 2 per cent. Some of the property is without any annual value. Take for instance, the old college of the Jesuits in Quebec, right to the centre of the city, opposite the Basilica. That property to-day does not give one cent of revenue, on the contrary it is a burden upon the Exchequer of the Province, whereas, were the property disposed of it would sell to advantage. Time and time again, the Government of Quebec have attempted to dispose of it, but every time the Government placed it in the market, the religious authorities came forward and claimed the property as their own, and rendered the attempts at sale abortive. Was that forever to remain thus? The question was opened more than once. M. DeBoucherville, in 1876 endeavored to enter into negotiations to settle the case with the religious authorities of the Province. He did not succeed. It has been asserted many times in the press, though the fact has never been stated officially, that Mr. Chapleau, when in office, entered into negotiations with the religious authorities, and went so far as to offer $500,000 for the removal of the claims of the religious authorities on these estates. Of this I do not know the exact truth. I can only speak from the rumors published in the press. But it is quite certain that Mr. Ross, who succeeded him as Premier a few years afterwards, entered into negotiations for the settlement of the estates. Nothing came of the negotiations, and why? Because it required some courage to deal with the question and to settle it, because it was certain that whoever dealt with it, would have to face much prejudice, as those events have proved. Mr. Mercier had the courage to grapple with this question and to settle it, and if nothing else in the career of Mr. Mercier remained to stamp him as a statesman, there would be this, that he had the courage to deal with this question, and this would give him that title. The question, I think, had to be settled. In what manner was it settled? It was settled just in the manner which was most fair to all: it was settled by compromise. Mr. Mercier in effect said to the religious authorities: I hold these estates as the representative of the Crown; the right belongs to the Province of Quebec: our title to them is legal; I do not admit that you have a legal title to them, while on the other hand you pretend you have a legal title. Be that as it may, he said, let us make a sacrifice each of our pretensions; I hold the property and the whole of the estates, and you claim the whole of them; let us compromise, and let us settle the question forever. Now, I ask every man in this House, no matter what his prejudice may be, I ask the hon. member for Muskoka (Mr. O'Brien) himself, in whose fairness I have the greatest confidence, was there ever a more fair method adopted of disposing of a public question than that which was adopted in this case?

Of course, it is quite easy for the editor in his easy chair, it is quite easy for the publisher in his office, it is quite easy for the clergyman in his study to settle questions according to fixed theories, but the public man in office or in Opposition cannot settle a question according to fixed theories, but he has to consult the wishes, not only the wishes, aye, but the passions and the prejudices of the people with whom he has to deal. And, in a country like the Province of Quebec where there are more than 1,000,000 of Catholic inhabitants, with a regularly constituted hierarchy, with such a claim as the Catholic ecclesiastical authorities could present, was it to be said that this question should ever remain open and these lands never be disposed of for the advantage of the exchequer of the Province? It seems to me that upon that question I can appeal again with confidence to the testimony of all those who will approach the question with an unbiassed mind. After all, Mr. Speaker, there is but one way which has been invented yet to govern men satisfactorily, and it is to govern them according to the wishes which are expressed by public opinion. I do not mean to say that public opinion is always right, the public opinion always comes up to the standard of eternal justice or truth; I do not mean to say that public opinion always comes up to the standard of wordly wisdom, but if you govern the people according to public opinion you are sure to have peace and harmony in the land and when this question was set led it was settled according to the wishes of the public opinion in the Province of Quebec and by so doing you have peace and harmony in the land. Now, if you are to attempt to override the well known wishes of the population of the Province of Quebec, instead of harmony and peace, you will have probably discord, the consequences of which I would fear to look at. Such is the reason why this question has been settled in the manner in which it has been settled. But it has been insisted by the hon. member for Simcoe (Mr. McCarthy) and by some other hon. members also that this legislation was offensive from a Protestant point of view. Well, strange to say, the Protestant minority is represented in the Legislature of the Province of Quebec. They have, if I remember rightly, some 12 members of the Protestant persuasion in the Provincial Legislature. When this question came to be discussed two members only protested, and they protested very mildly. And they protested against what? Only against one single feature of the Act, against the fact that the name of His Holiness the Pope appeared in the preamble of the Act. Mr. Mercier gave them at that moment the very answer quoted yesterday by the Minister of Justice, and he told them : If you do not want the name of the Pope in this matter, you will suggest the name of any one to put in his place. It was a compromise with the religious authorities of the Province of Quebec, and I think Mr. Mercier acted fairly and prudently in dealing direct with the head of the Roman Catholic church. His arguments were so convincing that those objections were not pressed, the Act passed unanimously, and Mr. Mercier was enabled to speak in the following terms of the attitude of his Protestant colleagues :—

" I thank the Protestant members for the moderation with which they have discussed this question. It is a good omen. The unanimity which now prevails is a proof that the different races of which our population is composed, has lived in peace and harmony and approaches the most delicate question with that spirit of conciliation which accomplished wonders when it is properly directed."

Well, this legislation is not satisfactory to our Protestant friends, or to some of them at least from Ontario. Still if the Protestants of Quebec are satisfied, who can object? I understood that it was said a moment ago by the hon. member for Huntingdon (Mr. Scriver), that the Protestants of Quebec are not all satisfied. They may not all be satisfied indeed. It is very seldom that upon any question that may come up men of the same creed, of the same race, will be entirely satisfied; but if anybody has a right to speak for the Protestant minority of the Province of Quebec, are they not those who are elected by the people of that Province to represent them in the Legislature, and if these do not choose to make any representation, if those on the contrary say that after all this question has been settled and approved, no one else has the right to complain. But the hon. member for Simcoe (Mr. McCarthy), it appears has no confidence in those who represent his fellow contrymen in the Province of Quebec. If I am to believe what he said yesterday, he has but a poor opinion of those who have been entrusted by his fellow religionists in the Province to take charge of their interests in the Legislature. These were his words yesterday :

" Does this look as if the Protestants of the Province of Quebec were desirous, and willing, and anxious that this legislation should remain unchanged, or does it not look as if, if the Protestant minority in that Province were given reasonable encouragement, they would get justice—and no more than justice are they entitled to, and no more than justice I hope they will ever ask for—from the Parliament of this country. Then they will be up and doing, to get their share of the legislation, but in the Legislature of that Province, composed as it is now, they cannot expect it. There was no Protestant representative in the Cabinet of that Province until recently, and, when one was chosen, he had to be elected in spite of the vote of the Protestant minority."

Now, without going any further, I wish to take issue upon this point with the hon. gentleman from North Simcoe (Mr. McCarthy), when he says here that Col. Rhodes was not elected in Megantic by the Protestant minority. The County of Megantic is a mixed county. Col. Rhodes, the Minister of Agriculture, was elected two or three months after this Act has been passed, and it was an issue upon which the electors had to pass. Col. Rhodes polled the majority of the French and Catholic votes, but I say that Col. Rhodes also polled the majority of the Protestant votes. As to this I do not give my own testimony. I have not yet had an occasion to look at the figures. But I give the testimony of Col. Rhodes himself, who, on the day of the election, telegraphed that he had been upheld by the majority of the Protestant electors of the County of Megantic. Then the hon. member for North Simcoe (Mr. McCarthy) goes on to say :

" I can understand that, if there were a fighting man in that House like the hon. member who leads the third party here, there might be a chance of obtaining something like justice, but men with that skill and ability, with parliamentary knowledge to back it, are not to be found every day, and we are not to judge the Protestant representatives of the Province of Quebec on that high standard."

And why not, Mr. Speaker, " of that high standard ? " Can it be that the Protestants of the Province of Quebec, who have placed themselves at the head of the trade of the country, still are so backward in this respect that they cannot send to the Legislature a man of standing to represent them ? Can it be that the Protestants of the Province of Quebec have to be taken under the fostering care of my hon. friend from Simcoe ? Can it be that they cannot manage their own affairs ? Can it be they cannot look after their own interests ? I have more confidence than my hon. friend in the ability of the Protestant representatives in the Province of Quebec, because I happen to know they are men of merit, men of ability, and some of the greatest ability. But, Mr. Speaker, if that is the opinion which the hon. gentleman entertains of his own countrymen and co-religionists in the Province of Quebec ; if he believes that they are not able to take care of their own interests, but that the Protestants of other Provinces must come to their rescue, perhaps he would be interested to know what is the opinion which is entertained by some of the Protestants of Quebec of those too zealous Protestants of the Province of Ontario who want to take up the cudgels on their behalf. I hold in my hand an extract from a paper published in the Eastern Townships, the Waterloo *Advertiser*, edited by a disciple and a life-long friend of the late Mr. Huntington, as good and as strong a Protestant as ever lived. This is how the paper speaks :

" Every patriotic Canadian must deplore the intemperate discussion that has been provoked by the Jesuits' Bill. The measure has become law, and no amount controversey can alter the fact. It is altogether the domestic concern of the Province of Quebec, and any outside interference is simply meddlesome and impertinent. The persons and the Orangemen of Ontario have joined hands to make war on the Catholics of Quebec. The Legislature has settled the old dispute over the Jesuits' estates in a manner satisfactory to the people. A source of irritation and discontent has been removed once for all. The Jesuits' Bill passed the Legislature, practically, without a dissenting voice. The chosen representatives of the Protestant minority accepted it as a fair settlement of a vexed question. The basis of settlement called for an expenditure of public funds, and to obviate any possibility of jealousy on the part of the Protestant minority a proportionate sum was at the same time voted for Protestant education. That was fair and just and it was so understood by the minority. The Protestant minority in this Province is quite able to take care of itself. In the purely domestic concerns of the Province it asks no assistance and expects no sympathy from outsiders. Taking it all in all, the minority has been fairly treated by the majority. There may have been friction at times, but there has not been in the history of the Province an instance in which the powers of the majority have been used to crush or injure the minority. If the Catholics and Protestants are able to get along together peaceably, why should Ontario interfere ? The Protestants minority as a whole has not and does not complain of the Jesuits settlement. It is recognized by broad-minded and patriotic men as being the best thing that could have been done under the circumstances."

Such, Mr. Speaker, is the opinion entertained in the Eastern Townships at least by one section of the people. Now, my hon. friend from Huntingdon (Mr. Scriver) a moment ago referred to the treatment of the minority in the Province of Quebec. I have the greatest respect as my friend knows for everything which he utters, and I am sure he will agree with me in one thing—if the Protestant minority in the Province of Quebec have anything to complain of—and I listened to what might be called the list of grievances which we heard read to-day by the hon. member for Norfolk (Mr. Charlton), but if the Protestant minority have anything to complain of, I ask : Are they not themselves responsible for it ? In all that list of grievances which were read is there an act of legislation against which they have ever protested ? Have they not always supported the Conservative party which has always been in power, and has not every one of these items in the list which we have heard recited as a grievance, been passed by the Conservative party which the Protestants of Quebec always supported. Sir, I have simply to say this, speaking as a Canadian of French origin, that if my fellow-countrymen of British origin have any grievances, real or imaginary, let them come before the Legislature of Quebec; and although I have not a seat in that Legislature I can claim that I have some influence there, nay I do not want any influence, I know that the majority of the members in that House, the Conservative minority as well, would be ever ready to give them what remedial legislation they may think for their benefit. But up to a few days ago, I never heard that the Protestant minority had anything to complain of in the treatment which they have received from the majority of the Province of Quebec, and if they had any serious grievances, can it be told upon the floor of this Parliament that these grievances would not have been ventilated before the representatives of the people ? I repeat what I said a moment ago. It is quite easy for the editor in his chair, or the clergyman in his study, or for any party who has no responsability to public at large—it is quite easy for them to determine questions by fixed theories, but it is another thing to fix them according to the will of the people, and I do not admit that there is any serious grievance so long as these grievances are not ventilated upon the floor of the House of the Provincial Parliament. The hon. member for Simcoe (Mr. McCarthy) also said something yesterday about Mr. Joly. He claimed that Mr. Joly had been ousted from public life. I do not know by whom, but I suppose he meant by the Liberal party.

Mr. McCARTHY. Hear, hear.

Mr. LAURIER. The hon. gentleman says " hear, hear." Mr. Joly has been in power for some eighteen months and he was ousted from power by the most dishonest warfare which every public man had to suffer in this country. Mr. Joly was ousted from power largely by a violation of the Constitution, perpetrated by this Parliament, and in which the hon. member for Simcoe was himself instrumental. If Mr. Joly had had anything like fair play, I believe that to this day he would have been in power in the Province of Quebec. Mr. Joly never had anything to suffer at the hands of the Liberal party; on the contrary, Mr. Joly is a man for whom we have the greatest respect. We have differed from him upon one question, and one question only, the question which arose out of the rebellion in the North-West. Upon that question Mr. Joly took one course, and we took a different course. I am not to argue this question over again, but I have simply to say this to the hon. member for Simcoe, that in the last election which took place in Megantic, where a Protestant representative of the Cabinet of Mr. Mercier was before the people, and when this very question was to be tested at the polls, Mr. Joly came down and supported the candidate and the policy of the Government. It is evident, Mr. Speaker, from the discussion which we have had in this Parliament since yesterday, that though the Act is objectionable to some people—and I find no fault with the hon. member for Muskoka, I find no fault with my hon. friend from Simcoe, for holding the views they hold; I would not attribute to them other than the motive of conscience, that they are doing what they think for the best, they are representing what they deem to be in the interest of the people at large—but it is manifest to me that their judgment has been considerably biassed by the fact that the name of the Jesuits has been introduced in that legislation. It seems to me manifest that the appearance of that name has evoked a fresh outburst of hostility which that celebrated order has been subjected to in many lands and in many ages. Now, it is said that they are dangerous men. Suppose all that has been said were true, would that be any reason to refuse them the justice to which they are entitled? Suppose they were dangerous men, as it is represented they are; that might perhaps be a reason to refuse them civil rights, to refuse them recognition. But they were incorporated by the Province of Quebec two years ago, and the Act which incorporated them received the approval of one of those weak Protestants, according to the member for Simcoe, who represent the minority in the Legislature of Quebec. Mr. Lynch, a fellow Conservative of the hon. member for Simcoe, speaking on that occasion, used this remarkable language:

" Mr. Lynch, on the Bill to incorporate the Jesuits, said that notwithstanding what might be thought in some quarters, there was nothing in the Bill alarming in its character. We were living in an age when wisdom prevailed, living in an age where freedom was supposed to exist the world over, and nowhere the Dominion of Her Majesty did liberty prevail more than in the Province of Quebec. In Committee, with a consideration of fairness which characterised members of the House, certain portions of the preamble were struck out. Now is it possible that the intelligent public opinion of the Province of Quebec should deny those Jesuit Fathers the civil rights which we have granted to everyone else ? If there is any religious aspect to this question it should be settled elsewhere than in this House. If there is anything in this Bill against civil rights, let us strike it out. Until this is shown I am prepared to support this Bill. "

And supported the Bill was, and became law. Under such circumstances, it seems to me that the explosion of bitterness which we have seen to-day and yesterday comes rather tardily. But, Sir, any man, be he friend or foe of the Jesuit Order, must at least give them credit for this, that they repel and deny all the charges which are made against them; they repeal and deny the dangerous doctrines which are attributed to them. Now, I would not enter upon that question for one moment were it not for the remarks which fell to-day from my friend the hon. member for North Norfolk (Mr. Charlton); but I cannot allow such views as those which have been expressed to pass without some comment, though this is not the proper sphere or time either to defend or attack the Jesuits. Every one familiar with French litterature knows that Pascal, in his celebrated " Lettres Provinciales," has quoted several paragraphs, which he attributes to Jesuits, of very objectionable character. I have not been able for my part to discover those extracts; I have often sought for the text books; but could not find them, and I cannot say whether they are right or wrong. But I know this, that writers of as great eminence as Pascal have asserted over and over again that all the statements upon which Pascal based his accusations have been refuted, time and again, by members of the Jesuit Order. Now, the Jesuits, it is admitted, are a body of able men, and, it must be admitted also, are a body of pure men, and they are characterised by knowledge and high attainments; but they are men, they are fallible, and it would be strange indeed if in such a numerous order some were not found to write objectionable things. But suppose one of an order were found to write objectionable thing would it follow that the whole order ought to be held responsible, as was said by one member? So are you to conclude that, because one of the order happens to write objectionable things, the whole order are to be condemned? It would be just as if you were to condemn all the Protestant divines of Ontario because the Rev. Dr Wild said, a few days ago, that to kill a Jesuit was no crime. I will not, Mr. Speaker, push this controversy any further. This is not the place, I say, to attack the Jesuits, nor the place to defend them. The place to attack the Jesuits, in so far as this Bill is concerned, was the Legislature of Quebec; but whether a man be a friend or a foe of the Jesuits, it seems to me that their history in Canada, whatever it may have been in other lands, has been such as to commend not only admiration, but the greatest admiration. They have been the pioneers of this country. In the language of a great historian, not a cape was turned, not a river was entered, but a Jesuit led the way. Every inch of the soil of Ontario was trodden by their weary feet at least 150 years before there was an English settler in that Province. Nay, the very soil of the Province has been consecrated by their blood, shed in their attempts to win over souls to the God of Protestants and Catholics alike. Of the Jesuits I have nothing more to say. The question, as I say, is not one fit for this audience; if it is to be discussed it should be discussed elsewhere than here. But the resolution asserts that they have been expelled. The hon. member for Simcoe stated yesterday that they have been expelled from several countries; and the hon. member for North Norfolk stated to-day that they have been expelled from twenty different countries. Sir, this is true; but, what is equally true, they have never yet been expelled from a free country. They have been expelled from countries where true principles of human freedom such as we understand them in British countries, were not understood. The hon. gentleman told us yesterday that they had been expelled from Germany in 1872. Why is it, in a British Assembly, that the example of Germany will be given to us to imitate? Does the hon. gentleman hold that because the Jesuits have been expelled from Germany—Germany ruled by a man of genius, but a despot after all—such an example should be followed here? We have been told that the Jesuits were expelled from France in 1880. Yes, they were; and to the shame of the French Republic be it said. But they are not the only men who were expelled by that Government. In 1880 six or seven different religious communities were expelled. Sisters of Charity were expelled—angels on earth, if there are any, women who renounce everything that life can give in order to give their life up to the daily maintenance and succor of those who are poor, helpless and suffering,. Not only those religious communities, but the princes of the House of Orleans were also expelled from France—men who were the *élite* of France, men of whom more than forty years ago, Prince Metternich said, when they were in their boyhood : "They are young men such they are few and princes such as they are none." The Duc d'Aumale, one of them, was expelled, one of the noblest soldiers of the French army, a man whose soul is so high that the only manner in which he requited the cruel treatment meted out to him was to make a gift to the ungrateful nation of the Chateau de Chantilly with all its art treasures. I have only this to say to an hon. gentleman who brings such arguments as these : I feel ten thousand times prouder of my native land, which can deal justly and generously with the Jesuits, than of the land of my ancestors, which though a republic, is to-day so retrogade in its constitution and practice of freedom, that it banishes those who do not come up to the standard of its own citizenship. In this matter, I am reminded that the hon. gentleman from Simcoe (Mr. McCarthy) yesterday stated that we of French origin sometimes forget that this is a British country. I have his words here and I want to quote them :

"We must never forget, said he, I am afraid that some of my friends from the Province of Quebec do sometimes forget that this is a British country, that by the fortunes of war that event was decided, and the greater half of this continent passed over to the British Crown."

What did the hon. gentleman mean by that ? I wish he had said a little more or a little less. I wish he had not contended himself with making an insinuation, but that if he had a charge to make, he should have had the pluck and the courage to make it. I tell this to the hon. gentleman. I am of French origin and I am proud of my origin, and I know my fellow countrymen of Anglo-Saxon race too well not to be aware that if I had not the pride of my origin in my heart they would never think of me but with the contempt which I should deserve. I am of French origin, but I am a British subject. The hon. member for North Norfolk (Mr. Charlton) said, a moment ago, that there should be but one race here.

Mr. McCARTHY. Hear, hear.

Mr. LAURIER. The hon. gentleman says "hear, hear." Well, what would that race be ? Is it the British lion that is to swallow the French lamb, or the French lamb that is to swallow the British lion ? There can be more than one race, but there shall be but one nation. Scotland has not forgotten her origin, as far as I know, but Scotland is British. I do not intend to forget my origin, but I am a Canadian before everything. Let me state this further to my hon. friend, I have the pride of my origin ; I feel the strenght of the blood which flows in my veins, but, in the language of the Latin poet, I say :

"Homo sum ; humani nihil a me alienum puto."

"I am a man ; nothing that relates to man is foreign to my sympathy; " but, at the same time, though I would never forget the language of my race, the langage which my mother taught me, I say to the hon. gentleman that if I had my choice to return to French allegiance, never would I consent to do so. I do not speak only my own feelings when I thus speak but I voice the feelings of every one of my countrymen. I do not give utterance merely to the feelings of those who sit beside me, but I am sure I speak the feelings of those French Canadians who sit on the other side as well. when I say that if to-day a poll was taken in the Province of Quebec, or all through the Dominion of Canada, giving a choice between allegiance to England or allegiance to France, there would not be one single vote cast in favor of a return to the allegiance to France. We would remain British subjects ; but because we are British subjects, is it to be expected that we shall turn traitors to our origin, traitors to everything that makes life valuable ? What would be life if a man had not in his veins and in his heart a feeling for the blood of his own country ? The hon. gentleman told us yesterday that he was an Irishman. Would he deny the land of his ancestors ? Well, I would pity him from my heart if he would. But, after all, if ever we were to forget that we are of French origin I am sure we could not forget it in view of the agitation which is now going on in the Province of Ontario, because from day to day, from week to week, in a certain press, we have been appealed to —we of French origin—as Liberals of French origin—to vote for disallowance against the Jesuits' Act. From day to day in a certain press, the Liberals of the Province of Quebec have been appealed to vote against the Government on this question; and in my hand I hold one of the last issues, in which after having recited all the villanies of which the Jesuits are accused, the editor continues as follows :—

" It is safe to say, therefore, that if the Liberals of England or of France were in the position of Mr. Laurier and his followers they would not hesitate a moment in killing this conspiracy in Quebec. Even if they did not hold the Acts to be absolutely unconstitutional they would certainly vote for their disallowance as being contrary to the public interest. "

Well, as far as reference is made to the Liberals of France, I have no doubt the editor is quite correct. No doubt, if the Liberals of France had the power to vote on this question, they would certainly disallow this Act; but I have this to say, that I am not and we are not Liberals of the French school. I have not said it once but ten times and twenty times in my own Province, that I am a Liberal of the English school, that I and my friends have nothing in common with the Liberals of France. A short time ago, I was sorry to hear my hon. friend from Norfolk (Mr. Charlton) express regret that there was no Protestant party, as far as I understood him. There are men of my own race, who entertain the same view as the hon. gentleman, and would desire to have a Catholic party. I have always raised my voice against that doctrine, and, as far back as 1877, speaking to a French audience in the French language in the city which I have the honor to represent now, the good old city of Quebec, I used to those who, like my hon. friend, would separate men upon the ground of creed, this language:

" You wish to organise all the Catholics in one party, without any other tie, without any other basis than the community of religion, but have you not reflected that, by that very fact, you will organise the Protestant population as one party, and that then, instead of the peace and harmony which exist to-day between the different elements of the Canadian population, you would bring on war, religious war, the most disastrous of all wars. "

Those were my sentiments ten years ago; those are my sentiments to-day. My hon. friend from Norfolk (Mr. Charlton) stated that we should not allow this Act because the Jesuits are inimical to liberty. Such a statement would not surprise me in the mouth of a Liberal from France, but it does surprise me to hear it on the floor of this Parliament. Are we to be told that, because men are inimical to liberty, they shall not be given liberty? In our own doctrine and in our own view, liberty shines not only for the friends of liberty but also for the enemies of liberty. We make no difference whatever : and, as far as the liberals of England are concerned, I am sure of one thing, that, if they were here, they would never vote as the editor of the *Mail* supposed they would. The Liberals of England have been for the last century and more the champions of freedom all over the world, and, if we have freedom to-day, as we understand it in this country, and in this age, it is largely due to the efforts of the Liberal party in England. They understood long ago that liberty is not only for the friends of liberty but for all. They understood long ago that the security of the State depends entirely upon the utmost freedom being given to all opinions, that no one is to be canvassed for his opinion, right or wrong, but that the utmost freedom shall be given to all opinions, and that the popular judgment will decide between the grain and the chaff, will select the one and reject the other. That is the principle which I have, in my humble way, endeavored to inculcate for many years amongst my fellow-countrymen of French origin. That, with a steadfast adherence to the broadest principles of constitutional freedom, is the guiding star which, in the station I now occupy and in any station I may have in life, I shall ever endeavor to follow.

Sir JOHN A. MACDONALD. (KINGSTON).

At this late hour, and after the subject before us has been so fully discussed, I do not feel myself warranted in addressing the House at any length, and I am too well pleased and satisfied with the course taken by my hon. friend who has just spoken in supporting the policy of the Government on this occasion to feel very indignant at the reproofs and reproaches thrown across the floor in the course of his speech. In fact it is a bitter pill for my hon. friend to be obliged to vote for us. He is obliged to to it. He dare not do otherwise. He could not face Quebec if he did anything else. So he takes his revenge by pitching into the Government generally, and that, I take it, is the means by which he reconciles it to his conscience to vote in favor of the Government. Like mine Ancient Pistol, " he eats his leek in earnest of revenge," and so he strays off to all kinds of irrelevant subjects. He brought in the Streams Bill, brought in the *modus vivendi*, he discussed the double-faced policy of the Conservative party, as he says, since 1854. As to that double-faced policy, I pardon my hon. friend for his great mistake in that regard. He is a young man. I cannot say of him, as the hon. member for Northumberland (Mr. Mitchell) said of my hon. friend here, that he is a fledging politician, but he is a young man, and he forgets the history of Canada since 1854. Why, he said that, while we professed to be the friends of Lower Canada and the friends of the French race and the friends of Catholicism in the Province of Quebec, we were equally strong as the advocates of Protestantism in the Province of Upper Canada, that we were avowing ourselves in that Province as Englishmen, as Anglo-Sexons, and as being opposed to French domination. The hon. gentleman has forgotten the history of his country. He has forgotten that for years, I was in a minority in my own Province. The hon. gentleman knows that I was attacked by the organ of the Liberal party in Upper Canada year after year as being recreant to Protestantism, as being recreant to the British race, as succumbing to French influence as being the tool and the subservient slave of the French people. Why, who opposed the cry of representation by population but myself and my party ; who supported the separate schools against the whole weight of the Liberal party of Ontario, headed at that time by the late Hon. George Brown, but myself and my party ? The opposition to both those cries was unpopular, especially in regard to representation by population, which seemed to be fair. My opposition to representation by population, in the interest of Lower Canada, was held out as being unjust and unfair to my own race and Province. Why did I oppose it ? The Liberal party and their leader—and he was a real leader of men—I mean the Hon George Brown, was supported by his party in that policy, and he had at his command the able newspaper which he conducted and owned, the *Globe*—abused and attacked me without stint because I opposed representation by population ; and why did I oppose it ? Because the leader of that party did not conceal the object for which he desired a majority in the United Legislature of Canada. He said that the French language must be put down. He said that the Anglo-Saxon race and English law must prevail, and that threat against our fellow-subjects in the Province of Lower Canada was so strongly pressed, and was so imminent, that I did not hesitate to incur the obloquy which was poured upon me for years, the result of which was that I was in the minority in my own Province during most of the time from 1854 to 1866. The hon. gentleman is rather ungrateful for the years and years during which I stood as the advocate for the Province of Lower Canada, of the French race, and of my Catholic fellow-countrymen. Aye, Sir, and more than that; although I was in a minority I had a very respectable Protestant Conservative support, and the main body of the Conservative support that I received in the Province of Ontario was from the Orange body. The majority of the Orange body was Conservative, and they stood by me. In the first place I had the Grand Master of the Orange body, the late George Benjamin, who, chief of the Orangemen as he was never failed in voting with me for the protection of the Lower Canadians, their country, their race, and their religion, from the persistent and factious attacks that were made upon them by the Liberal party of Ontario. Well, after a while Mr. George Benjamin disappeared, I had the support of another Grand Master of the Orangemen in the present Minister of Customs. Orangeman as he was, chief of the Orangemen as he was, he never failed in doing full justice to Lower Canada, its rights, its religion and its interests. The hon. gentleman then strayed off into the Streams Bill. Well, the hon. gentleman quoted what was said in the report on the Streams Bill. He forgot that the report and the action of the Government on the Streams Bill were ba-ed on the authority of a report of the Minister of Justice in the Government of which he was a member, which Government disallowed a Bill passed by the Legislature of Prince Edward Island on precisely the same grounds as the Streams Bill rejection was approved by us. Let the hon. gentleman look back, and he will find that the Government of that day notwithstanding their strong affection for provincial rights, disallowed a measure on the same grounds, first, because it was *ex post facto*, and, second, because it was *lis pendens*, and the subject already before the courts. Then my hon. friend says that although we are very slow in some things, we are very quick in others ; that, for instance, there was the *modus vivendi*, which we had to decline to grant, although my hon. friend had moved it, and then a few days afterwards we had agreed to continue it. The hon. gentleman must not lay the flattering unction to his soul that his motion had anything to do in the world with the action of the Government on that point. I can prove it in the clearest possible way. The hon. gentleman will, perhaps, remember my speech on the occasion in answer to that motion. I asked the hon. gentleman to allow the matter to stand over, not to press that subject while a Government was just going out in the United States, and to wait and see—I only asked for six days—whether the incoming Government were going to be friendly or were going to adopt a non intercourse policy. I said— the hon. gentleman must remember it —wait until we see if there is any evidence of hostility, if it is not going to be a non-intercourse Government, then it will be time enough to deal with that subject. I could not tell the hon. gentleman at that time, but I can tell him now. His motion was made on the 26th of February. On the 4th of February the first communication to the colony of Newfoundland was made. My telegram was :

" Have temporarily suspended granting of licenses under *modus vivendi* until the course of new president known. Wish co-operation. Am writing. "

So that the subject was under discussion between the Premier of Newfoundland and the Dominion of Canada long before we knew that my hon. friend was going to make his flourish. The papers I shall lay before the House, as I promised to do The hon. gentleman held us responsible for a debate in the Province of Ontario the other day, when Mr. Craig made a motion and Mr. Meredith made a speech. Well, Mr. Speaker, all that I can say is this, those gentlemen are free agents, they can make speeches as they like. We are responsible here in the Dominion Parliament for what we do in the Dominion Parliament. Even here the hon. gentleman would not like to be held responsible for this resolution, because his great friend and supporter, the hon. member for North Norfolk ( Mr. Charlton) happens to differ from him. These Conservative gentlemen in Toronto have taken their course. My hon. friend from North Norfolk is a supporter of the hon. gentleman, is a strong leader in the Liberal party. He has taken his course; the hon, gentleman was not bound by that, he has shown that he is not bound by it; and yet if we applied to him the same measure that he applies to us, we are to be held responsible, notwithstanding our own assertion, notwithstanding our own vote, notwithstanding our course of action—we are to be held responsible for the action of Conservatives in another and different sphere. My hon. friend from Northumberland (Mr. Mitchell) the other day, in his very effective speech, a very satisfactory speech from my point of view, said that the Government ought to have spoken early in this matter. Well, Mr. Speaker, if we had disallowed the Bill that would have been a true remark. If we had taken the responsibility of disallowing the Bill, of interfering with the legislation of the Province of Quebec, we ought to be called upon to state our reasons and to defend our course. But as a matter of course, the legislation of each Province is independent, subject to the restrictions in the Constitution. It requires no defence for the Government of the day to allow an Act of the Local Legislature to go into operation. That is their duty as a general rule and there is no defence required. An attack must be made if they have improperly allowed an Act to go into operation. Now, in this case I have no doubt, notwithstanding the able arguments of the hon. member from North Simcoe (Mr. McCarthy) that that measure was within the competence of the Provincial Legislature. My hon. friend who is a much higher authority than myself, the Minister of Justice, came to the same conclusion. I may say that we, laymen and lawyers in the Cabinet, were unanimous on the point; and if I had any doubt upon the subject the able and well reasoned argument and speech of my hon. friend from Bothwell (Mr. Mills) would have removed all doubts from my mind. Now, Mr. Speaker, the hon. gentleman seemed to intimate that there has been a change of front on this subject. He is wrong. We have carried out fully, in our opinion, the principles laid down in a report submitted by myself as Minister of Justice in 1869. That report was communicated to all the Governments of the Province, and it laid down what we considered were the principles which should govern the exercise of the power of disallowance by the Governor General on the advice of his Cabinet, and although that was not formally approved, it has really been acted upon and continually quoted by both sides of this House and by both parties in the press, as being a fair description of the instances in which the power and right of disallowance should be exercised. Now, this Bill, Mr. Speaker, was either within the competence of the Legislature or it was not. If within the competence of the Legislature, it must, as matter of course, be allowed to go into operation (I know some hon. gentlemen will not agree with the exception laid down in the report of 1869 and carried out ever since) unless in the opinion of the Government of the Dominion the Act, however much within the competence of the Province, was injurious to the Dominion as a whole. Of course, it is a great responsibility for any Government to take that course and to decide that any provincial measure is against the interests of the Dominion. But the provision was put into the British North America Act to meet such cases, so that if in any case the Government of the Dominion should believe that an Act within the competence of a Province was injurious to the whole Dominion, it was their duty as well as their right to disallow that measure, and for doing so they are responsible to the Parliament of the Dominion, in which Parliament every Province has its representatives, who, of course, are prepared, as is their duty, to defend their provincial rights. That is the doctrine in pursuance of which we have assumed the responsibility of allowing this Bill, not disallowing it, and for which we are held responsible. If it is not within the competence of the Province, it has not at all follow that it is the duty of the Dominion Government to interfere. Look at the returns laid before Parliament, amounting now to two volumes. You see again and again reports in which the Ministers of Justice have stated that they believed certain clauses of different measures were " ultra vires, " yet as they had a beneficial tendency, or as they did not affect the interests of the rest of the Dominion, the attention of the Provincial Legislatures and Provincial Governments were called to it, with the suggestion that, if they thought well of it, they should amend the Act in those clauses and in those particulars where, in the opinion of the Minister of Justice and the Government here, they had exceeded their legitimate powers. It does not at all follow that because a Bill is " ultra vires " and is beyond the competence of the Legislature, it should be disallowed. On the contrary, as has been urged by the hon. member for North-York (Mr. Mulock), and very correctly urged, it is just in those cases there is no necessity for disallowance, because there are the courts of law to appeal to. The allowance of a Bill which is " ultra vires " does not make it law. The courts can at once interfere and it is only in those cases where Acts are " ultra vires, " and where leaving them on the Statute-book would cause great injury to parties, that the right of disallowance should be exercised. Hon. members will readily understand that the moment an Act is passed by a Provincial Legislature people interested in the measure assume it is law, act on it, enter into large enterprises on it, and may be ruined if the Government did not immediately, with all convenient speed, interfere to protect those people from injury and ruin. In this case, as I have already said, we, the Government, including the legal members of it, had no doubt as to the fact that this Act was within the competence of the Local Legislature. And, Sir, I think it was not left for us, we could not as a Government, against the decisions of the Legislature of Old Canada, and against the repeated legislation of the Province of Quebec since Confederation, set up our own opinion against the various Acts that have been passed. Why, 37 years ago, by the Legislature of United Canada, where the majority of the reprensentatives of the people were Protestants, the St. Mary's College was incorporated with large powers. The hon. member for Norfolk (Mr. Charlton) says : because there were some few Jesuit professors, that did not make it a Jesuit college. Now, I tell the hon. gentleman that the corporators of the St. Mary's College were the Bishop of Montreal and six Jesuit priests. Just as Victoria College is a Methodist College and Queen's a Presbyterian institution, so St. Mary's College is a Jesuit teaching institution.

Mr. BLAKE. Everybody knew it was a Jesuit college.

Mr. BERGERON. It has never been disputed.

Sir JOHN A. MACDONALD. Let me call the attention of the House to the division on that occasion. Let the hon. gentleman remember that the majority that voted for the Bill was 54 and only seven members, on the third reading, were opposed to it. There was a larger vote against it in the second reading, but, after a full discussion, on the third reading the division was as I have stated. Of the 54 who voted for the incorporation of St. Mary's College 29 were Protestants and 25 Catholics. I will read to the House some of the names to show that, although it was known at the time that it was a Jesuit institution, although the objection was taken and arguments were used somewhat like the arguments used on this occasion, yet there was then no fear of the Jesuit body, no fear of their insidious attempt to unsettle the Constitution of Canada, no fear that the crown of Canada was trembling on the head of Her Majesty, no fear that this country was going to suffer any injury of any kind, and this will be shown when I read to this House some of the names. Judge Badgley, the leading lay representative in the Church of England of Montreal ; Hon. M. C. Cameron, a Free Church Presbyterian ; Mr. Clapham, a Church of England man from Quebec ; Hon. George Crawford, a strong North of Ireland Protestant, and I believe an Orangeman ; Mr. Dawson of London, who every one remembers as a strong Church of England man , Mr. Gamble, the special agent of Bishop Strachan in Parliament when the Clergy Reserves question was settled ; Sir Francis Hincks, whom we all know ; Mr. Langton, whom the older members of the House will remember ; myself, the member for Kingston ; Mr. McDougall (not the Honorable William), also a Protestant ; Mr. Hamilton Merritt, whom we all know as a Liberal in Parliament and afterwards a member of the Government ; Mr. Morrison, I am not sure whether that is Judge Morrison or his brother, Angus Morrison ; Mr. Page a prominent representative from the Province of Quebec ; Mr. Patrick, of Prescott, whom we all remember as being a good Liberal; Col. Prince, of Essex ; Sir William Richards, then the Attorney-General ; Mr. Ridout, the Conservative member for Toronto ; Hon. William Robinson, whom we all remember as the brother of Sir John Robinson, the leader of the old family compact party ; Dr. Rolph ; Sir John Rose ; Mr. Seymour, afterwards a Senator ; Honorable James Shaw, afterwards a Senator ; Mr. Stevenson, of Prince Edward ; the late Mr. Thomas Street ; the late the Hon. George O. Stuart, of Quebec ; Mr. C. Wilson, of Middlesex ; Mr. Wright, of West York, a leading Orangeman, and, as my friend from London can vouch, a staunch Protestant ; those were the gentlemen who voted for this Bill, and the members who voted against the Bill were all from Ontario. That is a sufficient answer to my hon. friend from Huntington (Mr. Scriver) that in 1852 not one single Protestant representative from the Province of Lower Canada—the Province of Quebec—voted against the Bill, and that is a full justification of the statement of my hon. friend from Stanstead (Mr. Colby) when he said that Protestants of the Province of Quebec were not opposed to the legislation of that subject. We find that so long as 37 years ago the Jesuit college was established in Montreal. I voted for that, Mr. Speaker, and I never have had cause to regret my vote. That institution has gone on in its work of usefulness. We do not hear one single complaint of its teaching, or of any perversion of the youth, nor any disloyal doctrines, or any doctrines which have brought censure on the college. We hear that that institution has gone on and continues to go on doing its work well and devotedly. Now, Mr. Speaker, one would suppose from the speeches we hear now, and the articles which we see in the newspapers, that this was a new invasion of the Jesuits, that they are coming in like the Huns and the Vandals over this country to sweep away civilisation. Well, 37 years ago they were in active and useful operation in Canada, and in 1871, 18 years ago, the Legislature of the Province of Quebec passed an Act incorporating the Society of Jesus. This Act of 1887 is not the first Act of incorporation. It is an Act altering the provisions of the Act of 1871 and, instead of enlarging their powers, it diminishes the powers given them by the Act of 1871. This Act of 1871 passed the Legislature of Quebec, and we find that there was no protest from the Protestants in Parliament or out of Parliament. We do not find or hear that there was any objection to this Act. Now, because an agitation has grown up in the country—I do not know how or why—it is found that the Act of 1871 ought never to have been passed, that the Act of 1878 limiting this Act of 1871 ought not to be passed, and that both those Acts, as well as the measure we are now dicussing, is deeply injurious to the people of all the Dominion of Canada. Now, Sir, this Act of 1871 provides :

" Whereas the Rev. Fathers Pierre Point, Superior, Firmin Vignon, Zéphirin Resther, and others, priests and religious members of the Company of Jesus, residing at Quebec, in the building of the ' Congrégation de Notre-Dame, ' from a body whose object is to perform the various functions of their office, in cities and in country places, such as the preaching of missions and retreats, and to assume the direction of religious congregations, brotherhoods and societies both of men and women ; can also, at the request or with the permission of their lordships the Roman Catholic Bishops, or of any one of them, to devote themselves to other works for spiritual or moral purposes, by preaching, precepts and education ; and, whereas, in order to consolidate their establishment and to favor its prosperity and progress, they have prayed for leave to form a corporate body enjoying civil and political rights ; Therefore, Her Majesty by and with the advice and consent of the Legislature of Quebec, enacts as follows :
" 1. The above named petitioners and all other persons who may in future be legally associated with them in virtue of the present Act, are hereby constituted a body politic, and shall form a corporation under the name of ' Les missionnaires de Notre-Dame, S. J. '
" 2. The said corporation shall, under the same name, have perpetual succession, and shall have all the rights, powers and privileges of other corporations, and particularly of those having a religious, spiritual or moral object. It may at all times admit other members and establish them in one or more places. It may also at all times and places by purchase, gift, devise, assignment, loan or in virtue of this Act, or by any other lawful means and legal title, acquire, possess, inherits take, have, accept and receive any movable or immovable property whatever, for the usages and purposes of the said corporation, and the same may hypothecate, sell, lease, farm out, exchange, alienate, and finally dispose of lawfully, in whole or in part, for the same purposes. "

And it goes on to say there must be the limit of $10,000 as to the extent of immovable property they should hold. How could the present Government, in the face of the solemn legislation of United Canada of 1852, and in the face of the legislation of the Province of Quebec in 1871—how could they now set up their own opinion and declare that this was a body that ought not to have existence in Canada ? But, Sir, let us look on it as a matter of common sense. What harm have the Jesuits done, and have they done any ? In 37 years, if their principles were so void of morality, if their morality was so doubtful, if their ambition was so inordinate they would have shown some evidence of it in 37 years or since their incorporation in 1871. They have gone on in their humble way acting like other Catholic orders in the Province of Quebec, doing their duty according to their lights. When you talk of their doctrines I have nothing to say about them ; all we know is this, their doctrines whatever they are, are such as to meet with the approbation of the Head of their Church or they would soon be informed of it in the authoritative way which the Head of that Church can govern all such religious bodies within the Catholic religion. Under these circumstances I say we would have been acting with a degree of presumption that I do not think any Canadian Government or any sensible Government in any country would think of exercising if we vetoed this Bill. We had no ground for doing so, we had the sanction of United Canada, as I said before for this Act ; we had positive legislation acted upon in the Province of Quebec for eighteen long years, and that we should set up our own opinion is absurd. If we did we would have been justly subject to the condemnation of every thinking man in Canada. But, Sir, we are told all about the expulsion of the Jesuits and the Act of Supremacy, and the unfavorable legislation that took place in England long long ago. It is too late for us to discuss this subject to-night, or I would like very much to do so. But those laws practically have been obsolete in England. England is a very Conservative country, and its general policy has been, in the chance of manners, in the advance of education and liberal ideas, not to rub out statute after statute whenever it may apparently infringe upon or be adverse to the thought of the day, but to allow them quietly to drop ; and what is the consequence ? Look at England. Are the people of England afraid of the insidious attempts of the Jesuit body to attack the supremacy of England ? Are they afraid that the Queen's crown would tremble on her head ? Sir, one of the greatest and finest educational institutions in the world is that of Stoneyhurst, which is altogether conducted as a Jesuit institution, where all the English Catholics, from the Duke of Norfolk down, are educated ; and anybody who knows the situation of parties in England must know that if there be a loyal body of men in the whole world, if there be a loyal body of men within the dominions of Her Majesty, it is the English Catholics, headed by the Duke of Norfolk, their great chief. In England they are not afraid ; and why should we be afraid ? Why, Mr. Speaker, there are known to be at least 300 Jesuits in England, Jesuit priests teaching. The collateral body, I think, is above 1,000 ; and there are 180 in Ireland. Besides the College at Stoneyhurst, there is the College of Mount St. Mary, and Beaumont College ; there are Jesuits teaching a collegiate institute at Canterbury ; there is a collegiate school at Liverpool ; and there is a Jesuit school in Jersey. The Jesuits are actively employed in educating the youth of England, and we do not find that there is a remonstrance anywhere. We do not find that the Acts which would affect their existence in England have ever been put in force. Why, it would be absurd. The Prince of Wales, the heir of Her Majesty, upon whose head the Crown of England will some day descend though we hold hope that Her Majesty may long continue to wear it—does not think his position as a Protestant sovereign will be affected by the fact that there are Jesuits in Canada or in England. At the requiem service at a Jesuit Church the other day, for the Archduke Rudulph, whose unhappy fate we all know, the Prince of Wales was present, and, strange to say, was so unconscious of the danger that he was running that after the service was over, he asked the superior, as a souvenir of the event, to make him a gift of his missal or mass book. And Canada is the only country in the world where there are Jesuits, which is afraid of their insidious attempts to unsettle the constitution.

There are Jesuits by the thousands in the United States, and if Canada is in danger, they can overflow into Canada just as well from the United States as they can from England, or be educated in the country. And, as a Presbyterian clergyman said in the pulpit here, this, after all, is a mere matter of money ; and that a religious excitement should be raised on a sum of money, and a small sum, shows how easily the public may be excited if only a cry is got up, especially on religious subjects. We know that public agitation may go on sometimes without reason, and to a great extent, one cannot but deeply regret that the hon. member for Muskoka felt it to be his duty to make this motion, which ought not to have been made—this motion which will be the cause of a great deal of discomfort in Canada. I look back, Mr. Speaker and I remember the great social evils that religious evils have caused in this country. I remember when the whole country was roused on the Clergy Reserve question William Lyon Mackenzie said in the Parliament of Canada, after he came back from his exile, that the proximate cause of the rebellion in Upper Canada was the Clergy Reserve question and the agitation upon it. One can also remember how neighbor was set against neighbor on the separate school question ; and, therefore, I feel deeply that this country is injured, greatly injured—of course my hon. friend does think so—by the projection of this subject in this popular assembly ; and we cannot see what the result may be. I hope and believe it will fade away like other cries, and I am induced to do so when I look back at the events connected with the Papal Aggression Bill of 1850. I happened to be in England in 1850. Then the excitement was tremendous, caused chiefly by the letter written by Lord John Russell, the Durham letter, and by the very unwise conduct of Cardinal Wiseman in making the announcement in the way he did. I remember the excitement in England. Cardinal Wiseman, although having an English name, was a foreigner, a Spaniard ; and when he flaunted the Papal decretals from over the Flaminian gate with a great deal of pomp and ceremony, it roused the sensibilities of the English people, and Lord John Russell took advantage of the excitement in order to make capital for himself. The agitation was so great in England that there was danger of a recurrence of the Lord George Gordon riots. As in those days, the streets and the doors were marked : " no Popery." Whenever I went along the streets I saw chalked on the houses : " No Popery." I think no one went so far as the celebrated clown Grimaldi in Lord George Gordon's days, when he wrote on his door : " No Religion." But we all remember the caustic cartoon in Punch, picturing Lord John Russell as a little boy in buttons, who wrote " No Popery " on the walls, and then ran away. What was the result of that cry ? I was a younger man then than now, and I must say I was for a time carried away. The excitement was contagious, wherever I went, at the theatres and elsewhere, the cry was : " God save the Queen, and down with the Pope." You could not go in to a place of public amusement but the crowds would assemble, and it was found necessary to put guards on the banks and to protect Roman Catholic chapels. But Mr. Gladstone and some cooler heads—

 Mr. MILLS (Bothwell). Sir James Graham.

 Sir JOHN A. MACDONALD. Yes ; Mr. Gladstone, Sir James Graham, and some others opposed the measure which had a most ignominious ending. Not one single prosecution took place under that Act. Not one single proceeding was taken under it, and a few years afterwards, in 1871, the Act was repealed in silence. Not a single observation was made to continue it in its wretched existence.

 Mr. BLAKE. Everybody was ashamed of it.

 Sir JOHN A. MACDONALD. Everybody, as the hon. member for the West Durham (Mr. Blake) says, was ashamed of it. The Bill was scouted out of Parliament, although the excitement had been originally so enormous. I cannot convey to you the excitement that existed in England at that time. I hope and believe that when this matter is fully understood in the Province of Ontario, when the exhaustive speeches that were made upon it are read and discussed and weighed, the country will see that their apprehensions are unfounded, and that the country is safe. Why, there are in all the Dominion of Canada 71 Jesuits. Are they going to conquer the whole of Canada? Is Protestantism to be subdued? Is the Dominion to be seduced from its faith by 71 Jesuit priests? They are armed with a string of beads, a sash around their waists and a mass book or missal. What harm can they do? I told my reverend and eloquent friend, Dr. Potts of Toronto, that I would match him physically and spiritually, against any follower of Ignatius Loyola in the whole Dominion of Canada. Now, only think of it. The Jesuits claim, and claimed with an appearance of right, that the effect of their restoration should be to give them back all their own property. They contended for that, and they had the right to fight the best battle they could. Look at the papers. They said that the value of the property was $2,000,000, but they came down, however, graciously, and said they would take $1,000,000, or, to be accurate, I think, $900,000. But the Government of the Province of Quebec said : No, you cannot have that : you can only have $400,000—not a very large sum. Why, Mr. Mercier has been granting in the interest of his country, sums as big as that for railways here and there through Quebec. We do the same thing here. It is no very large sum. But not only did Mr. Mercier confine the vote to $400,000 but he said : You shall have not the whole of it ; perhaps you shall have none of it. The other ecclesiastic institutions, Catholic colleges, said they had a right to their share. Now, it was a family matter, it was in *foro domestico*, and, as the hon. member for Bothwell (Mr. Mills) truly said, it was their own money, it was the property of the Province of Quebec and they could do with it as they liked. There is almost no subject to which the Quebec Government could not apply these moneys under the general phrase of " property and civil rights. " The lands themselves, if they came to the old Province of Canada by escheat, the moment that Upper and Lower Canada were severed, those lands, by the terms of the British North America Act, became, like any other public lands in the Province of Quebec, subject to be sold or kept or retained or applied for any purpose the Government of that Province chose. You cannot bind any Province to carry out the original intentions of the donors. This land became their property, and the representatives of the people, the legislators of the Province, have a right to apply their own property and the proceeds of their property for any purpose they have a right to deal with under the powers of the Act. How does it turn out? It was left to the Pope to settle in what proportion the different collegiate institutions should have this $400,000 ; and His Holiness, instead of being the special supporter of the Jesuit Order, instead of pressing their interest on the people of Canada, instead of giving them wealth in order to advance their insidious designs against the Crown and dignity of Canada, cut them down to the miserable sum of $160,000. He has given the rest of it to the other collegiate institutions and to the bishops for the purposes of higher education. I hear the argument stated that it is not stated, in so many words, that the money going to the Jesuits shall be devoted to educational purposes. Why, they are a teaching body in Canada exclusively now. There is not a single parish in the whole Province of Quebec which has a Jesuit as its *curé ;* there is not a single parish in which the Jesuits have any control. They are a teaching body in the Province of Quebec. They have a mission in which education and Christianity go hand in hand among the Indians and the Esquimaux on the Labrador coast, where they are doing a great deal of good, where they are suffering the hardships and miseries which we read in Parkman they were always ready to suffer in the cause of religion and humanity. And strange to say, if we go west, leaving the Eastern Province of Quebec, to the Province of Manitoba, we find there the College of St. Boniface with Archbishop Taché at its head, and the professors are six Jesuit priests. We do not hear of Manitoba raising up a cry against that institution. We know how easily popular excitement in a young country like that, full of ardent spirits, can be raised. I have occasion to know something about that. Well, they submit to the enormous wrong of having six Jesuit priests teaching in Manitoba with as much apathy as the Protestants in the Province of Quebec ; and more than that, strange to say, there is the Anglican clergy under the charge of the Bishop of the Church of England, there is the Presbyterian clergy under the charge of the Presbyterian body, and they are so recreant to their Protestantism. they are so apathetic, that they have joined hand-in-hand in forming a common university, that common university giving degrees, and the governing body of that university is composed of Catholics, Presbyterians, Anglicans And all this cry is for some $160,000, which, at four per cent., amounts to some $6,000 a year. I cannot but remember the story of the Jew going into an eating house and being seduced by a slice of ham. When he came out, it so happened there was a crash of thunder, and he said : Good heavens, what a row about a little bit of pork. It is a little bit of pork, and as the poor Jew escaped being crushed by the thunderbolt, I have no doubt Canada will escape from the enormous sum of $6,000 a year. If this Bill had been introduced in other terms it would have been fortunate. I agree with those gentlemen who say that the framers of the Bill, by the way it is drawn and the insertion of these recitals, almost court the opposition of the member for Muskoka. I agree that that is so, and, if the Bill had not mentioned the Society of Jesus it would have passed without any opposition. If the money had been given to the Sulpicians, the money had been given to the University of Laval, if the money had been given to the bishops of the different dioceses for higher education, no one would have objected to it, this Bill would not have excited any attention ; but, it is just because the Jesuits have got historically a bad name from Protestant history, and it was simply because their name was in the Bill that all this agitation has been aroused. This subject is not a new one. Years and years ago, long before Confederation, the subject was discussed in Parliament, and strong arguments were used against the recognition of the claim for Jesuits' estates, and the feeling of opposition was shown and emphasised in the sentence which was used by a worthy member of Parliament —a good Grit he was, by the way, and a very respectable and honest man, strange to say—but he exemplified the feeling of the country in one sentence. His speech was a very effective one. It was this: " Mr. Speaker, I don't like them there Jesuits." That was the feeling. There was a prejudice against the Jesuits, and it is from that same prejudice that all this agitation has been aroused. Now, I can only repeat that the Government would have performed an act of tyranny if they had disallowed the Bill. Believing as we do that it is perfectly within the competence of that Legislature, and does not in any way affect any other portion of Her Majesty's dominions, there would be no excuse for our interfering, even according to the rigid principles which my hon. friend opposite thinks govern us. I agree strongly with the language used by the hon. member for North York (Mr. Mulock). Supposing this Bill had been disallowed, Mr. Mercier would have gained a great object. He would have been the champion of his church. The moment it was announced that this Bill was disallowed there would have been a summons for a meeting of the Legislature of Quebec. They would have passed that Bill unanimously, and would have sent it back here, and what would have been the consequence ? No Government can be formed in Canada, either by myself, or by the hon. member who moves this resolution (Mr. O'Brien), or by my hon. friend who sits opposite (Mr. Laurier), having in view the disallowance of such a measure. What would be the consequence of a disallowance ? Agitation, a quarrel—a racial and a religious war would be aroused. The best interests of the country would be prejudiced, our credit would be ruined abroad, and our social relations destroyed at home. I cannot sufficiently picture, in my faint language, the misery and the wretchedness which would have been heaped upon Canada if this question, having been agitated as it has been, and would be, had culminated in a series of disallowances of this Act.

Some hon. MEMBERS. Question.

Sir RICHARD CARTWRIGHT. (OXFORD, S. RIDING.)

I sympathise entirely with the desires of hon. gentlemen, and I do not propose to occupy the time of the House at any length, but this is not a question on which I intend to record my vote without explicitly declaring the reasons which actuate me on this occasion. As to the speech which has been made by the hon. the Premier, I think the hon. gentleman certainly had very little ground for charging my hon. friend the member for Quebec East (Mr. Laurier) with any irrelevancy in his remarks, at any rate as compared with the remarks in which the hon. gentleman himself indulged, for he most assuredly travelled over a wider range and went back over a greater number of years than my hon. friend required to traverse on his part. There is one remark which the hon. gentleman made, having reference to a gentleman who has long since departed from amongst us, which, to the best of my knowledge and to the knowledge of other hon. gentlemen here who knew him betterthan I did, was not a just or a fair remark for the Premier to have made. That was the statement that the late Hon. George Brown had declared—as I took down the hon gentleman's words—that it was part of his policy to suppress the French language in Canada. If the hon. gentleman will show, if he will produce on the floor of this House any evidence that Mr. Brown did make use of such a statement, we will be willing to accept his assurance, but, although my acquaintance with Mr. Brown was not as long as that of the hon. gentleman, I knew him for a considerable number of years, and I cannot recollect having seen in his writings or heard from his lips any statement or any language at all warranting the assertion which has lately been made by the hon. gentleman. In reference to some of the remarks made, and most justly made, by my hon. friend from Quebec (Mr. Laurier), that the policy of the present Government, in wantonly and needlessly interfering with provincial rights, was largely and principally responsible for the present agitation which we must all deplore, the hon. gentleman opposite took refuge in the old *tu quoque* argument that, in the time of my hon. friend beside me (Mr. Mackenzie), certain Bills had been disallowed ; and he referred especially to one from Prince Edward Island which he asserted had been disallowed by us. My recollection is—and I have consulted my hon. friend the member for West Durham (Mr. Blake) in regard to it—that it was reserved by the Lieutenant Governor of that Province, and that, as was done by the hon. gentleman himself, in a certain memorable instance, it was not disallowed, but was sent back to the Province to be considered by the Lieutenant Governor. Perhaps the hon. gentleman recollects that, on a certain occasion, a Bill for the incorporation of the Orange Order was sent to him under precisely similar circumstances, and that he—good Orangeman as he is—sent back that Bill because it had been reserved by the Lieutenant Governor who, he stated, had no business to act in that way without instructions.

Sir JOHN A. MACDONALD. Yes ; that is the case.

Sir RICHARD CARTWRIGHT. That was exactly the case in regard to the Bill from Prince Edward Island.

Sir JOHN A. MACDONALD. My impression was that it was the other way.

Mr. BLAKE. It was the case of a reserved Bill.

Sir JOHN A. MACDONALD. The report was made by Mr. Scott ?

Mr. BLAKE. Yes.

Sir RICHARD CARTWRIGHT. So that we followed the example of the hon. gentleman in that matter. Now, I have no objection whatever to say that I believe the report which the hon. gentleman made in 1869 gave a very full and fair account of the lines which we ought to have been governed in dealing with provincial rights. But since that time, as we all know, the hon. gentleman fell from grace, but we are glad to see by the statements made the other night by the Minister of Justice, that here again the hon. gentleman is coming back to the identical principles, and is framing his policy on those identical lines, which were advocated from this side of the House. As my hon. friend truly said, we are getting used to these sudden extraordinary conversions on the part of the hon. gentleman. My hon. friend pointed out to him that before three weeks have elapsed from the time when we advised the *modus vivendi* to be put in force, we find the hon. gentleman and his colleagues, by their act in Council, giving effect to the proposition made by my hon. friend. Let me recall to the hon. gentleman's mind the language with which he received that proposition. Unless my recollection is wholly at fault, we were told that it would be to go down on our knees to the great American nation, it would disgrace Canada, it was unworthy of a free people, unworthy of a free Government; yet in three weeks he accedes to the proposition.

Sir JOHN A. MACDONALD. No, no. Look at *Hansard*.

Sir RICHARD CARTWRIGHT. I will not irritate or aggravate the hon. gentleman by reciting all the other summersaults that he has performed in the last few years. But that is very far from being the only case in which the hon. gentleman recently has chosen, for reasons of his own, to take a leaf out of our books and to put on the Statute-book the exact policy which we have over and over again pointed out to him, and pointed out to this country, as the only one which can be followed in the interests of the people of Canada. As my hon. friend beside me (Mr. Mackenzie) reminds me, that is no new thing on the part of the hon. gentleman. Almost all his life his business has been to make capital by opposing, as long as he thought it safe, all the Liberal ideas, all the improvements, all the useful suggestions that were made; and then when there was a chance of obtaining a reasonable amount of profit, the hon. gentleman was prepared to adopt them; nor did he ever in all his life do so more remarkably than in the case of the adoption of the scheme of Confederation itself, which to my certain knowledge—for I was a member of Parliament then—the hon. gentleman opposed with might and main, tooth and nail, until he was confronted with dissolution from which he knew he had not the ghost of a chance of emerging successfully. I will not spend any more time over the by gone proceedings of the hon. gentleman. I wish to say, however, a few words as to the question now in hand. I am in part disposed to agree with some of the hon. gentlemen who have spoken on this question in believing that this is not a light matter, that this may be attended with serious results indeed. I do not know, and none of us can tell, to what extent this agitation may ultimately spread. The vote that will be given to-night is a foregone conclusion, but it may well be that the end is not yet. Therefore, I hold that it is doubly our duty under these circumstances, speaking as men with a grave responsibility upon us, to declare why and wherefore we are not in a position at this moment to accept the motion recently made by the hon. member for Muskoka (Mr. O'Brien). As I have said, so far as the Government of Canada is concerned, this demand for interference with the legislation of the Province of Quebec is in a large degree due to the action which the Government have previously taken by their unjust interference with Acts passed by other Provincial Legislatures, passed by the Provincial Legislature of my own Province, passed by the Province Legislature of Manitoba, distinctly within their rights. The hon. gentlemen for their own reasons, and in pursuance of their own objects, chose to disallow these, and, therefore, they cannot blame their supporters if, under existing circumstances, they demand that they should put in force the same rule and law for the Province of Quebec that they have put in force for other Provinces of this Dominion. Sir, they chose to constitute themselves a court of appeal as to those Acts. I hold that the member for North Simcoe (Mr. McCarthy) was perfectly right in saying that when two gentlemen holding the position of the First Minister and the Minister of Customs and affiliating with the society to which they belong believe that this Act was a bad one, if they thought there was anything objectionable, in it, then they were bound by their own previous proceedings to disallow this Act and to take the consequence. Now, Sir, the position of three parties in this House is tolerably clearly defined. The position of the member for North Simcoe and his friends is clear enough. They maintain that we have a right to interfere and to sit in judgment on provincial legislature. They disapprove of this Act, and they consistently call upon the Goverment to disallow it. So the position of hon. gentlemen on this side is clearly defined. We have always declared that the Provinces had a full and perfect power to legislate on subjects which were formally assigned to them, and that on such subjets we ought not to interfere with them, even where some of us might believe that their action was unwise or indiscreet. But as to the Government, their position is wholly different. We find them on this occasion, as on almost all others, sometimes assuming one line and pursuing one policy, and sometimes on grounds, as they allege, of high moral conviction, disallowing an Act like that of the Province of Manitoba; but in cases like this, where there is too much at stake, we do not find the hon. gentlemen are troubled with any serious moral convictions which would lead them into collision with a powerful and united Province. Now, I do not in the least offer any opinion as to the legality of the preceedings. I am wholly in accord with the hon. member for West York (Mr. Mulock) and with other hon. gentlemen who have spoken here, in saying that if there be a question as to the legality of this Act, the proper place to settle it is the courts. I do not think this House is in any way constituted to act as a legal tribunal. I do not think the country would have confidence in us, acting as a legal tribunal, I am sure for one I would not. Now, we have two opinions from men eminent in their profession of the most possible opposite character on this question. There is no doubt whatever, I suppose, that there are very few questions of this nature on which legal gentlemen of the eminence of the Minister of Justice, or the hon. member for North Simcoe, or of the constitutional knowledge of my hon. friend from Bothwell (Mr. Mills), cannot make out at first sight a very good and a very plausible case, but with that I have nothing to do. What we are concerned with here is the question whether it is advisable for us to make use of this extreme power which we possess, which the Government possess, under the British North America Act, to disallow this legislation. Sir, I have always observed this plain principle in respect to such proceedings: I say that the position which the Dominion of Canada and the Government of Canada occupy with respect to the Provinces, is identically the same as that which the Parliament and the Government of England occupy with respect to this Dominion Parliament, and that we should imitate the example of the English Government and English Parliament in abstaining from interfering with the Provinces. They have scrupulously abstained, in all but a very few cases, growing yearly less and less—almost none I may say within the last few years—from interfering with our legislation, and so we in turn are bound carefully to abstain as the honorable gentleman knows right well and as all honorable gentlemen I suppose know, are precisely and identically the same, and just the same powers are given to the English Government to disallow the Acts of from interfering with the legislation of the Province. The words used in the Act this Parliament as is given to the Canadian Government to disallow provincial Acts, and it would be idle, it would be needless for me to waste the time of the House by reminding hon. members how they would resent any interference on the part of the British Government in a matter which came clearly and distinctly, as these I think come clearly and distinctly, within the jurisdiction of the Provincial Legislature.

All I desire to say with respect to the Bill now in hand is this: With the incorporation of the Jesuits we have nothing to do. The hon. gentleman was perfectly right as other hon. gentlemen were right, in calling the attention of the country and the House to the fact that over and over again other Acts of incorporation had been passed incorporating certain portions of this order. All, I say, we have to do with in these matters is the question, whether we were justified in interfering with this particular Act passed by Mr. Mercier. With respect to that question, I am bound to say that I myself entertain very great doubts of the wisdom and propriety of that Act. I doubt whether if I had lived in the Province of Quebec I would not have felt it to be my duty to have opposed it; but that is not the question, it is not what my opinion is and whether I approve of it or not, or whether it is justifiable on the whole. The question is this: Whether after the Legislature of Quebec has undertaken to deal with this subject, we, the Parliament of Canada, have a right to interfere with it? On that point, no more than the hon. gentleman do I entertain any doubt. I hold that it was fully within their constitutional rights, and I hold, therefore, that we have no business whatever to interfere with it or meddle with the disposal of the money entrusted to their care in any shape or way. If they have done wrong, let them answer for it to the people of the Province of Quebec, whom they specially represent. Let us not bring their Acts into controversy here, where, for various reasons, it is almost utterly impossible that we should come to a fair and equitable decision on the merits of any case passed on by a Provincial Legislature. More than that. Besides thinking it is beyond our right, I must add this, that I think it would be in the highest degree impolitic, in the highest degree contrary to good government, that it would impair the whole fabric of our Confederation if we took the advice of the hon. member for Muskoka ( Mr. O'Brien ) and proceed to disallow this Bill, I have seen, as well as the hon. gentleman, what the result of these religious feuds and discords sometimes is; and I say that I believe, il you were to disallow this Bill, most assuredly two results would flow from it: one would be that you would have a solid and united Lower Canada occupying to us approximately the same position that Ireland unhappily still holds in the British Parliament; and the other (if the hon. member for Muskoka (Mr. O'Brien) desires especially to achieve that end) that you would make the Order of Jesuits the most powerful religious body in Quebec, and probably in North America. These two results would flow from the adoption of the idea of the hon. member for Muskoka and the disallowance of the Act on the grounds set forth in his motion. I, for one, will be no party under any circumstances or for any consideration to stirring up religious strife among my contrymen. So far as my power goes, so far as my voice and vote can go, I desire to have the rights on my own Province respected, and I desire to see the rights of a sister Province respected. I desire to maintain my own rights, my own religious belief, my own right to act as a free man in this country, and these rights which I claim for myself I will also not merely give to my fellow-countrymen, but I am ready to champion and obtain for them in every shape and way that I can possibly do so. If I had any doubt as to the correctness of my conviction I would find it in the fact that we have to-night for the first time in many years my venerated friend (Mr. Mackenzie) coming here to record his vote against a proposition which would set man against man and kindle the flames of religious bigotry from one end of this Dominion to the other.

House divided on amendment (Mr. O'Brien):

YEAS:
Messieurs

Barron,
Bell,
Charlton,
Cockburn,
Denison,

Macdonald (Huron),
McCarthy,
McNeill,
O'Brien,

Scriver,
Sutherland,
Tyrwhitt, and
Wallace,—13.

NAYS:
Messieurs

Amyot,
Armstrong,
Audet,
Bain (Soulanges),
Bain (Wentworth),
Barnard,
Beausoleil,
Béchard,
Bergeron,
Bergin,
Bernier,
Blake,
Boisvert,
Borden,
Bourassa,
Bowell,
Bowman,
Boyle,
Brien,
Brown,
Bryson,
Burdett,
Burns,
Cameron,
Campbell,
Cargill,
Carling,
Carpenter,
Caron (Sir Adolphe),
Cartwright (Sir Richard),
Casey,
Casgrain,
Chisholm,
Choquette,
Chouinard,
Cimon,
Cochrane,
Colby,
Colter,
Cook,
Corby,
Coughlin,
Coulombe,
Couture,
Curran,
Daly,
Daoust,
Davies,
Davin,
Davis,
Dawson,
Desaulniers,
Desjardins,
Dessaint,
Dewdney,
Dickey,
Dickinson,
Doyon,
Dupont,
Edgar,
Edwards,
Eisenhauer,
Ellis,

Ferguson (Leeds & Gren),
Ferguson (Renfrew),
Ferguson (Welland),
Fiset,
Fisher,
Flynn,
Foster,
Freeman,
Gauthier,
Gigault,
Gillmor,
Girouard,
Godbout,
Gordon,
Grandbois,
Guay,
Guillet,
Haggart,
Hale,
Hall,
Hesson,
Hickey,
Halton,
Hudspeth,
Innes,
Ives,
Joncas,
Jones (Digby),
Jones (Halifax),
Kenny,
Kirk,
Kirkpatrick,
Labelle,
Labrosse,
Landerkin,
Landry,
Lang,
Langelier (Quebec),
Langevin (Sir Hector),
La Rivière,
Laurier,
Lépine,
Livingston,
Lovitt,
Macdonald (Sir John),
Macdowell,
Mackenzie,
McCulla,
McDonald (Victoria),
McDougall (Pictou),
McDougall (Cap Breton),
McGreevy,
McIntyre,
McKay,
McKeen,
McMillan (Huron),
McMillan (Vaudreuil),
McMullen,
Madill,
Mara,
Marshall,
Masson,
Meigs.

Mills (Annapolis),
Mills (Bothwell),
Mitchell,
Moffat,
Moncrieff,
Montplaisir,
Mulock,
Neveu,
Paterson (Brant),
Paterson (Essex),
Perley,
Perry,
Platt,
Porter,
Prefontaine,
Prior,
Purcell,
Putnam,
Rinfret,
Riopel,
Robertson,
Robillard,
Roome,
Ross,
Rowand,
Rykert,
Ste. Marie,
Scarth,
Semple,
Shanly,
Skinner,
Small,
Smith (Sir Donald)
Smith (Ontario),
Somerville,
Sproule,
Stevenson,
Taylor,
Temple,
Thérien,
Thompson (Sir John),
Tisdale,
Trow,
Tupper,
Turcot,
Vanasse,
Waldie,
Ward,
Watson,
Weldon (Albert),
Weldon (St. John),
Welsh,
White (Cardwell),
White (Renfrew),
Wilmot,
Wilson (Argenteuil),
Wilson (Elgin),
Wilson (Lennox),
Wood (Brockville),
Wood (Westmoreland),
Wright, and
Yeo.—188.

Amendment negatived.